Java™

software structures
designing and using data structures

Java™

software structures

designing and using data structures

JOHN LEWIS
Villanova University

JOSEPH CHASE
Radford University

PEARSON

Addison
Wesley

Boston San Francisco New York
London Toronto Sydney Tokyo Singapore Madrid
Mexico City Munich Paris Cape Town Hong Kong Montreal

Executive Editor	Susan Hartman Sullivan
Assistant Editor	Elizabeth Paquin
Marketing Manager	Nathan Schultz
Senior Production Supervisor	Jeffrey Holcomb
Project Management	Argosy Publishing
Copyeditor	William McManus
Proofreader	Kim Cofer
Indexer	Larry Sweazy
Composition and Art	Argosy Publishing
Text and Cover Designer	Joyce Cosentino Wells and Jennifer Powers
Text Image	© 2003 Photodisc, Getty Images
Cover Image	© 2003 Masterfile
Prepress and Manufacturing	Caroline Fell

Access the latest information about Addison-Wesley titles from our World Wide Web site: http://www.aw.com/cs

Many of the designations used by manufacturers and sellers to distinguish their products are claimed as trademarks. Where those designations appear in this book, and Addison-Wesley was aware of a trademark claim, the designations have been printed in initial caps or all caps.

The programs and applications presented in this book have been included for their instructional value. They have been tested with care, but are not guaranteed for any particular purpose. The publisher does not offer any warranties or representations, nor does it accept any liabilities with respect to the programs or applications.

Library of Congress Cataloging-in-Publication Data

Lewis, John, 1963-
    Java software structures : designing and using data structures / John Lewis, Joseph Chase.
        p. cm.
Includes index.
    ISBN 0-201-78878-0
    1. Java (Computer program language) 2. Computer software--Development. I. Chase, Joseph, 1964- II. Title.

QA76.73.J38L493 2003
005.13'3--dc21   2003052299
                                                           CIP

ISBN 0-201-78878-0
1 2 3 4 5 6 7 8 9 10-CRW-06 05 04 03

To Sharon, Justin, and Kayla Lewis
who give me cause to sing,
even though they'd prefer I not.

—J.L.

To my parents who taught me to fly,
my wife who flies with me providing both support and direction,
and our families that provide us a friendly place to roost.

—J.C.

This book is designed to serve as a text for a course on data structures and algorithms. This course is typically referred to as the CS2 course because it is often taken as the second course in a computing curriculum. We have designed this book to embrace the tenets of Computing Curricula 2001.

Pedagogically, this book follows the style and approach of the leading CS1 book *Java Software Solutions: Foundations of Program Design*, by John Lewis and William Loftus. Our book uses many of the highly regarded features of that book, such as the Key Concept boxes. Together, these two books support the classic introductory sequence for computing students with a solid and consistent approach.

That said, this book does not assume that students have used *Java Software Solutions* in a previous course. Material that might be presented in either course (such as recursion or sorting) is presented in this book as well. Appendix A provides an overview of object-oriented concepts and how they are realized in Java. This appendix can be used as a review or to bring students with varying backgrounds up to speed.

We understand the crucial role that the CS2 course plays in a curriculum and we think this book serves the needs of that course well.

our approach

Books of this type vary greatly in their overall approach. Our approach is founded on a few important principles that we fervently embraced. First, we present the various collections explored in the book in a consistent manner. Second, we emphasize the importance of sound software design techniques. Third, we organized the book to support and reinforce the big picture: the study of data structures and algorithms. Let's examine these principles further.

consistent presentation

When exploring a particular type of collection, we carefully address each of the following issues in order:

1. **Concept:** We discuss the collection conceptually, establishing the services it provides (its interface).

2. **Use:** We explore examples that illustrate how the particular nature of the collection, no matter how it's implemented, can be useful when solving problems.

3. **Implementation:** We explore various implementation options for the collection.

4. **Analysis:** We compare and contrast the implementations.

The Java Collections API is included in the discussion as appropriate. If there is support for a particular collection type in the API, we discuss it and its implementation. Thus we embrace the API, but are not completely tied to it. And we are not hesitant to point out its shortcomings.

The analysis is kept at a high level. We establish the concept of Big-Oh notation in Chapter 1 and use it throughout the book, but the analysis is more intuitive than it is mathematical.

sound program design

Throughout the book we keep sound software engineering practices a high priority. Our design of collection implementations and the programs that use them follow consistent and appropriate standards.

Of primary importance is the separation of a collection's interface from its underlying implementation. The services that a collection provides are always formally defined in a Java interface. The interface name is used as the type designation of the collection whenever appropriate to reinforce the collection as an abstraction.

In addition to practicing solid design principles, we stress them in the discussion throughout the text. We attempt to teach both by example and by continual reinforcement.

clean organization

The contents of the book have been carefully organized to minimize distracting tangents and reinforce the overall purpose of the book. The organization supports the book in its role as a pedagogical exploration of data structures and algorithms as well as its role as a valuable reference.

The book can be divided into three parts: Part I consists of the first five chapters of the book, which cover introductory and underlying issues that affect all aspects of data structures and algorithms. Part II covers linear collections (stacks, queues, and lists) in Chapters 6 through 8. Part III, in Chapters 9 through 14, covers the non-linear collections (trees, heaps, hashing, and graphs). Each type of collection, with the exception of trees, is covered in its own chapter. Trees are covered in a series of chapters that explore their various aspects and purposes.

Appendix A contains a discussion of fundamental object-oriented concepts and how those concepts are accomplished using Java. It can be used as a review for any students who have seen this material before, and can be covered before the main body of the book is tackled or as needed on a topic-by-topic basis. It can also serve as a Java-specific tutorial for those students who may have been introduced to object-oriented concepts in another language such as C++ or C# and who need to learn how those concepts are accomplished in Java.

Appendix B is a reference for many of the commonly used classes in the Java class library. Having this information on hand in the book makes it easier for students to develop their programs.

chapter breakdown

Chapter 1 (Software Engineering) discusses various aspects of software quality and provides an overview of software development issues. It is designed to establish the appropriate mindset before embarking on the details of data structure and algorithm design. This chapter also introduces the basic concepts underlying the analysis of algorithms.

Chapter 2 (Collections) establishes the concept of a collection, stressing the need to separate the interface from the implementation. As an example, it introduces a bag collection and discusses an array-based implementation.

Chapter 3 (Linked Structures) discusses the use of references to create linked data structures. It explores the basic issues regarding the management of linked lists, and then defines an alternative implementation of a bag collection (introduced in Chapter 2) using an underlying linked data structure.

Chapter 4 (Recursion) is a general introduction to the concept of recursion and how recursive solutions can be elegant. It explores the implementation details of recursion and discusses the basic idea of analyzing recursive algorithms.

Chapter 5 (Searching and Sorting) discusses the linear and binary search algorithms, as well as the algorithms for several sorts: selection sort, insertion sort, bubble sort, quick sort, and merge sort. Programming issues related to searching and sorting, such as using the `Comparable` interface as the basis of comparing objects, are stressed in this chapter. Searching and sorting that are based in particular data structures (such as heap sort) are covered in the appropriate chapter later in the book.

Chapter 6 (Stacks) begins the series of chapters that investigates particular collections. We begin with stacks, which is a fairly intuitive collection, both conceptually and from an implementation perspective. This chapter examines both array-based and linked implementation approaches and then compares them.

Chapter 7 (Queues) explores the concept and implementation of a first-in, first-out queue. Radix sort is discussed as an example of using queues effectively. The implementation options covered include an underlying linked list as well as both fixed and circular arrays.

Chapter 8 (Lists) covers three types of lists: ordered, unordered, and indexed. These three types of lists are compared and contrasted, discussing the operations that they share and those that are unique to each type. Inheritance is used appropriately in the design of the various types of lists, which are implemented using both array and linked representations.

Chapter 9 (Trees) provides an overview of trees, establishing key terminology and concepts. It discusses various implementation approaches and uses a binary tree to represent and evaluate an arithmetic expression.

Chapter 10 (Binary Search Trees) builds off of the basic concepts established in Chapter 9 to define a classic binary search tree. A linked implementation of a binary search tree is examined, followed by a discussion of how the balance in the tree nodes is key to its performance. That leads to exploring AVL and red-black implementations of binary search trees.

Chapter 11 (Heaps) explores the concept, use, and implementations of heaps. A heap sort is used as an example of its usefulness. Both linked and array-based implementations are explored.

Chapter 12 (Multi-Way Search Trees) is a natural extension of the discussion of the previous chapters. The concepts of 2-3 trees, 2-4 trees, and general B-trees are examined and implementation options are discussed.

Chapter 13 (Hashing) covers the concept of hashing and related issues, such as hash functions and collisions. Various Java Collections API options for hashing are discussed.

Chapter 14 (Graphs) explores the concept of undirected and directed graphs and establishes important terminology. It examines several common graph algorithms and discusses implementation options, including adjacency matrices.

Appendix A (Object-Oriented Concepts in Java) is a reference for anyone needing a review of fundamental object-oriented concepts and how they are accomplished in Java. Included are the concepts of abstraction, classes, encapsulation, inheritance, and polymorphism, as well as many related Java language constructs such as interfaces.

Appendix B (The Java Class Library) is a reference for commonly used classes from the standard Java API classes.

supplements

The following supplements are available to all readers of this book at www.aw.com/cssupport.

> **Source Code** for all programs presented in the book

The following instructor supplements are only available to qualified instructors. Please contact your local Addison-Wesley Sales Representative, or send e-mail to aw.cse@aw.com, for information about how to access them.

> **Instructor Manual with Solutions** containing author commentary and teaching tips
>
> **Solutions** for selected exercises and programming projects in the book
>
> **Test Bank** containing questions that can be used for exams
>
> **PowerPoint Slides** for the book content, including Appendix A
>
> **Applet Simulation** to illustrate the processing of some collections

acknowledgements

First and most importantly we want to thank our students for whom this book is written and without whom it never could have been. Your feedback helps us become better educators and writers. Please continue to keep us on our toes.

We would like to thank all of the reviewers, listed below, who took the time to share their insight on the content and presentation of the material in this book. Your input was invaluable.

Mary P. Boelk	Marquette University
Robert Burton	Brigham Young University
Bob Holloway	University of Wisconsin—Madison
Nisar Hundewale	Georgia State University
Chung Lee	California State Polytechnic University
Mark J. Llewellyn	University of Central Florida
Ronald Marsh	University of North Dakota
Eli C. Minkoff	Bates College; University of Maine—Augusta
Salam Salloum	California State Polytechnic University—Pomona
Don Slater	Carnegie Mellon University
Ashish Soni	University of Southern California

Special thanks go to Jack Davis and Ned Okie of Radford University. Jack provided continual feedback and insight during the development of the book, and Ned was always willing to discuss CS2 strategy and philosophy. Thank you both.

The folks at Addison-Wesley have gone to great lengths to support and develop this book along with us. It feels like a true team effort. Executive Editor Susan Hartman Sullivan and her assistant Beth Paquin have always been there to help. Michael Hirsch, Nathan Schultz, and Lesly Hershman work tirelessly to make sure that instructors understand the goals and benefits of the book. (We look forward to working with Michael in his new role as editor.) Patty Mahtani, Joyce Wells, and Jeff Holcomb head up the production of the book and are to be credited for the wonderful design. They are supported with amazing skill by Daniel Rausch and Edalin Michael at Argosy Publishing. Thank you all very much.

We'd be remiss if we didn't acknowledge the wonderful contributions of the ACM Special Interest Group on Computer Science Education. Their publications and conferences are crucial to anyone who takes the pedagogy of computing seriously. If you're not part of this group, you're missing out. The distinctly unfocused focus group that spontaneously occurred at the SIGCSE Symposium in Kentucky was particularly helpful!

Finally we want to thank our families who support and encourage us in whatever projects we find ourselves diving into. Ultimately, you are the reason we do what we do.

contents

index   **653**

software engineering

Our exploration of software development must begin with a discussion of the issues related to software engineering.

Rather than simply write programs, we should strive to engineer our software. We want to develop high-quality software systems that will stand the tests of users as well as the test of time. The principles of software engineering will lead us toward this goal. This chapter discusses a variety of issues related to software engineering and sets up some terminology that is crucial to our exploration of data structures and software design.

1.1 software development

Imagine a scenario where you are approaching a bridge that has recently been built over a large river. As you approach, you see a sign informing you that the bridge was designed and built by local construction workers and that engineers were not involved in the project. Would you continue across the bridge? Would it make a difference if the sign informed you that the bridge was designed by engineers and built by construction workers?

The word "engineer" in this context refers to an individual who has been educated in the history, theory, method, and practice of the engineering discipline. This definition includes fields of study such as electrical engineering, mechanical engineering, and chemical engineering. *Software engineering* is the study of the techniques and theory that underlie the development of high-quality software.

When the term "software engineering" was first coined in the 1970s, it was an aspiration—a goal set out by leaders in the industry who realized that much of the software being created was of poor quality. They wanted developers to move away from the simplistic idea of writing programs and toward the disciplined idea of engineering software. To engineer software we must first realize that this term is more than just a title—that it, in fact, represents a completely different attitude.

Many an argument has been started over the question of whether software engineering has reached the state of a true engineering discipline. We will leave that argument for software engineering courses. For our purposes, it is sufficient to understand that as software developers we share a common history, we are constrained by common theory, and we must understand current methods and practices in order to work together.

Ultimately, we want to satisfy the *client*, the person or organization who pays for the software to be developed, as well as the final *users* of the system. Clients and users may overlap depending on the situation.

The goals of software engineering are much the same as those for other engineering disciplines:

▸ Solve the right problem

▸ Deliver a solution on time and within budget

▸ Deliver a high-quality solution

It may sound strange that we need to be worried about solving the wrong problem, but that issue causes trouble for almost every project. Too often a software developer will deliver a product only to find out that it is not exactly what the client wanted. Therefore, one of the first steps in any software development process is to make sure we understand the details of the problem we intend to solve. To do so, we must develop an accurate specification of the requirements for the problem solution.

> **key concept**
> The first step in software development is to analyze the problem and develop a thorough and accurate set of requirements.

Problem analysis involves activities such as interviewing clients, observing existing processes, and analyzing existing solutions. The requirements developed from these activities must establish not only the functions that the solution must provide, such as allowing a user to log on to a system with a username and password, but also the constraints governing those functions and how they are developed, such as the specification of what characters can be used to make a valid password. By understanding the problem, we are better able to develop a solution that correctly solves the right problem.

professionalism and ethics

As professionals, if we agree to a client's requirements for a system to be delivered by a certain date for a particular price, then we are obligated to deliver on time and within budget. Obviously, a business cannot survive long if it continually disappoints its clients. But this issue goes beyond that practical aspect. Part of an engineering discipline is the need to be able to make accurate plans, schedules, and budgets. Failure to deliver on time and within budget not only may cause serious harm to the company or companies involved in the project but may also affect our shared reputation as a profession.

> **key concept**
> For both practical and philosophical reasons, a software engineer must strive to deliver on time and within budget.

True software engineers adhere to a code of ethics, which includes the concept of competence. If we do not think the project can be done under those requirements, then it is our responsibility to say so at the time that the requirements are being established.

To maximize the quality of our software, we must first realize that quality means different things to different people. Software quality issues are explored in the next section.

1.2 software quality

Of course, we want our software to be of high quality. But what does that mean? As is often the case, there are a variety of quality characteristics to consider. Figure 1.1 lists several aspects of high-quality software.

Quality Characteristic	Description
Correctness	The degree to which software adheres to its specific requirements.
Reliability	The frequency and criticality of software failure.
Robustness	The degree to which erroneous situations are handled gracefully.
Usability	The ease with which users can learn and execute tasks within the software.
Maintainability	The ease with which changes can be made to the software.
Reuseability	The ease with which software components can be reused in the development of other software systems.
Portability	The ease with which software components can be used in multiple computer environments.
Efficiency	The degree to which the software fulfills its purpose without wasting resources.

figure 1.1　Aspects of software quality

correctness

The concept of *correctness* goes back to our original goal to develop the appropriate solution. At each step of the way, we want to make sure that we are addressing the problem as defined by the requirements specification. Almost all other aspects of quality are meaningless if the software doesn't solve the right problem.

Correctness also implies that the solution produces the correct results. This concept goes beyond just performing numeric calculations to an appropriate level of accuracy. Software should also display graphics and user interface components in a well-organized and visually pleasing manner. It should produce text output (including error messages) that are carefully worded and spelled correctly.

reliability

key concept

Reliable software seldom fails and, when it does, minimizes the effects of that failure.

If you have ever attempted to access your bank account electronically and been unable to do so, or if you have ever lost all of your work because of a failure of the software or hardware you were using, you are already familiar with the concept of *reliability*. A software *failure* can be defined as any unacceptable behavior that occurs within permissible operating conditions. We can compute measures of reliability, such as the mean time between failures. Reliability also takes into account the fact that some failures are more critical than others. Above all, software should do no harm in the event of a failure.

In some situations, reliability is an issue of life and death. In the early 1980s, a piece of medical equipment called the Therac 25 was designed to deliver a dose of radiation according to the settings made by a technician on a special keyboard. An error existed in the software that controlled the device such that, when the technician made a very specific adjustment to the values on the keyboard, the internal settings of the device were changed drastically and a lethal dose of radiation was issued. The error occurred so infrequently that several people died before the source of the problem was determined.

In other cases, reliability repercussions are financial. On a particular day in November, 1998, the entire AT&T network infrastructure in the eastern United States failed, causing major interruption in communications capabilities. The problem was eventually traced back to a specific software error. That one failure cost millions of dollars in lost revenue to the companies affected.

robustness

Reliability is related to how *robust* a system is. A robust system handles problems gracefully. For example, if a particular input field is designed to handle numeric data, what happens when alphabetic information is entered? The program could be allowed to terminate abnormally because of the resulting error. However, a more robust solution would be to design the system to acknowledge and handle that situation with an appropriate error message.

One rule of thumb in software development is "never trust the user." That is, never assume the user will always interact with your system in normal or proper ways.

Developing a thoroughly robust system may or may not be worth the development cost. In some cases, it may be perfectly acceptable for a program to abnormally terminate if very strange conditions occur. On the other hand, if adding such protections is not unduly costly, it is simply considered to be good development practice. Furthermore, well-defined system requirements should carefully spell out the situations in which robust error handling is required.

usability

To be effective, a software system must be truly *usable*. If a system is too difficult to use, it doesn't matter if it provides wonderful functionality. Within computer science there is a field of study called Human-Computer Interaction (HCI) that focuses on the analysis and design of user interfaces of software systems. The interaction between the user and system must be well designed, including such things as help options, meaningful messages, consistent layout, appropriate use of color, error prevention, and error recovery.

maintainability

Software developers must *maintain* their software. That is, they make changes to software in order to fix errors or to enhance the functionality of the system. A useful software system may be maintained for many years after its original development. The software engineers that perform maintenance tasks are often not those who originally developed it. Thus, it is important that a software system be well structured, well written, and well documented in order to maximize its maintainability.

> **key concept**
>
> Software systems must be carefully designed, written, and documented to support the work of developers, maintainers, and users.

Large software systems are rarely written by a single individual or even a small group of developers. Instead, large teams, often working from widely distributed locations, are used to develop systems. For this reason, communication among developers is critical. Therefore, creating maintainable software for its long-term benefits also helps the initial development effort.

reusability

Suppose that you are a contractor involved in the construction of an office building. It is possible that you might design and build each door in the building from scratch. This would require a great deal of engineering and construction effort, not to mention money. Another option is to use pre-engineered, prefabricated doors for the doorways in the building. This approach represents a great savings of time and money because you can rely on a proven design that has been used many times before. You can be confident that it has been thoroughly tested and that you know its capabilities. However, this does not mean that there might not be a few doors in the building that will be custom engineered and custom built to fit a specific need.

When developing a software system, it often makes sense to use pre-existing software components if they fit the needs of the developer and the client. Why reinvent the wheel? Pre-existing components can range in scope from entire subsystems to individual classes and methods. They may come from part of another system developed earlier or from libraries of components that are created to support the development of future systems. Some pre-existing components are referred to as Commercial Off-The-Shelf (COTS) products. Pre-existing components are often reliable because they have usually been tested in other systems.

Using pre-existing components can reduce the development effort. However, reuse comes at a price. The developer must take the time to investigate potential components to find the right one. Often the component must be modified to fit the criteria of the new system. Thus, it is helpful if the component is truly *reusable*. That is, software should be written and documented so that it can be easily incorporated into new systems, and easily modified to accommodate new requirements.

Another form of reuse comes in the form of *software patterns*, which are processing steps that commonly occur in software. These recurring patterns allow designers to capitalize on expertise gained by generations of developers working on similar problems. Components that are designed with attention to the patterns that they manifest are generally more reusable. In recent years efforts have been made to identify and categorize the various patterns that occur in software development. It is unclear yet whether this approach will be significant in the world of software development, but it is viewed as promising by many developers because it is rooted in the fundamental and beneficial concept of software reuse.

portability

Software that is easily *portable* can be moved from one computing environment to another with little or no effort. Software developed using a particular operating system and underlying central processing unit (CPU) may not run well or at all in another environment. One obvious problem is a program that has been compiled into a particular CPU's machine language. Since each type of CPU has its own machine language, porting it to another machine would require another translated version. Differences in the various translations may cause the "same" program on two types of machines to behave differently.

The Java programming language addresses this issue by compiling into *bytecode*, which is a low-level language that is not the machine language for any particular CPU. Bytecode runs on a *Java Virtual Machine* (JVM), which is software that interprets the bytecode and executes it. Therefore, at least theoretically, any system that has a JVM can execute any Java program.

efficiency

The last software quality characteristic listed in Figure 1.1 is efficiency. Software systems should make *efficient* use of the resources allocated to them. Two key resources are CPU time and main memory. User demands on computers and their software have risen steadily ever since computers were first created. Software must always make the best use of its resources in order to meet those demands. The efficiency of individual algorithms is an important part of this issue and is discussed in more detail later in this chapter and throughout the book.

quality issues

To a certain extent, quality is in the eye of the beholder. That is, some quality characteristics are more important to certain people than to others. We must consider the needs of the various *stakeholders,* the people affected one way or another by the project. For example, the end user certainly wants to maximize reliability, usability, and efficiency, but doesn't necessarily care about the software's maintainability or reusability. The client wants to make sure the user is satisfied, but is also worried about the overall cost. The developers and maintainers want the internal system quality to be high.

Note also that some quality characteristics are in competition with each other. For example, to make a program more efficient, we may choose to use a complex algorithm that is difficult to understand and therefore hard to maintain. These types of trade-offs require us to carefully prioritize the issues related to a particular project and, within those boundaries, maximize all quality characteristics as much as possible. If we decide that we must use the more complex algorithm for efficiency, we can also document the code especially well to assist with future maintenance tasks.

1.3 development life cycle models

An engineer doesn't approach a project in a chaotic or ad hoc manner. To engineer a product, including a software system, we must develop a plan using the best techniques known to us, and execute that plan with care and precision.

One of the defining principles shared among all engineering disciplines is the concept of a *development life cycle,* which defines a process to be followed during the development of a product. This process defines the communication paths among developers and provides a context for the history and future of the project.

Many software development life cycle models have been defined over the years. Though they vary in emphasis and approach, every life cycle model addresses the fundamental development issues of analysis, design, implementation, and evaluation.

> **key concept**
> A development life cycle model defines a process to be followed during development.

The *analysis* process involves the specification of the problem. This is accomplished through a variety of activities including:

▶ Interviews and negotiation with the client

▶ Modeling the problem structure and data flow

▶ Observation of client activities

▶ Analysis of existing solutions and systems

The *design* process involves the specification of a solution or solutions to the problem. This is accomplished by specifying the structure of a solution, including objects, attributes, operations, relationships between objects within the system, and the user interface. We may sometimes design more than one solution to a problem so as to compare competing solutions.

The *implementation* process involves turning the design into a functional system. This may be accomplished through the reuse of existing code, the development of software from scratch, or, more likely, a combination of the two.

The implementation process also includes the concept of testing and debugging—finding and eliminating faults in the system. It is important to understand that exhaustive testing of most systems is not possible. Consider a simple program that requires the user to enter a 20-character string. Assuming a 256-character set, there are 256^{20} possible strings that the user could enter. Therefore, it is important to develop test plans that will effectively, if not exhaustively, test a system. Test plans usually involve both functional and structural testing. Using functional, or black-box, testing, the system is tested with a range of inputs without knowledge of the internal structure of the system. Output is evaluated against the specification for correctness. Using structural, or white-box, testing, the system is tested with a range of inputs specifically designed to test the known structure of the system.

The *evaluation* process involves verifying that the system that has been created conforms to the specifications derived in the analysis process. Note that evaluation is not simply testing and debugging. It is quite possible to build a system that has no bugs, or faults, in the code, and yet is completely wrong because it does not conform to its specifications.

> **key concept**
> Because exhaustive testing of most systems is not possible, we must develop test plans that are effective.

After a system is initally developed, it must be maintained. The *maintenance* process involves the ongoing modification and evolution of the system to meet changing requirements. This is often time-consuming and expensive. The better the earlier stages of the development process are done, the easier maintenance will be. Systems that are well thought out, well designed, and well written are also much easier and cheaper to maintain.

the waterfall model

One of the earliest formal software development life cycle models is called the *waterfall model,* depicted in Figure 1.2. Traditional engineering disciplines have long used a waterfall process for development of a product. The name of the waterfall model comes from the way one phase flows into the next. That is, the information generated in one phase is used to guide the next.

The waterfall process begins with an analysis phase, which focuses on identifying the problem. During analysis, requirements are gathered and eventually synthesized into a requirements document. The requirements document becomes the basis for the design phase, in which potential solutions to the problem are explored until one solution is chosen and fully documented in a design document. The design document becomes the basis for the implementation phase in which the product is developed. The implemented system flows into the evaluation phase. Finally, evaluation yields to maintenance.

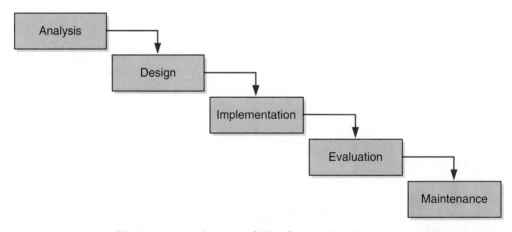

figure 1.2   The waterfall software development model

The waterfall model has several distinct advantages. First, the model lays out very clearly a set of milestones and deliverables. *Milestones* are points in time that mark the endpoint of some process activity. *Deliverables* are products, or pieces of products, that are delivered to the client.

Second, from a management perspective, the waterfall model is said to have high visibility. *Visibility* means that managers and clients can easily see the status of the devlopment process: what has been completed, and what is yet to be done.

Third, since the waterfall model is a traditional engineering model used in the development of hardware, if there is hardware being developed as part of our system, then the hardware and software can be developed using the same life cycle.

While the traditional waterfall model has been very successful in engineering disciplines where the products are tangible and often based upon principles of science, software development deals with a far less tangible product. For this reason, one major disadvantage of the waterfall model is the lateness of evaluation in the process. If this model were strictly followed for a software system, the entire system would be written before any evaluation was done. The waterfall model is based upon an old engineering notion sometimes referred to as "throw it over the wall" engineering, where one group would do the analysis work, throw their results over the wall to another group that would design a solution and throw their design over the wall to the next group that would build it, and so on. In software engineering, we must be prepared for the next group to throw it back as our understanding of our less tangible problem grows over time.

the spiral model

Given the inflexibility of the waterfall model, a variety of other software development models have emerged. The *spiral model* of software development was developed by Barry Boehm in the mid-1980s. A depiction of this model is shown in Figure 1.3. The spiral model was specifically designed to reduce the two most serious risks in the software development process: building the wrong system and building the system wrong.

> The spiral model is designed to reduce the risks inherent in software development.
>
> **key concept**

This model follows a spiral that continually refines the requirements for the system being developed, addressing the fact that software requirements are difficult to ascertain because of their very nature. Software is both invisible and intangible. Thus, this model allows for an iterative refinement of those requirements through the use of a series of expanding prototypes and high-level designs.

Each cycle in the spiral represents a phase of the process and therefore each phase goes through the four main quadrants of the spiral. Initially, the objectives

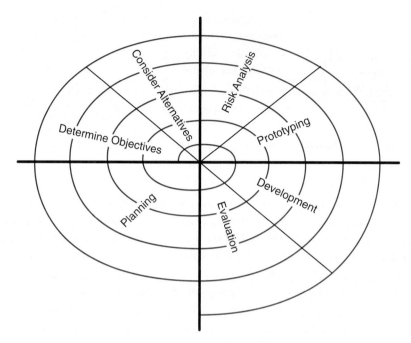

figure 1.3   The spiral model of software development

of the phase are determined, considering possible alternatives. Then the risks for following this approach are assessed and minimized. For example, what is the risk that the new database system we are planning to use will not process enough transactions per second to meet our requirements? Prototypes are then often developed to explore the issue further. Then the objectives of this phase are developed and evaluated. Finally, given the status of the evolving product, plans are made for the next phase.

The spiral model is much more flexible than the waterfall model. Each phase can be tailored to address issues that have come up in previous phases. The spiral model's iterative nature is simply more realistic than the more static waterfall model.

the evolutionary development model

Another development model created to address the unique nature of software is the *evolutionary development* model, shown in Figure 1.4. Like the spiral model,

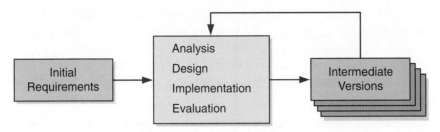

figure 1.4   The evolutionary development model

the evolutionary development model also utilizes the concept of iterative refinement. However, unlike the spiral model, this model iteratively refines the requirements, the design, and the software product, not just the requirements and the high-level design.

The evolutionary development model has proven to be very effective for the development of relatively small systems and for short duration systems that will not require evolution and maintenance. Systems developed using this process typically are not as well structured as systems developed using the other methods and therefore are more difficult to maintain or evolve.

1.4 the unified modeling language (UML)

Software engineering deals with the analysis, synthesis, and communication of ideas in the development of software systems. In order to facilitate the methods and practices necessary to accomplish these goals, software engineers have developed various notations to capture and communicate information. While there are a great number of notations available, a few have become popular and one in particular has become a de facto standard in the industry.

The *Unified Modeling Language* (UML) was developed in the mid-1990s, but is actually the synthesis of three separate and long-standing design notations, each popular in its own right. We use UML notation throughout this book to illustrate program designs, and this section describes the key aspects of UML diagrams. Keep in mind that UML is language-independent. It uses generic terms and contains features that are not relevant to the Java programming language. We focus on aspects of UML that are particularly appropriate for its use in this book.

> **key concept**
>
> The Unified Modeling Language (UML) provides a notation with which we can capture and illustrate program designs.

A UML *class diagram* describes the classes in the system, the static relationships among them, the attributes and operations associated with a class, and the constraints on the connections among objects. The terms "attribute" and "operation" are generic object-oriented terms. An *attribute* is any class-level data including variables and constants. An *operation* is essentially equivalent to a method.

A class is represented in UML by a rectangle that is usually divided into three sections containing the class name, its attributes, and its operations. Figure 1.5 illustrates a class named `LibraryItem`. There are two attributes associated with the class, `title` and `callNumber`, and there are two operations associated with the class, `checkout` and `return`.

In the notation for a class, the attributes and operations are optional. Therefore, a class may be represented by a single rectangle containing only the class name, if desired. We can include the attributes and/or operations whenever they help convey important information in the diagram. If attributes or operations are included, then both sections are shown (though not necessarily filled) to make it clear which is which.

There are many additional pieces of information that can be included in the UML class notation. An annotation bracketed using << and >> is called a *stereotype* in UML terminology. The `<<abstract>>` stereotype or the `<<interface>>` stereotype could be added above the name to indicate that it is representing an abstract class or an interface. The visibility of a class is assumed to be public by default, though nonpublic classes can be identified using a property string in curly braces, such as `{private}`.

Attributes listed in a class can also provide several pieces of additional information. The full syntax for showing an attribute is

visibility name : type = default-value

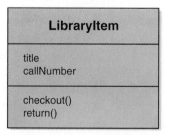

figure 1.5   LibraryItem class diagram

The visibility may be spelled out as `public`, `protected`, or `private`, or you may use the symbols + to represent public visibility, # for protected visibility, or − for private visibility. For example, we might have listed the title of a `LibraryItem` as

    - title : String

indicating that the attribute `title` is a private variable of type `String`. A default value is not provided in this case. Also, the stereotype <<final>> may be added to an attribute to indicate that it is a constant.

Similarly, the full syntax for an operation is

visibility name (parameter-list) : *return-type { property-string }*

As with the syntax for attributes, all of the items other than the name are optional. The visibility modifiers are the same as they are for attributes. The *parameter-list* can include the name and type of each parameter, separated by a colon. The *return-type* is the type of the value returned from the operation.

UML relationships

There are several kinds of relationships among classes that UML diagrams can represent. Usually they are shown as lines or arrows connecting one class to another. Specific types of lines and arrowheads have specific meaning in UML.

> **key concept**
>
> Various kinds of relationships can be represented in a UML class diagram.

One type of relationship shown between two classes in a UML diagram is an *inheritance relationship*. Figure 1.6 shows two classes that are derived from the `LibraryItem` class. Inheritance is shown using an arrow with an open arrowhead pointing from the child class to the parent class. This example shows that both the `Book` class and the `Video` class inherit all of the attributes and operations of `LibraryItem`, but they also extend that definition with attributes of their own. Note that in this example, neither subclass has any additional operations other than those provided in the parent class.

Another relationship shown in a UML diagram is an *association*, which represents relationships between instances (objects) of the classes. An association is indicated by a solid line between the two classes involved, and can be annotated with the *cardinality* of the relationship on either side. For example, Figure 1.7 shows an association between a `LibraryCustomer` and a `LibraryItem`. The cardinality of 0..* means "zero or more", in this case indicating that any given library customer may check out 0 or more items, and that any given library item may be checked out by multiple customers. The cardinality of an association may

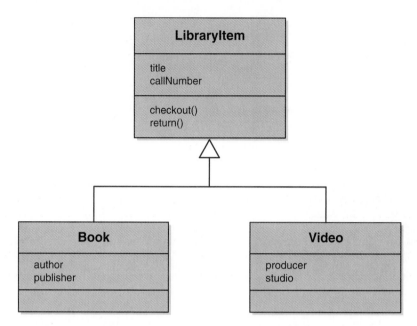

figure 1.6   A UML class diagram showing inheritance relationships

indicate other relationships, such as an exact number or a specific range. For example, if a customer is allowed to check out no more than five items, the cardinality could have been indicated by 0..5.

A third type of relationship between classes is the concept of *aggregation*. This is the situation in which one class is essentially made up, at least in part, of other classes. For example, we can extend our library example as shown in Figure 1.8 to show a CourseMaterials class that is made up of books, course notes, and

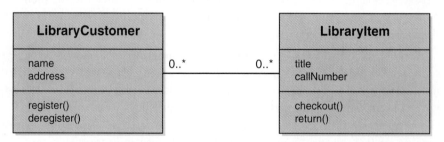

figure 1.7   A UML class diagram showing an association

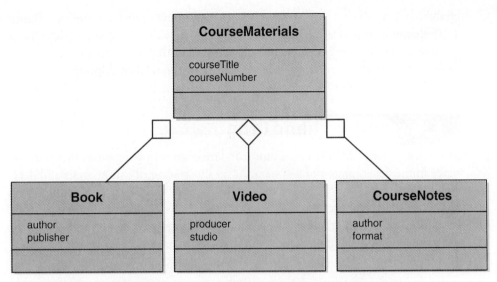

figure 1.8   One class shown as an aggregate of other classes

videos. Aggregation is shown using an open diamond on the aggregate end of the relationship.

A fourth relationship that we may wish to represent is the concept of *implementation*. This relationship occurs between an interface and any class that implements that interface. Figure 1.9 shows an interface called `Copyrighted` that contains two abstract methods. The dotted arrow with the open arrowhead indicates that the `Book` class implements the `Copyrighted` interface.

A fifth type of relationship between classes is the concept of one class *using* another. Examples of this concept include such things as an instructor using a

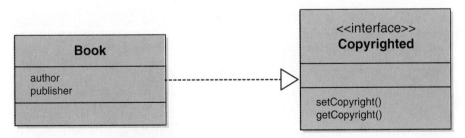

figure 1.9   A UML diagram showing a class implementing an interface

chalkboard, a driver using a car, or a library customer using a computer. Figure 1.10 illustrates this relationship, showing that a `LibraryCustomer` might use a `Computer`. The uses relationship is indicated by a dotted line with an open arrowhead that is usually annotated with the nature of the relationship.

1.5   error handling

There are a variety of very important software engineering decisions that must be made in the development of a system. As an illustration of this analysis and decision making process, let's take a closer look at how errors are handled in a system. As discussed in section 1.2, a robust program is one that handles erroneous or unusual situations gracefully. Therefore, the way a program is designed to handle these situations is fundamental to the software engineering process.

key concept

A Java error represents an unrecoverable problem, whereas a Java exception represents an unusual situation that may or may not be recoverable.

In Java, a program might throw an error or an exception, depending on the situation. An *error* almost always represents an unrecoverable situation and results in the abnormal termination of the program. An *exception*, as the name implies, represents an exceptional situation. That is, an exception represents a situation that does not occur in the normal or usual state of affairs. However, an exceptional situation does not necessarily mean that the program should terminate. An exception can be caught and handled using a `try-catch` statement.

Furthermore, in Java an exception is an object that can be created and used as needed. We can design, instantiate, and throw our own exceptions under whatever conditions we choose. Exceptions we design are essentially no different than the exceptions that are predefined in the Java class libraries and thrown by the runtime environment or other Java API classes.

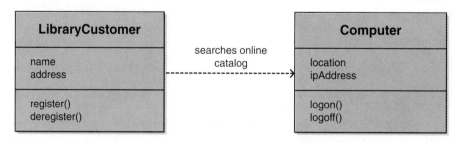

figure 1.10   One class indicating its use of another

How exceptions are handled is one of the most important decisions made when designing a software system. There are many questions to consider. What custom exception classes should be defined? When should those classes be instantiated and thrown? How and when should they be caught and handled?

As we explore the larger world of software development, especially when it involves the management of large amounts of data, we must carefully consider these questions. Perhaps the most important step is to establish a clear and consistent policy regarding how and when exceptions are used.

When a method is called that causes some kind of erroneous situation, the program could respond in any of the following ways:

▶ Return a value that represents the error rather than a valid return value.

▶ Throw an exception that the user must handle or ignore.

▶ If possible, handle the situation inside the method so that the calling object never needs to worry about it.

Before languages were designed with specific exception handling techniques, the first option was often used. However, it requires finding a return value that can be used to indicate the error and explicitly checking for that value in the calling object. The second option is more versatile and isn't a function of the return value at all. The last option is the most robust, but might not be possible. That is, the called method may not have enough information to handle the situation, or it may be best left to the calling object to decide.

> The manner in which exceptions are generated and handled is an important design decision.

key concept

Error handling is a function of many factors regarding the design of software systems. We examine these factors as they come up throughout the book.

1.6 analysis of algorithms

Another quality characteristic discussed in section 1.2 is the efficient use of resources. One of the most important resources is CPU time. The efficiency of an algorithm we use to accomplish a particular task is a major factor that determines how fast a program executes. Although we can analyze an algorithm relative to the amount of memory it uses, CPU time is usually the more interesting issue.

The *analysis of algorithms* is a fundamental computer science topic and involves a variety of techniques and concepts. It is a primary theme that we return to throughout the book. This section introduces the issues related to algorithm analysis and lays the groundwork for using analysis techniques.

Algorithm analysis is a fundamental computer science topic.

Let's start with an everyday example: washing dishes by hand. If we assume that washing a dish takes 30 seconds and drying a dish takes an additional 30 seconds, then we can see quite easily that it would take n minutes to wash and dry n dishes. This computation could be expressed as follows:

Time (n dishes)   = n * (30 seconds wash time + 30 seconds dry time)

                   = 60n seconds

On the other hand, suppose we were careless while washing the dishes and splashed too much water around. Suppose each time we washed a dish, we had to dry not only that dish but also all of the dishes we had washed before that one. It would still take 30 seconds to wash each dish, but now it would take 30 seconds to dry the last dish (once), 2 * 30 or 60 seconds to dry the second-to-last dish (twice), 3 * 30 or 90 seconds to dry the third-to-last dish (three times), and so on. This computation could be expressed as follows:

Time (n dishes) $= n * (30 \text{ seconds wash time}) + \sum_{i=1}^{n} (i * 30)$

                   = 30n + 30n(n+1)/2

                   $= 15n^2 + 45n$ seconds

If there were 30 dishes to wash, the first approach would take 30 minutes, whereas the second (careless) approach would take 247.5 minutes. The more dishes we wash the worse that discrepancy becomes.

growth functions and big O() notation

For every algorithm we want to analyze, we need to define the size of the problem. For our dishwashing example, the size of the problem is the number of dishes to be washed and dried. We also must determine the value that represents efficient use of time or space. For time considerations, we often pick an appropriate key processing step that we'd like to minimize, such as our goal to minimize the number of times a dish has to be washed and dried. The overall amount of time spent at the task is directly related to how many times we have to perform that task. The algorithm's efficiency can be defined in terms of the problem size and the processing step.

Consider an algorithm that sorts a list of numbers into increasing order. One natural way to express the size of the problem would be the number of values to be sorted. The processing step we are trying to optimize could be expressed as the number of comparisons we have to make for the algorithm to put the values in order. The more comparisons we make, the more CPU time is used.

A *growth function* shows the relationship between the size of the problem (n) and the value we hope to optimize. This function represents the *time complexity* or *space complexity* of the algorithm.

> A growth function shows time or space utilization relative to the problem size.
>
> **key concept**

The growth function for our second dishwashing algorithm is

$t(n) = 15n^2 + 45n$

However, it is not typically necessary to know the exact growth function for an algorithm. Instead, we are mainly interested in the *asymptotic complexity* of an algorithm. That is, we want to focus on the general nature of the function as n increases. This characteristic is based on the *dominant term* of the expression—the term that increases most quickly as n increases. As n gets very large, the value of the dishwashing growth function approaches n^2 because the n^2 term grows much faster than the n term. The constants and the secondary term quickly become irrelevant as n increases.

The asymptotic complexity is called the *order* of the algorithm. Thus, our dishwashing algorithm is said to have order n^2 time complexity, written $O(n^2)$. This is referred to as Big O() or Big-Oh notation. A growth function that executes in constant time regardless of the size of the problem is said to have $O(1)$. Figure 1.11 shows several growth functions and their asymptotic complexity.

Because the order of the function is the key factor, the other terms and constants are often not even mentioned. All algorithms within a given order are considered to be generally equivalent in terms of efficiency. For example, all sorting algorithms of $O(n^2)$ are considered to be equally efficient in general.

Growth Function	Order
$t(n) = 17$	$O(1)$
$t(n) = 20n - 4$	$O(n)$
$t(n) = 12n \log n + 100n$	$O(n \log n)$
$t(n) = 3n^2 + 5n - 2$	$O(n^2)$
$t(n) = 2^n + 18n^2 + 3n$	$O(2^n)$

figure 1.11   Some growth functions and their asymptotic complexity

comparing growth functions

One might assume that, with the advances in the speed of processors and the availability of large amounts of inexpensive memory, algorithm analysis would no longer be necessary. However, nothing could be farther from the truth. Processor speed and memory cannot make up for the differences in efficiency of algorithms.

Another way of looking at the effect of algorithm complexity was developed by Aho, Hopcroft, and Ullman (1974). The table in Figure 1.12 compares four algorithms with various time complexities and the effects of speeding up the processor by a factor of 10. Algorithm A_1, with a time complexity of n, is indeed improved by a factor of 10. However, algorithm A_2, with a time complexity of n^2, is only improved by a factor of 3.16. Similarly, algorithm A_3 is only improved by a factor of 2.15. For algorithms with *exponential complexity*, in which the size variable is in the exponent of the complexity term, the situation is far worse. In the grand scheme of things, if an algorithm is inefficient, speeding up the processor will not help.

> **key concept**
>
> If the algorithm is inefficient, a faster processor will not help in the long run.

Figure 1.13 illustrates various growth functions graphically. Note that, when n is small, there is little difference between the algorithms. That is, if you can guarantee a very small problem size (5 or less), it doesn't really matter which algorithm is used. However, as n gets larger, the differences between the growth functions become obvious.

analyzing loop execution

To determine the order of an algorithm, we often have to determine how often a particular statement or set of statements gets executed. Therefore, we often have to determine how many times the body of a loop is executed. To analyze loop exe-

Algorithm	Time Complexity	Max problem size before speed up	Max problem size after speed up
A_1	n	s_1	$10s_1$
A_2	n^2	s_2	$3.16s_2$
A_3	n^3	s_3	$2.15s_3$
A_4	n^4	s_4	$s_4 + 3.3$

Figure 1.12   Increase in problem size with a ten-fold increase in processor speed

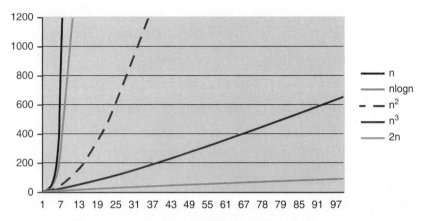

figure 1.13   Comparison of typical growth functions

cution, first determine the order of the body of the loop, and then multiply that by the number of times the loop will execute relative to n. Keep in mind that n represents the problem size.

Assuming that the body of a loop is O(1), then a loop such as this:

```
for (int count = 0; count < n; count++)
{
    /* some sequence of O(1) steps */
}
```

would have O(n) time complexity. This is due to the fact that the body of the loop has O(1) complexity but is executed n times by the loop structure. In general, when a loop structure steps through n items in a linear fashion and the body of the loop is O(1), then the loop is O(n). Even in a case where the loop is designed to skip some number of elements, as long as the progression of elements to skip is linear, the loop is still O(n). For example, if the preceding loop skipped every other number, the growth function of the loop would be n/2, but since constants don't affect the asymptotic complexity, the order is still O(n).

Let's look at another example. If the progression of the loop is logarithmic such as the following:

```
count = 1
while (count < n)
{
    count *= 2;
    /* some sequence of O(1) steps */
}
```

then the loop is said to be $O(\log n)$. Note that when we use a logarithm in an algorithm complexity, we almost always mean log base 2. This can be explicitly written as $O(\log_2 n)$. Since each time through the loop the value of count is multiplied by 2, the number of times the loop is executed is $\log_2 n$.

nested loops

A slightly more interesting scenario arises when loops are nested. In this case, we must multiply the complexity of the outer loop by the complexity of the inner loop to find the resulting complexity. For example, the following nested loops:

```
for (int count = 0; count < n; count++)
{
    for (int count2 = 0; count2 < n; count2++)
    {
        /* some sequence of O(1) steps */
    }
}
```

key concept

The analysis of nested loops must take into account both the inner and outer loops.

would have complexity $O(n^2)$. Both the inner and outer loops have complexity $O(n)$, which, when multiplied together, results in $O(n^2)$.

What is the complexity of the following nested loop?

```
for (int count = 0; count < n; count++)
{
    for (int count2 = count; count2 < n; count2++)
    {
        /* some sequence of O(1) steps */
    }
}
```

In this case, the inner loop index is initialized to the current value of the index for the outer loop. The outer loop executes n times. The inner loop executes n times the first time, n–1 times the second time, etc. However, remember that we are only interested in the dominant term, not in constants or any lesser terms. If the progression is linear, regardless of whether some elements are skipped, the order is still $O(n)$. Thus the resulting complexity for this code is $O(n^2)$.

1.7 software engineering and data structures

Why spend so much time talking about software engineering in a text that focuses on data structures and their algorithms? Well, as you begin to develop more complex programs, it's important to evolve a more mature outlook on the process. As we discussed at the beginning of this chapter, the goal should be to engineer software, not just write code. The data structures we examine in this book lay the foundation for complex software that must be carefully designed.

For each data structure that we study, we first need to know its purpose: why, how, and when it should be used. From this analysis, we will be able to design an interface to the data structure that is independent of its implementation. We will also design solutions that provide the required functionality. We will document these designs using UML class diagrams and examine multiple solutions for each data structure. We will examine our solutions for the proper use of exception handling and analyze their use of resources, especially CPU time and memory space.

> **key concept**
>
> Data structure design requires solid software engineering practices.

The topics of data structure design and software engineering are intertwined. Throughout this text, as we discuss data structures, we will also practice good software engineering.

summary of key concepts

- The first step in software development is to analyze the problem and develop a thorough and accurate set of requirements.

- For both practical and philosophical reasons, a software engineer must strive to deliver on time and within budget.

- Reliable software seldom fails and, when it does, minimizes the effects of that failure.

- Software systems must be carefully designed, written, and documented to support the work of developers, maintainers, and users.

- Software must make efficient use of resources such as CPU time and memory.

- Quality characteristics must be prioritized, and then maximized to the extent possible.

- A development life cycle model defines a process to be followed during development.

- Because exhaustive testing of most systems is not possible, we must develop test plans that are effective.

- Systems that are well designed and implemented are much easier to maintain.

- The waterfall model defines a specific set of milestones and deliverables.

- The spiral model is designed to reduce the risks inherent in software development.

- The Unified Modeling Language (UML) provides a notation with which we can capture and illustrate program designs.

- Various kinds of relationships can be represented in a UML class diagram.

- A Java error represents an unrecoverable problem, whereas a Java exception represents an unusual situation that may or may not be recoverable.

- The manner in which exceptions are generated and handled is an important design decision.

- Algorithm analysis is a fundamental computer science topic.

- A growth function shows time or space utilization relative to the problem size.

▸ If the algorithm is inefficient, a faster processor will not help in the long run.

▸ Analyzing algorithm complexity often requires analyzing the execution of loops.

▸ The analysis of nested loops must take into account both the inner and outer loops.

▸ Data structure design requires solid software engineering practices.

self-review questions

1.1   What is the difference between software engineering and programming?

1.2   Name several software quality characteristics.

1.3   What aspects of software creation do all development models include?

1.4   What is the main problem with the waterfall software development model?

1.5   What is the difference between a milestone and a deliverable?

1.6   What do the spiral and evolutionary development models have in common?

1.7   What does a UML class diagram represent?

1.8   What are the different types of relationships represented in a class diagram?

1.9   What is an exception?

1.10 What is the difference between the growth function of an algorithm and the order of that algorithm?

1.11 Why does speeding up the CPU not necessarily speed up the process by the same amount?

exercises

1.1   Compare and contrast software engineering with other engineering disciplines.

1.2   Give a specific example that illustrates each of the software quality characteristics listed in Figure 1.1.

1.3   Explain the difference between debugging and evaluation.

1.4   Compare and contrast the waterfall, spiral, and evolutionary models of software development.

1.5   Define the concept of visibility and describe why it is important in the software development process.

1.6   Create a UML class diagram for the organization of a university, where the university is made up of colleges, which are made up of departments, which contain faculty and students.

1.7   Complete the UML class description for a library system outlined in this chapter.

1.8   What is the order of the following growth functions?

   a. $10n^2 + 100n + 1000$

   b. $10n^3 - 7$

   c. $2^n + 100n^3$

   d. $n^2 \log n$

1.9   Arrange the growth functions of the previous exercise in ascending order of efficiency for n=10 and again for n=1,000,000.

1.10   Write the code necessary to find the largest element in an unsorted array of integers. What is the time complexity of this algorithm?

1.11   Determine the growth function and order of the following code fragment:

```
for (int count=0; count < n; count++)
{
   for (int count2=0; count2 < n; count2=count2*2)
   {
      /* some sequence of O(1) steps */
   }
}
```

answers to self-review questions

1.1   Software engineering is concerned with the larger goals of system design and development, not just the writing of code. Programmers mature into software engineers as they begin to understand the issues related to the development of high-quality software and adopt the appropriate practices.

1.2   Software quality characteristics include: correctness, reliability, robustness, usability, maintainability, reusability, portability, and efficiency.

1.3   In one way or another, all software development models include the processes of requirements analysis, design, implementation, evaluation, and maintenance.

1.4   The waterfall model is an engineering process developed for traditional engineering fields dealing with a more tangible product with more completely specified requirements. Iterative processes work better for software development simply because of the intangible nature of the product.

1.5   Milestones mark the end of a process activity. Deliverables are some product delivered to the client.

1.6   Both the spiral and evolutionary development models are iterative, easily allowing the developer to revisit previous activities.

1.7   A class diagram describes the types of objects or classes in the system, the static relationships among them, the attributes and operations of a class, and the constraints on the connections among objects.

1.8   Relationships shown in a UML class diagram include subtypes or extensions, associations, aggregates, and the implementation of interfaces.

1.9   An exception is an object that represents an unusual situation that can occur in a program. Some exceptions represent serious problems that are unrecoverable, while others represent processing that is out of the norm but can be handled appropriately under program control.

1.10 The growth function of an algorithm represents the exact relationship between the problem size and the time complexity of the solution. The order of the algorithm is the asymptotic time complexity. As the size of the problem grows, the complexity of the algorithm approaches the asymptotic complexity.

1.11 Linear speed up only occurs if the algorithm has a linear order, $O(n)$. As the complexity of the algorithm grows, faster processors have significantly less impact.

references

Aho, A. V., J. E. Hopcroft, and J. D. Ullman. *The Design and Analysis of Computer Algorithms*. Reading, Mass.: Addison-Wesley, 1974.

Boehm, B. "A Spiral Model for Software Development and Enhancement." *Computer* 21, no. 5 (May 1988): 61–72.

Sommerville, I. *Software Engineering*. 6th Ed. Harlow, England: Addison-Wesley, 2001.

This chapter begins our exploration of collections and the underlying data structures used to implement them. It lays the groundwork for the study of collections by carefully defining the issues and goals related to their design. This chapter also introduces a collection called a bag and uses it to exemplify the issues related to the design, implementation, and use of collections.

chapter
objectives

▷ Define the concepts and terminology related to collections

▷ Explore the basic structure of the Java Collections API

▷ Discuss the abstract design of collections

▷ Define a bag collection

▷ Use a bag collection to solve a problem

▷ Examine an array implementation of a bag

2.1 introduction to collections

A *collection* is an object that gathers and organizes other objects. It defines the specific ways in which those objects, which are called *elements* of the collection, can be accessed and managed. The user of a collection, which is usually another class or object in the software system, must interact with the collection only in the prescribed ways.

Over the past 50 years, several specific types of collections have been defined by software developers and researchers. Each type of collection lends itself to solving particular kinds of problems. A large portion of this book is devoted to exploring these classic collections.

Collections can be separated into two broad categories: linear and nonlinear. As the name implies, a *linear collection* is one in which the elements of the collection are organized in a straight line. A *nonlinear collection* is one in which the elements are organized in something other than a straight line, such as a hierarchy or a network. For that matter, a nonlinear collection may not have any organization at all.

Figure 2.1 shows a linear and a nonlinear collection. It usually doesn't matter if the elements in a linear collection are depicted horizontally or vertically.

The organization of the elements in a collection, relative to each other, is usually determined by one of two things:

▸ The order in which they were added to the collection.

▸ Some inherent relationship among the elements themselves.

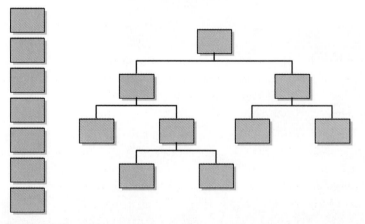

figure 2.1   A linear and a nonlinear collection

For example, one linear collection may always add new elements to one end of the line, so the order of the elements is determined by the order in which they are added. Another linear collection may be kept in sorted order based on some characteristic of the elements. For example, a list of people may be kept in alphabetical order based on the characters that make up their name. The specific organization of the elements in a nonlinear collection can be determined in either of these two ways as well.

abstraction

An *abstraction* hides or ignores certain details at certain times. It's easier to deal with an abstraction than it is to deal with too many details at one time. In fact, we couldn't get through a day without relying on abstractions. For example, we couldn't possibly drive a car if we had to worry about all the details that make the car work: the spark plugs, the pistons, the transmission, and so on. Instead, we can focus on the *interface* to the car: the steering wheel, the pedals, and a few other controls. These controls are an abstraction, hiding the underlying details and allowing us to control an otherwise very complicated machine.

> **A collection is an abstraction where the details of the implementation are hidden.**
>
> key concept

A collection, like any well-designed object, is an abstraction. A collection defines the interface operations through which the user can manage the objects in the collection, such as adding and removing elements. The user interacts with the collection through this interface, as depicted in Figure 2.2. However, the details of how a collection is implemented in order to fulfill that definition are another issue altogether. A class that implements the collection's interface must fulfill the conceptual definition of the collection, but can do so in many ways.

Abstraction is another important software engineering concept. In large software systems, it is virtually impossible for any one person to grasp all of the details of the system at once. Instead, the system is divided into abstract subsystems such that the purpose of and the interactions among those subsystems can be specified. Subsystems may then be assigned to different developers or groups of developers that will develop the subsystem to meet its specification.

An object is the perfect mechanism for creating a collection because, if it is designed correctly, the internal workings of an object are *encapsulated* from the rest of the system. In almost all cases, the instance variables defined in a class should be declared with private visibility. Therefore, only the methods of that class can access and modify them. The only interaction a user has with an object should be through its public methods that represent the services that that object provides.

Interface

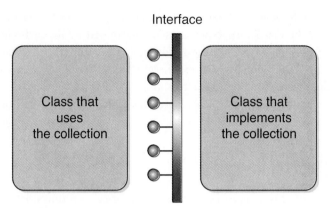

figure 2.2   A well-defined interface masks the implementation of the collection

As we progress through our exploration of collections, we will always stress the idea of separating the interface from the implementation. Therefore, for every collection we examine, we should consider the following:

- How does the collection operate, conceptually?
- How do we formally define the interface to the collection?
- What kinds of problems does the collection help us solve?
- What various ways might we implement the collection?
- What are the benefits and costs of each implementation?

Before we continue, let's carefully define some other terms related to the exploration of collections. A *data type* is a group of values and the operations defined on those values. The primitive data types defined in Java are the primary examples. For example, the integer data type defines a set of numeric values and the operations (addition, subtraction, etc.) that can be used on them.

An *abstract data type* (ADT) is a data type whose values and operations are not inherently defined within a programming language. It is abstract only in that the details of its implementation must be defined and should be hidden from the user. A collection, therefore, is an abstract data type.

A *data structure* is the collection of programming constructs used to implement a collection. For example, a collection might be implemented using a fixed-size structure such as an array. One interesting artifact of these definitions and our design decision to separate the interface from the implementation (i.e., the collection from the data structure that implements it) is that we may, and often do, end up with a linear data structure, such as an array, being used to implement a nonlinear collection, such as a tree.

> **A data structure is the underlying programming constructs used to implement a collection.**
>
> key concept

Historically, the terms ADT and data structure have been used in various ways. We carefully define them here to avoid any confusion, and will use them consistently. Throughout this book we will examine various data structures and how they can be used to implement various collections.

the Java Collections API

The Java programming language is accompanied by a huge library of classes that can be used to support the development of software. Parts of the library are organized into *application programming interfaces* (APIs). The *Java Collections API* is a set of classes that represent a few specific types of collections, implemented in various ways.

You might ask why we should learn how to design and implement collections if a set of collections has already been provided for us. There are several reasons. First, the Java Collections API only provides a subset of the collections you may want to use. Second, the classes they provide may not implement the collections in the ways you desire. Third, and perhaps most important, the study of software development requires a deep understanding of the issues involved in the design of collections and the data structures used to implement them.

As we explore various types of collections, we will also examine the appropriate classes of the Java Collections API. In each case, we analyze the various implementations that we develop and compare them to the approach used by the classes in the standard library.

2.2 a bag collection

Let's look at an example of a collection. A *bag* can be defined as a collection that groups elements with no particular positional relationship at all. Conceptually it is similar to a physical bag into which elements are placed. Once an element is put in a bag, there is no guarantee about where that element is in relation to any other element in the bag. If you reach into the bag and pull out an element without looking, you are equally likely to get any of the elements. If you want to get a particular element out of the bag, you'll have to search for it. Figure 2.3 depicts a bag collection holding its otherwise unorganized elements.

figure 2.3   The conceptual view of a bag collection

A bag is a nonlinear collection. There is essentially no organization to the elements in the collection at all. The elements in a bag have no inherent relationship to each other, and there is no significance to the order in which they have been added to the bag.

key concept

A bag is a nonlinear collection in which there is essentially no organization to the elements in the collection.

The specific manner in which a collection is defined is important. For the classic collection types, there is general agreement among software developers about their role. However, a specific set of operations is not carved in stone. There are many variations possible for any given collection type, though it's appropriate that the defined operations adhere to its underlying purpose. The operations we define for a bag collection are listed in Figure 2.4.

Operation	Description
`add`	Adds an element to the bag.
`addAll`	Adds the elements of one bag to another.
`removeRandom`	Removes an element at random from the bag.
`remove`	Removes a particular element from the bag.
`union`	Combines the elements of two bags to create a third.
`contains`	Determines if a particular element is in the bag.
`equals`	Determines if two bags contain the same elements.
`isEmpty`	Determines if the bag is empty.
`size`	Determines the number of elements in the bag.
`iterator`	Provides an iterator for the bag.
`toString`	Provides a string representation of the bag.

figure 2.4   The operations on a bag collection

Every collection has operations that allow the user to add and remove elements, though they vary in their details. Some operations such as `isEmpty` and `size` are common to almost all collections as well. A bag collection is somewhat unique in that it incorporates an element of randomness. The very nature of a bag collection lends itself to being able to pick an element out of the bag at random.

interfaces

To facilitate the separation of the interface operations from the methods that implement them, we can define a Java interface structure for a collection. A Java interface provides a formal mechanism for defining the set of operations for any collection.

> **key concept**
>
> A Java interface defines a set of abstract methods and is useful in separating the concept of an abstract data type from its implementation.

Recall that a Java interface defines a set of abstract methods, specifying each method's signature but not its body. A class that implements an interface provides definitions for the methods defined in the interface. The interface name can be used as the type of a reference, which can be assigned any object of any class that implements the interface.

Listing 2.1 defines a Java interface for a bag collection. We name a collection interface using the collection name followed by the abbreviation ADT (for abstract data type). Thus, `BagADT.java` contains the interface for a bag collection. It is defined as part of the `jss2` package, which contains all of the collection classes and interfaces presented in this book.

Note that in some methods, the return type is given as `BagADT`. This indicates that the method returns a bag collection. But by using the interface name as the return type, the interface doesn't commit the method to the use of any particular class that implements a bag. This is important for the definition of the interface, which is deliberately not tied to a particular implementation. This same argument can be made about the methods that accept a bag collection as a parameter.

> **key concept**
>
> By using the interface name as a return type, the interface doesn't commit the method to the use of any particular class that implements a bag.

Each time we introduce an interface, a class, or a system in this text, we will accompany that description with the UML description of that interface, class, or system. This should help you become accustomed to reading UML descriptions and creating them for other classes and systems. Figure 2.5 illustrates the UML description of the `BagADT` interface. Note that UML provides flexibility in describing the methods associated with a class or interface. In this case, we have chosen to identify each of the methods as public (+) but we have not listed the parameters for each.

listing
    2.1

```java
//********************************************************************
//  BagADT.java        Authors: Lewis/Chase
//
//  Defines the interface to a bag collection.
//********************************************************************

package jss2;

import java.util.Iterator;

public interface BagADT
{
    //  Adds one element to this bag
    public void add (Object element);

    //  Removes and returns a random element from this bag
    public Object removeRandom ();

    //  Removes and returns the specified element from this bag
    public Object remove (Object element);

    //  Returns the union of this bag and the parameter
    public BagADT union (BagADT set);

    //  Returns true if this bag contains the parameter
    public boolean contains (Object target);

    //  Returns true if this bag and the parameter contain exactly
    //  the same elements
    public boolean equals (BagADT bag);

    //  Returns true if this set contains no elements
    public boolean isEmpty();

    //  Returns the number of elements in this set
    public int size();

    //  Returns an iterator for the elements in this bag
    public Iterator iterator();

    //  Returns a string representation of this bag
    public String toString();
}
```

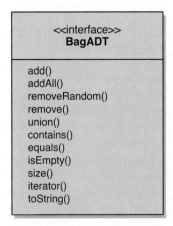

figure 2.5   UML description of the `BagADT` interface

iterators

An *iterator* is an object that provides the means to iterate over a collection. That is, it provides methods that allow the user to acquire and use each element in a collection in turn. Most collections provide one or more ways to iterate over their elements. In the case of the `BagADT` interface, we define a method called `iterator` that returns an `Iterator` object.

> **key concept**
>
> An iterator is an object that provides a means to iterate over a collection.

The `Iterator` interface is defined in the Java standard class library. The two primary abstract methods defined in the `Iterator` interface are:

- `hasNext`, which returns true if there are more elements in the iteration
- `next`, which returns the next element in the iteration

The `iterator` method of the `BagADT` interface returns an object that implements this interface. The user can then interact with that object, using the `hasNext` and `next` methods, to access the elements in the bag.

Note that there is no assumption about the order in which an `Iterator` object delivers the elements from the collection. In the case of a bag, there is no particular order to the elements, so the order will be arbitrary. In other cases, an iterator may follow a particular order that makes sense for that collection.

Another issue surrounding the use of iterators is what happens if the collection is modified while the iterator is in use. Most of the collections in the Java Collections API are implemented to be *fail-fast*. This simply means that they will, or should, throw an exception if the collection is modified while the iterator is in use. However, the documentation regarding these collections is very explicit that this behavior cannot be guaranteed. We will illustrate a variety of alternative possibilities for iterator construction throughout the examples in the book. These include creating iterators that allow concurrent modification and reflect those changes in the iteration, and iterators that iterate over a snapshot of the collection for which concurrent modifications have no impact.

exceptions

As discussed in Chapter 1, the manner in which exceptions are used is important to the definition of a software system. Exceptions could be thrown in many situations in a collection. Usually it's best to throw exceptions whenever an invalid operation is attempted. For example, in the case of a bag, we will throw an exception whenever the user attempts to remove an element from an empty bag. The user then has the choice of checking the situation beforehand to avoid the exception:

```
if (! theBag.isEmpty())
    element = theBag.removeRandom();
```

Or the user can use a `try-catch` statement to handle the situation when it does occur:

```
try {
    element = theBag.removeRandom()
}
catch (EmptyBagException exception)
{
    System.out.println ("No elements available.");
}
```

As we explore particular implementation techniques for a collection, we will also discuss the appropriate use of exceptions.

2.3 using a bag: bingo

We can use the game called bingo to demonstrate the use of a bag collection. In bingo, numbers are chosen at random from a limited set, usually 1 to 75. The numbers in the range 1 to 15 are associated with the letter B, 16 to 30 with the letter I, 31 to 45 with the letter N, 46 to 60 with the letter G, and 61 to 75 with the letter O. The person managing the game (the "caller") selects a number randomly, and then announces the letter and the number. The caller then sets aside that number so that it cannot be used again in that game. All of the players then mark any squares on their card that match the letter and number called. Once any player has five squares in a row marked (vertically, horizontally, or diagonally), they announce BINGO! and claim their prize. Figure 2.6 shows a sample bingo card.

A bag is perfectly suited for assisting the caller in selecting randomly from the possible numbers. To solve this problem, we would simply need to create an object for each of the possible numbers and add them to a bag. Then, each time the caller needs to select a number, we would call the removeRandom method. Listing 2.2 shows the BingoBall class needed to represent each possible selection. The program in Listing 2.3 adds the 75 bingo balls to the bag and then selects some of them randomly to illustrate the task.

Figure 2.7 shows the relationship between the Bingo and BingoBall classes illustrated in UML.

B	I	N	G	O
9	25	34	48	69
15	19	31	59	74
2	28	FREE	52	62
7	16	41	58	70
4	20	38	47	64

figure 2.6   A bingo card

listing
    2.2

```java
//********************************************************************
//   BingoBall.java        Authors: Lewis/Chase
//
//   Represents a ball used in a BINGO game.
//********************************************************************

public class BingoBall
{
   private char letter;
   private int number;

   //-----------------------------------------------------------------
   //   Sets up this BINGO ball with the specified number and the
   //   appropriate letter.
   //-----------------------------------------------------------------
   public BingoBall (int num)
   {
      number = num;

      if (num <= 15)
         letter = 'B';
      else
         if (num <= 30)
            letter = 'I';
         else
            if (num <= 45)
               letter = 'N';
            else
               if (num <= 60)
                  letter = 'G';
               else
                  letter = 'O';
   }

   //-----------------------------------------------------------------
   //   Returns a string representation of this BINGO ball.
   //-----------------------------------------------------------------
   public String toString ()
   {
      return (letter + " " + number);
   }
}
```

listing
    2.3

```java
//*****************************************************************
//  Bingo.java         Authors: Lewis/Chase
//
//  Demonstrates the use of a bag collection.
//*****************************************************************

import jss2.ArrayBag;

public class Bingo
{
   //-----------------------------------------------------------------
   //  Creates all 75 bingo balls and stores them in a bag. Then
   //  pulls several balls from the bag at random and prints them.
   //-----------------------------------------------------------------
   public static void main (String[] args)
   {
      final int NUM_BALLS = 75, NUM_PULLS = 10;

      ArrayBag bingoBag = new ArrayBag();
      BingoBall ball;

      for (int num = 1; num <= NUM_BALLS; num++)
      {
         ball = new BingoBall (num);
         bingoBag.add (ball);
      }

      System.out.println ("Size: " + bingoBag.size());
      System.out.println ();

      for (int num = 1; num <= NUM_PULLS; num++)
      {
         ball = (BingoBall) bingoBag.removeRandom();
         System.out.println (ball);
      }
   }
}
```

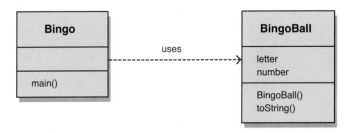

`figure 2.7`   UML description of the `Bingo` and `BingoBall` classes

2.4 `implementing a bag: with arrays`

So far in our discussion of a bag collection we've described its basic conceptual nature and the operations that allow the user to interact with it. In software engineering terms, we would say that we have done the analysis and perhaps the high-level design for a bag collection. We've also used a bag, without knowing the details of how it was implemented, to solve a particular problem. Now let's turn our attention to the implementation details. There are various ways to implement a class that represents a bag. In this section we examine an implementation strategy that uses an array to store the objects contained in the bag. In the next chapter we examine a second technique for implementing a bag.

To explore this implementation we must recall several key characteristics of Java arrays. The elements stored in an array are indexed from 0 to n–1, where n is the total number of cells in the array. An array is an object, which is instantiated separately from the objects it holds. And when we talk about an array of objects, we are actually talking about an array of references to objects, as pictured in Figure 2.8.

Keep in mind the separation between the collection and the underlying data structure used to implement it. Our goal is to design an efficient implementation that provides the functionality of every operation defined in the bag abstract data type. In this case, as we discussed earlier, we happen to be using an array (a linear data structure) to represent a bag (a nonlinear collection). The array is just a convenient data structure in which to store the objects. The fact that an array stores objects in a particular order is not relevant in this case because, in a bag collection, there is no defined order among the elements. Therefore, our solution for implementing each operation of a bag collection will give no relevance to the order in which objects are held in the array.

> The implementation of the collection operations should not affect the way users interact with the collection.

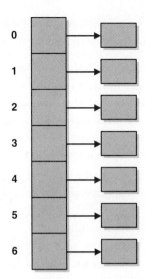

figure 2.8   An array of object references

managing capacity

When an array object is created, it is allocated a specific number of cells into which elements can be stored. For example, the following instantiation creates an array that can store 500 elements, indexed from 0 to 499:

```
Object[] collection = Object[500];
```

The number of cells in an array is called its *capacity*. This value is stored in the `length` constant of the array. The capacity of an array cannot be changed once the array has been created.

When using an array to implement a collection, we have to deal with the situation in which all cells of the array are being used to store elements. That is, because we are using a fixed-size data structure, at some point the collection may become "full."

A crucial question in the design of a collection is what to do in the case when a new element is added to a full data structure. Three basic options exist:

▸ We could implement operations that add an element to the collection such that they throw an exception if the data structure is full.

▸ We could implement the `add` operations to return a status indicator that can be checked by the user to see if the `add` operation was successful.

▸ We could automatically expand the capacity of the underlying data structure whenever necessary so that, essentially, it would never become full.

In the first two cases, the user of the collection must be aware that the collection could get full and take steps to deal with it when needed. For these solutions we would also provide extra operations that allow the user to check to see if the collection is full and to expand the capacity of the data structure as desired. The advantage of these approaches is that it gives the user more control over the capacity.

However, given our goal to separate the interface from the implementation, the third option is attractive. The capacity of the underlying data structure is an implementation detail that, in general, should be hidden from the user. Furthermore, the capacity issue is particular to this implementation. Other techniques used to implement the collection, such as the one we explore in the next chapter, are not restricted by a fixed capacity and therefore never have to deal with this issue.

In the solutions presented in this book, we opt to implement fixed data structure solutions by automatically expanding the capacity of the underlying data structure. Occasionally other options are explored as programming projects.

the ArrayBag class

In the Java Collections API framework, class names indicate both the underlying data structure and the collection. We follow that naming convention in this book. Thus, we define a class called ArrayBag that represents an array-based implementation of a bag collection. We present various pieces of the ArrayBag class throughout this section.

The ArrayBag class implements the BagADT interface presented earlier in this chapter, and therefore must define the methods listed in that interface. Keep in mind that a class that implements an interface may also define additional methods as well.

The key instance data for the ArrayBag class includes the array that holds the contents of the bag and the integer variable count that keeps track of the number of elements in the collection. We also define a Random object to support the drawing of a random element from the bag, and a constant to define a default capacity. Another constant called NOT_FOUND is also created to assist in the operations that search for particular elements. The ArrayBag instance data is declared as follows:

```
private static Random rand = new Random( );

private final int DEFAULT_CAPACITY = 100;
private final int NOT_FOUND = -1;

private int count;
private Object[] contents;
```

Note that the Random object is declared as a static variable, and is instantiated in its declaration (rather than in a constructor). Because it is static, the Random object is shared among all instances of the ArrayBag class. This strategy avoids the problem of creating two bags that have random-number generators using the same seed value.

The value of the variable count actually represents two related pieces of information. First, it represents the number of elements that are currently stored in the bag collection. Second, because Java array indexes start at zero, it also represents the next open slot into which a new element can be stored in the array. On one hand the value of count represents the abstract state of the collection, and on the other it helps us with the internal implementation of that collection.

In this implementation, the elements contained in the bag are gathered contiguously at one end of the array. This strategy simplifies various aspects of the operations, though it does require operations that remove elements to "fill in the gaps" created in the elements. Figure 2.9 depicts the use of an array to store the elements of a bag.

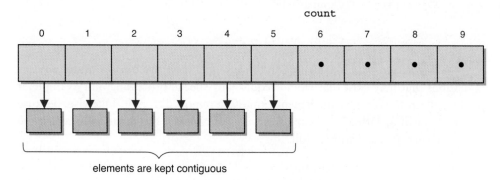

figure 2.9   An array implementation of a bag

The following constructor is defined for the `ArrayBag` class to set up an initially empty bag. The value of `count` is set to zero and the array that will store the elements of the bag is instantiated. This constructor uses a default value for the initial capacity of the `contents` array.

```
//------------------------------------------------------------------
//  Creates an empty bag using the default capacity.
//------------------------------------------------------------------
public ArrayBag()
{
   count = 0;
   contents = new Object[DEFAULT_CAPACITY];
}
```

We can also provide a second constructor that accepts a single integer parameter representing the initial capacity of the `contents` array. In a particular situation, the user may know approximately how many elements will be stored in a bag, and can specify that value from the beginning. This overloaded constructor can be defined as follows:

```
//------------------------------------------------------------------
//  Creates an empty bag using the specified capacity.
//------------------------------------------------------------------
public ArrayBag (int initialCapacity)
{
   count = 0;
   contents = new Object[initialCapacity];
}
```

As we design the implementation of each operation, we must consider any situations that may exist that would require any special processing. For example, if the collection is empty, an element cannot be removed from it. Likewise, because we are dealing with a fixed capacity, we must consider the situation in which the underlying data structure is full.

the `size` and `isEmpty` operations

The operations `size` and `isEmpty` are found in almost any collection. In the `ArrayBag` class, the count instance variable represents the number of elements in the bag, and can therefore be used to provide efficient solutions to these operations.

The size method simply returns the value of the count variable:

```
//-----------------------------------------------------------------
//   Returns the number of elements currently in this bag.
//-----------------------------------------------------------------
public int size()
{
    return count;
}
```

The isEmpty method returns true if the value of count is zero:

```
//-----------------------------------------------------------------
//   Returns true if this bag is empty and false otherwise.
//-----------------------------------------------------------------
public boolean isEmpty()
{
    return (count == 0);
}
```

The ArrayBag implementation relies on the value of count in several situations. It is fundamental to the representation of the collection. Therefore, all operations that change the state of the bag collection must carefully maintain the integrity of the count value.

the add operation

The purpose of the add method is to incorporate the Object that it accepts as a parameter into the bag collection. For our array implementation, that means storing it in an empty slot in the array. The instance variable count represents the next empty space in the array, so we can simply store the new element at that location.

However, the add operation for a fixed-capacity structure must take into account the situation in which the array is filled. As we discussed earlier in this chapter, our solution is to automatically expand the capacity of the array when this situation arises.

The following method implements the `add` operation for the `ArrayBag` class:

```
//--------------------------------------------------------------
//   Adds the specified element to the bag, expanding the capacity
//   of the bag array if necessary.
//--------------------------------------------------------------
public void add (Object element)
{
   if (size() == contents.length)
      expandCapacity();

   contents[count] = element;
   count++;
}
```

The `add` method uses the `size` method to determine the number of elements currently in the collection. If this value equals the total number of cells in the array, indicated by the `length` constant, then the `expandCapacity` method is called. Whether the capacity is expanded or not, the element is then stored in the array and the number of elements in the bag collection is incremented. Note that after the `add` method finishes, the value of the `count` variable continues to represent both the number of elements in the bag and the next open slot in the array.

Instead of calling the `size` method, the `add` method could have examined the value of the `count` variable to determine if the capacity of the array needed to be expanded. The value of `count` is, after all, exactly what the `size` method returns. However, in situations like this in which there is a method to play a particular role (determine the size), we are better off using the method. If the design is later changed to determine the size of the bag in a different way, the `add` method would still work without a problem.

The `expandCapacity` method increases the size of the array storing the elements of the bag. More precisely, it creates a second array that is twice the size of the one currently storing the contents of the bag, copies all of the current references into the new array, then resets the `contents` instance variable to refer to the larger array. The `expandCapacity` method is implemented as follows:

```
//-----------------------------------------------------------------
//  Creates a new array to store the contents of the bag with
//  twice the capacity of the old one.
//-----------------------------------------------------------------
private void expandCapacity()
{
    Object[] larger = new Object[contents.length*2];

    for (int index=0; index < contents.length; index++)
        larger[index] = contents[index];

    contents = larger;
}
```

Note that the expandCapacity method is declared with private visibility. It is designed as a support method, not as a service provided for the user of the bag collection.

Also note that the expandCapacity method doubles the size of the contents array. It could have tripled the size, or simply added ten more cells, or even just one. The amount of the increase determines how soon we'll have to increase the size again. We don't want to have to call the expandCapacity method too often, because it copies the entire contents of the collection from one array to another. We also don't want to have too much unused space in the array, though this is probably the less serious offense. There is some mathematical analysis that could be done to determine the most effective size increase, but at this point we will simply make reasonable choices.

the addAll operation

The purpose of the addAll method is to incorporate all of the objects from one bag, that it accepts as a parameter, into the bag collection. For our array implementation, this means that we can use our iterator method to step through the contents of one bag and our add method to add those elements to the current bag. One advantage of using the add method in this way is that the add method already checks capacity and expands the array if necessary.

The following method implements the `addAll` operation for the `ArrayBag` class:

```
//--------------------------------------------------------------------
//  Adds the contents of the parameter to this bag.
//--------------------------------------------------------------------
public void addAll (BagADT bag)
{
   Iterator scan = bag.iterator();

   while (scan.hasNext())
      add (scan.next());
}
```

the `removeRandom` operation

The `removeRandom` operation must choose an element from the collection at random, remove that element from the collection, and return it to the calling method. This operation relies on the static `Random` object called `rand` that is defined as instance data.

The only special case for this operation is when an attempt is made to remove an element from an empty bag. If the bag collection is empty, this method throws an `EmptyBagException`. This processing is consistent with our philosophy of using exceptions.

The `removeRandom` method of the `ArrayBag` class is written as follows:

```
//--------------------------------------------------------------------
//  Removes a random element from the bag and returns it. Throws
//  an EmptyBagException if the bag is empty.
//--------------------------------------------------------------------
public Object removeRandom() throws EmptyBagException
{
   if (isEmpty())
      throw new EmptyBagException();

   int choice = rand.nextInt(count);

   Object result = contents[choice];

   contents[choice] = contents[count-1];  // fill the gap
   contents[count-1] = null;
   count--;

   return result;
}
```

The nextInt method of the Random class is used to determine a pseudorandom value in the range from 0 to count-1. This range represents the indices of all elements currently stored in the array. Once the random element is chosen, it is stored in the local variable called result, which is returned to the calling method when this method is complete.

Recall that this implementation of the bag collection keeps all elements in the bag stored contiguously at one end of the contents array. Because this method removes one of the elements, we must "fill the gap" in some way. We could use a loop to shift all of the elements down one, but that is unnecessary. Since there is no ordering implied by the array, we can simply take the last element in the list (at index count-1) and put it in the cell of the removed element, which requires no looping.

the remove operation

The remove operation removes one occurrence of the specified element from the bag and returns it. Keep in mind that bags allow duplicates. This means that if there are two occurrences of a particular element in the bag and we remove one of them, the other one will remain. This method will throw an EmptyBagException if the bag is empty and a NoSuchElementException if the target element is not in the bag.

With our array implementation, the remove operation is simply a matter of searching the array for the target element, removing it, and replacing it with the element stored at count-1, or the last element stored in the array. Since the elements of a bag are not stored in any particular order, there is no need to shift more than the one element. We then decrement the count.

```
//-----------------------------------------------------------------
//   Removes one occurrence of the specified element from the bag
//   and returns it. Throws an EmptyBagException if the bag is
//   empty and a NoSuchElemetnException if the target is not in
//   the bag.
//-----------------------------------------------------------------
public Object remove (Object target) throws EmptyBagException,
                                      NoSuchElementException
{
    int search = NOT_FOUND;

    if (isEmpty())
        throw new EmptyBagException();
```

```
      for (int index=0; index < count && search == NOT_FOUND; index++)
         if (contents[index].equals(target))
            search = index;

      if (search == NOT_FOUND)
         throw new NoSuchElementException();

      Object result = contents[search];

      contents[search] = contents[count-1];
      contents[count-1] = null;
      count--;

      return result;
   }
```

the union operation

The union operation returns a new bag that is the union of this bag and the parameter; i.e., a new bag that contains all of the elements from both bags. Again, we can make use of our existing operations. We use our constructor to create a new bag and then step through our array and use the add method to add each element of our current bag to the new bag. Next we create an iterator for the bag passed as a parameter, step through each element of that bag, and add each of them to the new bag. Since there is no inherent order in a bag, it does not matter which bag's contents we add first.

There are several interesting design possibilities with this operation. First, since the method is returning a new bag that is the combination of this bag and another bag, one could argue that the method should simply be a static method accepting two bags as input parameters. For consistency, we have chosen not to use that solution. A second possibility is to use the addAll method (i.e., both.addAll(this) followed by both.addAll(bag)). However, we have deliberately chosen to use a for loop and an iterator in this implementation to demonstrate an important concept. Since the process occurs "inside" one bag, we have access to its private instance data and thus can use a for loop to traverse the array. However, for the bag passed as a parameter, we use an iterator to access its elements.

```
//----------------------------------------------------------------
//  Returns a new bag that is the union of this bag and the
//  parameter.
//----------------------------------------------------------------
public BagADT union (BagADT bag)
{
   ArrayBag both = new ArrayBag();

   for (int index = 0; index < count; index++)
      both.add (contents[index]);

   Iterator scan = bag.iterator();
   while (scan.hasNext())
      both.add (scan.next());

   return both;
}
```

the contains operation

The contains operation returns true if this bag contains the specified target element. As with the remove operation, because of our array implementation, this operation becomes a simple search of an array to locate a particular element.

```
//----------------------------------------------------------------
//  Returns true if this bag contains the specified target
//  element.
//----------------------------------------------------------------
public boolean contains (Object target)
{
   int search = NOT_FOUND;

   for (int index=0; index < count && search == NOT_FOUND; index++)
      if (contents[index].equals(target))
         search = index;

   return (search != NOT_FOUND);
}
```

the equals operation

The equals operation will return true if the current bag contains exactly the same elements as the bag passed as a parameter. If the two bags are of different sizes, then there is no reason to continue the comparison. However, if the two bags are the same size, we create a deep copy of each bag and then use an iterator to step through the elements of the bag passed as a parameter and use the contains method to confirm that each of those elements are also in the current bag. As we find elements in both bags, we remove them from the copies, being careful not to affect the original bags. If both of the copies are empty at the end of the process, then the bags are indeed equal. Notice that we iterate over the original bag passed as a parameter while removing matching elements from the copies. This avoids any problems associated with modifying a bag while using the associated iterator.

```java
//-----------------------------------------------------------------
//  Returns true if this bag contains exactly the same elements
//  as the parameter.
//-----------------------------------------------------------------
public boolean equals (BagADT bag)
{
   boolean result = false;
   ArrayBag temp1 = new ArrayBag();
   ArrayBag temp2 = new ArrayBag();
   Object obj;

   if (size() == bag.size())
   {
      temp1.addAll(this);
      temp2.addAll(bag);

      Iterator scan = bag.iterator();

      while (scan.hasNext())
      {
         obj = scan.next();
         if (temp1.contains(obj))
         {
            temp1.remove(obj);
            temp2.remove(obj);
         }

      }
```

```
            result = (temp1.isEmpty() && temp2.isEmpty());
        }

        return result;
    }
```

the `iterator` operation

We have emphasized the idea thus far that we should reuse code whenever possible and design our solutions such that we can reuse them. The `iterator` operation is an excellent example of this philosophy. It would be possible to create an `iterator` method specifically for the array implementation of a bag. However, instead we have created a general `ArrayIterator` class that will work with any array-based implementation of any collection. The `iterator` method for the array implementation of a bag creates an instance of the `ArrayIterator` class. Listing 2.4 shows the `ArrayIterator` class.

```
    //-----------------------------------------------------------------
    //  Returns an iterator for the elements currently in this bag.
    //-----------------------------------------------------------------
    public Iterator iterator()
    {
        return new ArrayIterator (contents, count);
    }
```

the `toString` operation

The `toString` operation simply returns a string made up of the letter and number of each ball in the bag as provided by the `toString` operation of the `BingoBall` class.

listing
   2.4

```java
//*********************************************************************
//   ArrayIterator.java         Authors: Lewis/Chase
//
//   Represents an iterator over the elements of an array.
//*********************************************************************

package jss2;

import java.util.*;

public class ArrayIterator implements Iterator
{
   private int count;      // the number of elements in the collection
   private int current;    // the current position in the iteration
   private Object[] items;

   //-------------------------------------------------------------------
   //   Sets up this iterator using the specified items.
   //-------------------------------------------------------------------
   public ArrayIterator (Object[] collection, int size)
   {
      items = collection;
      count = size;
      current = 0;
   }

   //-------------------------------------------------------------------
   //   Returns true if this iterator has at least one more element
   //   to deliver in the iteration.
   //-------------------------------------------------------------------
   public boolean hasNext()
   {
      return (current < count);
   }

   //-------------------------------------------------------------------
   //   Returns the next element in the iteration. If there are no
   //   more elements in this iteration, a NoSuchElementException is
   //   thrown.
   //-------------------------------------------------------------------
```

listing
2.4   continued

```java
    public Object next()
    {
       if (! hasNext())
          throw new NoSuchElementException();

       current++;
       return items[current - 1];
    }

    //------------------------------------------------------------------
    //   The remove operation is not supported in this collection.
    //------------------------------------------------------------------
    public void remove() throws UnsupportedOperationException
    {
       throw new UnsupportedOperationException();
    }
}
```

```java
    //------------------------------------------------------------------
    //   Returns a string representation of this bag.
    //------------------------------------------------------------------
    public String toString()
    {
       String result = "";

       for (int index=0; index < count; index++)
          result = result + contents[index].toString() + "\n";

       return result;
    }
```

UML description

Now that we have all of our classes defined, it is possible to see a UML representation of the entire class diagram, as illustrated in Figure 2.10.

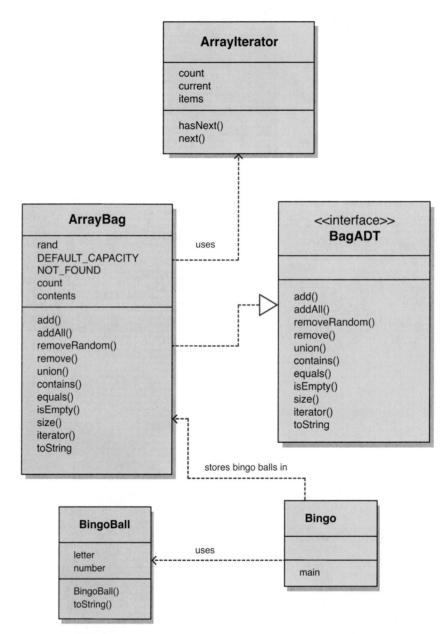

figure 2.10 UML description of the bingo system

2.5 analysis of the array implementation of a bag

The analysis of the space complexity of the array implementation of a bag is typical of the array implementations we will see for other collections. Array implementations are very effecient with each element, only allocating enough space per element for the object reference variable. However, array implementations typically allocate space for more elements than are currently stored in the array. If managed properly, using an appropriate initial capacity and then expanding capacity as needed, this additional space is not a problem.

The analysis of the time complexity of the operations for the array implementation of a bag is quite simple. Let's address each operation separately.

analysis of add

The add operation for the array implementation consists of the following steps:

▸ Check to make sure that the array is not full, expanding capacity if needed.

▸ Set the pointer in position count of the array to the object being added to the bag.

▸ Increment the count.

If the array is not full, each of these steps is O(1). Thus the operation is O(1). If the array is full, the expandCapacity method must create a new array twice as large as the original and copy all of the elements of the bag into the new array. This process is O(n). However, this case happens so seldom that, taken across all instances of add, expanding capacity has virtually no effect on the analysis. Thus we say that the add method is O(1).

analysis of remove

The remove operation for the array implementation consists of the following steps:

▸ Check to make sure the bag is not empty.

▸ Find the element to be removed.

▸ Move the last element in the array down to fill the position.

▸ Decrement the count.

All of these steps are also O(1) except for finding the element. This step requires best case 1 comparison if the element is the first one we check, worst case n comparisons if the elment is the last one we check, and expected case n/2 comparisons. Because we ignore constants when considering the complexity the `remove` operation for the array implementation has time complexity O(n).

analysis of `removeRandom`

The `removeRandom` operation for the array implementation is similar to the `remove` method except that we do not have to search for the element to be removed. We simply choose an index at random and remove that element. Thus the `removeRandom` operation is O(1).

analysis of `addAll`

The `addAll` operation for the array implementation makes use of an iterator to step through the contents of a bag, adding each element in turn to the current bag. Since the `add` method is O(1), and the iterator will step through n elements, this operation is also O(n).

analysis of `find` and `contains`

Both the `find` and `contains` methods step through the elements of a bag searching for a particular element. Like the discussion of the `remove` method, the best case is 1 comparsion, the worst case is n comparisons, and the expected case is n/2 comparisons. Thus these methods are both O(n).

analysis of `union`

The `union` operation for the array implementation steps through both the current bag and the bag passed as a parameter, adding each of their elements one at a time to a new bag. Assuming that the total number of elements between the two bags is n, then this operation is O(n). Another way to look at this is to assume that their are n elements in the current bag and m elements in the bag passed as a parameter. Then the operation would be O(n + m).

analysis of `equals`

The `equals` method for the array implementation makes use of three iterators, one each as copies of the bags are made using `addAll`, and then one to step through checking the contents of the copies. Assuming that each of the bags has roughly n elements, then the time complexity would be roughly 3*n or O(n).

summary of key concepts

- A collection is an object that gathers and organizes other objects.
- Elements in a collection are typically organized by the order of their addition to the collection or by some inherent relationship among the elements.
- A collection is an abstraction where the details of the implementation are hidden.
- A data structure is the underlying programming constructs used to implement a collection.
- A bag is a nonlinear collection in which there is essentially no organization to the elements in the collection.
- A Java interface defines a set of abstract methods and is useful in separating the concept of an abstract data type from its implementation.
- By using the interface name as a return type, the interface doesn't commit the method to the use of any particular class that implements a bag.
- An iterator is an object that provides a means to iterate over a collection.
- The implementation of the collection operations should not affect the way users interact with the collection.
- How we handle exceptional conditions determines whether the collection or the user of the collection controls the particular behavior.
- In the Java Collections API and throughout this text, class names indicate both the underlying data structure and the collection.

self-review questions

2.1   What is a collection?

2.2   What is a data type?

2.3   What is an abstract data type?

2.4   What is a data structure?

2.5   What is abstraction and what advantage does it provide?

2.6   What is a bag?

2.7   Why is a class an excellent representation of an abstract data type?

2.8   What is an iterator and why is it useful for ADTs?

2.9   Why develop collections if they are provided in the Java Collections API?

2.10 How should exceptional conditions be handled in ADTs?

2.11 What would the time complexity be for the `size` operation if there were not a `count` variable?

2.12 What would the time complexity be for the `add` operation if there were not a `count` variable?

exercises

2.1   Compare and contrast data types, abstract data types, and data structures.

2.2   List the collections in the Java Collections API and mark the ones that are covered in this text.

2.3   Define the concept of abstraction and explain why it is important in software development.

2.4   Define the concept of a bag. List additional operations that might be considered for a bag.

2.5   List each occurrence of one method in the `ArrayBag` class calling on another method from the same class. Why is this good programming practice?

2.6   Write an algorithm for the `add` method that would place each new element in position 0 of the array. What would the time complexity be for this algorithm?

2.7   A set is a very similar construct to a bag except that there are no duplicates in a set. What changes would have to be made to our methods to create an implementation of a set?

programming projects

2.1   Modify the `ArrayBag` class such that it puts the user in control of the bag's capacity. Eliminate the automatic expansion of the array. The revised class should throw a `FullBagException` when an element is added to a full bag. Add a method called `isFull` that returns true if the bag is full. And add a method that the user can call to expand the capacity by a particular number of cells.

2.2   An additional operation that might be implemented for a bag is
       `difference`. This operation would take a bag as a parameter and sub-
       tract the contents of that bag from the current bag if they exist in the
       current bag. The result would be returned in a new bag. Implement this
       operation. Be careful to consider possible exceptional situations.

2.3   Another operation that might be implemented for a bag is
       `intersection`. This operation would take a bag as a parameter and
       would return a bag containing those elements that exist in both bags.

2.4   Another operation that might be implemented for a bag is `count`. This
       operation would take an element as a parameter and return the number
       of copies of that element in the bag. Implement this operation. Be care-
       ful to consider possible exceptional situations.

2.5   A set is a very similar construct to a bag except that there are no dupli-
       cates in a set. Implement a set collection by creating both a `SetADT`
       interface and an `ArraySet` class. Include the additional operations
       described in the earlier projects.

2.6   Create a simple graphical application with a button labeled Add that,
       when pressed, will take a string from a text field and add it to a bag,
       and a button labeled Remove Random that, when pressed, will remove
       a random element from the bag. After processing in either case, the
       contents of a text area should be set to the bag's `toString` method to
       display the contents of the bag.

answers to self-review questions

2.1   A collection is an object that gathers and organizes other objects.

2.2   A data type is a set of values and operations on those values defined
       within a programming language.

2.3   An abstract data type is a data type that is not defined within the pro-
       gramming language and must be defined by the programmer.

2.4   A data structure is the set of objects necessary to implement an abstract
       data type.

2.5   Abstraction is the concept of hiding the underlying implementation of
       operations and data storage in order to simplify the use of a collection.

2.6   A bag is a collection in which there is no particular order or relation-
       ship among the elements in the collection.

2.7   Classes naturally provide abstraction since only those methods that provide services to other classes have public visibility.

2.8   An iterator is an object that provides a means of stepping through the elements of a collection one at a time.

2.9   The Java Collections API provides implementations of many ADTs but not all of them. Further, developers may wish to provide their own definitions in order to customize the behavior of the ADT.

2.10 The question should always be asked, "Is this a condition that should be handled automatically, or is this a condition over which the user of the ADT should have control?" An excellent example of this dilemma is the issue of automatically resizing the array in the array-based implementation of a bag.

2.11 Without a `count` variable, the most likely solution would be to traverse the array using a `while` loop, counting as you go, until you encounter the first null element of the array. Thus, this operation would be O(n).

2.12 Without a `count` variable, the most likely solution would be to traverse the array using a `while` loop until you encounter the first null element of the array. The new element would then be added into this position. Thus, this operation would be O(n).

This chapter explores a technique for creating data structures that uses references to create links between objects. Linked structures are fundamental in the development of software, especially the design and implementation of collections. This approach has both advantages and disadvantages when compared to a solution using arrays.

3

linked structures

chapter
objectives

- Describe the use of references to create linked structures

- Compare linked structures to array-based structures

- Explore the techniques for managing a linked list

- Discuss the need for a separate node object to form linked structures

- Implement a bag collection using a linked list

3.1   references as links

In Chapter 2 we discussed the concept of collections and explored one collection in particular: a bag. We defined the operations on a bag collection and designed an implementation using an underlying array-based data structure. In this chapter we explore an entirely different approach to designing a data structure.

A *linked structure* is a data structure that uses object reference variables to create links between objects. Linked structures are the primary alternative to an array-based implementation of a collection. After discussing various issues involved in linked structures, we will define a new implementation of a bag collection that uses an underlying linked data structure.

> **key concept**
>
> Object reference variables can be used to create linked structures.

Recall that an object reference variable holds the address of an object, indicating where the object is stored in memory. The following declaration creates a variable called obj that is only large enough to hold the numeric address of an object:

```
Object obj;
```

Usually the specific address that an object reference variable holds is irrelevant. That is, while it is important to be able to use the reference variable to access an object, the specific location in memory where it is stored is unimportant. Therefore, instead of showing addresses, we usually depict a reference variable as a name that "points to" an object, as shown in Figure 3.1. A reference variable, used in this context, is sometimes called a *pointer*.

Consider the situation in which a class defines as instance data a reference to another object of the same class. For example, suppose we have a class named Person that contains a person's name, address, and other relevant information. Now suppose that in addition to this data, the Person class also contains a reference variable to another Person object:

```
public class Person
{
    private String name;
    private String address;

    private Person next;   // a link to another Person object

    //  whatever else
}
```

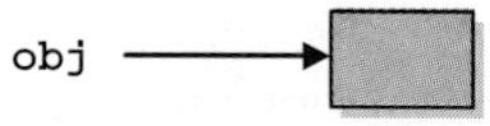

obj ——————▶ □

figure 3.1   An object reference variable pointing to an object

Using only this one class, a linked structure can be created. One `Person` object contains a link to a second `Person` object. This second object also contains a reference to a `Person`, which contains another, and so on. This type of object is sometimes called *self-referential*.

This kind of relationship forms the basis of a *linked list,* which is a linked structure in which one object refers to the next, creating a linear ordering of the objects in the list. A linked list is depicted in Figure 3.2. Often the objects stored in a linked list are referred to generically as the *nodes* of the list.

> **key concept**
>
> A linked list is composed of objects that each point to the next object in the list.

Note that a separate reference variable is needed to indicate the first node in the list. The list is terminated in a node whose `next` reference is `null`.

A linked list is only one kind of linked structure. If a class is set up to have multiple references to objects, a more complex structure can be created, such as the one depicted in Figure 3.3. The way in which the links are managed dictates the specific organization of the structure.

For now, we will focus on the details of a linked list. Many of these techniques apply to more complicated linked structures as well.

Unlike an array, which has a fixed size, a linked list has no upper bound on its capacity other than the limitations of memory in the computer. A linked list is considered to be a *dynamic* structure because its size grows and shrinks as needed to accommodate the number of elements stored. In Java, all objects are created dynamically from an area of memory called the system *heap,* or *free store*.

> **key concept**
>
> A linked list dynamically grows as needed and essentially has no capacity limitations.

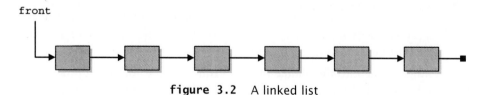

figure 3.2   A linked list

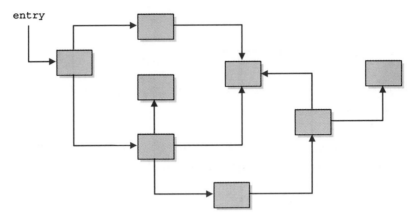

entry

figure 3.3   A complex linked structure

The next section explores some of the primary ways in which a linked list is managed.

3.2 managing linked lists

No matter what a linked list is used to store, there are a few basic techniques involved in managing the nodes on the list. Specifically, nodes are added to a list and they are removed from the list. Special care must be taken when dealing with the first node in the list so that the reference to the entire list is maintained appropriately.

inserting nodes

A node may be inserted into a linked list at any location: at the front of the list, among the interior nodes in the middle of the list, or at the end of the list. Adding a node to the front of the list requires resetting the reference to the entire list, as shown in Figure 3.4. First, the next reference of the added node is set to point to the current first node in the list. Second, the reference to the front of the list is reset to point to the newly added node.

Note that difficulties would arise if these steps were reversed. If we reset the front reference first, we would lose the only reference to the existing list and it could not be retrieved.

Inserting a node into the middle of a list requires some additional processing. First we have to find the node in the list that will immediately precede the new

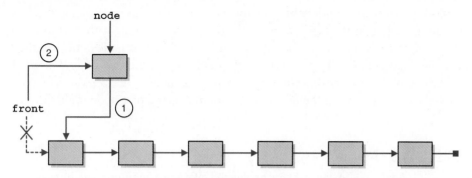

figure 3.4   Inserting a node at the front of a linked list

node being inserted. Unlike an array, in which we can access elements using subscripts, a linked list requires that we use a separate reference to move through the nodes of the list until we find the one we want. This type of reference is often called current, because it indicates the current node in the list that is being examined.

Initially, current is set to point to the first node in the list. Then a loop is used to move the current reference along the list of nodes until the desired node is found. Once it is found, the new node can be inserted, as shown in Figure 3.5.

First, the next reference of the new node is set to point to the node *following* the one to which current refers. Then, the next reference of the current node is reset to point to the new node. Once again, the order of these steps is important.

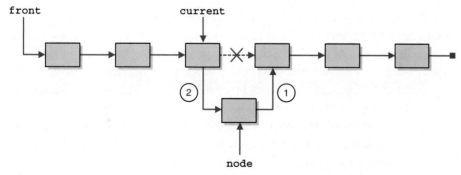

figure 3.5   Inserting a node in the middle of a linked list

This process will work wherever the node is to be inserted along the list, including making it the new second node in the list or making it the last node in the list. If the new node is inserted immediately after the first node in the list, then current and front will refer to the same (first) node. If the new node is inserted at the end of the list, the next reference of the new node is set to null. The only special case occurs when the new node is inserted as the first node in the list.

deleting nodes

key concept

Dealing with the first node in a linked list often requires special handling.

Any node in the list can be deleted. We must maintain the integrity of the list no matter which node is deleted. As with the process of inserting a node, dealing with the first node in the list represents a special case.

To delete the first node in a linked list, the reference to the front of the list is reset so that it points to the current second node in the list. This process is shown in Figure 3.6. If the deleted node is needed elsewhere, a separate reference to it must be set up before resetting the front reference.

To delete a node from the interior of the list, we must first find the node *in front of* the node that is to be deleted. This processing often requires the use of two references: one to find the node to be deleted and another to keep track of the node immediately preceding that one. Thus, they are often called current and previous, as shown in Figure 3.7.

Once these nodes have been found, the next reference of the previous node is reset to point to the node pointed to by the next reference of the current node. The deleted node can then be used as needed.

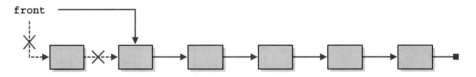

figure 3.6   Deleting the first node in a linked list

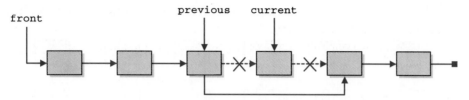

figure 3.7   Deleting an interior node from a linked list

dummy nodes

Thus far, we have described insertion into and deletion from a list as having two cases: the case when dealing with the first node and the case when dealing with any other node. It is possible to eliminate the special case involving the first node by introducing a *dummy node* at the front of the list. A dummy node serves as a false first node and doesn't actually represent an element in the list. By using a dummy node, all insertions and deletions will fall under the second case and the implementations won't have as many special situations to consider. However, the use of a dummy node adds an artificial aspect to the implementation that does not sit well with some developers.

3.3   elements without links

Now that we've explored some of the techniques needed to manage the nodes of a linked list, we can turn our attention to using a linked list as an alternative implementation approach for a collection. However, to do so we need to carefully examine one other key aspect of linked lists. We must separate the details of the linked list structure from the elements that the list stores.

Earlier in this chapter we discussed the idea of a Person class that contains, among its other data, a link to another Person object. The flaw in this approach is that the self-referential Person class must be designed so that it "knows" it may become a node in a linked list of Person objects. This assumption is impractical, and it violates our goal of separating the implementation details from the parts of the system that use the collection.

> **key concept**
>
> Objects that are stored in a collection should not contain any implementation details of the underlying data structure.

The solution to this problem is to define a separate node class that serves to link the elements together. A node class is fairly simple, containing only two important references: one to the next node in the linked list and another to the element that is being stored in the list. This approach is depicted in Figure 3.8.

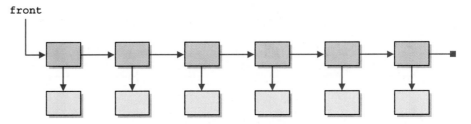

`figure 3.8`   Using separate node objects to store and link elements

The linked list of nodes can still be managed using the techniques discussed in the previous section. The only additional aspect is that the actual elements stored in the list are accessed using a separate reference in the node objects.

doubly linked lists

An alternative implementation for linked structures is the concept of a doubly linked list, as illustrated in Figure 3.9. In a doubly linked list, two references are maintained: one to point to the first node in the list and another to point to the last node in the list. Each node in the list stores both a reference to the next element and a reference to the previous one. We discuss doubly linked lists further in Chapter 8.

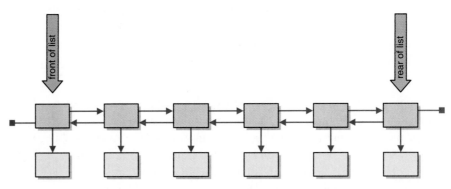

`figure 3.9`   A doubly linked list

3.4   implementing a bag: with links

Let's use a linked list to implement a bag collection as defined in Chapter 2. Note that we are not changing the way in which a bag works. Its conceptual nature remains the same, as does the set of operations defined for it. We are merely changing the underlying data structure used to implement it.

The purpose of the bag, and the solutions it helps us to create, also remain the same. The bingo example from Chapter 2 used the `ArrayBag` class, but any valid implementation of a bag could be used instead. Once we create the `LinkedBag` class to define an alternative implementation, it could be substituted into the bingo solution without having to change anything but the class name. That is the beauty of abstraction.

> **key concept**
>
> Any implementation of a collection can be used to solve a problem as long as it validly implements the appropriate operations.

In the following discussion, we show and discuss the methods that are important to understanding the linked list implementation of a bag. Some of the bag operations are left as programming projects.

the `LinkedBag` class

The `LinkedBag` class implements the `BagADT` interface, just as the `ArrayBag` class does. Both provide the operations defined for a bag collection.

Because we are using a linked list approach, there is no array in which we store the elements of the collection. Instead, we need only a single reference to the first node in the list. We will also maintain a count of the number of elements in the list. Finally, we need a `Random` object to support the `removeRandom` operation. The instance data of the `LinkedBag` class is therefore:

```java
private static Random rand = new Random();

private int count;  // the current number of elements in the bag

private LinearNode contents;
```

The `LinearNode` class serves as the node class, containing a reference to the next `LinearNode` in the list and a reference to the element stored in that node. It also contains methods to set and get these values. The `LinearNode` class is shown in Listing 3.1.

listing
    3.1

```java
//**********************************************************************
//  LinearNode.java        Authors: Lewis/Chase
//
//  Represents a node in a linked list.
//**********************************************************************

package jss2;

public class LinearNode
{
   private LinearNode next;
   private Object element;

   //------------------------------------------------------------------
   //  Creates an empty node.
   //------------------------------------------------------------------
   public LinearNode()
   {
      next = null;
      element = null;
   }


   //------------------------------------------------------------------
   //  Creates a node storing the specified element.
   //------------------------------------------------------------------
   public LinearNode (Object elem)
   {
      next = null;
      element = elem;
   }


   //------------------------------------------------------------------
   //  Returns the node that follows this one.
   //------------------------------------------------------------------
   public LinearNode getNext()
   {
      return next;
   }
```

listing
  3.1   continued

```
//----------------------------------------------------------------
//  Sets the node that follows this one.
//----------------------------------------------------------------
public void setNext (LinearNode node)
{
   next = node;
}


//----------------------------------------------------------------
//  Returns the element stored in this node.
//----------------------------------------------------------------
public Object getElement()
{
   return element;
}


//----------------------------------------------------------------
//  Sets the element stored in this node.
//----------------------------------------------------------------
public void setElement (Object elem)
{
   element = elem;
}
}
```

Note that the LinearNode class is not tied to the implementation of a bag collection. It can be used in any linear linked list implementation of a collection. We will use it for other collections as needed.

Using the LinearNode class and maintaining a count of elements in the collection creates the implementation strategy depicted in Figure 3.10.

The constructor of the LinkedBag class, shown on the following page, sets the count of elements to zero and the front of the list, represented by the variable contents, to null. Note that because a linked list implementation does not have to worry about capacity limitations, there is no need to create a second constructor as we did in the ArrayBag class.

count: 6

contents

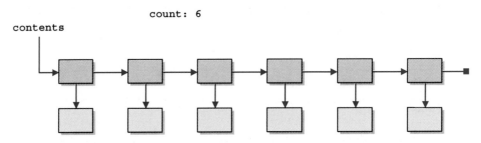

figure 3.10   A linked implementation of a bag collection

```
//----------------------------------------------------------------
//  Creates an empty bag.
//----------------------------------------------------------------
public LinkedBag()
{
    count = 0;
    contents = null;
}
```

the add operation

The add method incorporates the element passed as a parameter into the collection. Because there is no inherent order among the elements of a bag, we can simply add the new element to the front of the list:

```
//----------------------------------------------------------------
//  Adds the specified element to the bag.
//----------------------------------------------------------------
public void add (Object element)
{
    LinearNode node = new LinearNode (element);
    node.setNext(contents);
    contents = node;
    count++;
}
```

The add method first creates a new LinearNode object, using its constructor to store the element. Then the new node's next reference is set to the fist node in the list, the reference to the first node is reset to point to the newly created one, and the count is incremented. This processing is consistent with that shown in Figure 3.4.

the removeRandom operation

The removeRandom method demonstrates how a linked list solution is sometimes more complicated than its array-based counterpart. In the ArrayBag class, the removeRandom method simply chose an index into the array and returned that element. In this version of removeRandom, we must traverse the list, counting the elements until we get to the one that has been randomly selected for removal:

```java
//---------------------------------------------------------------
//  Removes a random element from the bag and returns it. Throws
//  an EmptyBagException if the bag is empty.
//---------------------------------------------------------------
public Object removeRandom() throws EmptyBagException
{
    LinearNode previous, current;
    Object result = null;

    if (isEmpty())
        throw new EmptyBagException();

    int choice = rand.nextInt(count) + 1;

    if (choice == 1)
    {
        result = contents.getElement();
        contents = contents.getNext();
    }
    else
    {
        previous = contents;
        for (int skip=2; skip < choice; skip++)
            previous = previous.getNext();
        current = previous.getNext();
        result = current.getElement();
        previous.setNext(current.getNext());
    }

    count--;

    return result;
}
```

Like the `ArrayBag` version, this method throws an `EmptyBagException` if there are no elements in the bag. If there is at least one, a random number is chosen in the proper range. If the first element is chosen for removal, that situation is handled separately to maintain the reference to the front of the list. If any other element has been chosen, a `for` loop is used to traverse the list to the proper point and the node is deleted using the technique depicted in Figure 3.7.

the remove operation

The `remove` method follows somewhat similar logic to the `removeRandom` method, except that it is looking for a particular element to remove. If the first element matches the target element, it is removed. Otherwise, `previous` and `current` references are used to traverse the list to the appropriate point.

```
//-------------------------------------------------------------------
//   Removes one occurence of the specified element from the bag
//   and returns it. Throws an EmptyBagException if the bag is
//   empty and a NoSuchElemetnException if the target is not in
//   the bag.
//-------------------------------------------------------------------
public Object remove (Object target) throws EmptyBagException,
                                             NoSuchElementException
{
   boolean found = false;
   LinearNode previous, current;
   Object result = null;

   if (isEmpty())
      throw new EmptyBagException();

   if (contents.getElement().equals(target))
   {
      result = contents.getElement();
      contents = contents.getNext();
   }
   else
   {
      previous = contents;
      current = contents.getNext();
      for (int look=0; look < count && !found; look++)
         if (current.getElement().equals(target))
            found = true;
         else
```

```
        {
            previous = current;
            current = current.getNext();
        }

        if (!found)
            throw new NoSuchElementException();

        result = current.getElement();
        previous.setNext(current.getNext());
    }

    count--;

    return result;
}
```

There is always the possibility that the target element is not found in the collection. In that case, a NoSuchElementException is thrown. If the exception is not thrown, the element found is stored so that it can be returned at the end of the method. The node is deleted from the list by adjusting the references as depicted in Figure 3.7.

the iterator operation

The iterator method simply returns a new LinkedIterator object:

```
//------------------------------------------------------------------
//  Returns an iterator for the elements currently in this bag.
//------------------------------------------------------------------
public Iterator iterator()
{
    return new LinkedIterator (contents, count);
}
```

Like the ArrayIterator class discussed in Chapter 2, the LinkedIterator class is written so that it can be used with multiple collections. It stores the contents of the linked list and the count of elements, as shown in Listing 3.2.

```java
//********************************************************************
//  LinkedIterator.java        Authors: Lewis/Chase
//
//  Represents an iterator for a linked list of linear nodes.
//********************************************************************

package jss2;

import java.util.*;

public class LinkedIterator implements Iterator
{
   private int count;  // the number of elements in the collection
   private LinearNode current;  // the current position

   //-------------------------------------------------------------------
   //  Sets up this iterator using the specified items.
   //-------------------------------------------------------------------
   public LinkedIterator (LinearNode collection, int size)
   {
      current = collection;
      count = size;
   }

   //-------------------------------------------------------------------
   //  Returns true if this iterator has at least one more element
   //  to deliver in the iteration.
   //-------------------------------------------------------------------
   public boolean hasNext()
   {
      return (current != null);
   }

   //-------------------------------------------------------------------
   //  Returns the next element in the iteration. If there are no
   //  more elements in this iteration, a NoSuchElementException is
   //  thrown.
   //-------------------------------------------------------------------
   public Object next()
   {
      if (! hasNext())
         throw new NoSuchElementException();
```

listing
3.2   continued

```
        Object result = current.getElement();
        current = current.getNext();
        return result;
    }

    //----------------------------------------------------------------
    //  The remove operation is not supported.
    //----------------------------------------------------------------
    public void remove() throws UnsupportedOperationException
    {
        throw new UnsupportedOperationException();
    }
}
```

The `LinkedIterator` constructor sets up a reference that is designed to move across the list of elements in response to calls to the `next` method. The iteration is complete when `current` becomes null, which is the condition returned by the `hasNext` method. As in the case of the `ArrayIterator` from Chapter 2, the `remove` method is left unsupported. Figure 3.11 shows the UML description for the `LinkedBag` class.

The remaining methods are similar to their counterparts in the `ArrayBag` class from Chapter 2.

3.5   analysis of the linked implementation of a bag

The analysis of the space complexity of the linked implementation of a bag is typical of the linked implementations we will see for other collections. Linked implementations are typically dynamic, meaning that they only allocate as much space as they need and the amount of space allocated can grow and shrink as needed. However, linked implementations do come with an additional space requirement for the references associated with each element.

Let's address the analysis of the time complexity of each operation separately.

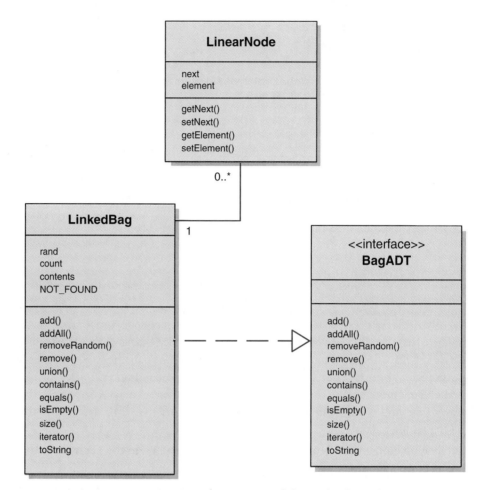

figure 3.11   UML description of the LinkedBag class

analysis of add

Since the order of elements within a bag is irrelevant, we can simply add each new element to the front of the list. Thus, adding an elment to a linked bag consists of the following steps:

▸ Create a new node pointing to the element to be added.

▸ Set the next reference of the new node to the current front of the list.

▸ Set the front reference to the new node.

▸ Increment the count.

Each of these steps is O(1), and thus the add operation is O(1).

analysis of remove

The remove operation for the linked implementation consists of the following steps:

▸ Check to make sure the bag is not empty.

▸ Find the element to be removed.

▸ Remove it.

▸ Decrement the count.

Like the array implementation, all of these steps are also O(1) except for finding the element. This step requires best case 1 comparison if the element is the first one we check, worst case n comparisons if the elment is the last one we check, and expected case n/2 comparisons. Because we ignore constants when considering order, the remove operation for the array implementation has time complexity O(n).

analysis of removeRandom

The removeRandom operation for the linked implementation is similar to the remove method except that we do not have to search for the element to be removed. However, unlike the array implementation, we cannot simply choose an index at random and remove that element. Instead, we must choose a random number and then traverse the list to that position. The best case would be index 0 requiring no traversal, the worst case would require traversal of all n nodes, and the expected case is traversal of n/2 nodes. Thus the removeRandom operation is O(n).

summary of key concepts

- Object reference variables can be used to create linked structures.

- A linked list is composed of objects that each point to the next object in the list.

- A linked list dynamically grows as needed and essentially has no capacity limitations.

- The order in which references are changed is crucial to maintaining a linked list.

- Dealing with the first node in a linked list often requires special handling.

- Objects that are stored in a collection should not contain any implementation details of the underlying data structure.

- Any implementation of a collection can be used to solve a problem as long as it validly implements the appropriate operations.

self-review questions

3.1   How do object references help us define data structures?

3.2   Compare and contrast a linked list and an array.

3.3   What special case exists when managing linked lists?

3.4   Why should a linked list node be separate from the element stored on the list?

3.5   What do the `LinkedBag` and `ArrayBag` classes have in common?

3.6   What would be the time complexity of the `add` operation if we chose to add at the end of the list instead of the front?

3.7   What is the difference between a doubly linked list and a singly linked list?

3.8   What impact would the use of dummy records have upon a doubly linked list implementation?

exercises

3.1 Explain what will happen if the steps depicted in Figure 3.4 are reversed.

3.2 Explain what will happen if the steps depicted in Figure 3.5 are reversed.

3.3 Draw a UML diagram showing the relationships among the classes involved in the linked list implementation of a bag.

3.4 Write an algorithm for the add method that will add at the end of the list instead of the beginning. What is the time complexity of this algorithm?

3.5 Modify the algorithm from Exercise 3.4 so that it makes use of a rear reference. How does this affect the time complexity of this and the other operations?

3.6 Discuss the effect on all the operations if there were not a count variable in the implementation.

3.7 Discuss the impact (and draw an example) of using a dummy record at the head of the list.

programming projects

3.1 Complete the implementation of the LinkedBag class by providing the definitions for the size, isEmpty, addAll, union, contains, equals, and toString methods.

3.2 Modify the Bingo program from Chapter 2 so that it uses the LinkedBag class instead of the ArrayBag class.

3.3 An additional operation that might be implemented for a bag is difference. This operation would take a bag as a parameter and subtract the contents of that bag from the current bag if they exist in the current bag. The result would be returned in a new bag. Implement this operation. Be careful to consider possible exceptional situations.

3.4 Another operation that might be implemented for a bag is intersection. This operation would take a bag as a parameter and would return a bag containing those elements that exist in both bags. Implement this operation. Be careful to consider possible exceptional situations.

3.5   Another operation that might be implemented for a bag is `count`. This operation would take an element as a parameter and return the number of copies of that element in the bag. Implement this operation. Be careful to consider possible exceptional situations.

3.6   A set is a very similar construct to a bag except that there are no duplicates in a set. Implement a set collection by creating both a `SetADT` interface and a `LinkedSet` class. Include the additional operations described in the earlier projects.

3.7   Create a new version of the `LinkedBag` class that makes use of a dummy record at the head of the list.

3.8   Create a simple graphical application that will allow a user to perform `add`, `remove`, and `removeRandom` operations on a bag and display the resulting bag (using `toString`) in a text area.

answers to self-review questions

3.1   An object reference can be used as a link from one object to another. A group of linked objects can form a data structure, such as a linked list, on which a collection can be based.

3.2   A linked list has no capacity limitations, while an array does. However, arrays provide direct access to elements using indexes, whereas a linked list must be traversed one element at a time to reach a particular point in the list.

3.3   The primary special case in linked list processing occurs when dealing with the first element in the list. A special reference variable is maintained that specifies the first element in the list. If that element is deleted, or a new element is added in front of it, the `front` reference must be carefully maintained.

3.4   It is unreasonable to assume that every object that we may want to put in a collection can be designed to cooperate with the collection implementation. Furthermore, the implementation details are supposed to be kept distinct from the user of the collection, including the elements the user chooses to add to the collection.

3.5   Both the `LinkedBag` and `ArrayBag` classes implement the `BagADT` interface. This means that they both represent a bag collection, providing the necessary operations needed to use a bag. Though they both have distinct approaches to managing the collection, they are functionally interchangeable from the user's point of view.

3.6   To add at the end of the list, we would have to traverse the list to reach the last element. This traversal would cause the time complexity to be O(n). An alternative would be to modify the solution to add a `rear` reference that always pointed to the last element in the list. This would help the time complexity for `add` but would have consequences if we try to remove the last element.

3.7   A singly linked list maintains a reference to the first element in the list and then a `next` reference from each node to the following node in the list. A doubly linked list maintains two references: `front` and `rear`. Each node in the doubly linked list stores both a `next` and a `previous` reference.

3.8   It would take two dummy records in a doubly linked list, one at the front and one at the rear, in order to eliminate the special cases when dealing with the first and last node.

Recursion is a powerful programming
technique that provides elegant solutions
to certain problems.

It is particularly helpful in the
implementation of various data
structures and in the process of
searching and sorting data. This
chapter provides an introduction
to recursive processing. It contains an explanation of the basic
concepts underlying recursion,
and then explores the use of
recursion in programming.

chapter
objectives

▸ Explain the underlying concepts of
recursion

▸ Examine recursive methods and
unravel their processing steps

▸ Define infinite recursion and
discuss ways to avoid it

▸ Explain when recursion should and
should not be used

▸ Demonstrate the use of recursion
to solve problems

4.1 `recursive thinking`

We know that one method can call another method to help it accomplish its goal. Similarly, a method can also call itself to help accomplish its goal. *Recursion* is a programming technique in which a method calls itself in order to fulfill its overall purpose.

Before we get into the details of how we use recursion in a program, we need to explore the general concept of recursion first. The ability to think recursively is essential to being able to use recursion as a programming technique.

In general, recursion is the process of defining something in terms of itself. For example, consider the following definition of the word *decoration*:

decoration: n. any ornament or adornment used to decorate something

The word *decorate* is used to define the word *decoration*. You may recall your grade-school teacher telling you to avoid such recursive definitions when explaining the meaning of a word. However, in many situations, recursion is an appropriate way to express an idea or definition. For example, suppose we want to formally define a list of one or more numbers, separated by commas. Such a list can be defined recursively as either a number or as a number followed by a comma followed by a list. This definition can be expressed as follows:

A list is a: `number`

or a: `number   comma   list`

This recursive definition of a list defines each of the following lists of numbers:

```
24, 88, 40, 37
96, 43
14, 64, 21, 69, 32, 93, 47, 81, 28, 45, 81, 52, 69
70
```

No matter how long a list is, the recursive definition describes it. A list of one element, such as in the last example, is defined completely by the first (nonrecursive) part of the definition. For any list longer than one element, the recursive part of the definition (the part that refers to itself) is used as many times as necessary, until the last element is reached. The last element in the list is always defined by the nonrecursive part of the definition. Figure 4.1 shows how one particular list of numbers corresponds to the recursive definition of list.

```
LIST:  number  comma   LIST
         24       ,     88, 40, 37
                       number  comma   LIST
                         88      ,     40, 37
                               number  comma   LIST
                                 40      ,       37
                                              number
                                                37
```

figure 4.1   Tracing the recursive definition of a list

infinite recursion

Note that this definition of a list contains one option that is recursive, and one option that is not. The part of the definition that is not recursive is called the *base case*. If all options had a recursive component, then the recursion would never end. For example, if the definition of a list was simply "a number followed by a comma followed by a list," then no list could ever end. This problem is called *infinite recursion*. It is similar to an infinite loop, except that the "loop" occurs in the definition itself.

As in the infinite loop problem, a programmer must be careful to design algorithms so that they avoid infinite recursion. Any recursive definition must have a base case that does not result in a recursive option. The base case of the list definition is a single number that is not followed by anything. In other words, when the last number in the list is reached, the base case option terminates the recursive path.

recursion in math

Let's look at an example of recursion in mathematics. The value referred to as N! (which is pronounced *N factorial*) is defined for any positive integer N as the product of all integers between 1 and N inclusive. Therefore:

    3! = 3*2*1 = 6

and

    5! = 5*4*3*2*1 = 120.

Mathematical formulas are often expressed recursively. The definition of N! can be expressed recursively as:

```
1! = 1
N! = N * (N-1)! for N > 1
```

Mathematical problems and formulas are often expressed recursively.

The base case of this definition is 1!, which is defined to be 1. All other values of N! (for N > 1) are defined recursively as N times the value (N–1)!. The recursion is that the factorial function is defined in terms of the factorial function.

Using this definition, 50! is equal to 50 * 49!. And 49! is equal to 49 * 48!. And 48! is equal to 48 * 47!. This process continues until we get to the base case of 1. Because N! is defined only for positive integers, this definition is complete and will always conclude with the base case.

The next section describes how recursion is accomplished in programs.

4.2 recursive programming

Let's use a simple mathematical operation to demonstrate the concepts of recursive programming. Consider the process of summing the values between 1 and N inclusive, where N is any positive integer. The sum of the values from 1 to N can be expressed as N plus the sum of the values from 1 to N–1. That sum can be expressed similarly, as shown in Figure 4.2.

$$\sum_{i=1}^{N} i = N + \sum_{i=1}^{N-1} i = N + N{-}1 + \sum_{i=1}^{N-2} i$$

$$= N + N{-}1 + N{-}2 + \sum_{i=1}^{N-3} i$$

$$= N + N{-}1 + N{-}2 + \ldots + 2 + 1$$

figure 4.2   The sum of the numbers 1 through N, defined recursively

For example, the sum of the values between 1 and 20 is equal to 20 plus the sum of the values between 1 and 19. Continuing this approach, the sum of the values between 1 and 19 is equal to 19 plus the sum of the values between 1 and 18. This may sound like a strange way to think about this problem, but it is a straightforward example that can be used to demonstrate how recursion is programmed.

In Java, as in many other programming languages, a method can call itself. Each call to the method creates a new environment in which to work. That is, all local variables and parameters are newly defined with their own unique data space every time the method is called. Each parameter is given an initial value based on the new call. Each time a method terminates, processing returns to the method that called it (which may be an earlier invocation of the same method). These rules are no different from those governing any "regular" method invocation.

> **key concept**
> Each recursive call to a method creates new local variables and parameters.

A recursive solution to the summation problem is defined by the following recursive method called sum:

```java
// This method returns the sum of 1 to num
public int sum (int num)
{
   int result;
   if (num == 1)
      result = 1;
   else
      result = num + sum (num-1);
   return result;
}
```

Note that this method essentially embodies our recursive definition that the sum of the numbers between 1 and N is equal to N plus the sum of the numbers between 1 and N–1. The sum method is recursive because sum calls itself. The parameter passed to sum is decremented each time sum is called, until it reaches the base case of 1. Recursive methods usually contain an if-else statement, with one of the branches representing the base case.

Suppose the main method calls sum, passing it an initial value of 1, which is stored in the parameter num. Since num is equal to 1, the result of 1 is returned to main and no recursion occurs.

Now let's trace the execution of the sum method when it is passed an initial value of 2. Since num does not equal 1, sum is called again with an argument of num-1, or 1. This is a new call to the method sum, with a new parameter num and a new local variable result. Since this num

> **key concept**
> A careful trace of recursive processing can provide insight into the way it is used to solve a problem.

is equal to 1 in this invocation, the result of 1 is returned without further recursive calls. Control returns to the first version of sum that was invoked. The return value of 1 is added to the initial value of num in that call to sum, which is 2. Therefore, result is assigned the value 3, which is returned to the main method. The method called from main correctly calculates the sum of the integers from 1 to 2, and returns the result of 3.

The base case in the summation example is when N equals 1, at which point no further recursive calls are made. The recursion begins to fold back into the earlier versions of the sum method, returning the appropriate value each time. Each return value contributes to the computation of the sum at the higher level. Without the base case, infinite recursion would result. Each call to a method requires additional memory space; therefore, infinite recursion often results in a runtime error indicating that memory has been exhausted.

Trace the sum function with different initial values of num until this processing becomes familiar. Figure 4.3 illustrates the recursive calls when main invokes sum to determine the sum of the integers from 1 to 4. Each box represents a copy of the method as it is invoked, indicating the allocation of space to store the formal parameters and any local variables. Invocations are shown as solid lines, and returns as dotted lines. The return value result is shown at each step. The recursive path is followed completely until the base case is reached; then the calls begin to return their result up through the chain.

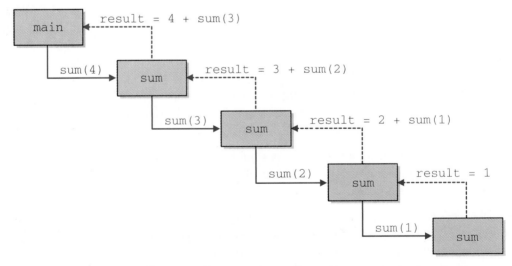

figure 4.3   Recursive calls to the sum method

recursion vs. iteration

Of course, there is a nonrecursive solution to the summation problem we just explored. One way to compute the sum of the numbers between 1 and num inclusive in an iterative manner is as follows:

```
sum = 0;
for (int number = 1; number <= num; number++)
    sum += number;
```

This solution is certainly more straightforward than the recursive version. We used the summation problem to demonstrate recursion because it is a simple problem to understand, not because you would use recursion to solve it under normal conditions. Recursion has the overhead of multiple method invocations and, in this case, presents a more complicated solution than its iterative counterpart.

> **key concept**
>
> Recursion is the most elegant and appropriate way to solve some problems, but for others it is less intuitive than an iterative solution.

A programmer must learn when to use recursion and when not to use it. Determining which approach is best is another important software engineering decision that depends on the problem being solved. All problems can be solved in an iterative manner, but in some cases the iterative version is much more complicated. Recursion, for some problems, allows us to create relatively short, elegant programs.

direct vs. indirect recursion

Direct recursion occurs when a method invokes itself, such as when sum calls sum. *Indirect recursion* occurs when a method invokes another method, eventually resulting in the original method being invoked again. For example, if method m1 invokes method m2, and m2 invokes method m1, we can say that m1 is indirectly recursive. The amount of indirection could be several levels deep, as when m1 invokes m2, which invokes m3, which invokes m4, which invokes m1. Figure 4.4 depicts a situation with indirect recursion. Method invocations are shown with solid lines, and returns are shown with dotted lines. The entire invocation path is followed, and then the recursion unravels following the return path.

Indirect recursion requires all of the same attention to base cases that direct recursion requires. Furthermore, indirect recursion can be more difficult to trace because of the intervening method calls. Therefore, extra care is warranted when designing or evaluating indirectly recursive methods. Ensure that the indirection is truly necessary and clearly explained in documentation.

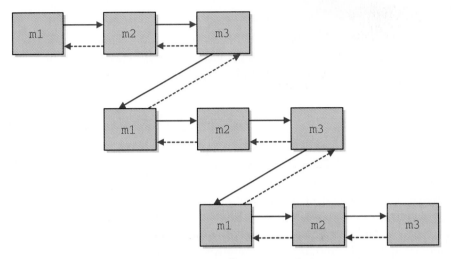

figure 4.4   Indirect recursion

4.3   using recursion

The following sections describe problems that we then solve using a recusive technique. For each one, we examine exactly how recursion plays a role in the solution and how a base case is used to terminate the recursion. As you explore these
examples, consider how complicated a nonrecursive solution for each problem
would be.

traversing a maze

Solving a maze involves a great deal of trial and error: following a path, back-
tracking when you cannot go farther, and trying other untried options. Such
activities often are handled nicely using recursion. The program shown in Listing
4.1 creates a `Maze` object and attempts to traverse it.

listing
4.1

```
//*****************************************************************
//  MazeSearch.java        Authors: Lewis/Chase
//
//  Demonstrates recursion.
//*****************************************************************
```

listing
    4.1   continued

```java
public class MazeSearch
{
    //-----------------------------------------------------------------
    //  Creates a new maze, prints its original form, attempts to
    //  solve it, and prints out its final form.
    //-----------------------------------------------------------------
    public static void main (String[] args)
    {
        Maze labyrinth = new Maze();

        System.out.println (labyrinth);

        if (labyrinth.traverse (0, 0))
            System.out.println ("The maze was successfully traversed!");
        else
            System.out.println ("There is no possible path.");

        System.out.println (labyrinth);
    }
}
```

output

```
1110110001111
1011101111001
0000101010100
1110111010111
1010000111001
1011111101111
1000000000000
1111111111111

The maze was successfully traversed!

7770110001111
3077707771001
0000707070300
7770777070333
7070000773003
7077777703333
7000000000000
7777777777777
```

The `Maze` class, shown in Listing 4.2, uses a two-dimensional array of integers to represent the maze. The goal is to move from the top-left corner (the entry point) to the bottom-right corner (the exit point). Initially, a 1 indicates a clear path, and a 0 indicates a blocked path. As the maze is solved, these array elements are changed to other values to indicate attempted paths and ultimately a successful path through the maze if one exists. Figure 4.5 shows the UML illustration of this solution.

The only valid moves through the maze are in the four primary directions: down, right, up, and left. No diagonal moves are allowed. In this example, the maze is 8 rows by 13 columns, although the code is designed to handle a maze of any size.

Let's think this through recursively. The maze can be traversed successfully if it can be traversed successfully from position (0, 0). Therefore, the maze can be traversed successfully if it can be traversed successfully from any positions adjacent to (0, 0), namely position (1, 0), position (0, 1), position (–1, 0), or position (0, –1). Picking a potential next step, say (1, 0), we find ourselves in the same type of situation we did before. To successfully traverse the maze from the new current position, we must successfully traverse it from an adjacent position. At any point, some of the adjacent positions may be invalid, may be blocked, or may represent a possible successful path. We continue this process recursively. If the base case, position (7, 12), is reached, the maze has been traversed successfully.

The recursive method in the `Maze` class is called `traverse`. It returns a `boolean` value that indicates whether a solution was found. First the method

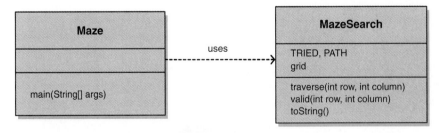

figure 4.5   UML description of the Maze and MazeSearch classes

listing
   4.2

```
//*********************************************************************
//  Maze.java         Authors: Lewis/Chase
//
//  Represents a maze of characters. The goal is to get from the
//  top left corner to the bottom right, following a path of 1s.
//*********************************************************************

public class Maze
{
   private final int TRIED = 3;
   private final int PATH = 7;

   private int[][] grid = { {1,1,1,0,1,1,0,0,0,1,1,1,1},
                            {1,0,1,1,1,0,1,1,1,1,0,0,1},
                            {0,0,0,0,1,0,1,0,1,0,1,0,0},
                            {1,1,1,0,1,1,1,0,1,0,1,1,1},
                            {1,0,1,0,0,0,0,1,1,1,0,0,1},
                            {1,0,1,1,1,1,1,1,0,1,1,1,1},
                            {1,0,0,0,0,0,0,0,0,0,0,0,0},
                            {1,1,1,1,1,1,1,1,1,1,1,1,1} };

   //----------------------------------------------------------------
   //  Attempts to recursively traverse the maze. Inserts special
   //  characters indicating locations that have been tried and that
   //  eventually become part of the solution.
   //----------------------------------------------------------------
   public boolean traverse (int row, int column)
   {
      boolean done = false;

      if (valid (row, column))
      {
         grid[row][column] = TRIED;  // this cell has been tried

         if (row == grid.length-1 && column == grid[0].length-1)
            done = true;  // the maze is solved
         else
         {
            done = traverse (row+1, column);     // down
            if (!done)
               done = traverse (row, column+1);  // right
            if (!done)
               done = traverse (row-1, column);  // up
            if (!done)
               done = traverse (row, column-1);  // left
```

listing
   4.2   continued

```
      }

      if (done)  // this location is part of the final path
         grid[row][column] = PATH;
   }

   return done;
}

//------------------------------------------------------------------
//  Determines if a specific location is valid.
//------------------------------------------------------------------
private boolean valid (int row, int column)
{
   boolean result = false;

   // check if cell is in the bounds of the matrix
   if (row >= 0 && row < grid.length &&
         column >= 0 && column < grid[row].length)

      //  check if cell is not blocked and not previously tried
      if (grid[row][column] == 1)
         result = true;

   return result;
}

//------------------------------------------------------------------
//  Returns the maze as a string.
//------------------------------------------------------------------
public String toString ()
{
   String result = "\n";

   for (int row=0; row < grid.length; row++)
   {
      for (int column=0; column < grid[row].length; column++)
         result += grid[row][column] + "";
      result += "\n";
   }

   return result;
}
}
```

determines if a move to the specified row and column is valid. A move is considered valid if it stays within the grid boundaries and if the grid contains a 1 in that location, indicating that a move in that direction is not blocked. The initial call to traverse passes in the upper-left location (0, 0).

If the move is valid, the grid entry is changed from a 1 to a 3, marking this location as visited so that later we don't retrace our steps. Then the traverse method determines if the maze has been completed by having reached the bottom-right location. Therefore, there are actually three possibilities of the base case for this problem that will terminate any particular recursive path:

▸ An invalid move because the move is out of bounds or blocked

▸ An invalid move because the move has been tried before

▸ A move that arrives at the final location

If the current location is not the bottom-right corner, we search for a solution in each of the primary directions, if necessary. First, we look down by recursively calling the traverse method and passing in the new location. The logic of the traverse method starts all over again using this new position. A solution either is ultimately found by first attempting to move down from the current location, or is not found. If it's not found, we try moving right. If that fails, we try up. Finally, if no other direction has yielded a correct path, we try left. If no direction from the current location yields a correct solution, then there is no path from this location, and traverse returns false.

If a solution is found from the current location, then the grid entry is changed to a 7. The first 7 is placed in the bottom-right corner. The next 7 is placed in the location that led to the bottom-right corner, and so on until the final 7 is placed in the upper-left corner. Therefore, when the final maze is printed, the 0s still indicate a blocked path, a 1 indicates an open path that was never tried, a 3 indicates a path that was tried but failed to yield a correct solution, and a 7 indicates a part of the final solution of the maze.

Note that there are several opportunities for recursion in each call to the traverse method. Any or all of them might be followed, depending on the maze configuration. Although there may be many paths through the maze, the recursion terminates when a path is found. Carefully trace the execution of this code while following the maze array to see how the recursion solves the problem. Then consider the difficulty of producing a nonrecursive solution.

the Towers of Hanoi

The *Towers of Hanoi* puzzle was invented in the 1880s by Edouard Lucas, a French mathematician. It has become a favorite among computer scientists because its solution is an excellent demonstration of recursive elegance.

The puzzle consists of three upright pegs and a set of disks with holes in the middle so that they slide onto the pegs. Each disk has a different diameter. Initially, all of the disks are stacked on one peg in order of size such that the largest disk is on the bottom, as shown in Figure 4.6.

The goal of the puzzle is to move all of the disks from their original (first) peg to the destination (third) peg. We can use the "extra" peg as a temporary place to put disks, but we must obey the following three rules:

▶ We can move only one disk at a time.

▶ We cannot place a larger disk on top of a smaller disk.

▶ All disks must be on some peg except for the disk in transit between pegs.

These rules imply that we must move smaller disks "out of the way" in order to move a larger disk from one peg to another. Figure 4.7 shows the step-by-step solution for the Towers of Hanoi puzzle using three disks. In order to ultimately move all three disks from the first peg to the third peg, we first have to get to the point where the smaller two disks are out of the way on the second peg so that the largest disk can be moved from the first peg to the third peg.

The first three moves shown in Figure 4.7 can be thought of as "moving the smaller disks out of the way." The fourth move puts the largest disk in its final place. Then the last three moves put the smaller disks to their final place on top of the largest one.

figure 4.6   The Towers of Hanoi puzzle

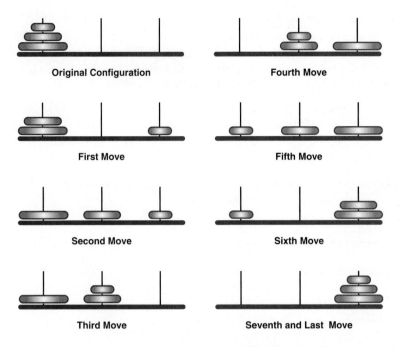

figure 4.7   A solution to the three-disk Towers of Hanoi puzzle

Let's use this idea to form a general strategy. To move a stack of N disks from the original peg to the destination peg:

▶ Move the topmost N–1 disks from the original peg to the extra peg.

▶ Move the largest disk from the original peg to the destination peg.

▶ Move the N–1 disks from the extra peg to the destination peg.

This strategy lends itself nicely to a recursive solution. The step to move the N–1 disks out of the way is the same problem all over again: moving a stack of disks. For this subtask, though, there is one less disk, and our destination peg is what we were originally calling the extra peg. An analogous situation occurs after we've moved the largest disk, and we have to move the original N–1 disks again.

The base case for this problem occurs when we want to move a "stack" that consists of only one disk. That step can be accomplished directly and without recursion.

The program in Listing 4.3 creates a `TowersOfHanoi` object and invokes its `solve` method. The output is a step-by-step list of instructions that describe how the disks should be moved to solve the puzzle. This example uses four disks, which is specified by a parameter to the `TowersOfHanoi` constructor. Figure 4.8 shows the UML description for this solution.

listing
4.3

```
//********************************************************************
//   SolveTowers.java        Authors: Lewis/Chase
//
//   Demonstrates recursion.
//********************************************************************

public class SolveTowers
{
    //----------------------------------------------------------------
    //   Creates a TowersOfHanoi puzzle and solves it.
    //----------------------------------------------------------------
    public static void main (String[] args)
    {
        TowersOfHanoi towers = new TowersOfHanoi (4);

        towers.solve();
    }
}
```

output

```
Move one disk from 1 to 2
Move one disk from 1 to 3
Move one disk from 2 to 3
Move one disk from 1 to 2
Move one disk from 3 to 1
Move one disk from 3 to 2
Move one disk from 1 to 2
Move one disk from 1 to 3
Move one disk from 2 to 3
Move one disk from 2 to 1
Move one disk from 3 to 1
Move one disk from 2 to 3
Move one disk from 1 to 2
Move one disk from 1 to 3
Move one disk from 2 to 3
```

The TowersOfHanoi class, shown in Listing 4.4, uses the solve method to make an initial call to moveTower, the recursive method. The initial call indicates that all of the disks should be moved from peg 1 to peg 3, using peg 2 as the extra position.

listing
   4.4

```java
//********************************************************************
//  TowersOfHanoi.java        Authors: Lewis/Chase
//
//  Represents the classic Towers of Hanoi puzzle.
//********************************************************************

public class TowersOfHanoi
{
   private int totalDisks;

   //-----------------------------------------------------------------
   //  Sets up the puzzle with the specified number of disks.
   //-----------------------------------------------------------------
   public TowersOfHanoi (int disks)
   {
      totalDisks = disks;
   }

   //-----------------------------------------------------------------
   //  Performs the initial call to moveTower to solve the puzzle.
   //  Moves the disks from tower 1 to tower 3 using tower 2.
   //-----------------------------------------------------------------
   public void solve ()
   {
      moveTower (totalDisks, 1, 3, 2);
   }

   //-----------------------------------------------------------------
   //  Moves the specified number of disks from one tower to another
   //  by moving a subtower of n-1 disks out of the way, moving one
   //  disk, then moving the subtower back. Base case of 1 disk.
   //-----------------------------------------------------------------
   private void moveTower (int numDisks, int start, int end, int temp)
   {
      if (numDisks == 1)
         moveOneDisk (start, end);
      else
```

listing
  4.4   continued

```
      {
          moveTower (numDisks-1, start, temp, end);
          moveOneDisk (start, end);
          moveTower (numDisks-1, temp, end, start);
      }
   }

   //-----------------------------------------------------------------
   //  Prints instructions to move one disk from the specified start
   //  tower to the specified end tower.
   //-----------------------------------------------------------------
   private void moveOneDisk (int start, int end)
   {
      System.out.println ("Move one disk from " + start + " to " +
                          end);
   }
}
```

The moveTower method first considers the base case (a "stack" of one disk). When that occurs, it calls the moveOneDisk method that prints a single line describing that particular move. If the stack contains more than one disk, we call moveTower again to get the N–1 disks out of the way, then move the largest disk, then move the N–1 disks to their final destination with yet another call to moveTower.

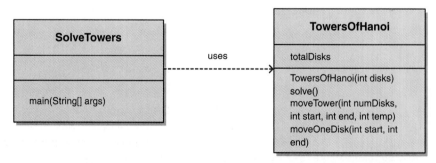

figure 4.8   UML description of the SolveTowers and
              TowersOfHanoi classes

Note that the parameters to moveTower describing the pegs are switched around as needed to move the partial stacks. This code follows our general strategy, and uses the moveTower method to move all partial stacks. Trace the code carefully for a stack of three disks to understand the processing. Compare the processing steps to Figure 4.8.

4.4 analyzing recursive algorithms

In Chapter 1 we explored the concept of analyzing an algorithm to determine its complexity (usually its time complexity) and expressed it in terms of a growth function. The growth function gave us the order of the algorithm, which can be used to compare it to other algorithms that accomplish the same task.

When analyzing a loop, we determined the order of the body of the loop and multiplied it by the number of times the loop was executed. Analyzing a recursive algorithm uses similar thinking. Determining the order of a recursive algorithm is a matter of determining the order of the recursion (the number of times the recursive definition is followed) and multiplying that by the order of the body of the recursive method.

> **key concept**
>
> The order of a recursive algorithm can be determined using techniques similar to analyzing iterative processing.

Consider the recursive method presented in section 4.2 that computes the sum of the integers from 1 to some positive value. We reprint it here for convenience:

```
// This method returns the sum of 1 to num
public int sum (int num)
{
    int result;
    if (num == 1)
        result = 1;
    else
        result = num + sum (num-1);
    return result;
}
```

The size of this problem is naturally expressed as the number of values to be summed. Because we are summing the integers from 1 to num, the number of values to be summed is num. The operation of interest is the act of adding two values together. The body of the recursive method performs one addition operation, and therefore is $O(1)$. Each time the recursive method is invoked, the value of num is decreased by 1. Therefore, the recursive method is called num times, so the recursive iterator is $O(n)$. Therefore, the order of the entire algorithm is $O(n)$.

We will see that in some algorithms the recursive step operates on half as much data as the previous call, thus creating an order of recursion of O(log n). If the body of the method is O(1), then the whole algorithm is O(log n). If the body of the method is O(n), then the whole algorithm is O(n log n).

Now consider the Towers of Hanoi puzzle. The size of the puzzle is naturally the number of disks, and the processing operation of interest is the step of moving one disk from one peg to another. Except for the base case, each recursive call results in calling itself *twice more*, and each call operates on a stack of disks that is only one less than the stack that is passed in as the parameter.

> **key concept**
>
> The Towers of Hanoi solution has exponential complexity, which is very inefficient. Yet the implementation of the solution is remarkably short and elegant.

Contrary to its short and elegant implementation, the solution to the Towers of Hanoi puzzle is terribly inefficient. To solve the puzzle with a stack of N disks, we have to make $2^N - 1$ individual disk moves. Therefore, the Towers of Hanoi algorithm is $O(2^n)$. As we discussed in Chapter 1, this order is an example of exponential complexity. As the number of disks increases, the number of required moves increases exponentially.

Legend has it that priests of Brahma are working on this puzzle in a temple at the center of the world. They are using 64 gold disks, moving them between pegs of pure diamond. The downside is that when the priests finish the puzzle, the world will end. The upside is that even if they move one disk every second of every day, it will take them over 584 billion years to complete it. That's with a puzzle of only 64 disks! It is certainly an indication of just how intractable exponential algorithm complexity is.

summary of key concepts

- Recursion is a programming technique in which a method calls itself. A key to being able to program recursively is to be able to think recursively.
- Any recursive definition must have a nonrecursive part, called the base case, which permits the recursion to eventually end.
- Mathematical problems and formulas are often expressed recursively.
- Each recursive call to a method creates new local variables and parameters.
- A careful trace of recursive processing can provide insight into the way it is used to solve a problem.
- Recursion is the most elegant and appropriate way to solve some problems, but for others it is less intuitive than an iterative solution.
- The order of a recursive algorithm can be determined using techniques similar to analyzing iterative processing.
- The Towers of Hanoi solution has exponential complexity, which is very inefficient. Yet the implementation of the solution is incredibly short and elegant.

self-review questions

4.1   What is recursion?

4.2   What is infinite recursion?

4.3   When is a base case needed for recursive processing?

4.4   Is recursion necessary?

4.5   When should recursion be avoided?

4.6   What is indirect recursion?

4.7   Explain the general approach to solving the Towers of Hanoi puzzle. How does it relate to recursion?

exercises

4.1   Write a recursive definition of a valid Java identifier.

4.2   Write a recursive definition of x^y (x raised to the power y), where x and y are integers and $y > 0$.

4.3   Write a recursive definition of $i * j$ (integer multiplication), where $i > 0$. Define the multiplication process in terms of integer addition. For example, 4 * 7 is equal to 7 added to itself 4 times.

4.4   Write a recursive definition of the Fibonacci numbers. The Fibonacci numbers are a sequence of integers, each of which is the sum of the previous two numbers. The first two numbers in the sequence are 0 and 1. Explain why you would not normally use recursion to solve this problem.

4.5   Modify the method that calculates the sum of the integers between 1 and N shown in this chapter. Have the new version match the following recursive definition: The sum of 1 to N is the sum of 1 to (N/2) plus the sum of (N/2 + 1) to N. Trace your solution using an N of 7.

4.6   Write a recursive method that returns the value of N! (N factorial) using the definition given in this chapter. Explain why you would not normally use recursion to solve this problem.

4.7   Write a recursive method to reverse a string. Explain why you would not normally use recursion to solve this problem.

4.8   Design or generate a new maze for the MazeSearch program in this chapter and rerun the program. Explain the processing in terms of your new maze, giving examples of a path that was tried but failed, a path that was never tried, and the ultimate solution.

4.9   Annotate the lines of output of the SolveTowers program in this chapter to show the recursive steps.

4.10   Produce a chart showing the number of moves required to solve the Towers of Hanoi puzzle using the following number of disks: 2, 3, 4, 5, 6, 7, 8, 9, 10, 15, 20, and 25.

4.11   Determine and explain the order of your solution to Exercise 4.4.

4.12   Determine and explain the order of your solution to Exercise 4.5.

4.13   Determine and explain the order of your solution to Exercise 4.6.

4.14   Determine the order of the recursive maze solution presented in this chapter.

programming projects

4.1 Design and implement a program that implements Euclid's algorithm for finding the greatest common divisor of two positive integers. The greatest common divisor is the largest integer that divides both values without producing a remainder. In a class called DivisorCalc, define a static method called gcd that accepts two integers, num1 and num2. Create a driver to test your implementation. The recursive algorithm is defined as follows:

```
gcd (num1, num2) is num2 if num2 <= num1 and num2 divides num1
gcd (num1, num2) is gcd (num2, num1) if num1 < num2
gcd (num1, num2) is gcd (num2, num1%num2) otherwise
```

4.2 Modify the Maze class so that it prints out the path of the final solution as it is discovered without storing it.

4.3 Design and implement a program that traverses a 3D maze.

4.4 Design and implement a recursive program that solves the Non-attacking Queens problem. That is, write a program to determine how eight queens can be positioned on an eight-by-eight chessboard so that none of them are in the same row, column, or diagonal as any other queen. There are no other chess pieces on the board.

4.5 In the language of an alien race, all words take the form of Blurbs. A Blurb is a Whoozit followed by one or more Whatzits. A Whoozit is the character 'x' followed by zero or more 'y's. A Whatzit is a 'q' followed by either a 'z' or a 'd', followed by a Whoozit. Design and implement a recursive program that generates random Blurbs in this alien language.

4.6 Design and implement a recursive program to determine if a string is a valid Blurb as defined in the previous project description.

4.7 Design and implement a recursive program to determine and print the Nth line of Pascal's Triangle, as shown on the next page. Each interior value is the sum of the two values above it. (*Hint*: use an array to store the values on each line.)

```
                                 1
                          1             1
                   1             2             1
            1             3             3             1
     1             4             6             4             1
1             5            10            10             5             1
      6            15            20            15             6             1
1     7            21            35            35            21             7             1
1     8            28            56            70            56            28             8             1
```

4.8   Design and implement a graphic version of the Towers of Hanoi puzzle. Allow the user to set the number of disks used in the puzzle. The user should be able to interact with the puzzle in two main ways. The user can move the disks from one peg to another using the mouse, in which case the program should ensure that each move is legal. The user can also watch a solution take place as an animation, with pause/resume buttons. Permit the user to control the speed of the animation.

answers to self-review questions

4.1   Recursion is a programming technique in which a method calls itself, solving a smaller version of the problem each time, until the terminating condition is reached.

4.2   Infinite recursion occurs when there is no base case that serves as a terminating condition, or when the base case is improperly specified. The recursive path is followed forever. In a recursive program, infinite recursion will often result in an error that indicates that available memory has been exhausted.

4.3   A base case is always required to terminate recursion and begin the process of returning through the calling hierarchy. Without the base case, infinite recursion results.

4.4   Recursion is not necessary. Every recursive algorithm can be written in an iterative manner. However, some problem solutions are much more elegant and straightforward when written recursively.

4.5   Avoid recursion when the iterative solution is simpler and more easily understood and programmed. Recursion has the overhead of multiple method calls and is not always intuitive.

4.6   Indirect recursion occurs when a method calls another method, which calls another method, and so on until one of the called methods invokes the original. Indirect recursion is usually more difficult to trace than direct recursion, in which a method calls itself.

4.7   The Towers of Hanoi puzzle of N disks is solved by moving N–1 disks out of the way onto an extra peg, moving the largest disk to its destination, then moving the N–1 disks from the extra peg to the destination. This solution is inherently recursive because, to move the substack of N–1 disks, we can use the same process.

searching and sorting

Two common tasks in the world of software development are searching for a particular element within a group and sorting a group of elements into a particular order. There are a variety of algorithms that can be used to accomplish these tasks, and the differences between them are worth exploring carefully. These topics go hand in hand with our study of collections and data structures.

chapter
objectives

- Examine the linear search and binary search algorithms

- Examine several sorting algorithms

- Discuss the complexity of these algorithms

5.1   searching

Searching is the process of finding a designated *target element* within a group of items, or determining that the target does not exist within the group. The group of items to be searched is sometimes called the *search pool*.

This section examines two common approaches to searching: a linear search and a binary search. Later in this book other search techniques are presented that use the characteristics of particular data structures to facilitate the search process.

Our goal is to perform the search as efficiently as possible. In terms of algorithm analysis, we want to minimize the number of comparisons we have to make in order to find the target. In general, the more items there are in the search pool, the more comparisons it will take to find the target. Thus the size of the problem is defined by the number of items in the search pool.

To be able to search for an object, we must be able to compare one object to another. Our implementations of these algorithms search an array of `Comparable` objects. Therefore, the elements involved must implement the `Comparable` interface.

Recall that the `Comparable` interface contains one method, `compareTo`, which is designed to return an integer that is less than zero, equal to zero, or greater than zero (respectively) if the object is less than, equal to, or greater than the object to which it is being compared. Therefore, any class that implements the `Comparable` interface defines the relative order of any two objects of that class.

linear search

If the search pool is organized into a list of some kind, one straightforward way to perform the search is to start at the beginning of the list and compare each value in turn to the target element. Eventually, either the target will be found or we will come to the end of the list and conclude that the target doesn't exist in the group. This approach is called a *linear search* because it begins at one end and scans the search pool in a linear manner. This process is depicted in Figure 5.1.

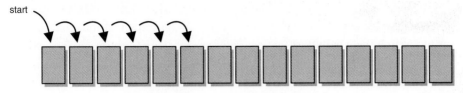

figure 5.1   A linear search

The following method implements a linear search. It accepts the array of elements to be searched and the target value sought. The method returns a `boolean` value that indicates whether or not the target element was found.

```
//---------------------------------------------------------------
//   Searches the specified array of objects for the target value
//   using a linear search algorithm.
//---------------------------------------------------------------
public static boolean linearSearch (Comparable[] data,
                                    Comparable target)
{
    int index = 0;
    boolean found = false;

    while (!found && index < data.length)
    {
        if (data[index].compareTo(target) == 0)
            found = true;
        index++;
    }

    return found;
}
```

The `while` loop steps through the elements of the array, terminating either when the element is found or the end of the array is reached. The `boolean` variable `found` is initialized to `false` and is only changed to `true` if the target element is located.

Variations on this implementation could return the element found in the array if it is found and return a null reference if it is not found. Alternatively, an exception could be thrown if the target element is not found.

The linearSearch method could be incorporated into any class. Our version of this method is defined as part of a class containing static methods that provide various searching capabilities.

The linear search algorithm is fairly easy to understand, though it is not particularly efficient. Note that a linear search does not require the elements in the search pool to be in any particular order within the array. The only criterion is that we are able to examine them one at a time in turn. The binary search algorithm, described next, improves on the efficiency of the search process, but only works if the search pool is ordered.

binary search

If the group of items in the search pool is sorted, then our approach to searching can be much more efficient than that of a linear search. A *binary search* algorithm eliminates large parts of the search pool with each comparison by capitalizing on the fact that the search pool is in sorted order.

Instead of starting the search at one end or the other, a binary search begins in the middle of the sorted list. If the target element is not found at that middle element, then the search continues. And because the list is sorted, we know that if the target is in the list, it will be on one side of the array or the other, depending on whether the target is less than or greater than the middle element. Thus, because the list is sorted, we eliminate half of the search pool with one carefully chosen comparison. The remaining half of the search pool represents the *viable candidates* in which the target element may yet be found.

The search continues in this same manner, examining the middle element of the viable candidates, eliminating half of them. Each comparison reduces the viable candidates by half until eventually the target element is found or there are no more viable candidates, which means the target element is not in the search pool. The process of a binary search is depicted in Figure 5.2.

Let's look at an example. Consider the following sorted list of integers:

10   12   18   22   31   34   40   46   59   67   69   72   80   84   98

Suppose we were trying to determine if the number 67 is in the list. Initially, the target could be anywhere in the list (all items in the search pool are viable candidates).

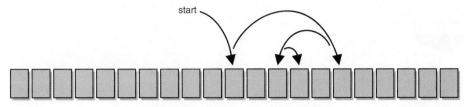

figure 5.2   A binary search

The binary search approach begins by examining the middle element, in this case 46. That element is not our target, so we must continue searching. But since we know that the list is sorted, we know that if 67 is in the list, it must be in the second half of the data, because all data to the left of the middle have values of 46 or less. This leaves the following viable candidates to search (shown in bold):

10   12   18   22   31   34   40   46   **59   67   69   72   80   84   98**

Continuing the same approach, we examine the middle value of the viable candidates (72). Again, this is not our target value, so we must continue the search. This time we can eliminate all values higher than 72, leaving:

10   12   18   22   31   34   40   46   **59   67   69**   72   80   84   98

Note that, in only two comparisons, we have reduced the viable candidates from 15 items down to 3 items. Employing the same approach again, we select the middle element, 67, and find the element we are seeking. If it had not been our target, we would have continued with this process until we either found the value or eliminated all possible data.

With each comparison, a binary search eliminates approximately half of the remaining data to be searched (it also eliminates the middle element as well). That is, a binary search eliminates half of the data with the first comparison, another quarter of the data with the second comparison, another eighth of the data with the third comparison, and so on.

> **key concept**
> A binary search eliminates half of the viable candidates with each comparison.

The following method implements a binary search. Like the `linearSearch` method, it accepts an array of `Comparable` objects to be searched as well as the target value. It also takes integer values representing the minimum index and maximum index that define the portion of the array to search (the viable candidates).

```
//------------------------------------------------------------
//  Searches the specified array of objects for the target value
//  using a binary search algorithm.
//------------------------------------------------------------
public static boolean binarySearch (Comparable[] data, int min,
                                     int max, Comparable target)
{
   boolean found = false;
   int midpoint = (min + max) / 2;   // determine the midpoint

   if (data[midpoint].compareTo(target) == 0)
      found = true;
   else
      if (data[midpoint].compareTo(target) > 0)
         if (min <= midpoint-1)
            found = binarySearch(data, min, midpoint-1, target);
         else
            if (midpoint+1 <= max)
               found = binarySearch(data, midpoint+1, max, target);

   return found;
}
```

Note that the binarySearch method is implemented recursively. If the target element is not found, and there is more data to search, the method calls itself, passing parameters that shrink the size of viable candidates within the array. The min and max indexes are used to determine if there is still more data to search. That is, if the reduced search area does not contain at least one element, the method does not call itself and a value of false is returned.

At any point in this process, we may have an even number of values to search, and therefore we have two "middle" values. As far as the algorithm goes, the midpoint used could be either of the two middle values. In this implementation of the binary search, the calculation that determines the midpoint index discards any fractional part, and therefore picks the first of the two middle values.

comparing search algorithms

For a linear search, the best case occurs when the target element happens to be the first item we examine in the group. The worst case occurs when the target is not in the group, and we have to examine every element before we determine that it isn't present. The expected case is that we would have to search half of the list before we find the element. That is, if there are n elements in the search pool, on average we would have to examine n/2 elements before finding the one for which we were searching.

Therefore, the linear search algorithm has a linear time complexity of $O(n)$. Because the elements are searched one at a time in turn, the complexity is linear—in direct proportion to the number of elements to be searched.

A binary search, on the other hand, is generally much faster. Because we can eliminate half of the remaining data with each comparison, we can find the element much more quickly. The best case is that we find the target in one comparison—that is, that the target element happens to be at the midpoint of the array. The worst case occurs if the element is not present in the list, in which case we have to make approximately $\log_2 n$ comparisons before we eliminate all of the data. Thus, the expected case for finding an element that is in the search pool is approximately $(\log_2 n)/2$ comparisons.

Therefore, a binary search is a *logarithmic algorithm* and has a time complexity of $O(\log_2 n)$. Compared to a linear search, a binary search is much faster for large values of n.

The question might be asked, if a logarithmic search is more efficient than a linear search, why would we ever use a linear search? First, a linear search is generally simpler than a binary search, and thus easier to program and debug. Second, a linear search does not require the additional overhead that the search list be sorted. There is a trade-off between the effort to keep the search pool sorted and the efficiency of the search.

For small problems, there is little practical difference between the two types of algorithms. However, as n gets large, the binary search becomes increasingly attractive. Suppose a given set of data contains one million elements. In a linear search, we'd have to examine each of the one million elements to determine that a particular target element is not in the group. In a binary search, we could make that conclusion in roughly 20 comparisons.

> **key concept**
> A binary search has logarithmic complexity, making it very efficient for a large search pool.

5.2   sorting

Sorting is the process of arranging a group of items into a defined order, either ascending or descending, based on some criteria. For example, you may want to alphabetize a list of names or put a list of survey results into descending numeric order.

> **key concept**
> Sorting is the process of arranging a list of items into a defined order based on some criteria.

Many sorting algorithms have been developed and critiqued over the years. In fact, sorting is considered to be a classic area of study in computer science. Similar to searching algorithms, sorting algorithms generally are divided into two categories based on efficiency: *sequential sorts,* which typically use a pair of nested loops and require roughly n² comparisons to sort n elements, and *logarithmic sorts,* which typically require roughly nlog₂n comparisons to sort n elements. As with the search algorithms, when n is small, there is little practical difference between the two categories of algorithms.

In this chapter we examine three sequential sorts—selection sort, insertion sort, and bubble sort—and two logarithmic sorts—quick sort and merge sort. Other search techniques are examined later in the book based on particular data structures.

Before we dive into particular sorting algorithms, let's look at a general sorting problem to solve. The `SortPhoneList` program, shown in Listing 5.1, creates an array of `Contact` objects, sorts these objects, and then prints the sorted list. In this implementation, the `Contact` objects are sorted using a call to the `selectionSort` method, which we examine later in this chapter. However, any sorting method described in this chapter could be used instead to achieve the same results.

listing
  5.1

```
//********************************************************************
//   SortPhoneList.java        Authors: Lewis/Chase
//
//   Driver for testing an object selection sort.
//********************************************************************

public class SortPhoneList
{
    //----------------------------------------------------------------
    //   Creates an array of Contact objects, sorts them, then prints
    //   them.
    //----------------------------------------------------------------
    public static void main (String[] args)
    {
        Contact[] friends = new Contact[7];
```

listing
   5.1   continued

```
        friends[0] = new Contact ("John", "Smith", "610-555-7384");
        friends[1] = new Contact ("Sarah", "Barnes", "215-555-3827");
        friends[2] = new Contact ("Mark", "Riley", "733-555-2969");
        friends[3] = new Contact ("Laura", "Getz", "663-555-3984");
        friends[4] = new Contact ("Larry", "Smith", "464-555-3489");
        friends[5] = new Contact ("Frank", "Phelps", "322-555-2284");
        friends[6] = new Contact ("Marsha", "Grant", "243-555-2837");

        Sort.selectionSort(friends);

        for (int index = 0; index < friends.length; index++)
            System.out.println (friends[index]);
    }
}
```

output

```
Barnes, Sarah      215-555-3827
Getz, Laura        663-555-3984
Grant, Marsha      243-555-2837
Phelps, Frank      322-555-2284
Riley, Mark        733-555-2969
Smith, John        610-555-7384
Smith, Larry       464-555-3489
```

Each Contact object represents a person with a last name, a first name, and a phone number. The Contact class is shown in Listing 5.2. The UML description of these classes is left as an exercise.

The Contact class implements the Comparable interface and therefore provides a definition of the compareTo method. In this case, the contacts are sorted by last name; if two contacts have the same last name, their first names are used.

Now let's examine several sorting algorithms and their implementations. Any of these could be used to put the Contact objects into sorted order.

listing
    5.2

```java
//***********************************************************
//   Contact.java        Authors: Lewis/Chase
//
//   Represents a phone contact.
//***********************************************************

public class Contact implements Comparable
{
   private String firstName, lastName, phone;

   //-----------------------------------------------------------------
   //  Sets up this contact with the specified information.
   //-----------------------------------------------------------------
   public Contact (String first, String last, String telephone)
   {
      firstName = first;
      lastName = last;
      phone = telephone;
   }

   //-----------------------------------------------------------------
   //  Returns a description of this contact as a string.
   //-----------------------------------------------------------------
   public String toString ()
   {
      return lastName + ", " + firstName + "\t" + phone;
   }

   //-----------------------------------------------------------------
   //  Uses both last and first names to determine lexical ordering.
   //-----------------------------------------------------------------
   public int compareTo (Object other)
   {
      int result;

      if (lastName.equals(((Contact)other).lastName))
         result = firstName.compareTo(((Contact)other).firstName);
      else
         result = lastName.compareTo(((Contact)other).lastName);

      return result;
   }
}
```

selection sort

The *selection sort* algorithm sorts a list of values by repetitively putting a particular value into its final, sorted, position. In other words, for each position in the list, the algorithm selects the value that should go in that position and puts it there.

The general strategy of the selection sort algorithm is as follows: Scan the entire list to find the smallest value. Exchange that value with the value in the first position of the list. Scan the rest of the list (all but the first value) to find the smallest value, and then exchange it with the value in the second position of the list. Scan the rest of the list (all but the first two values) to find the smallest value, and then exchange it with the value in the third position of the list. Continue this process for each position in the list. When complete, the list is sorted. The selection sort process is illustrated in Figure 5.3.

The following method defines an implementation of the selection sort algorithm. It accepts an array of `Comparable` objects as a parameter. When it returns to the calling method, the elements within the array are sorted.

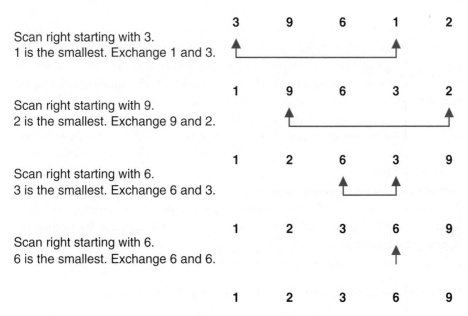

figure 5.3   Illustration of selection sort processing

```
//--------------------------------------------------------------------
//   Sorts the specified array of objects using the selection
//   sort algorithm.
//--------------------------------------------------------------------
public static void selectionSort (Comparable[] data)
{
    int min;
    Comparable temp;
    for (int index = 0; index < data.length-1; index++)
    {
        min = index;
        for (int scan = index+1; scan < data.length; scan++)
            if (data[scan].compareTo(data[min])<0)
                min = scan;

        // Swap the values
        temp = data[min];
        data[min] = data[index];
        data[index] = temp;
    }
}
```

The implementation of the selectionSort method uses two loops to sort an array of integers. The outer loop controls the position in the array where the next smallest value will be stored. The inner loop finds the smallest value in the rest of the list by scanning all positions greater than or equal to the index specified by the outer loop. When the smallest value is determined, it is exchanged with the value stored at index. This exchange is accomplished by three assignment statements using an extra variable called temp. This type of exchange is called *swapping*.

Note that because this algorithm finds the smallest value during each iteration, the result is an array sorted in ascending order (i.e., smallest to largest). The algorithm can easily be changed to put values in descending order by finding the largest value each time.

insertion sort

The *insertion sort* algorithm sorts a list of values by repetitively inserting a particular value into a subset of the list that has already been
sorted. One at a time, each unsorted element is inserted at the appropriate position in that sorted subset until the entire list is in order.

The general strategy of the insertion sort algorithm is as follows: Sort the first
two values in the list relative to each other by exchanging them if necessary. Insert
the list's third value into the appropriate position relative to the first two (sorted)
values. Then insert the fourth value into its proper position relative to the first
three values in the list. Each time an insertion is made, the number of values in
the sorted subset increases by one. Continue this process until all values in the list
are completely sorted. The insertion process requires that the other values in the
array shift to make room for the inserted element. Figure 5.4 illustrates the insertion sort process.

> The insertion sort algorithm
> sorts a list of values by repeti-
> tively inserting a particular
> value into a subset of the list
> that has already been sorted.
>
> key concept

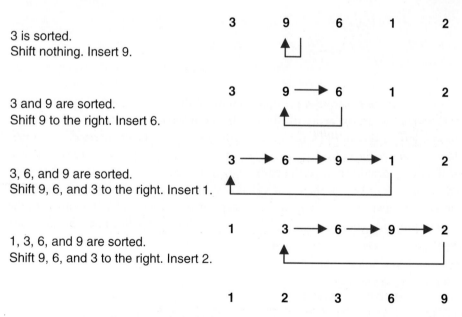

figure 5.4   Illustration of insertion sort processing

The following method implements an insertion sort:

```
//------------------------------------------------------------
//  Sorts the specified array of objects using an insertion
//  sort algorithm.
//------------------------------------------------------------
public static void insertionSort (Comparable[] data)
{
    for (int index = 1; index < data.length; index++)
    {
        Comparable key = data[index];
        int position = index;

        // Shift larger values to the right
        while (position > 0 && data[position-1].compareTo(key) > 0)
        {
            data[position] = data[position-1];
            position--;
        }

        data[position] = key;
    }
}
```

Similar to the selection sort implementation, the insertionSort method uses two loops to sort an array of objects. In the insertion sort, however, the outer loop controls the index in the array of the next value to be inserted. The inner loop compares the current insert value with values stored at lower indexes (which make up a sorted subset of the entire list). If the current insert value is less than the value at position, then that value is shifted to the right. Shifting continues until the proper position is opened to accept the insert value. Each iteration of the outer loop adds one more value to the sorted subset of the list, until the entire list is sorted.

bubble sort

key concept

The bubble sort algorithm sorts a list by repeatedly comparing neighboring elements and swapping them if necessary.

A *bubble sort* is another sequential sorting algorithm that uses two nested loops. It sorts values by repeatedly comparing neighboring elements in the list and swapping their position if they are not in order relative to each other.

The general strategy of the bubble sort algorithm is as follows: Scan through the list comparing adjacent elements and exchange them if they are not in relative order. This has the effect of "bubbling" the largest value to the last position in the list, which is its appropriate position in the final sorted list. Then scan through the list again, bubbling up the second-to-last value. This process continues until all elements have been bubbled into their correct positions.

Each pass through the bubble sort algorithm moves the largest value to its final position. A pass may also reposition other elements as well. For example, if we started with the list:

9   6   8   12   3   1   7

we would first compare 9 and 6 and, finding them not in the correct order, we would swap them, yielding:

6   9   8   12   3   1   7

Then we would compare 9 to 8, and again, finding them not in the correct order, we would swap them, yielding:

6   8   9   12   3   1   7

Then we would compare 9 to 12. Since they are in the correct order, we don't swap them. Instead, we move to the next pair of values to compare. That is, we then compare 12 to 3. Since they are not in order, we swap them, yielding:

6   8   9   3   12   1   7

We then compare 12 to 1 and swap them, yielding:

6   8   9   3   1   12   7

We then compare 12 to 7 and swap them, yielding:

6   8   9   3   1   7   12

This completes one pass through the data to be sorted. After this first pass, the largest value in the list (12) is in its correct position, but we cannot be sure about any of the other numbers. Each subsequent pass through the data guarantees that one more element is put into the correct position. Thus we make n−1 passes through the data, since if n−1 elements are in the correct sorted positions, the nth item must also be in the correct location.

An implementation of the bubble sort algorithm is shown in the following method:

```
//------------------------------------------------------------------
//   Sorts the specified array of objects using a bubble sort
//   algorithm.
//------------------------------------------------------------------
public static void bubbleSort (Comparable[] data)
{
    int position, scan;
    Comparable temp;

    for (position = data.length-1; position >= 0; position--)
    {
        for (scan = 0; scan <= position-1; scan++)
        {
            if (data[scan].compareTo(data[scan+1]) > 0)
            {
                // Swap the values
                temp = data[scan];
                data[scan] = data[scan + 1];
                data[scan + 1] = temp;
            }
        }
    }
}
```

The outer for loop in the bubbleSort method represents the n–1 passes through the data. The inner for loop scans through the data, performs the pairwise comparisons of the neighboring data, and swaps them if necessary.

Note that the outer loop also has the effect of decreasing the position that represents the maximum index to examine in the inner loop. That is, after the first pass, which puts the last value in its correct position, there is no need to consider that value in future passes through the data. After the second pass, we can forget about the last two, and so on. Thus the inner loop examines one less value on each pass.

quick sort

The sorting algorithms we have discussed thus far in this chapter (selection sort, insertion sort, and bubble sort) are relatively simple, but they are inefficient sequential sorts that use a pair of nested loops and require roughly n² comparisons to sort a list of n elements. Now we can turn our attention to more efficient sorts that lend themselves to a recursive implementation.

The *quick sort* algorithm sorts a list by partitioning the list using an arbitrarily chosen *partition element* and then recursively sorting the sublists on either side of the partition element. The general strategy of the quick sort algorithm is as follows: First, choose one element of the list to act as a partition element. Next, partition the list so that all elements less than the partition element are to the left of that element and all elements greater than the partition element are to the right. Finally, apply this quick sort strategy (recursively) to both partitions.

> **key concept**
> The quick sort algorithm sorts a list by partitioning the list and then recursively sorting the two partitions.

The choice of the partition element is arbitrary, and we will use the first element in the list. For efficiency reasons, it would be nice if the partition element divided the list roughly in half, but the algorithm will work no matter what element is chosen as the partition.

Let's look at an example of creating a partition. If we started with the following list:

90   65   7   305   120   110   8

we would choose 90 as our partition element. We would then rearrange the list, swapping the elements that are less than 90 to the left side and those that are greater than 90 to the right side, yielding:

8   65   7   **90**   120   110   305

We would then apply the quick sort algorithm separately to both partitions. This process continues until a partition contains only one element, which is inherently sorted. Thus, after the algorithm is applied recursively to either side, the entire list is sorted. Once the initial partition element is determined and placed, it is never considered or moved again.

The following method implements the quick sort algorithm. It accepts an array of Comparable data to sort and the minimum and maximum index values used for a particular call to the method. For the initial call to the method, the values of min and max would encompass the entire set of elements to be sorted.

```
//-------------------------------------------------------------------
//  Sorts the specified array of objects using the quick sort
//  algorithm.
//-------------------------------------------------------------------
public static void quickSort (Comparable[] data, int min, int max)
{
   int indexOfPartition;

   if (max-min  > 0)
   {
      // Create partitions
      indexOfPartition = findPartition (data, min, max);

      // Sort the left side
      quickSort (data, min, indexOfPartition-1);

      // Sort the right side
      quickSort (data, indexOfPartition+1, max);
   }
}
```

The quickSort method relies heavily on the findPartition method, which it calls initially to divide the sort area into two partitions. The findPartition method returns the index of the partition value. Then the quicksort method is called twice (recursively) to sort the two partitions. The base case of the recursion, represented by the if statement in the quickSort method, is a list of one element or less, which is already inherently sorted. The findPartition method is shown below:

```
//-------------------------------------------------------------------
//  Rearranges the elements in the sort area into two partitions.
//-------------------------------------------------------------------
private static int findPartition (Comparable[] data, int min, int max)
{
   int left, right;
   Comparable temp, partitionelement;

   // Use the first element as the partition element
   partitionelement = data[min];

   left = min;
   right = max;
```

```
        while (left < right)
        {
            // search for an element that is > the partition element
            while (data[left].compareTo(partitionelement) <=0 &&
                            left < right)
                left++;

            // search for an element that is < the partition element
            while (data[right].compareTo(partitionelement) > 0)
                right--;

            // swap the elements
            if (left < right)
            {
                temp = data[left];
                data[left] = data[right];
                data[right] = temp;
            }
        }

        // Move partition element to partition index
        temp = data[min];
        data[min] = data[right];
        data[right] = temp;

        return right;
    }
```

The two inner while loops of the findPartition method are used to find elements that are in the wrong partitions to swap. The first loop scans from left to right looking for an element that is greater than the partition element. The second loop scans from right to left looking for an element that is less than the partition element. When these two elements are found, they are swapped. This process continues until the right and left indexes meet in the "middle" of the list. The location where they meet also indicates where the partition element (which isn't moved from its initial location until the end) will ultimately reside.

merge sort

Now we can examine another recursive sorting algorithm. The *merge sort* algorithm sorts a list by recursively dividing the list in half until each sublist has one element and then recombining these sublists in order.

The general strategy of the merge sort algorithm is as follows: begin by dividing the list in two roughly equal parts and then recursively calling itself with each of those lists. Continue the recursive decomposition of the list until base case of the recursion is reached, where the list is divided into lists of length one, which are by definition sorted. Then, as control passes back up the recursive calling structure, the algorithm merges into one sorted list the two sorted sublists resulting from the two recursive calls.

For example, if we started with the initial list from our example in the previous section, the recursive decomposition portion of the algorithm would yield the results shown in Figure 5.5.

The merge portion of the algorithm would then recombine the list as shown in Figure 5.6.

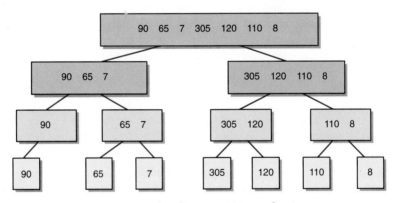

figure 5.5 The decomposition of merge sort

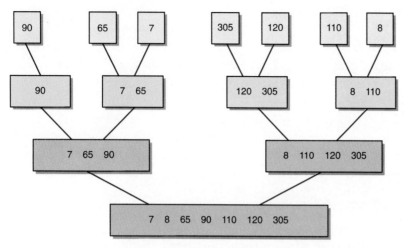

figure 5.6   The merge portion of the merge sort algorithm

An implementation of the merge sort algorithm is shown below:

```
//-------------------------------------------------------------------
//   Sorts the specified array of objects using the merge sort
//   algorithm.
//-------------------------------------------------------------------
public static void mergeSort (Comparable[] data, int min, int max)
{
    Comparable temp[];
    int index1, left, right;

    // Return on list of length one
    if (min == max)
        return;

    // Find the length and the midpoint of the list
    int size = max - min + 1;
    int pivot = (min + max) / 2;

    temp = new Comparable[size];

    // Sort left half of list
    mergeSort(data, min, pivot);
```

```
// Sort right half of list
mergeSort(data, pivot + 1, max);

// Copy sorted data into workspace
for (index1 = 0; index1 < size; index1++)
   temp[index1] = data[min + index1];

// Merge the two sorted lists
left = 0;
right = pivot - min + 1;
for (index1 = 0; index1 < size; index1++)
{
   if (right <= max - min)
      if (left <= pivot - min)
         if (temp[left].compareTo(temp[right]) > 0)
            data[index1 + min] = temp[right++];
         else
            data[index1 + min] = temp[left++];
      else
         data[index1 + min] = temp[right++];
   else
      data[index1 + min] = temp[left++];
}
}
```

summary of key concepts

▸ Searching is the process of finding a designated target within a group of items or determining that it doesn't exist.

▸ An efficient search minimizes the number of comparisons made.

▸ A binary search capitalizes on the fact that the search pool is sorted.

▸ A binary search eliminates half of the viable candidates with each comparison.

▸ A binary search has logarithmic complexity, making it very efficient for a large search pool.

▸ Sorting is the process of arranging a list of items into a defined order based on some criteria.

▸ The selection sort algorithm sorts a list of values by repetitively putting a particular value into its final, sorted, position.

▸ The insertion sort algorithm sorts a list of values by repetitively inserting a particular value into a subset of the list that has already been sorted.

▸ The bubble sort algorithm sorts a list by repeatedly comparing neighboring elements and swapping them if necessary.

▸ The quick sort algorithm sorts a list by partitioning the list and then recursively sorting the two partitions.

▸ The merge sort algorithm sorts a list by recursively dividing the list in half until each sublist has one element and then merging these sublists into the sorted order.

self-review questions

5.1   When would a linear search be preferable to a logarithmic search?

5.2   Which searching method requires that the list be sorted?

5.3   When would a sequential sort be preferable to a recursive sort?

5.4   The insertion sort algorithm sorts using what technique?

5.5   The bubble sort algorithm sorts using what technique?

5.6   The selection sort algorithm sorts using what technique?

5.7   The quick sort algorithm sorts using what technique?

5.8   The merge sort algorithm sorts using what technique?

exercises

5.1   Compare and contrast the linearSearch and binarySearch algorithms searching for the numbers 45 and 54 in the following list (3, 8, 12, 34, 54, 84, 91, 110).

5.2   Using the list from Exercise 5.1, construct a table showing the number of comparisons required to sort that list for each of the sort algorithms (selection sort, insertion sort, bubble sort, quick sort, and merge sort).

5.3   Using the same list from Exercise 5.1, what happens to the number of comparisons for each of the sort algorithms if the list is already sorted?

5.4   Given the following list:

    90   8   7   56   123   235   9   1   653

Show a trace of execution for:

    a. selection sort

    b. insertion sort

    c. bubble sort

    d. quick sort

    e. merge sort

5.5   Given the resulting sorted list from Exercise 5.4, show a trace of execution for a binary search, searching for the number 235.

5.6   Draw the UML description of the SortPhoneList example.

programming projects

5.1   The bubble sort algorithm shown in this chapter is less efficient than it could be. If a pass is made through the list without exchanging any elements, this means that the list is sorted and there is no reason to continue. Modify this algorithm so that it will stop as soon as it recognizes that the list is sorted. DO NOT use a break statement!

5.2   There is a variation of the bubble sort algorithm called gap sort that, rather than comparing neighboring elements each time through the list, compares elements that are some number (i) positions apart, where i is an integer less than n. For example, the first element would be compared to the (i + 1) element, the second element would be compared to the (i + 2) element, the nth element to the (n–i) element, etc. A single iteration is completed when all of the elements that can be compared, have been compared. On the next iteration, i is reduced by some number greater than 1 and the process continues until i is less than 1. Implement a gap sort.

5.3   Modify the sorts listed in the chapter (selection sort, insertion sort, bubble sort, quick sort, and merge sort) by adding code to each to tally the total number of comparisons and total execution time of each algorithm. Execute the sort algorithms against the same list, recording information for the total number of comparisons and total execution time for each algorithm. Try several different lists, including at least one that is already in sorted order.

answers to self-review questions

5.1   A linear search would be preferable for relatively small, unsorted lists, and in languages where recursion is not supported.

5.2   Binary search.

5.3   A sequential sort would be preferable for relatively small data sets, and in languages where recursion is not supported.

5.4   The insertion sort algorithm sorts a list of values by repetitively inserting a particular value into a subset of the list that has already been sorted.

5.5   The bubble sort algorithm sorts a list by repeatedly comparing neighboring elements in the list and swapping their position if they are not already in order.

5.6   The selection sort algorithm, which is an $O(n^2)$ sorting algorithm, sorts a list of values by repetitively putting a particular value into its final, sorted, position.

5.7   The quick sort algorithm sorts a list by partitioning the list using an arbitrarily chosen partition element and then recursively sorting the sublists on either side of the partition element.

5.8   The merge sort algorithm sorts a list by recursively dividing the list in half until each sublist has one element and then recombining these sublists in order.

stacks

A stack may have been the first organized collection that we all learned about as children. From the very first time we stacked blocks one upon another, we learned that we usually should not try to get to the ones on the bottom of the stack without first removing the ones on top. Other common examples include a stack of plates, a stack of chairs, and a stack of trays in a cafeteria. The stack data structure we examine in this chapter operates on similar principles and has many uses in the world of computing.

chapter objectives

▶ Examine stack processing

▶ Define a stack abstract data type

▶ Demonstrate how a stack can be used to solve problems

▶ Examine various stack implementations

▶ Compare stack implementations

6.1   a stack ADT

key
concept

Stack elements are processed in a LIFO manner—the last element in is the first element out.

A *stack* is a linear collection whose elements are added and removed from the same end. We say that a stack is processed in a *last in, first out* (LIFO) manner. That is, the last element to be put on a stack will be the first one that gets removed. Said another way, the elements of a stack are removed in the reverse order of their placement on it.

The processing of a stack is shown in Figure 6.1. Usually a stack is depicted vertically, and we refer to the *top* of the stack as the end to which elements are added and from which they are removed.

Recall from Chapter 3 that we define an abstract data type (ADT) using a specific set of operations that establish the valid ways in which we can manage the elements stored in the data structure. We always want to use this concept to formally define the operations for a collection and work within the functionality it provides. That way, we can cleanly separate the interface to the collection from any particular implementation technique used to create it.

The operations for a stack ADT are listed in Figure 6.2. We say we *push* an element onto a stack and that we *pop* it off. We can also *peek* at the top element of a stack, examining it or using it as needed, without actually removing it from the collection. There are also the general operations that allow us to determine if the stack is empty or, more specifically, how many elements it contains.

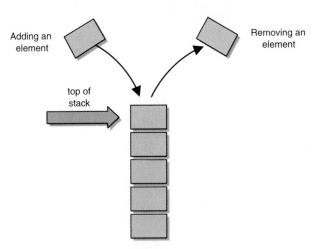

Adding an element

Removing an element

top of stack

figure 6.1   A conceptual view of a stack

Operation	Description
push	Adds an element to the top of the stack.
pop	Removes an element from the top of the stack.
peek	Examines the element at the top of the stack.
isEmpty	Determines if the stack is empty.
size	Determines the number of elements on the stack.

figure 6.2   The operations on a stack

Sometimes there are variations on the naming conventions for the operations on a data structure. For a stack, the use of the terms push and pop are relatively standard. The peek operation is sometimes referred to as *top*.

Keep in mind that the definition of a collection is not universal. You will find variations in the operations defined for specific data structures from one book to another. We've been very careful in this book to define the operations on each data structure so that they are consistent with its purpose.

For example, note that none of the stack operations in Figure 6.2 allow us to reach down into the stack to remove or reorganize the elements in the stack. That is the very nature of a stack—all activity occurs at one end. If we discover that, in order to solve a particular problem, we need to access the elements in the middle or bottom of the collection, then a stack is not the appropriate data structure to use.

> **key concept**
> A programmer should choose the structure that is appropriate for the type of data management needed.

As we did with the bag collection in Chapters 3 and 4, we also provide a toString operation for the collection. This is not a classic operation defined for a stack, but provides a convenient means to traverse and display its contents without allowing modification of the stack. Notice that we did not provide an iterator method. An iterator would violate the basic premise of a stack that you can only access the top of the stack.

The operations on a stack can be defined in a Java interface, such as the one shown in Listing 6.1. Any class that implements the StackADT interface must provide a definition for the methods listed in the interface. Note that the methods of this interface refer to generic Object reference variables, which allows a stack to store any kind of object. Later in this chapter we examine two classes that implement these methods in different ways. For now, our abstract understanding of how a stack operates allows us to explore situations in which stacks help us solve particular problems.

The StackADT interface can be depicted in UML as shown in Figure 6.3.

listing
     6.1

```java
//***********************************************************************
//  StackADT.java        Authors: Lewis/Chase
//
//  Defines the interface to a stack collection.
//***********************************************************************

package jss2;

public interface StackADT
{
   public void push (Object element);

   public Object pop();

   public Object peek();

   public boolean isEmpty();

   public int size();

   public String toString();
}
```

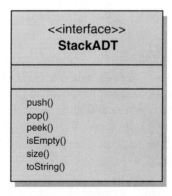

figure 6.3   The StackADT interface in UML

Stacks are used quite frequently in the computing world. For example, the undo operation in a word processor is usually implemented using a stack. As we make changes to a document (add data, delete data, make format changes, etc.), the word processor keeps track of each operation by pushing some representation of it onto a stack. If we choose to undo an operation, the word processing software pops the most recently performed operation off the stack and reverses it. If we choose to undo again (undoing the second-to-last operation we performed), another element is popped from the stack. In most word processors, many operations can be reversed in this manner.

> A data structure often lends itself to the solution of particular kinds of problems.
>
> key concept

The following sections explore in detail other examples of using stacks to solve problems.

6.2 using stacks: evaluating postfix expressions

Traditionally, arithmetic expressions are written in an *infix* notation, meaning that the operator is placed between its operands in the form

    <operand> <operator> <operand>

such as in the expression

    4 + 5

When evaluating an infix expression, we rely on precedence rules to determine the order of operator evaluation. For example, the expression

    4 + 5 * 2

evaluates to 14 rather than 18 because of the precedence rule that says in the absence of parentheses, multiplication evaluates before addition.

In a *postfix* expression, the operator comes after its two operands. Therefore a postfix expression takes the form

    <operand> <operand> <operator>

For example, the postfix expression

    6 9 -

is equivalent to the infix expression

    6 - 9

A postfix expression is generally easier to evaluate than an infix expression because precedence rules and parentheses do not have to be taken into account. The order of the values and operators in the expression are sufficient to determine the result. Programming language compilers and runtime environments often use postfix expressions in their internal calculations for this reason.

The process of evaluating a postfix expression can be stated in one simple rule: Scanning from left to right, apply each operation to the two operands immediately preceding it. At the end we are left with the final value of the expression.

Consider the infix expression we looked at earlier:

```
4 + 5 * 2
```

In postfix notation, this expression would be written

```
4 5 2 * +
```

Let's use our evaluation rule to determine the final value of this expression. We scan from the left until we encounter the multiplication (*) operator. We apply this operator to the two operands immediately preceding it (5 and 2) and replace it with the result (10), leaving us with

```
4 10 +
```

Continuing our scan from left to right, we immediately encounter the plus (+) operator. Applying this operator to the two operands immediately preceding it (4 and 10) yields 14, which is the final value of the expression.

Let's look at a slightly more complicated example. Consider the following infix expression:

```
(3 * 4 − (2 + 5)) * 4 / 2
```

The equivalent postfix expression is

```
3 4 * 2 5 + − 4 * 2 /
```

Applying our evaluation rule results in:

	12 2 5 + − 4 * 2 /
then	12 7 − 4 * 2 /
then	5 4 * 2 /
then	20 2 /
then	10

Now let's think about the design of a program that will evaluate a postfix expression. The evaluation rule relies on being able to retrieve the previous two operands whenever we encounter an operator. Furthermore, a large postfix expression will have many operators and operands to manage. It turns out that a stack is the perfect data structure to use in this case. The operations provided by a stack coincide nicely with the process of evaluating a postfix expression.

> A stack is the ideal data structure to use when evaluating a postfix expression.

The algorithm for evaluating a postfix expression using a stack can be expressed as follows: Scan the expression from left to right, identifying each token (operator or operand) in turn. If it is an operand, push it onto the stack. If it is an operator, pop the top two elements off of the stack, apply the operation to them, and push the result onto the stack. When we reach the end of the expression, the element on top of the stack will be the result of the expression. Figure 6.4 depicts the use of a stack to evaluate a postfix expression.

The program in Listing 6.2 evaluates multiple postfix expressions entered by the user. It uses the PostfixEvaluator class shown in Listing 6.3.

To keep things simple, this program assumes that the operands to the expression are integers and that they are literal values (not variables). When executed, the program repeatedly accepts and evaluates postfix expressions until the user chooses not to.

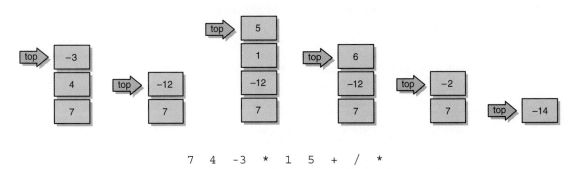

7   4   -3   *   1   5   +   /   *

figure 6.4   Using a stack to evaluate a postfix expression

listing
   6.2

```java
//*********************************************************************
//  Postfix.java          Authors: Lewis/Chase
//
//  Demonstrates the use of a stack to evaluate postfix expressions.
//*********************************************************************

import java.util.StringTokenizer;
import java.io.*;

public class Postfix
{
   //-----------------------------------------------------------------
   //  Reads and evaluates multiple postfix expressions.
   //-----------------------------------------------------------------
   public static void main (String[] args)
   {
      String expression, again;
      int result;

      try
      {
         BufferedReader in = new
            BufferedReader( new InputStreamReader(System.in));

         PostfixEvaluator evaluator = new PostfixEvaluator();

         do
         {
            System.out.println ("Enter a valid postfix expression: ");
            expression = in.readLine();

            result = evaluator.evaluate (expression);
            System.out.println();
            System.out.println ("That expression equals " + result);

            System.out.print ("Evaluate another expression [Y/N]? ");
            again = in.readLine();
            System.out.println();
         }
         while (again.equalsIgnoreCase("y"));
      }
      catch (Exception IOException)
      {
```

listing
    6.2   continued

```
        System.out.println("Input exception reported");
      }
   }
}
```

output

```
Enter a valid postfix expression:
20 5 - 3 *

That expression equals 45
Evaluate another expression [Y/N]? y

Enter a valid postfix expression:
99 3 / 2 * 3 +

That expression equals 69
Evaluate another expression [Y/N]? n
```

listing
    6.3

```
//***********************************************************************
//  PostfixEvaluator.java        Authors: Lewis/Chase
//
//  Represents an evaluator of postfix expressions. Assumes the
//  operands are integer literals.
//***********************************************************************

import jss2.ArrayStack;
import java.util.StringTokenizer;

public class PostfixEvaluator
{
   private final char ADD = '+', SUBTRACT = '-';
   private final char MULTIPLY = '*', DIVIDE = '/';

   private ArrayStack stack;
```

listing
6.3   continued

```java
//------------------------------------------------------------------
//  Sets up this evalutor by creating a new stack.
//------------------------------------------------------------------
public PostfixEvaluator()
{
   stack = new ArrayStack();
}


//------------------------------------------------------------------
//  Evaluates the specified postfix expression. If an operand is
//  encountered, it is pushed onto the stack. If an operator is
//  encountered, two operands are popped, the operation is
//  evaluated, and the result is pushed onto the stack.
//------------------------------------------------------------------
public int evaluate (String expr)
{
   int op1, op2, result = 0;
   String token;
   StringTokenizer tokenizer = new StringTokenizer (expr);

   while (tokenizer.hasMoreTokens())
   {
      token = tokenizer.nextToken();

      if (isOperator(token))
      {
         op2 = ((Integer)stack.pop()).intValue();
         op1 = ((Integer)stack.pop()).intValue();
         result = evalSingleOp (token.charAt(0), op1, op2);
         stack.push (new Integer(result));
      }
      else
         stack.push (new Integer(Integer.parseInt(token)));
   }

   return result;
}
```

listing
   6.3   continued

```java
//-----------------------------------------------------------------
//  Determines if the specified token is an operator.
//-----------------------------------------------------------------
private boolean isOperator (String token)
{
   return ( token.equals("+") || token.equals("-") ||
            token.equals("*") || token.equals("/") );
}


//-----------------------------------------------------------------
//  Evaluates a single expression consisting of the specified
//  operator and operands.
//-----------------------------------------------------------------
private int evalSingleOp (char operation, int op1, int op2)
{
   int result = 0;

   switch (operation)
   {
      case ADD:
         result = op1 + op2;
         break;
      case SUBTRACT:
         result = op1 - op2;
         break;
      case MULTIPLY:
         result = op1 * op2;
         break;
      case DIVIDE:
         result = op1 / op2;
   }

   return result;
}
}
```

The `evaluate` method performs the evaluation algorithm described earlier, supported by the `isOperator` and `evalSingleOp` methods. Note that in the `evaluate` method, only operands are pushed onto the stack. Operators are used as they are encountered and are never put on the stack. This is consistent with the evaluation algorithm we discussed. An operand is put on the stack as an `Integer` object, instead of as an `int` primitive value, because the stack data structure is designed to store objects. Also, because the stack's `pop` operation is defined to return a generic `Object` reference, we must cast the value returned from the `pop` method into an `Integer` before invoking the `intValue` method.

When an operator is encountered, the most recent two operands are popped off of the stack. Note that the first operand popped is actually the second operand in the expression, and the second operand popped is the first operand in the expression. This order doesn't matter in the cases of addition and multiplication, but it certainly matters for subtraction or division.

Note also that the postfix expression program assumes that the postfix expression entered is valid, meaning that it contains a properly organized set of operators and operands. A postfix expression is invalid if either (1) two operands are not available on the stack when an operator is encountered or (2) there is more than one value on the stack when the tokens in the expression are exhausted. Either situation indicates that there was something wrong with the format of the expression, and both can be caught by examining the state of the stack at the appropriate point in the program. Checking for these erroneous situations is left as a programming project.

Perhaps the most important aspect of this program is the use of the class that defined the stack collection. At this point, we don't know how the stack was implemented. We simply trusted the class to do its job. In this example, we used the class `ArrayStack`, but we could have used any class that implemented a stack as long as it performed the stack operations (defined by the `StackADT` interface) as expected. From the point of view of evaluating postfix expressions, the manner in which the stack is implemented is largely irrelevant. Figure 6.5 shows a UML class diagram for the postfix expression evaluation program.

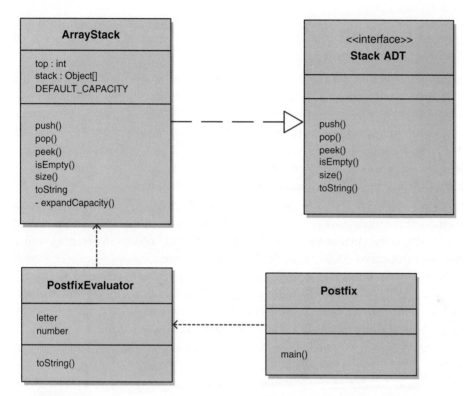

figure 6.5   A UML class diagram for the postfix expression program

6.3 using stacks: simulating recursion

Another classic use of a stack data structure occurs when the runtime environment executes a program. A *program stack* (or *runtime stack*) is used to keep track of methods that are invoked. Every time a method is called, an *activation record* that represents the invocation is created and pushed onto the program stack. Therefore, the elements on the stack represent the series of method invocations that occurred to reach a particular point in an executing program.

For example, when the main method of a program is called, an activation record for it is created and pushed onto the program stack. When main calls another method (say m2), then an activation record for m2 is created and pushed onto the stack. If m2 calls method m3, then an activation record for m3 is created and pushed onto the stack. When method m3 terminates, its activation record is popped off of the stack and control returns to the calling method (m2), which is now on the top of the stack.

If an exception occurs during the execution of a Java program, the programmer can examine the *call stack trace* to see in what method the problem occurred and what method calls were made to arrive at that point.

An activation record contains various administrative data to help manage the execution of the program. It also contains a copy of the method's data (local variables and parameters) for that invocation of the method.

The program stack works the same way when recursive calls are made. As discussed in Chapter 4, a recursive method calls itself, and each invocation of the method maintains its own copy of the local data. It is the program stack that keeps track of the data for each activation of the method.

Recall the maze traversal problem presented in Chapter 4. The `traverse` method of the `Maze` class is a recursive method that keeps track of three pieces of information: the current row in the grid, the current column in the grid, and a `boolean` flag called `done` that indicates whether or not a solution has been found.

Each time the `traverse` method calls itself, an activation record is created with a copy of these three variables and their current values. Each time an instance of the `traverse` method completed execution, the associated activation record was popped off the stack.

> **key concept**
>
> Recursive processing can be simulated using a stack to keep track of the appropriate data.

Because of the relationship between stacks and recursion, we can always rewrite a recursive program into a nonrecursive program that uses a stack. Instead of using recursion to keep track of the data, we can create our own stack to do so.

A version of the `traverse` method that uses a stack might look something like this:

```
//--------------------------------------------------------------
//  Attempts to iteratively traverse the maze.  It inserts special
//  characters indicating locations that have been tried.
//--------------------------------------------------------------
public boolean traverse ()
{
    boolean done = false;
    Position pos = new Position();
    Stack stack = new Stack();
    stack.push(pos);

    while (!(done))
    {
        pos = (Position)stack.pop();
        grid[pos.getx()][pos.gety()] = TRIED;  // this cell has been tried
        if (pos.getx() == grid.length-1 && pos.gety() == grid[0].length-1)
            done = true;  // the maze is solved
```

```
        else
        {
            stack = pushNewPos (pos.getx(), pos.gety() - 1, stack);
            stack = pushNewPos (pos.getx(), pos.gety() + 1, stack);
            stack = pushNewPos (pos.getx() - 1, pos.gety(), stack);
            stack = pushNewPos (pos.getx() + 1, pos.gety(), stack);
        }
    }

    return done;
}
```

This solution does not behave exactly like the recursive solution from Chapter 4. It uses a class called `Position` to encapsulate the coordinates of a position within the maze. The `traverse` method loops, popping the top position off of the stack, marking it as tried, and then testing to see if we are done. If we are not done, then all of the valid moves from this position are pushed onto the stack and the loop continues. A private method called `pushNewPos` has been created to handle the task of putting the valid moves from the current position onto the stack:

```
private Stack pushNewPos (int x, int y, Stack stack)
{
    Position npos = new Position();
    npos.setx(x);
    npos.sety(y);
    if (valid(npos.getx(),npos.gety()))
        stack.push(npos);
    return stack;
}
```

This solution also does not mark the successful path the way that our `traverse` method from Chapter 4 did. Completing this solution is left as a programming project.

6.4 implementing stacks: with links

Similar to our approach to the linked implementation of the bag collection in Chapter 3, we can define a class called `LinkedStack` that represents a linked implementation of a stack. And we can reuse the `LinearNode` class defined in Chapter 3 to maintain a linked list of nodes that represent the stack. We will maintain a reference variable called `top` to point to the top of the stack. Each node contains a reference to the element stored at that point in the stack, and a reference to the next node (below it) in the stack.

Figure 6.6 illustrates this configuration for a stack containing four elements A, B, C, and D that have been pushed onto the stack in that order.

Let's explore the implementation of the stack operations for the `LinkedStack` class.

the `push` operation

Every time a new element is pushed onto the stack, a new `LinearNode` object must be created to store it in the linked list. To position the newly created node at the top of the stack, we must set its `next` reference to the current top of the stack, and reset the `top` reference to point to the new node. We must also increment the `count` variable.

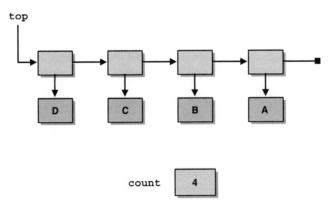

figure 6.6   A linked implementation of a stack

Implementing these steps results in the following code:

```
//-----------------------------------------------------------------
//  Adds the specified element to the top of the stack.
//-----------------------------------------------------------------
public void push (Object element)
{
    LinearNode temp = new LinearNode (element);

    temp.setNext(top);
    top = temp;
    count++;
}
```

Figure 6.7 shows the result of pushing the element E onto the stack depicted in Figure 6.6.

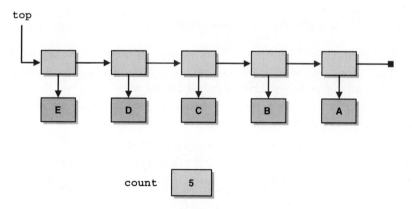

figure 6.7   The stack after pushing element E

the `pop` operation

The `pop` operation is implemented by returning a reference to the element currently stored at the top of the stack and adjusting the `top` reference to the new top of the stack. Before attempting to return any element, however, we must first ensure that there is at least one element to return. This operation can be implemented as follows:

```
//-------------------------------------------------------------------
//   Removes the element at the top of the stack and returns a
//   reference to it. Throws an EmptyStackException if the stack
//   is empty.
//-------------------------------------------------------------------
public Object pop() throws EmptyStackException
{
    if (isEmpty())
        throw new EmptyStackException();

    Object result = top.getElement();
    top = top.getNext();
    count--;

    return result;
}
```

If the stack is empty, as determined by the `isEmpty` method, an `EmptyStackException` is thrown. If there is at least one element to pop, it is stored in a temporary variable so that it can be returned. Then the reference to the top of the stack is set to the next element in the list, which is now the new top of the stack. The count of elements is decremented as well.

Figure 6.8 illustrates the result of a `pop` operation on the stack from Figure 6.7. Notice that this figure is identical to our original configuration in Figure 6.6. This illustrates the fact that the `pop` operation is the inverse of the `push` operation.

other operations

Using a linked implementation, the `peek` operation is implemented by returning a reference to the element pointed to by the node pointed to by the top pointer. The `isEmpty` operation returns true if the count of elements is 0, and false oth-

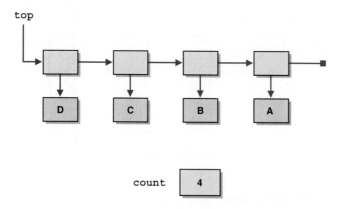

figure 6.8   The stack after a pop operation

erwise. The `size` operation simply returns the count of elements in the stack. The `iterator` and `toString` operations can be implemented using a similar approach to the one used in the bag collection in Chapter 3. These operations are left as programming projects.

6.5 implementing stacks: with arrays

An array implementation of a stack, defined by a class called `ArrayStack`, can be designed by making the following four assumptions: the array is an array of object references, the bottom of the stack is always at index 0 of the array, the elements of the stack are stored in order and contiguously in the array, and there is an integer variable `top` that stores the index of the array immediately following the top element in the stack.

Figure 6.9 illustrates this configuration for a stack that currently contains the elements A, B, C, and D, assuming that they have been pushed on in that order. To simplify the figure, the elements are shown in the array itself rather than as objects referenced from the array. Note that the variable `top` represents both the next cell into which a pushed element should be stored as well as the count of the number of elements currently in the stack.

In this implementation, the bottom of the stack is always held at index 0 of the array, and the stack grows and shrinks at the higher indexes. This is considerably more efficient than if the stack were reversed within the array. Consider the processing that would be necessary if the top of the stack were kept at index 0.

For efficiency, an array-based stack implementation keeps the bottom of the stack at index 0.

key concept

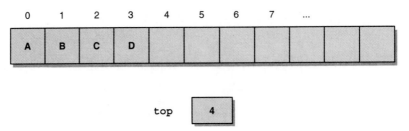

figure 6.9   An array implementation of a stack

the `push` operation

To push an element on the stack, we simply insert it in the next available position in the array, which is specified by the current value of `top`. Before doing so, however, we must determine if the array has reached its capacity and expand it if necessary. After storing the value, we must update the value of `top` so that it continues to represent the number of elements in the stack.

Implementing these steps results in the following code:

```java
//-----------------------------------------------------------------
//  Adds the specified element to the top of the stack, expanding
//  the capacity of the stack array if necessary.
//-----------------------------------------------------------------
public void push (Object element)
{
   if (size() == stack.length)
      expandCapacity();

   stack[top] = element;
   top++;
}
```

The `expandCapacity` method is implemented similarly to the version of that method we saw in Chapter 3 with the bag collection. It serves as a support method of the class and can therefore be implemented with private visibility.

Figure 6.10 illustrates the result of pushing an element E onto the stack that was depicted in Figure 6.9.

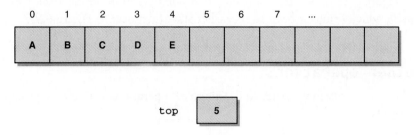

figure 6.10   The stack after pushing element E

the pop operation

The pop operation removes and returns the element at the top of the stack. For an array implementation, that means returning the element at index top–1. Before attempting to return an element, however, we must ensure that there is at least one element in the stack to return.

The array-based version of the pop operation can be implemented as follows:

```
//------------------------------------------------------------------
//   Removes the element at the top of the stack and returns a
//   reference to it. Throws an EmptyStackException if the stack
//   is empty.
//------------------------------------------------------------------
public Object pop() throws EmptyStackException
{
    if (isEmpty())
        throw new EmptyStackException();

    top--;
    Object result = stack[top];
    stack[top] = null;

    return result;
}
```

If the stack is empty when the pop method is called, an EmptyStackException is thrown. Otherwise, the value of top is decremented and the element stored at that location is stored into a temporary variable so that it can be returned. That cell in the array is then set to null. Note that the value of top ends up with the appropriate value relative to the now smaller stack.

Figure 6.11 illustrates the results of a pop operation on the stack from Figure 6.10, which brings it back to its earlier state (identical to Figure 6.9).

other operations

The peek, isEmpty, size, and iterator operations are left as programming projects.

6.6 implementing stacks: the java.util.Stack class

Class java.util.Stack is an implementation of a stack provided in the Java Collections framework. This implementation provides either the same or similar operations to the ones that we have been discussing:

- The push operation accepts a parameter item that is a reference to an object to be placed on the stack.
- The pop operation removes the object on top of the stack and returns a reference to it.
- The peek operation returns a reference to the object on top of the stack.
- The empty operation behaves the same as the isEmpty operation that we have been discussing.
- The size operation returns the number of elements in the stack.

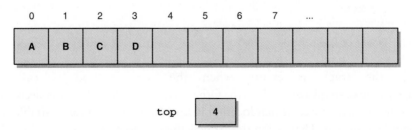

figure 6.11   The stack after popping the top element

The `java.util.Stack` class is derived from the `Vector` class and uses its inherited capabilities to store the elements in the stack. Since this implementation is built upon a vector, it exhibits the characteristics of both of these collections. This implementation keeps track of the top of the stack using an index similar to the array implementation and thus does not require the additional overhead of storing a `next` reference in each node. Further, like the linked implementation, the `java.util.Stack` implementation only allocates additional space as needed.

unique operations

The `java.util.Stack` class provides an additional operation called `search`. Given an object to search for, the `search` operation returns the distance from the top of the stack to the first occurrence of that object on the stack. If the object is found at the top of the stack, the `search` method returns the value 1. If the object is not found on the stack, `search` will return the value –1.

Unfortunately, since the `java.util.Stack` implementation is derived from the `Vector` class, quite a number of other operations are inherited from the `Vector` class that are available for use. In some cases, these additional capabilities violate the basic assumptions of a stack. Most software engineers consider this a bad use of inheritance. Since a stack is not everything a vector is (conceptually), the `Stack` class should not be derived from the `Vector` class. Well-disciplined developers can, of course, limit themselves to only those operations appropriate to a stack.

> **key concept**
> The `java.util.Stack` class is derived from `Vector`, which gives a stack inappropriate operations.

inheritance and implementation

The class `java.util.Stack` is an extension of the class `java.util.Vector`, which is an extension of `java.util.AbstractList`, which is an extension of `java.util.AbstractCollection`, which is an extension of `java.lang.Object`. The `java.util.Stack` implements the `cloneable`, `collection`, `list`, and `serializable` interfaces. These relationships are illustrated in the UML diagram of Figure 6.12.

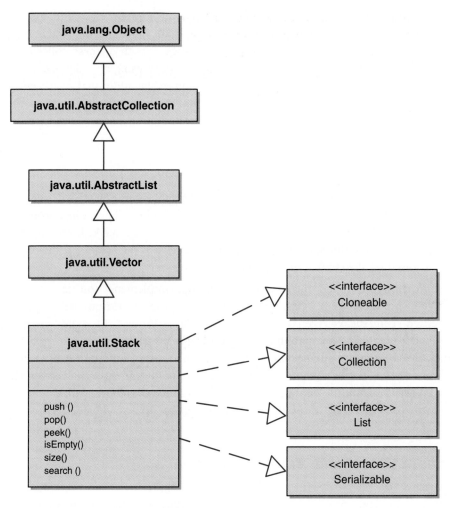

figure 6.12   A UML description of the `java.util.Stack` class

6.7 analysis of stack implementations

There is a space complexity difference between the stack implementations we have discussed. The linked implementation requires more space per node since it has to store both the object and the link to the next object. However, it only allocates space as it needs it and then can store as many elements as needed up to the limitations of the hardware.

The array implementation does not require the additional space per element for the pointer. However, typically array implementations allocate more space than is required and thus may be wasteful.

The analysis of the time complexity of the operations for the various implementations of a stack is quite simple compared to other collections. Let's address each operation separately.

analysis of push

The push operation for the linked implementation consists of the following steps:

- ‣ Create a new node containing a reference to the object to be placed on the stack.
- ‣ Set the next reference of the new node to point to the current top of the stack (which will be null if the stack is empty).
- ‣ Set the top reference to point to the new node.
- ‣ Increment the count of elements in the stack.

All of these steps have time complexity O(1) because they require only one processing step regardless of the number of elements already in the stack. Each of these steps would have to be accomplished once for each of the elements to be pushed. Thus, using this method, the push operation would be O(1).

The push operation for the array implementation consists of the following steps:

- ‣ Check to make sure that the array is not full.
- ‣ Set the reference in position top of the array to the object being added to the stack.
- ‣ Increment the values of top and count.

As with the steps for the push operation in the linked representation, each of these steps is O(1). Thus the operation is O(1).

The push operation for the java.util.Stack implementation is virtually the same as that for the array implementation and is also O(1).

From a time complexity point of view, there is not a substantial difference between the push operations for the three implementations, so let us move on to the pop operation.

analysis of pop

The pop operation for the linked implementation consists of the following steps:

- Check to make sure the stack is not empty.
- Set a temporary reference equal to the element on top of the stack.
- Set the top reference equal to the next reference of the node at the top of the stack.
- Decrement the count of elements in the stack.
- Return the element pointed to by the temporary reference.

As with our previous examples, each of these operations consists of a single comparison or a simple assignment and is therefore O(1). Thus, the pop operation for the linked implementation is O(1).

The pop operation for the array implementation consists of the following steps:

- Check to make sure the stack is not empty.
- Decrement the top counter.
- Set a temporary reference equal to the element in stack[top].
- Set stack[top] equal to null.
- Return the temporary reference.

All of these steps are also O(1). Thus, the pop operation for the array implementation has time complexity O(1).

The pop operation for the java.util.Stack implementation is virtually identical to the pop operation in the array implementation and is also O(1).

> **key concept**
> The order of every operation in every implementation of a stack collection is O(1).

Thus, there is no significant difference in the time complexity of the three implementations of the pop operation.

The front, isEmpty, and size operations for all three implementations are O(1).

The search operation for the java.util.Stack implementation will search from the top of the stack to the bottom of the stack looking for the particular object. In the best case, the object we are looking for is on top of the stack, requiring only one comparison. In the worst case, the object we are looking for is not on the stack so that it requires n comparisons to find that out. The expected case would be roughly n/2 comparisons. This operation would be considered O(n).

summary of
key concepts

- Stack elements are processed in a LIFO manner—the last element in is the first element out.
- A programmer should choose the structure that is appropriate for the type of data management needed.
- A data structure often lends itself to the solution of particular kinds of problems.
- A stack is the ideal data structure to use when evaluating a postfix expression.
- Recursive processing can be simulated using a stack to keep track of the appropriate data.
- A linked implementation of a stack adds and removes elements from one end of the linked list.
- For efficiency, an array-based stack implementation keeps the bottom of the stack at index 0.
- The `java.util.Stack` class is derived from `Vector`, which gives a stack inappropriate operations.
- The order of every operation in every implementation of a stack collection is O(1).

self-review questions

6.1   What is the characteristic behavior of a stack?

6.2   What are the five basic operations on a stack?

6.3   What are some of the other operations that might be implemented for a stack?

6.4   What are the advantages to using a linked implementation as opposed to an array implementation?

6.5   What are the advantages to using an array implementation as opposed to a linked implementation?

6.6   What are the advantages of the `java.util.Stack` implementation of a stack?

6.7   What is the potential problem with the `java.util.Stack` implementation?

6.8   What is the advantage of postfix notation?

exercises

6.1   Hand trace a stack X through the following operations:

```
X.push(new Integer(4));
X.push(new Character('T'));
Object Y = X.pop();
X.push(new Character('b'));
X.push(new Integer(2));
X.push(new Integer(5));
X.push(new Character('j'));
Object Y = X.pop();
X.push(new Character('q'));
X.push(new Integer(9));
```

6.2   Given the resulting stack X from the previous exercise, what would be the result of each of the following?

    a. `Y = X.peek();`

    b. `Y = X.pop();`

      `Z = X.peek();`

    c. `Y = X.pop();`

      `Z = X.peek();`

6.3   What would be the time complexity of the `size` operation for the linked implementation if there were no `count` variable?

6.4   Show how the undo operation in a word processor can be supported by the use of a stack. Give specific examples and draw the contents of the stack after various actions are taken.

6.5   In the postfix expression evaluation example, the two most recent operands are popped when an operator is encountered so that that subexpression can be evaluated. The first operand popped is treated as the second operand in the subexpression, and the second operand popped is the first. Give and explain an example that demonstrates the importance of this aspect of the solution.

6.6   Draw an example using the five integers (12, 23, 1, 45, 9) of how a stack could be used to reverse the order (9, 45, 1, 23, 12) of these elements.

6.7   Explain what would happen to the algorithms and the time complexity of an array implementation of the stack if the top of the stack were at position 0.

programming projects

6.1   Complete the implementation of the LinkedStack class presented in this chapter. Specifically, complete the implementations of the peek, isEmpty, size, iterator, and toString methods.

6.2   Complete the implementation of the ArrayStack class presented in this chapter. Specifically, complete the implementations of the peek, isEmpty, size, iterator, and toString methods.

6.3   Design and implement an application that reads a sentence from the user and prints the sentence with the characters of each word backwards. Use a stack to reverse the characters of each word.

6.4   Modify the solution to the postfix expression evaluation problem so that it checks for the validity of the expression that is entered by the user. Issue an appropriate error message when an erroneous situation is encountered.

6.5   Complete the solution to the iterative maze solver. Be sure that your solution marks the successful path the way that it was done in Chapter 4.

6.6   The linked implementation in this chapter uses a count variable to keep track of the number of elements in the stack. Rewrite the linked implementation without a count variable.

6.7   The array implementation in this chapter keeps the top variable pointing to the next array position above the actual top of the stack. Rewrite the array implementation such that stack[top] is the actual top of the stack.

6.8   There is a data structure called a drop-out stack that behaves like a stack in every respect except that if the stack size is n, when the n+1 element is pushed, the first element is lost. Implement a drop-out stack using links.

6.9   Implement the drop-out stack from the previous project using an array implementation. (*Hint:* a circular array implementation would make sense.)

6.10   Implement an integer adder using three stacks.

6.11   Implement an infix-to-postfix translator using stacks.

6.12   Implement a search operation like the one in `java.util.Stack` for the linked implementation.

6.13   Implement a search operation like the one in `java.util.Stack` for the array implementation.

6.14   Implement a class called `reverse` that uses a stack to output a set of elements input by the user in reverse order.

6.15   Create a graphical application that provides a button for push and pop from a stack, a text field to accept a string as input for push, and a text area to display the contents of the stack after each operation.

answers to self-review questions

6.1   A stack is a last in, first out (LIFO) structure.

6.2   The operations are:

   `push`—adds an element to the end of the stack

   `pop`—removes an element from the front of the stack

   `peek`—returns a reference to the element at the front of the stack

   `isEmpty`—returns true if the stack is empty, returns false otherwise

   `wsize`—returns the number of elements in the stack

6.3   `makeEmpty()`, `destroy()`, `full()`

6.4   A linked implementation only allocates space as it is needed and has a theoretical limit of the size of the hardware.

6.5   An array implementation uses less space per object since it only has to store the object and not an extra pointer. However, the array implementation will allocate much more space than it needs initially.

6.6 Since the `java.util.Stack` implementation is an extension of the `Vector` class, it can keep track of the positions of elements in the stack using an index and thus does not require each node to store an additional pointer. This implementation also only allocates space as it is needed, like the linked implementation.

6.7 The `java.util.Stack` implementation is an extension of the `Vector` class and thus inherits a large number of operations that violate the basic assumptions of a stack.

6.8 Postfix notation avoids the need for precedence rules that are required to evaluate infix expressions.

A queue is another collection with which we are inherently familiar. A queue is a waiting line, such as the line of customers waiting in a bank for their opportunity to talk to a teller. In fact, in many countries the word queue is used habitually in this way. In such countries, a person might say "join the queue" rather than "get in line." Other examples of queues include the check-out line at the grocery store or cars waiting at a stop-light. In any queue, an item enters on one end and leaves from the other. Queues have a variety of uses in computer algorithms.

chapter objectives

▶ Examine queue processing

▶ Define a queue abstract data type

▶ Demonstrate how a queue can be used to solve problems

▶ Examine various queue implementations

▶ Compare queue implementations

7.1 a queue ADT

A *queue* is a linear collection whose elements are added on one end and removed from the other. Therefore, we say that queue elements are processed in a *first in, first out* (FIFO) manner. Elements are removed from a queue in the same order in which they are placed on the queue.

This is consistent with the general concept of a waiting line. When a customer arrives at a bank, he or she begins waiting at the end of the line. When a teller becomes available, the customer at the beginning of the line leaves the line to receive service. Eventually every customer that started out at the end of the line moves to the front of the line and exits. For any given set of people, the first person to get in line is the first person to leave it.

The processing of a queue is pictured in Figure 7.1. Usually a queue is depicted horizontally. One end is established as the *front* of the queue and the other as the *rear* of the queue. Elements go onto the rear of the queue and come off of the front. Sometimes the front of the queue is called the *head* and the rear of the queue the *tail*.

Compare and contrast the processing of a queue to the LIFO (last in, first out) processing of a stack, which was discussed in Chapter 6. In a stack, the processing occurs at only one end of the collection. In a queue, processing occurs at both ends.

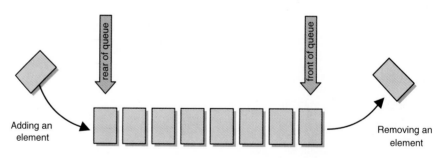

figure 7.1   A conceptual view of a queue

Operation	Description
enqueue	Adds an element to the rear of the queue.
dequeue	Removes an element from the front of the queue.
first	Examines the element at the front of the queue.
isEmpty	Determines if the queue is empty.
size	Determines the number of elements on the queue.
toString	Returns a string representation of the queue.

figure 7.2   The operations on a queue

The operations defined for a queue ADT are listed in Figure 7.2. The term *enqueue* is used to refer to the process of adding a new element to the end of a queue. Likewise, *dequeue* refers to removing the element at the front of a queue. The *first* operation allows the user to examine the element at the front of the queue without removing it from the collection.

Remember that naming conventions are not universal for collection operations. Sometimes enqueue is simply called add or insert. The dequeue operation is sometimes called remove or serve. The first operation is sometimes called front.

Note that there is a general similarity between the operations of a queue and those of a stack. The enqueue, dequeue, and first operations correspond to the stack operations push, pop, and peek. Similar to a stack, there are no operations that allow the user to "reach into" the middle of a queue and reorganize or remove elements. If that type of processing is required, perhaps the appropriate collection to use is a generic list of some kind, such as those discussed in the next chapter.

As we did with stacks, we define a generic QueueADT interface that represents the queue operations, separating the general purpose of the operations from the variety of ways they could be implemented. A Java version of the QueueADT interface is shown in Listing 7.1, and its UML description is shown in Figure 7.3.

```
listing
    7.1
```

```
//*****************************************************************
//   QueueADT.java        Authors: Lewis/Chase
//
//   Defines the interface to a queue collection.
//*****************************************************************

package jss2;

import java.util.Iterator;

public interface QueueADT
{
    //  Adds one element to the rear of the queue
    public void enqueue (Object element);

    //  Removes and returns the element at the front of the queue
    public Object dequeue();

    //  Returns without removing the element at the front of the queue
    public Object first();

    //  Returns true if the queue contains no elements
    public boolean isEmpty();

    //  Returns the number of elements in the queue
    public int size();

    //  Returns a string representation of the queue
    public String toString();
}
```

Note that in addition to the standard queue operations we have also included a toString method, as we did with previous collections. It is included for convenience and is not generally considered a classic operation on a queue. As we did with stacks, we have deliberately excluded an iterator since it would violate the premise of a queue.

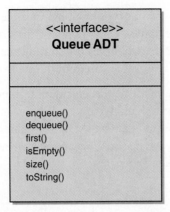

figure 7.3   The `QueueADT` interface in UML

Queues have a wide variety of application within computing. Before exploring various ways to implement a queue, let's examine some ways in which a queue can be used to solve problems.

7.2 using queues: code keys

A *Caesar cipher* is a simple approach to encoding messages by shifting each letter in a message along the alphabet by a constant amount k. For example, if k equals 3, then in an encoded message, each letter is shifted three characters forward: a is replaced with d, b with e, c with f, and so on. The end of the alphabet wraps back around to the beginning. Thus, w is replaced with z, x with a, y with b, and z with c.

To decode the message, each letter is shifted the same number of characters backwards. Therefore, if k equals 3, the encoded message

```
vlpsolflwb iroorzv frpsohalwb
```

would be decoded into

```
simplicity follows complexity
```

Julius Caesar actually used this type of cipher in some of his secret government correspondence (hence the name). Unfortunately, the Caesar cipher is fairly easy to break. There are only 26 possibilities for shifting the characters and the code can be broken by trying various key values until one works.

An improvement can be made to this encoding technique if we use a *repeating key*. Instead of shifting each character by a constant amount, we can shift each character by a different amount using a list of key values. If the message is longer than the list of key values, we just start using the key over again from the beginning. For example, if the key values are

3 1 7 4 2 5

then the first character is shifted by three, the second character by one, the third character by seven, etc. After shifting the sixth character by five, we start using the key over again. The seventh character is shifted by three, the eighth by one, etc.

Figure 7.4 shows the message "knowledge is power" encoded using this repeating key. Note that this encryption approach encodes the same letter into different characters, depending on where it occurs in the message and thus which key value is used to encode it. Conversely, the same character in the encoded message is decoded into different characters.

The program in Listing 7.2 uses a repeating key to encode and decode a message. The key of integer values is stored in a queue. After using a key value, it is put back on the end of the queue so that the key continually repeats as needed for long messages. The key in this example uses both positive and negative values. Figure 7.5 illustrates the UML description of the `Codes` class.

> **key concept**
>
> A queue is a convenient collection for storing a repeating code key.

Encoded Message:	n	o	v	a	n	j	g	h	l		m	u		u	r	x	l	v
Key:	3	1	7	4	2	5	3	1	7		4	2		5	3	1	7	4
Decoded Message:	k	n	o	w	l	e	d	g	e		i	s		p	o	w	e	r

figure 7.4   An encoded message using a repeating key

listing
  7.2

```
//**********************************************************************
//   Codes.java          Authors: Lewis/Chase
//
//   Demonstrates the use of queues to encrypt and decrypt messages.
//**********************************************************************

import jss2.LinkedQueue;

public class Codes
{
   //---------------------------------------------------------------
   //   Encode and decode a message using a key of values stored in
   //   a queue.
   //---------------------------------------------------------------
   public static void main ( String[] args)
   {
      int[] key = {5, 12, -3, 8, -9, 4, 10};
      int keyValue;

      String encoded = "", decoded = "";

      String message = "All programmers are playwrights and all " +
                       "computers are lousy actors.";

      LinkedQueue keyQueue1 = new LinkedQueue();
      LinkedQueue keyQueue2 = new LinkedQueue();

      // load key queue
      for (int scan=0; scan < key.length; scan++)
      {
         keyQueue1.enqueue (new Integer(key[scan]));
         keyQueue2.enqueue (new Integer(key[scan]));
      }

      // encode message
      for (int scan=0; scan < message.length(); scan++)
      {
         keyValue = ((Integer) keyQueue1.dequeue()).intValue();
         encoded += (char) ((int)message.charAt(scan) + keyValue);
         keyQueue1.enqueue (new Integer(keyValue));
      }
```

listing
    7.2   continued

```
System.out.println ("Encoded Message:\n" + encoded + "\n");

// decode message
for (int scan=0; scan < encoded.length(); scan++)
{
   keyValue = ((Integer) keyQueue2.dequeue()).intValue();
   decoded += (char) ((int)encoded.charAt(scan) - keyValue);
   keyQueue2.enqueue (new Integer(keyValue));
}

System.out.println ("Decoded Message:\n" + decoded);
   }
}
```

output

```
Encoded Message:
Fxi(gvyl~^udi|x,^z\$zqmv_imqm?p(Xrn%mit_gyr|r|\v}%mom_pyz_v(Xg~t~p6

Decoded Message:
All programmers are playwrights and all computers are lousy actors.
```

This program actually uses two copies of the key stored in two separate queues. The idea is that the person encoding the message has one copy of the key, and the person decoding the message has another. Two copies of the key are helpful in this program as well because the decoding process needs to match up the first character of the message with the first value in the key.

Also, note that this program doesn't bother to wrap around the end of the alphabet. It encodes any character in the Unicode character set by shifting it to some other position in the character set. Therefore we can encode any character, including uppercase letters, lowercase letters, and punctuation. Even spaces get encoded.

Using a queue to store the key makes it easy to repeat the key by putting each key value back onto the queue as soon as it is used. The nature of a queue keeps the key values in the proper order, and we don't have to worry about reaching the end of the key and starting over.

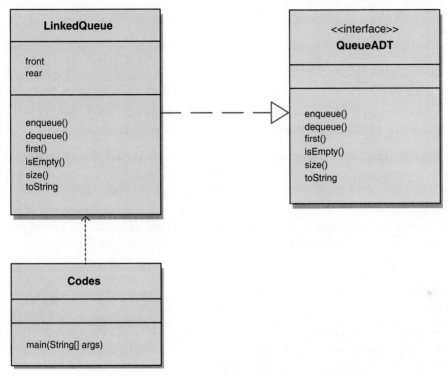

figure 7.5   UML description of the Codes program

7.3   using queues: ticket counter simulation

Consider the situation in which you are waiting in line to purchase tickets at a movie theatre. In general, the more cashiers there are, the faster the line moves. The theatre manager wants to keep his customers happy, but doesn't want to employ any more cashiers than he has to. Suppose the manager wants to keep the total time needed by a customer to less than seven minutes. Being able to simulate the effect of adding more cashiers during peak business hours allows the manager to plan more effectively. And, as we've discussed, a queue is the perfect collection for representing a waiting line.

> Simulations are often implemented using queues to represent waiting lines.

key concept

Our simulated ticket counter will use the following assumptions:

▸ There is only one line and it is first come first served (a queue).

▸ Customers arrive on average every 15 seconds.

▸ If there is a cashier available, processing begins immediately upon arrival.

▸ Processing a customer request and getting them on their way takes on average two minutes (120 seconds) from the time they reach a cashier.

First we can create a `Customer` class, as shown in Listing 7.3. A `Customer` object keeps track of the time the customer arrives and the time the customer departs after purchasing a ticket. The total time spent by the customer is therefore the departure time minus the arrival time. To keep things simple, our simulation will measure time in elapsed seconds, so a time value can be stored as a single integer. Our artificial simulation world will begin at time 0.

listing
7.3

```java
//***********************************************************************
//   Customer.java        Authors: Lewis/Chase
//
//   Represents a waiting customer.
//***********************************************************************

public class Customer
{
    private int arrivalTime, departureTime;

    //-------------------------------------------------------------------
    //  Creates a new customer with the specified arrival time.
    //-------------------------------------------------------------------
    public Customer (int arrives)
    {
        arrivalTime = arrives;
        departureTime = 0;
    }
```

listing
  7.3   continued

```java
//-----------------------------------------------------------------
//   Returns the arrival time of this customer.
//-----------------------------------------------------------------
public int getArrivalTime()
{
    return arrivalTime;
}

//-----------------------------------------------------------------
//   Sets the departure time for this customer.
//-----------------------------------------------------------------
public void setDepartureTime (int departs)
{
    departureTime = departs;
}

//-----------------------------------------------------------------
//   Returns the departure time of this customer.
//-----------------------------------------------------------------
public int getDepartureTime()
{
    return departureTime;
}

//-----------------------------------------------------------------
//   Computes and returns the total time spent by this customer.
//-----------------------------------------------------------------
public int totalTime()
{
    return departureTime - arrivalTime;
}
}
```

Our simulation will create a queue of customers, then see how long it takes to process those customers if there is only one cashier. Then we'll process the same queue of customers with two cashiers. Then we'll do it again with three cashiers. We'll continue this process for up to ten cashiers. At the end we'll compare the average time it takes to process a customer.

Because of our assumption that customers arrive every 15 seconds (on average), we can preload a queue with customers. We will process 100 customers in this simulation.

The program shown in Listing 7.4 conducts our simulation. The outer loop determines how many cashiers are used in each pass of the simulation. For each pass, the customers are taken from the queue in turn and processed by a cashier. The total elapsed time is tracked, and at the end of each pass the average time is computed. Figure 7.6 shows the UML description of the `TicketCounter` and `Customer` classes.

listing
  7.4

```
//*******************************************************************
//   TicketCounter.java        Authors: Lewis/Chase
//
//   Demonstrates the use of a queue for simulating a waiting line.
//*******************************************************************

import jss2.*;

public class TicketCounter
{
    final static int PROCESS = 120;
    final static int MAX_CASHIERS = 10;
    final static int NUM_CUSTOMERS = 100;

    public static void main ( String[] args)
    {
        Customer customer;
        LinkedQueue customerQueue = new LinkedQueue();
        int[] cashierTime = new int[MAX_CASHIERS];
        int totalTime, averageTime, departs;

        // process the simulation for various number of cashiers
        for (int cashiers=1; cashiers <= MAX_CASHIERS; cashiers++)
        {
            // set each cashier's time to zero initially
            for (int count=0; count < cashiers; count++)
                cashierTime[count] = 0;
```

listing 7.4   continued

```java
    // load customer queue
    for (int count=1; count <= NUM_CUSTOMERS; count++)
        customerQueue.enqueue(new Customer(count*15));

    totalTime = 0;

    // process all customers in the queue
    while (!(customerQueue.isEmpty()))
    {
        for (int count=0; count < cashiers; count++)
        {
            if (!(customerQueue.isEmpty()))
            {
                customer = (Customer) customerQueue.dequeue();
                if (customer.getArrivalTime() > cashierTime[count])
                    departs = customer.getArrivalTime() + PROCESS;
                else
                    departs = cashierTime[count] + PROCESS;
                customer.setDepartureTime (departs);
                cashierTime[count] = departs;
                totalTime += customer.totalTime();
            }
        }
    }

    // output results for this simulation
    averageTime = totalTime / NUM_CUSTOMERS;
    System.out.println ("Number of cashiers: " + (cashiers));
    System.out.println ("Average time: " + averageTime + "\n");
    }
  }
}
```

```
listing
    7.4        continued
```

output

```
Number of cashiers: 1
Average time: 5317

Number of cashiers: 2
Average time: 2325

Number of cashiers: 3
Average time: 1332

Number of cashiers: 4
Average time: 840

Number of cashiers: 5
Average time: 547

Number of cashiers: 6
Average time: 355

Number of cashiers: 7
Average time: 219

Number of cashiers: 8
Average time: 120

Number of cashiers: 9
Average time: 120

Number of cashiers: 10
Average time: 120
```

The results of the simulation are shown in Figure 7.7. Note that with eight cashiers, the customers do not wait at all. The time of 120 seconds reflects only the time it takes to walk up and purchase the ticket. Increasing the number of cashiers to nine or ten or more will not improve the situation. Since the manager has decided he wants to keep the total average time to less than seven minutes (420 seconds), the simulation tells him that he should have six cashiers.

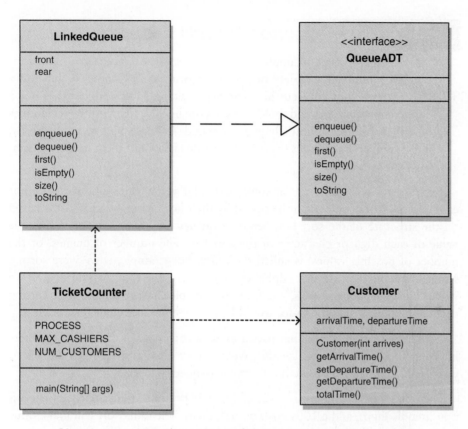

figure 7.6   UML description of the TicketCounter program

Number of Cashiers:	1	2	3	4	5	6	7	8	9	10
Average Time (sec):	5317	2325	1332	840	547	355	219	120	120	120

figure 7.7   The results of the ticket counter simulation

7.4 using queues: radix sort

Another interesting application of queues is the concept of a *radix sort*. We examined a variety of sorting algorithms in Chapter 5, but radix sort was not covered there for two reasons. First, radix sort is not a comparison sort and thus has very little in common with the techniques that we discussed in Chapter 5. Second, to implement them effectively, a radix sort requires the use of a queue (several of them in fact) or similar collection.

Recall that a sort is based on some particular value, called the *sort key*. For example, a set of people might be sorted by their last name. A radix sort is based on the structure of the sort key. Separate queues are created for each possible value of each digit or character of the sort key. The number of queues, or the number of possible values, is called the *radix*. For example, if we were sorting strings made up of lowercase alphabetic characters, the radix would be 26. We would use 26 separate queues, one for each possible character. If we were sorting decimal numbers, then the radix would be ten, one for each digit 0 through 9.

Let's look at an example that uses a radix sort to put ten three-digit numbers in order. To keep things manageable, we'll restrict the digits of these numbers to 0 through 5, which means we'll only need six queues.

Each three-digit number to be sorted has a 1s position (right digit), a 10s position (middle digit), and a 100s position (left digit). The radix sort will make three passes through the values, one for each digit position. On the first pass, each number is put on the queue corresponding to its 1s digit. On the second pass, each number is put on the queue corresponding to its 10s digit. And finally, on the third pass, each number is put on the queue corresponding to its 100s digit.

Originally, the numbers are loaded into the queues from the original list. On the second pass, the numbers are taken from the queues in a particular order. They are retrieved from the digit 0 queue first, and then the digit 1 queue, etc. For each queue, they are processed in the order in which they come off the queue. This processing order is crucial to the operation of a radix sort. Likewise, on the third pass, the numbers are again taken from the queues in the same way. When the numbers are pulled off of the queues after the third pass, they will be completely sorted.

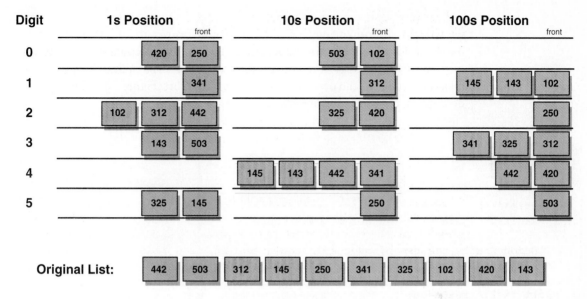

figure 7.8   A radix sort of ten three-digit numbers

Figure 7.8 shows the processing of a radix sort for ten three-digit numbers. The number 442 is taken from the original list and put onto the queue corresponding to digit 2. Then 503 is put onto the queue corresponding to digit 3. Then 312 is put onto the queue corresponding to digit 2 (following 442). This continues for all values, resulting in the set of queues for the 1s position.

Assume, as we begin the second pass, that we have a fresh set of six empty digit queues. In actuality, the queues can be used over again if processed carefully. To begin the second pass, the numbers are taken from the 0 digit queue first. The number 250 is put onto the queue for digit 5, and then 420 is put onto the queue for digit 2. Then we can move to the next queue, taking 341 and putting it onto the queue for digit 4. This continues until all numbers have been taken off of the 1s position queues, resulting in the set of queues for the 10s position.

For the third pass, the process is again repeated. First, 102 is put onto the queue for digit 1, then 503 is put onto the queue for digit 5, then 312 is put onto the queue for digit 3. This continues until we have the final set of digit queues for the 100s position. These numbers are now in sorted order if taken off of each queue in turn.

Let's now look at a program that implements the radix sort. For this example, we will sort four-digit numbers, and we won't restrict the digits used in those numbers. Listing 7.5 shows the RadixSort class, which contains a single main method. Using an array of ten queue objects (one for each digit 0 through 9), this method carries out the processing steps of a radix sort. Figure 7.9 show the UML description of the RadixSort class.

**listing
  7.5**

```java
//********************************************************************
//   RadixSort.java        Authors: Lewis/Chase
//
//   Demonstrates the use of queues in the execution of a radix sort.
//********************************************************************

import jss2.ArrayQueue;

public class RadixSort
{
    //----------------------------------------------------------------
    //   Perform a radix sort on a set of numeric values.
    //----------------------------------------------------------------
    public static void main ( String[] args)
    {
        int[] list = {7843, 4568, 8765, 6543, 7865, 4532, 9987, 3241,
                      6589, 6622, 1211};

        String temp;
        Integer numObj;
        int digit, num;

        ArrayQueue[] digitQueues = new ArrayQueue[10];
        for (int digitVal = 0; digitVal <= 9; digitVal++)
            digitQueues[digitVal] = new ArrayQueue();
```

listing
    7.5   continued

```java
        // sort the list
        for (int position=0; position <= 3; position++)
        {
            for (int scan=0; scan < list.length; scan++)
            {
                temp = String.valueOf (list[scan]);
                digit = Character.digit (temp.charAt(3-position), 10);
                digitQueues[digit].enqueue (new Integer(list[scan]));
            }

            // gather numbers back into list
            num = 0;
            for (int digitVal = 0; digitVal <= 9; digitVal++)
            {
                while (!(digitQueues[digitVal].isEmpty()))
                {
                    numObj = (Integer) digitQueues[digitVal].dequeue();
                    list[num] = numObj.intValue();
                    num++;
                }
            }
        }

        // output the sorted list
        for (int scan=0; scan < list.length; scan++)
            System.out.println (list[scan]);
    }
}
```

output

```
1211
3241
4532
4568
6543
6589
6622
7843
7865
8765
9987
```

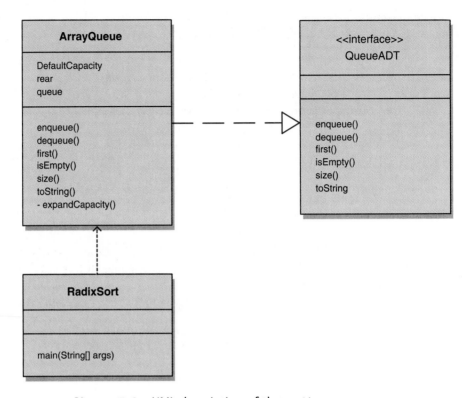

figure 7.9   UML description of the RadixSort program

In the RadixSort program, the numbers are originally stored in an array called list. After each pass, the numbers are pulled off of the queues and stored back into the list array in the proper order. This allows the program to reuse the original array of ten queues for each pass of the sort.

The concept of a radix sort can be applied to any type of data as long as the sort key can be dissected into well-defined positions. Note that unlike the sorts covered in Chapter 5, it's not reasonable to create a generic radix sort for any object, because dissecting the key values is an integral part of the process.

7.5 implementing queues: with links

Since it is a linear collection, we can implement a queue as a linked list of `LinearNode` objects, as we did with stacks. The primary difference is that we will have to operate on both ends of the list. Therefore, in addition to a reference (called `front`) pointing to the first element in the list, we will also keep track of a second reference (called `rear`) that points to the last element in the list. We will also use an integer variable called `count` to keep track of the number of elements in the queue.

> A linked implementation of a queue is facilitated by references to the first and last elements of the linked list.
>
> *key concept*

Figure 7.10 depicts this strategy for implementing a queue. It shows a queue that has had the elements A, B, C, and D added to the queue, in that order.

Remember that Figure 7.10 depicts the general case. We always have to be careful to accurately maintain our references in special cases. For an empty queue, the `front` and `rear` references are both null and the `count` is zero. If there is exactly one element in the queue, both the `front` and `rear` references point to the same object.

Let's explore the implementation of the queue operations using this linked list approach.

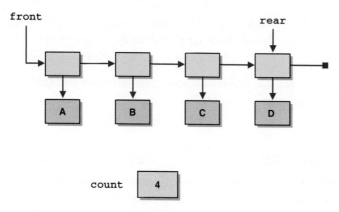

figure 7.10   A linked implementation of a queue

the enqueue operation

The enqueue operation requires that we put the new element on the rear of the list. In the general case, that means setting the next reference of the current last element to the new one, and resetting the rear reference to the new last element. However, if the queue is currently empty, the front reference must also be set to the new (and only) element. This operation can be implemented as follows:

```
//------------------------------------------------------------
//  Adds the specified element to the rear of the queue.
//------------------------------------------------------------
public void enqueue (Object element)
{
    LinearNode node = new LinearNode(element);

    if (isEmpty())
        front = node;
    else
        rear.setNext (node);

    rear = node;
    count++;
}
```

Note that if the queue is empty, the next reference of the new node need not be set, because it has already been set to null in the LinearNode class. The rear reference is set to the new node in either case, and the count is incremented.

Figure 7.11 shows the linked list implementation of the queue from Figure 7.10 after element E has been added.

the dequeue operation

The first issue to address when implementing the dequeue operation is to ensure that there is at least one element to return. If not, an EmptyCollectionException is thrown. Note that in the case of our bag collections from Chapters 3 and 4, and our stack collections from Chapter 7, we created specific exceptions (EmptyBagException and EmptyStackException). However, as we did with ArrayIterator and LinkedIterator, it makes sense to create a generic EmptyCollectionException to which we can pass a param-

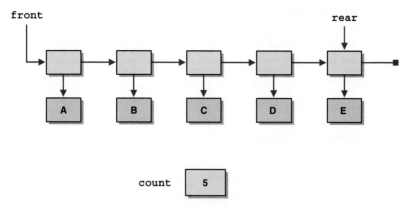

figure 7.11   The queue after adding element E

eter specifying which collection we are dealing with. If there is at least one element in the queue, the first one in the list is returned and the front reference is updated:

```
//-------------------------------------------------------------------
//   Removes the element at the front of the queue and returns a
//   reference to it. Throws an EmptyCollectionException if the
//   queue is empty.
//-------------------------------------------------------------------
public Object dequeue() throws EmptyCollectionException
{
    if (isEmpty())
        throw new EmptyCollectionException ("queue");

    Object result = front.getElement();
    front = front.getNext();
    count--;

    if (isEmpty())
        rear = null;

    return result;
}
```

For the dequeue operation, we must consider the situation in which we are returning the only element in the queue. If, after removing the front element, the queue is now empty, the rear reference is set to null. Note that in this case, the front will be null because it was set equal to the next reference of the last element in the list.

Figure 7.12 shows the result of a dequeue operation on the queue from Figure 7.11. The element A at the front of the list is removed and returned to the user.

key concept

The enqueue and dequeue operations work on opposite ends of the collection.

Note that, unlike the pop and push operations on a stack, the dequeue operation is not the inverse of enqueue. That is, Figure 7.12 is not identical to our original configuration shown in Figure 7.10, because the enqueue and dequeue operations are working on opposite ends of the collection.

other operations

The remaining operations in the linked queue implementation are fairly straightforward and are similar to the stack and bag collections. The first operation is implemented by returning a reference to the element at the front of the queue. The isEmpty operation returns true if the count of elements is 0, and false otherwise. The size operation simply returns the count of elements in the queue. Finally, the toString operation returns a string made up of the toString results of each individual element. These operations are left as programming projects.

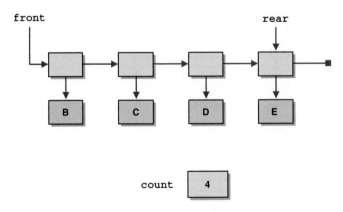

figure 7.12   The queue after a dequeue operation

7.6 implementing queues: with arrays

One array-based strategy for implementing a queue is to fix one end of the queue (say, the front) at index 0 of the array. The elements are stored contiguously in the array. Figure 7.13 depicts a queue stored in this manner, assuming elements A, B, C, and D have been added to the queue in that order.

The integer variable `rear` is used to indicate the next open cell in the array. Note that it also represents the number of elements in the queue.

This strategy assumes that the first element in the queue is always stored at index 0 of the array. Because queue processing affects both ends of the collection, this strategy will require that we shift the elements whenever an element is removed from the queue. Later in this chapter, we examine a different array-based implementation that eliminates element shifting. First, though, let's examine the queue operations using an array-based, fixed-end approach.

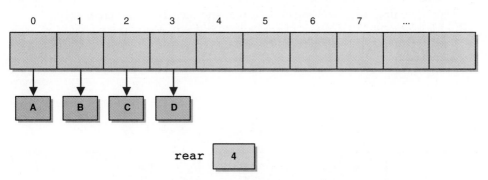

figure 7.13   An array implementation of a queue

the enqueue operation

The enqueue operation adds a new element to the rear of the queue, which in this implementation strategy is stored at the high end of the array. As long as there is room in the array for an additional element, it can be stored in the location indicated by the integer `rear`. This operation can be implemented as follows:

```
//----------------------------------------------------------------
//  Adds the specified element to the rear of the queue, expanding
//  the capacity of the queue array if necessary.
//----------------------------------------------------------------
public void enqueue (Object element)
{
    if (size() == queue.length)
        expandCapacity();

    queue[rear] = element;
    rear++;
}
```

The technique for expanding the capacity of the queue array is the same as the one used for other collections. Recall that the value of `rear` indicates both the number of elements in the queue and the next available slot in the array. Therefore, first the new element is stored, and then `rear` is incremented.

Figure 7.14 shows the queue implementation of Figure 7.13 after element E is enqueued.

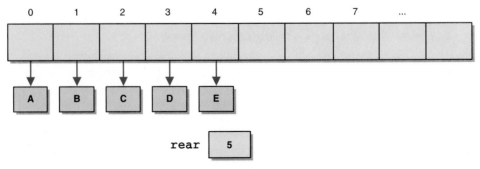

figure 7.14   The queue after adding element E

the `dequeue` operation

With this implementation strategy, the `dequeue` operation must assure that after removing the first element of the queue, the new first element (currently the second element in the list) is stored at index 0 of the array. Furthermore, because we store the elements contiguously, we cannot have gaps in the list. Therefore, all elements must be shifted down one cell in the array. This operation can be implemented as follows:

```
//----------------------------------------------------------------
//   Removes the element at the front of the queue and returns a
//   reference to it. Throws an EmptyCollectionException if the
//   queue is empty.
//----------------------------------------------------------------
public Object dequeue() throws EmptyCollectionException
{
   if (isEmpty())
      throw new EmptyCollectionException ("queue");

   Object result = queue[0];

   // shift the elements
   for (int scan=0; scan < rear; scan++)
      queue[scan] = queue[scan+1];

   rear--;
   queue[rear] = null;

   return result;
}
```

This method first checks to see if the queue has at least one element to dequeue. If not, it throws an `EmptyCollectionException`, consistent with how we've been dealing with such situations. If there is at least one element, it is stored for return, the elements are shifted, and the value of `rear` is decremented to reflect that we now have one less element in the queue. For completeness, the copy of the reference to the last element in the queue is overwritten with `null`.

Figure 7.15 illustrates the results of the `dequeue` operation on the queue from Figure 7.14. As with our linked strategy, the `dequeue` operation does not bring us back to the original configuration shown in Figure 7.13 because `enqueue` and `dequeue` modify opposite ends of the queue.

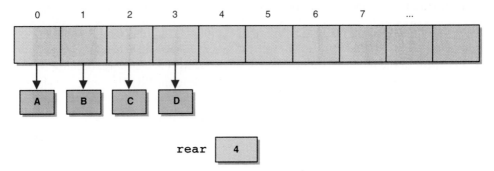

figure 7.15 The queue after removing the first element

other operations

The implementation of the `first`, `isEmpty`, `size`, and `toString` operations using this strategy are left as programming projects.

7.7 implementing queues: with circular arrays

The main problem with the array-based strategy discussed in the previous section is that the front end of the queue is fixed at index 0. Therefore, every time a `dequeue` operation is performed, all elements stored in the queue array have to be shifted down. If the queue is large, or if many `dequeue` operations are performed, this creates a lot of shifting operations that we'd like to avoid. This section describes another array-based approach that eliminates the shifting of elements.

Turning around the queue so that the rear of the queue is at index 0 does not solve the problem. That approach would simply cause the element shifting to occur in the `enqueue` method (before the element is added) rather than in the `dequeue` method (after the element is removed).

The key is to not fix either end. As elements are dequeued, the front of the queue will move further into the array. As elements are enqueued, the rear of the queue will also move further into the array. The challenge comes when the rear of the queue reaches the end of the array. Enlarging the array at this point is not a practical solution, and does not make use of the now empty space in the lower indexes of the array.

To make this solution work, we will use a *circular array* to implement the queue, defined in a class called `CircularArrayQueue`. A circular array is not a new construct—it is just a way to think about the array used to store the collection. Conceptually, the array is used as a circle, whose last index is followed by the first index. A circular array storing a queue is shown in Figure 7.16.

Two integer values are used to represent the front and rear of the queue. These values change as elements are added and removed. Note that the value of `front` represents the location where the first element in the queue is stored, and the value of `rear` represents the next available slot in the array (not where the last element is stored). Using `rear` in this manner is consistent with our other array implementation. Note, however, that the value of `rear` no longer represents the number of elements in the queue. We will use a separate integer value to keep a count of the elements.

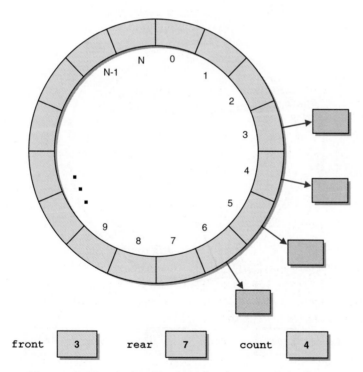

front [3]   rear [7]   count [4]

figure 7.16   A circular array implementation of a queue

When the rear of the queue reaches the end of the list, it "wraps around" to the front of the array. The elements of the queue can therefore straddle the end of the array, as shown in Figure 7.17, which assumes the array can store 100 elements.

Using this strategy, once an element has been added to the queue, it stays in one location in the array until it is removed with a `dequeue` operation. No elements need to be shifted as elements are added or removed. This approach requires, however, that we carefully manage the values of `front` and `rear`.

Let's look at another example. Figure 7.18 shows a circular array (drawn linearly) with a capacity of ten elements. Initially it is shown after elements A

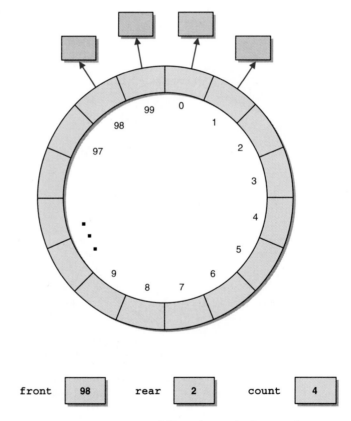

figure 7.17 A queue straddling the end of a circular array

through H have been enqueued. It is then shown after the first four elements (A through D) have been dequeued. Finally, it is shown after elements I, J, K, and L have been enqueued, which causes the queue to wrap around the end of the array.

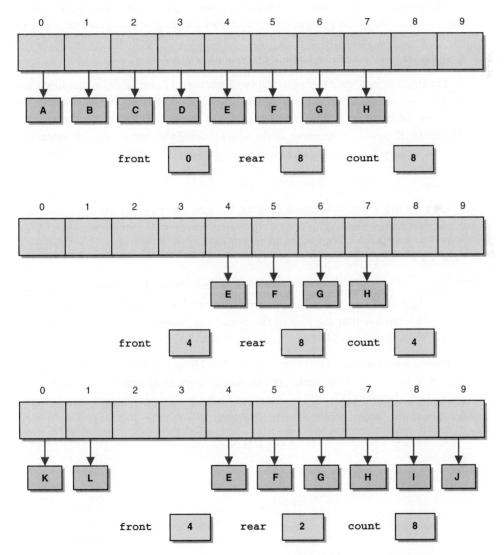

figure 7.18   Changes in a circular array implementation of a queue

In general, after an element is enqueued, the value of `rear` is incremented. But when an `enqueue` operation fills the last cell of the array (at the largest index), the value of `rear` must be set to 0, indicating that the next element should be stored at index 0.

Likewise, after an element is dequeued, the value of `front` is incremented. After enough `dequeue` operations, the value of `front` will reach the last index of the array. After removing the element at the largest index, the value of `front` must be set to 0 instead of being incremented.

The appropriate update to the values of `rear` and `front` can be accomplished in one calculation using the remainder operator (`%`). Recall that the remainder operator returns the remainder after dividing the first operand by the second. Therefore, if `queue` is the name of the array storing the queue, the following line of code will update the value of `rear` appropriately:

```
rear = (rear+1) % queue.length;
```

Let's try this calculation, assuming we have an array of size 10. If `rear` is currently 5, it will be set to 6%10, or 6. If `rear` is currently 9, it will be set to 10%10 or 0. Try this calculation using various situations to see that it works no matter how big the array is.

Note that this implementation strategy can still allow the array to reach capacity. As with any array-based implementation, all cells in the array may become filled. This implies that the rear of the queue has "caught up" to the front of the queue. To add another element, the array would have to be enlarged.

Operations such as `toString` become a bit more complicated using this approach because the elements are not stored starting at index 0 and may wrap around the end of the array. These methods have to take the current situation into account.

All of the operations for a circular array queue are left as programming projects.

7.8 analysis of queue implementations

As with our previous collections, there is a difference in space complexity among the implementations of a queue. The linked implementation requires more space per node since it has to store both the object and the link to the next object. However, it only allocates space as it needs it and then can store as many elements as needed up to the limitations of the hardware.

The array implementations do not require the additional space per element for the reference. However, typically array implementations allocate more space than is required and thus may be wasteful.

The analysis of the time complexity of the operations for the various implementations of a queue is quite simple. We will address each operation for each of the three implementations.

enqueue

The enqueue operation for the linked implementation consists of the following steps:

- ▸ Create a new node with the `element` reference pointing to the object to be added to the queue and with the `next` reference set to null.
- ▸ Set the `next` reference of the current node at the rear of the queue to point to the new object.
- ▸ Set the `rear` reference to point to the new object.
- ▸ Increment the `count` of elements in the queue.

All of these steps have time complexity O(1) since they require only one processing step regardless of the number of elements already in the queue. Each of these steps has to be accomplished once for each of elements enqueued. Thus, using this method, the enqueue operation is O(1).

The enqueue operation for the noncircular array implementation consists of the following steps:

- Check to make sure that the array is not full (if it is, throw an exception).
- Set the reference at the rear of the queue to point to the object being added to the queue.
- Increment the values of rear and count.

As with the steps for the enqueue operation in the linked representation, each of these steps is O(1). Thus the operation is O(1).

The enqueue operation for the circular array implementation consists of the following steps:

- Check to make sure that the array is not full (if it is, throw an exception).
- Set the reference at the rear of the queue to point to the object being added to the queue.
- Set rear to the appropriate value.
- Increment the count.

As with the enqueue operation for the linked implementation and the noncircular array implementation, each of these operations is O(1) and thus the operation is O(1).

From a time complexity point of view, there is not a substantial difference between the enqueue operations for the three implementations, so let us move on to the dequeue operation.

dequeue

The dequeue operation for the linked implementation consists of the following steps:

- Check to make sure the queue is not empty (throw an exception if it is).
- Set a temporary reference equal to the element pointed to by the element reference of the node pointed to by the front reference.
- Set the front reference equal to the next reference of the node at the head of the queue.

▸ Decrement the count of elements in the queue.

▸ Return the element pointed to by the temporary reference.

As with our previous examples, each of these operations consists of a single comparison or a simple assignment and is therefore O(1). Thus, the dequeue operation for the linked implementation is O(1).

The dequeue operation for the noncircular array implementation consists of the following steps:

▸ Check to make sure the queue is not empty (throw an exception if it is).

▸ Set a temporary object equal to the first element in the array.

▸ Shift all of the elements in the array one position to the left.

▸ Decrement the values of rear and count.

▸ Return the temporary object.

All of these steps are O(1) with the exception of shifting all of the remaining elements in the array to the left, which is O(n). Thus, the dequeue operation for the noncircular array implementation has time complexity O(n).

> The shifting of elements in a noncircular array implementation creates an O(n) complexity.
>
> key concept

The dequeue operation for the circular array implementation consists of the following steps:

▸ Check to make sure the queue is not empty (throw an exception if it is).

▸ Set a temporary object equal to the object at the front of the queue.

▸ Set the position at front of the queue to null.

▸ Decrement the count.

▸ Return the temporary object.

All of these steps are O(1) resulting in the dequeue operation for the circular array implementation being O(1).

The front, isEmpty, and size operations for all three implementations are O(1).

As you can see, we do pay a time complexity penalty for dequeue operations on the noncircular array implementation.

summary of key concepts

▸ Queue elements are processed in a FIFO manner—the first element in is the first element out.

▸ A queue is a convenient collection for storing a repeating code key.

▸ Simulations are often implemented using queues to represent waiting lines.

▸ A radix sort is inherently based on queue processing.

▸ A linked implementation of a queue is facilitated by references to the first and last elements of the linked list.

▸ The enqueue and dequeue operations work on opposite ends of the collection.

▸ Because queue operations modify both ends of the collection, fixing one end at index 0 requires that elements be shifted.

▸ Treating arrays as circular eliminates the need to shift elements in an array queue implementation.

▸ The shifting of elements in a noncircular array implementation creates an O(n) complexity.

self-review questions

7.1   What is the difference between a queue and a stack?

7.2   What are the five basic operations on a queue?

7.3   What are some of the other operations that might be implemented for a queue?

7.4   How many queues would it take to use a radix sort to sort names stored as all lowercase?

7.5   Is it possible for the front and rear references in a linked implementation to be equal?

7.6   Is it possible for the front and rear references in a noncircular array implementation to be equal?

7.7 Is it possible for the `front` and `rear` references in a circular array implementation to be equal?

7.8 Which implementation has the worst time complexity?

7.9 Which implementation has the worst space complexity?

exercises

7.1 Hand trace a queue X through the following operations:

```
X.enqueue(new Integer(4));

X.enqueue(new Character('T'));

Object Y = X.dequeue();

X.enqueue(new Character('b'));

X.enqueue(new Integer(2));

X.enqueue(new Integer(5));

X.enqueue(new Character('j'));

Object Y = X.dequeue();

X.enqueue(new Character('q'));

X.enqueue(new Integer(9));
```

7.2 Given the resulting queue X from Exercise 7.1, what would be the result of each of the following?

```
a. X.front();

b. Y = X.dequeue();

   X.front();

c. Y = X.dequeue();

   X.front();
```

7.3 What would be the time complexity of the `size` operation for each of the three implementations if there were not a `count` variable?

7.4 Under what circumstances could the `front` and `rear` references be equal for each of the three implementations?

7.5   Hand trace the ticket counter problem for 22 customers and 4 cashiers. Graph the total process time for each person. What can you surmise from these results?

7.6   Hand trace a radix sort for the following list of six-digit student ID numbers assuming that each digit must be between 1 and 5:

13224

32131

54355

12123

22331

21212

33333

54312

7.7   What is the time complexity of a radix sort compared to the sorting algorithms discussed in Chapter 5?

7.8   Compare and contrast the enqueue method of the LinkedQueue class to the push method of the LinkedStack class from Chapter 6.

7.9   Describe two different ways the isEmpty method of the LinkedQueue class could be implemented.

7.10   Name five everyday examples of a queue other than those discussed in this chapter.

7.11   Explain why the array implementation of a stack does not require elements to be shifted but the noncircular array implementation of a queue does.

7.12   Suppose the count variable was not used in the CircularArrayQueue class. Explain how you could you use the values of front and rear to compute the number of elements in the list.

programming projects

7.1   Complete the implementation of the LinkedQueue class presented in this chapter. Specifically, complete the implementations of the first, isEmpty, size, and toString methods.

7.2 Complete the implementation of the `ArrayQueue` class presented in this chapter. Specifically, complete the implementations of the `first`, `isEmpty`, `size`, and `toString` methods.

7.3 Complete the implementation of the `CircularArrayQueue` class described in this chapter, including all methods.

7.4 Write a version of the `ArrayQueue` class that keeps the rear of the queue fixed at index 0.

7.5 Write a version of the `CircularArrayQueue` class that grows the list in the opposite direction than the version described in this chapter.

7.6 All of the implementations in this chapter use a `count` variable to keep track of the number of elements in the queue. Rewrite the linked implementation without a `count` variable.

7.7 All of the implementations in this chapter use a `count` variable to keep track of the number of elements in the queue. Rewrite the noncircular array implementation without a `count` variable.

7.8 All of the implementations in this chapter use a `count` variable to keep track of the number of elements in the queue. Rewrite the circular array implementation without a `count` variable.

7.9 A data structure called a deque (pronounced like "deck") is closely related to a queue. The name deque stands for double ended queue. The difference between the two is that with a deque, you can insert or remove from either end of the queue. Implement a deque using arrays.

7.10 Implement the deque from Programming Project 7.9 using links. (*Hint:* each node will need a `next` and a `previous` reference.)

7.11 Implement the `front`, `isEmpty`, and `size` operations for the noncircular array implementation of a queue.

7.12 Create a graphical application that provides buttons for `enqueue` and `dequeue` from a queue, a text field to accept a string as input for `enqueue`, and a text area to display the contents of the queue after each operation.

answers to self-review questions

7.1 A queue is a first in, first out (FIFO) collection, whereas a stack is a last in, first out (LIFO) collection.

7.2   The basic queue operations are:

   enqueue—adds an element to the end of the queue

   dequeue—removes an element from the front of the queue

   first—returns a reference to the element at the front of the queue

   isEmpty—returns true if the queue is empty, returns false otherwise

   size—returns the number of elements in the queue

7.3   makeEmpty(), destroy(), full()

7.4   27, one for each of the 26 letters in the alphabet and 1 to store the whole list before, during, and after sorting.

7.5   Yes, it happens when the queue is empty (both front and rear are null) and when there is only one element on the queue.

7.6   There is no front reference in this implementation. The first element in the queue is always in position 0 of the array. However, when the queue is empty, the rear also points to position 0.

7.7   Yes, it can happen under two circumstances: when the queue is empty, and when the queue is full.

7.8   The noncircular array implementation with an O(n) dequeue operation has the worst time complexity.

7.9   Both of the array implementations waste space for unfilled elements in the array. The linked implementation uses more space per element stored.

The concept of a list is inherently familiar to us. We make "to-do" lists, and lists of items to buy at the grocery store, and lists of friends to invite to a party. We may number the items in a list or we may keep them in alphabetical order. For other lists we may keep the items in a particular order that simply makes the most sense to us. This chapter explores the concept of a list collection and some ways they can be managed.

chapter
objectives

- Examine list processing and various ordering techniques

- Define a list abstract data type

- Demonstrate how a list can be used to solve problems

- Examine various list implementations

- Compare list implementations

8.1 a list ADT

There are three types of list collections:

▸ *Ordered lists,* whose elements are ordered by some inherent characteristic of the elements

▸ *Unordered lists,* whose elements have no inherent order

▸ *Indexed lists,* whose elements can be referenced using a numeric index

> **key concept**
>
> List collections can be categorized as ordered, unordered, and indexed.

An ordered list is based on some particular characteristic of the elements in the list. For example, you may keep a list of names ordered alphabetically, or you may keep an inventory list ordered by part number. The list is sorted based on some key value. Any element added to an ordered list has a proper location in the list, given its key value and the key values of the elements already in the list. Figure 8.1 shows a conceptual view of an ordered list, in which the elements are ordered by an integer key value. Adding a value to the list involves finding the new elements' proper sorted position among the existing elements.

> **key concept**
>
> The elements of an ordered list have an inherent relationship defining their order.

> **key concept**
>
> The elements of an unordered list are kept in whatever order the client chooses.

An unordered list is not based on any inherent characteristic of the elements. Don't let the name mislead you. The elements in an unordered list can be kept in a particular order, but that order is not based on the elements themselves. The client using the list determines the order of the elements. Figure 8.2 shows a conceptual view of an unordered list. A new element can be put on the front or rear of the list, or it can be inserted after a particular element already in the list.

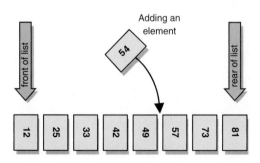

figure 8.1   A conceptual view of an ordered list

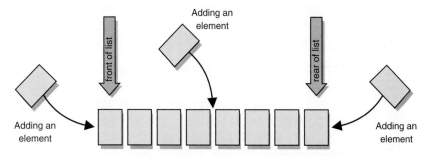

figure 8.2   A conceptual view of an unordered list

An indexed list is similar to an unordered list in that there is no inherent relationship among the elements that determines their order in the list. The client using the list determines the order of the elements. However, in addition, each element can be referenced by a numeric index that begins at 0 at the front of the list and continues contiguously until the end of the list. Figure 8.3 shows a conceptual view of an indexed list. A new element can be inserted into the list at any position, including at the front or rear of the list. Every time a change occurs in the list, the indexes are adjusted to stay in order and contiguous.

> **key concept**
>
> An indexed list maintains a contiguous numeric index range for its elements.

Note the primary difference between an indexed list and an array: an indexed list keeps its indexes contiguous. If an element is removed, the indexes of other elements "collapse" to eliminate the gap. When an element is inserted, the indexes of other elements are shifted to make room.

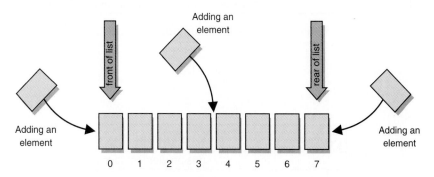

figure 8.3   A conceptual view of an indexed list

Keep in mind that these are conceptual views of lists. As with any collection, they can be implemented in many ways. The implementations of these lists don't even have to keep the elements in the order that their conceptual view indicates, though that may be easiest.

There is a set of operations that is common to all three types of lists. These common operations are shown in Figure 8.4. They include operations to remove and examine elements, as well as classic operations such as isEmpty and size. The contains operation is also supported by all list types, which allows the user to determine if a list contains a particular element. We saw a similar operation defined for a bag collection in Chapters 2 and 3.

The differences in the various types of lists generally center on how elements are added to the list. In an ordered list, we need only specify the new element to add. Its position in the list is based on its key value. This operation is shown in Figure 8.5.

Operation	Description
removeFirst	Removes the first element from the list.
removeLast	Removes the last element from the list.
remove	Removes a particular element from the list.
first	Examines the element at the front of the list.
last	Examines the element at the rear of the list.
contains	Determines if the list contains a particular element.
isEmpty	Determines if the list is empty.
size	Determines the number of elements on the list.

figure 8.4   The common operations on a list

Operation	Description
add	Adds an element to the list.

figure 8.5   The operation particular to an ordered list

Operation	Description
addToFront	Adds an element to the front of the list.
addToRear	Adds an element to the rear of the list.
addAfter	Adds an element after a particular element already in the list.

figure 8.6   The operations particular to an unordered list

An unordered list supports three variations of the add operation. Elements can be added to the front or rear of the list, or after a particular element that is already in the list. These operations are shown in Figure 8.6.

The operations particular to an indexed list make use of its ability to reference elements by their index. These operations are shown in Figure 8.7. A new element can be inserted into the list at a particular index, or it can be added to the rear of the list without specifying an index at all. Note that if an element is inserted, the elements at higher indexes are shifted up to make room. Alternatively, the element at a particular index can be set, which overwrites the element currently at that index and therefore does not cause other elements to shift. In addition, the get operation returns the element stored at that index without removing it from the list. The indexOf operation determines the index of a particular element, if it exists. Also, an indexed list supports another variation of the remove operation, in which the element to be removed is specified by its index.

We can capitalize on the fact that all versions of a list collection share a common set of operations. These need only be defined once. Therefore, we will define four list interfaces: one with the common operations and three with the operations particular to each list type. Inheritance can be used with interfaces just as it can with classes. The interfaces of the particular list types extend the common list definition. This relationship among the interfaces is shown in Figure 8.8.

Operation	Description
add	Inserts an element at a particular index or at the rear of the list.
set	Sets the element at a particular index.
get	Examines the element at a particular index.
indexOf	Determines the index of an element in the list.
remove	Removes the element at a particular index.

figure 8.7   The operations particular to an indexed list

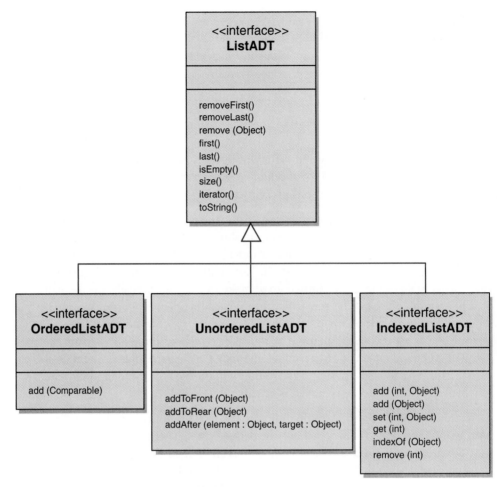

figure 8.8   The various list interfaces

When interfaces are inherited, the child interface contains all abstract methods defined in the parent. Therefore, any class implementing a child interface must implement all methods from both the parent and the child.

Listings 8.1 through 8.4 show the Java interfaces corresponding to the UML diagram in Figure 8.8.

listing
   8.1

```
//*******************************************************************
//  ListADT.java        Authors: Lewis/Chase
//
//  Defines the interface to a general list collection. Specific
//  types of lists will extend this interface to complete the
//  set of necessary operations.
//*******************************************************************

package jss2;

import java.util.Iterator;

public interface ListADT
{
    //  Removes and returns the first element from this list
    public Object removeFirst ();

    //  Removes and returns the last element from this list
    public Object removeLast ();

    //  Removes and returns the specified element from this list
    public Object remove (Object element);

    //  Returns a reference to the first element on this list
    public Object first ();

    //  Returns a reference to the last element on this list
    public Object last ();

    //  Returns true if this list contains the specified target element
    public boolean contains (Object target);

    //  Returns true if this list contains no elements
    public boolean isEmpty();

    //  Returns the number of elements in this list
    public int size();

    //  Returns an iterator for the elements in this list
    public Iterator iterator();

    //  Returns a string representation of this list
    public String toString();
}
```

listing
    8.2

```
//***********************************************************************
//   OrderedListADT.java        Authors: Lewis/Chase
//
//   Defines the interface to an ordered list collection. Only
//   Comparable elements are stored, kept in the order determined by
//   the inherent relationship among the elements.
//***********************************************************************

package jss2;

public interface OrderedListADT extends ListADT
{
    //  Adds the specified element to this list at the proper location
    public void add (Comparable element);
}
```

listing
    8.3

```
//***********************************************************************
//   UnorderedListADT.java        Authors: Lewis/Chase
//
//   Defines the interface to an unordered list collection. Elements
//   are stored in any order the user desires.
//***********************************************************************

package jss2;

public interface UnorderedListADT extends ListADT
{
    //  Adds the specified element to the front of this list
    public void addToFront (Object element);

    //  Adds the specified element to the rear of this list
    public void addToRear (Object element);

    //  Adds the specified element after the specified target
    public void addAfter (Object element, Object target);
}
```

listing
   8.4

```java
//************************************************************************
//   IndexedListADT.java        Authors: Lewis/Chase
//
//   Defines the interface to an indexed list collection. Elements
//   are referenced by contiguous numeric indexes.
//************************************************************************

package jss2;

public interface IndexedListADT extends ListADT
{
    //  Inserts the specified element at the specified index
    public void add (int index, Object element);

    //  Sets the element at the specified index
    public void set (int index, Object element);

    //  Adds the specified element to the rear of this list
    public void add (Object element);

    //  Returns a reference to the element at the specified index
    public Object get (int index);

    //  Returns the index of the specified element
    public int indexOf (Object element);

    //  Removes and returns the element at the specified index
    public Object remove (int index);
}
```

Before exploring how these various kinds of lists can be implemented, let's first see how they might be used.

8.2 using ordered lists: tournament maker

Sporting tournaments, such as the NCAA basketball tournament or a championship tournament at a local bowling alley, are often organized by the number of wins achieved during the regular season. Ordered lists can be used to help organize the tournament play. An ordered list can be used to store teams ordered by number of wins. To form the match-ups for the first round of the tournament, teams can be selected from the front and back of the list in pairs.

key concept An ordered list is a convenient collection to use when creating a tournament schedule.

For example, consider the eight bowling teams listed in Figure 8.9. This table indicates the number of wins each team accomplished during the regular season.

To create the first-round tournament matches, the teams would be stored in a list ordered by the number of wins. The first team on the list (the team with the best record) is removed from the list and matched up with the last team on the list (the team with the worst record) to form the first game of the tournament. The process is repeated, matching up the team with the next best record with the team with the next worst record to form the second game. This process continues until the list is empty. Interestingly, the same process would be used to form the second-round match-ups, only for the second round, the teams would be

Team Name	Wins
GutterBalls	9
KingPins	8
PinDoctors	7
Scorecards	10
Spares	5
Splits	4
Tenpins	3
Woodsplitters	2

figure 8.9 Bowling league team names and number of wins

ordered by game number from the first round. For the third round, the teams would be ordered by game number from the second round. This process would continue with half as many games per round until there was only one game left. Thus, from our example in Figure 8.9 we would end up with the tournament as laid out in Figure 8.10.

To create a program to create the first-round tournament match-ups first requires that we create a class to represent the information we wish to store about teams. This `Team` class will need to store both the name of the team and the number of wins. The class will also need to provide us with some sort of comparison operation. For purposes of this discussion, we have created an interface called `Comparable`, which the `Team` class will implement. This interface provides for a `lessThan` operation, which is unique from the traditional `compareTo` operation. The `lessThan` operation will return true if the new element, the one being inserted in the list, is less than the current element in the list. For example, this means that if two teams have the same number of wins, the team that is entered first will hold the higher position in the list. Figure 8.11 illustrates the UML relationships among the classes used to solve this problem. Listing 8.5 shows the `Tournament` class and sample output. Listing 8.6 shows the `Team` class, and Listing 8.7 illustrates the `TournamentMaker` class.

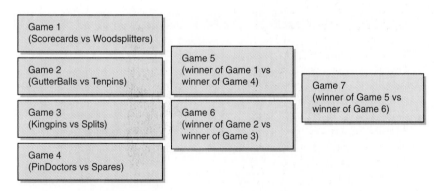

figure 8.10   Sample tournament layout for a bowling league tournament

listing
   8.5

```java
//************************************************************************
//   Tournament.java        Authors: Lewis/Chase
//
//   Demonstrates the use of an ordered list to create the match-ups
//   in a sporting tournament.
//************************************************************************
public class Tournament
{
   //----------------------------------------------------------------
   //   Determines and prints the tournament organization.
   //----------------------------------------------------------------
   public static void main (String[] args)
   {
      try
      {
         TournamentMaker temp = new TournamentMaker();
         temp.make();
      }
      catch (Exception IOException)
      {
         System.out.println("Invalid input reported");
      }
   }
}
```

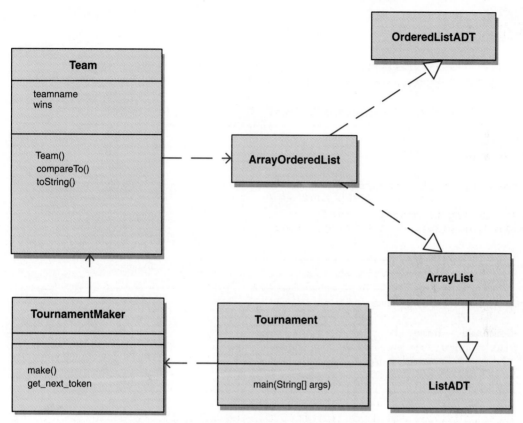

figure 8.11 UML description of the Tournament class

listing
    8.6

```java
//*********************************************************************
//  Team.java          Authors: Lewis/Chase
//
//  Represents a sports team and its wins.
//*********************************************************************

import java.util.*;

class Team implements Comparable
{
   public String teamname;
   private int wins;

   //-----------------------------------------------------------------
   //  Sets up this team with the specified information.
   //-----------------------------------------------------------------
   public Team (String name, int numwins)
   {
      teamname = name;
      wins = numwins;
   }

   //-----------------------------------------------------------------
   //  Returns -1, 0, 1 for less = >.
   //-----------------------------------------------------------------
   public int compareTo (Object other)
   {
      if (this.wins < (((Team)other).wins))
         return -1;
      else
        if (this.wins == (((Team)other).wins))
           return 0;
        else
           return 1;
   }

   //-----------------------------------------------------------------
   //  Returns the name of the team.
   //-----------------------------------------------------------------
   public String toString()
   {
     return teamname;
   }
}
```

listing
   8.7

```java
//********************************************************************
//  TournamentMaker.java        Authors: Lewis/Chase
//
//  Supports the generation of tournaments.
//********************************************************************

import jss2.*;
import jss2.exceptions.*;
import java.util.StringTokenizer;
import java.io.*;

public class TournamentMaker
{
   //---------------------------------------------------------------
   //  Gets the next token from the input stream.
   //---------------------------------------------------------------
   private String getNextToken() throws IOException
   {
      String temptoken, instring;
      StringTokenizer tokenizer;
      BufferedReader in = new
         BufferedReader(new InputStreamReader(System.in));

      instring = in.readLine();
      tokenizer = new StringTokenizer(instring);
      temptoken = (tokenizer.nextToken());
      return temptoken;
   }


   //---------------------------------------------------------------
   //  Determines and prints the tournament organization.
   //---------------------------------------------------------------
   public void make( ) throws IOException
   {
      ArrayOrderedList tournament = new ArrayOrderedList();
      String team1, team2, teamname;
      int numwins, numteams = 0;

      System.out.println("Tournament Maker");
```

listing
    8.7   continued

```java
while (((numteams % 2) != 0) || (numteams == 0))
{
   System.out.println ("Enter the number of teams (must be even):");
   numteams = Integer.parseInt(get_next_token());
}

System.out.println ("Enter " + numteams + " team names and number "
                  + "of wins:");
System.out.println("Teams may be entered in any order ");

for (int count=1; count <= numteams; count++)
{
   System.out.println("Enter team name: ");
   teamname = getNextToken();
   System.out.println("Enter number of wins: ");
   numwins = Integer.parseInt(getNextToken());
   tournament.add(new Team(teamname, numwins));
}

System.out.println("The first round match-ups are: ");

for (int count=1; count <= (numteams/2); count++)
{
   team1 = ((Team)(tournament.removeFirst())).teamname;
   team2 = ((Team)(tournament.removeLast())).teamname;
   System.out.println ("Game " + count + " is " + team1 +
      " against " + team2);
   System.out.println ("with the winner to play the winner of game "
      + (((numteams/2)+1) - count));
}

   }
}
```

listing 8.7 continued

output

```
Enter the number of teams (must be even):
4
Enter 4 team names and number of wins:
Teams may be entered in any order
Enter team name:
PinDoctors
Enter number of wins:
11
Enter team name:
GutterBalls
Enter number of wins:
5
Enter team name:
Spares
Enter number of wins:
8
Enter team name:
FirstStrikes
Enter number of wins:
12
The first round match-ups are:
Game 1 is GutterBalls against FirstStrikes
with the winner to play the winner of game 2
Game 2 is Spares against PinDoctors
with the winner to play the winner of game 1
```

8.3 using indexed lists: the Josephus problem

Flavius Josephus was a Jewish historian of the first century. Legend has it that he was one of a group of 41 Jewish rebels trapped by the Romans who decided to kill themselves rather than surrender. They decided to form a circle and to kill every third person until no one was left. Josephus, not wanting to die, calculated where he needed to stand so that he would be the last one alive and thus would not have to die. Thus was born a class of problems referred to as the Josephus problem. These problems involve

> **key concept**
>
> The Josephus problem is a classic computing problem that is appropriately solved with indexed lists.

finding the order of events when events in a list are not taken in order, but rather are taken every i^th element in a cycle until there are none remaining.

For example, let us suppose that we have a list of seven elements numbered from 1 to 7:

1 2 3 4 5 6 7

If we were to remove every third element from the list, the first element to be removed would be number 3, leaving the list:

1 2 4 5 6 7

The next element to be removed would be number 6, leaving the list:

1 2 4 5 7

The elements are thought of as in a continuous cycle, so that when we reach the end of the list, we continue counting at the beginning. Therefore, the next element to be removed would be number 2, leaving the list:

1 4 5 7

The next element to be removed would be number 7, leaving the list:

1 4 5

The next element to be removed would be number 5, leaving the list:

1 4

The next to last element to be removed would be number 1, leaving the number 4 as the last element on the list.

Listing 8.8 illustrates a generic implementation of the Josephus problem, allowing the user to input the number of items in the list and the gap between elements. Note that the original list is placed in an indexed list. Each element is then removed from the list one at a time by computing the next index position in the list to be removed. The one complication in this is the computation of the next index position to be removed. This is particularly interesting since the list collapses on itself as elements are removed. For example, the element number 6 from our previous example should be the second element removed from the list. However, once element 3 has been removed from the list, element 6 is no longer in its original position. Instead of being at index position 5 in the list, it is now at

listing
    8.8

```java
//*******************************************************************
//    Josephus.java        Authors: Lewis/Chase
//*******************************************************************

import java.util.ArrayList;
import java.util.StringTokenizer;
import java.io.*;

public class Josephus
{

    //---------------------------------------------------------------
    //    Continue around the circle eliminating every nth soldier
    //    until all of the soldiers have been eliminated
    //---------------------------------------------------------------
    public static void main ( String[] args) throws IOException
    {
        String instring;
        int numpeople, gap, newgap, counter;
        StringTokenizer tokenizer;
        ArrayList list = new ArrayList();
        Object tempelement;
        BufferedReader in = new
            BufferedReader(new InputStreamReader(System.in));

        // get the initial number of soldiers
        System.out.println("Enter the number of soldiers: ");
        instring = in.readLine();
        tokenizer = new StringTokenizer(instring);
        numpeople = Integer.parseInt (tokenizer.nextToken());

        // get the gap between soldiers
        System.out.println("Enter the gap between soldiers: ");
        instring = in.readLine();
        tokenizer = new StringTokenizer(instring);
        gap = Integer.parseInt (tokenizer.nextToken());

        // load the initial list of soldiers
        for (int count=1; count <= numpeople; count++)
        {
            list.add(new Integer(count));
        }
        counter = gap - 1;
```

listing
   8.8   continued

```
      newgap = gap;

      //  Treating the list as circular, remove every nth element
      //  until the list is empty

      System.out.println("The order is: ");


      while (!(list.isEmpty()))
      {
          tempelement = list.remove(counter);
          numpeople = numpeople - 1;
          if (numpeople > 0)
              counter = (counter + gap - 1) % numpeople;
          System.out.println(tempelement);
      }
   }
}
```

output

```
Enter the number of soldiers:
11
Enter the gap between soldiers:
3
The order is:
3
6
9
1
5
10
4
11
8
2
7
```

index position 4. Figure 8.12 illustrates the UML for the Josephus problem. Notice that we have chosen to use the `ArrayList` implementation from the Java Collections API, which is actually an indexed list implementation.

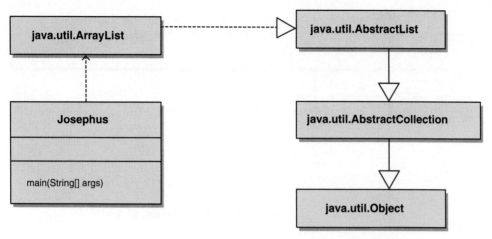

figure 8.12   UML description of the Josephus program

8.4 implementing lists: with arrays

An array-based implementation of a list could fix one end of the list at index 0 and shift elements as needed. This is similar to the first array-based implementation of a queue from the previous chapter. The primary difference is that we will now also insert elements into the middle of the list. We could also use a circular array approach as we did with our second array-based queue implementation. That approach is left as a programming project.

Figure 8.13 shows an array implementation of a list with the front of the list fixed at index 0. The integer variable rear represents the number of elements in the list and the next available slot for adding an element to the rear of the list.

Note that Figure 8.13 applies to all three variations of the list. First we will explore the common operations.

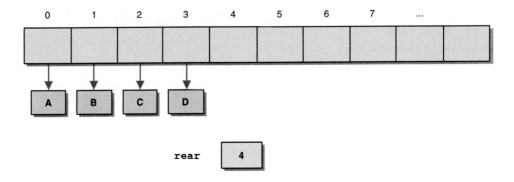

figure 8.13   An array implementation of a list

the remove operation

This variation of the remove operation requires that we search for the element passed in as a parameter and remove it from the list if it is found. Then any appropriate elements are shifted down in the list to fill in the gap. This operation can be implemented as follows:

```java
//-------------------------------------------------------------------
//  Removes and returns the specified element.
//-------------------------------------------------------------------
public Object remove (Object element)
{
   Object result;
   int index = find (element);

   if (index == NOT_FOUND)
      throw new NoSuchElementException("list");

   result = list[index];

   // shift the appropriate elements
   for (int scan=index; scan < rear; scan++)
      list[scan] = list[scan+1];

   rear--;
   list[rear] = null;

   return result;
}
```

The remove method makes use of a method called find, which finds the element in question, if it exists in the list, and returns its index. The find method returns a constant called NOT_FOUND if the element is not in the list. The NOT_FOUND constant is equal to –1 and is defined in the ArrayList class. If the element is not found, a NoSuchElementException is generated. If it is found, the elements at higher indexes are shifted down, the rear value is updated, and the element is returned.

The find method supports the implementation of a public operation on the list, rather than defining its own operation. Therefore, the find method should be declared with private visibility. The find method can be implemented as follows:

```
//----------------------------------------------------------------
//  Returns the array index of the specified element, or the
//  constant NOT_FOUND if it is not found.
//----------------------------------------------------------------
private int find (Object target)
{
    int scan = 0, result = NOT_FOUND;
    boolean found = false;

    if (! isEmpty())
        while (! found && scan < rear)
            if (target.equals(list[scan])
                found = true;
            else
                scan++;

    if (found)
        result = scan;

    return result;
}
```

Note that the find method relies on the equals method to determine if the target has been found. It's possible that the object passed into the method is an exact copy of the element being sought. In fact, it may be an alias of the element in the list. However, if the parameter is a separate object, it may not contain all aspects of the element being sought. Only the key characteristics on which the equals method is based are important.

The logic of the `find` method could have been incorporated into the `remove` method, though it would have made the `remove` method somewhat complicated. When appropriate, such support methods should be defined to keep each method readable. Furthermore, in this case, the `find` support method is useful in implementing the `contains` operation, as we will now explore.

the `contains` operation

The purpose of the `contains` operation is to determine if a particular element is currently contained in the list. We saw a similar operation in the bag collection in Chapter 2. This time, however, we can make use of the `find` support method to create a fairly straightforward implementation:

```
//----------------------------------------------------------------
//  Returns true if this list contains the specified element.
//----------------------------------------------------------------
public boolean contains (Object target)
{
    return (find(target) != NOT_FOUND)
}
```

If the target element is not found, the `contains` method returns false. If it is found, it returns true. A carefully constructed `return` statement ensures the proper return value.

The remaining common list operations are left as programming projects. Let's turn our attention now to the operations that are particular to a specific type of list.

the `add` operation for an ordered list

The `add` operation is the only way an element can be added to an ordered list. No location is specified in the call because the elements themselves determine their order. The `add` operation can be implemented as follows:

```
//-----------------------------------------------------------
//  Adds the specified Comparable element to the list, keeping
//  the elements in sorted order.
//-----------------------------------------------------------
public void add (Comparable element)
{
   if (size() == list.length)
      expandCapacity();

   int scan = 0;
   while (scan < rear && element.compareTo(list[scan]) > 0)
      scan++;

   for (int scan2=rear; scan2 > scan; scan2--)
      list[scan2] = list[scan2-1];

   list[scan] = element;
   rear++;
}
```

Note that the parameter to the method is a `Comparable` object. Thus, only `Comparable` objects can be stored in an ordered list. This guarantees that the objects in the list can be compared to each other to determine their relative order.

> **key concept**
> Only `Comparable` objects can be stored in an ordered list.

Recall that the `Comparable` interface defines the `compareTo` method that returns a negative, zero, or positive integer value if the executing object is less than, equal to, or greater than the parameter, respectively. The `Comparable` interface was crucial in our discussion of sorting in Chapter 5. It therefore makes sense that it comes into play again for an ordered list collection, because we are keeping the elements in the list in sorted order.

The unordered and indexed versions of a list do not require that the elements they store be `Comparable`. It is a testament to object-oriented programming that the various classes that implement these list variations can exist in harmony despite these differences.

operations particular to unordered lists

The three `add` operations for an unordered list are left as programming projects. The `addToFront` and `addToRear` operations are similar to operations from other collections. Keep in mind that the `addToFront` operation must shift the current elements in the list first to make room at index 0 for the new element.

The `addAfter` operation accepts two `Object` objects: one that represents the element to be added and one that represents the target element that determines the placement of the new element. The `addAfter` method must first find the target element, and then insert the new element after it.

operations particular to indexed lists

The Java Collections API provides implementations for an indexed list. In fact, it provides two implementations for lists: `ArrayList` and `LinkedList`. Both of these classes extend the abstract class `java.util.AbstractList`, which implements the `java.util.List` interface. These are part of the Java class library and are distinct from the interfaces and classes we've discussed so far in this chapter. The `java.util.AbstractList` class is an extension of the `java.util.AbstractCollection` class, which implements the `java.util.Collection` interface. Both of the list implementations provided in the Java Collections framework are indexed lists, even though the class names do not identify them as such.

The `ArrayList` implementation of an indexed list is, as its name implies, an array-based implementation. Thus, many of the issues discussed in the array implementations of stacks, queues, unordered lists, and ordered lists apply here as well. For example, using an array implementation of a list, an `add` operation that specifies an index in the middle of the list will require all of the elements above that position in the list to be shifted one position higher in the list. Likewise, a `remove` operation that removes an element from the middle of the list will require all of the elements above that position in the list to be shifted one position lower in the list.

The `ArrayList` implementation is resizable, meaning that if adding the next element would overflow the `ArrayList`, the underlying array is automatically resized. To do this, the `ArrayList` class contains two additional operations: `ensureCapacity` increases the size of the array to the specified size if it is not already that large or larger, and `trimToSize` trims the array to the actual current size of the list.

The `ArrayList` implementation is very similar to the implementation of a `Vector`. However, the `Vector` operations are synchronized and `ArrayList` operations are not.

Like arrays, one advantage of the `ArrayList` implementation is the ability to access any element in the list in equal time. However, the penalty for that access is the added cost of shifting remaining elements either as part of an insertion into the list or a deletion from the list.

8.5 implementing lists: with links

As we've seen with other collections, the use of a linked list is often another convenient way to implement a linear collection. Both the common operations that apply for all three types of a list collection, as well as the particular operations for the three types, can be implemented with techniques similar to the ones we've used before. We will examine a couple of the more interesting operations but will leave most of these as programming projects.

the `remove` operation

The `remove` operation is part of the `LinkedList` class shared by all three implementations: unordered, ordered, and indexed lists. The `remove` operation consists of checking to make sure that the list is not empty, finding the element to be removed, and then handling one of four cases: the element to be removed is the only element in the list, the element to be removed is the first element in the list, the element to be removed is the last element in the list, or the element to be removed is in the middle of the list. In all cases, the `count` is decremented by one. An implementation of the `remove` operation is shown below.

```
//===============================================================
//  Removes the first instance of the specified element from the
//  list if it is found in the list and returns a reference to it.
//  Throws an EmptyListException if the list is empty.  Throws a
//  NoSuchElementException if the specified element is not found
//  on the list.
//===============================================================
```

```
public Object remove (Object targetElement) throws
   EmptyCollectionException, ElementNotFoundException
{
   if (isEmpty())
      throw new EmptyCollectionException ("List");

   boolean found = false;

   LinearNode previous = null;
   LinearNode current = head;

   while (current != null && !found)
      if (targetElement.equals (current.getElement()))
         found = true;
      else
      {
         previous = current;
         current = current.getNext();
      }

   if (!found)
      throw new ElementNotFoundException ("List");

   if (size() == 1)
      head = tail = null;
   else
      if (current.equals (head))
         head = current.getNext();
      else
         if (current.equals (tail))
         {
            tail = previous;
            tail.setNext(null);
         }
         else
            previous.setNext(current.getNext());

   count--;

   return current.getElement();
}
```

doubly linked lists

Note how much code in this method is devoted to finding the target element and keeping track of a current and a previous reference. This seems like a missed opportunity to reuse code since we already have a find method in the LinkedList class. What if this list were *doubly linked*, meaning that each node stores a reference to the next element, as well as to the previous element? Would this make the remove operation simpler? First, we would need a DoubleNode class, as shown in Listing 8.9.

listing
8.9

```java
//********************************************************************
//   DoubleNode.java        Authors: Lewis/Chase
//
//   Represents a node in a doubly linked list.
//********************************************************************

public class DoubleNode
{
   private DoubleNode next;
   private Object element;
   private DoubleNode previous;

   //----------------------------------------------------------------
   //  Creates an empty node.
   //----------------------------------------------------------------
   public DoubleNode()
   {
      next = null;
      element = null;
      previous = null;
   }

   //----------------------------------------------------------------
   //  Creates a node storing the specified element.
   //----------------------------------------------------------------
   public DoubleNode (Object elem)
   {
      next = null;
      element = elem;
      previous = null;
   }
```

listing
8.9   continued

```
//----------------------------------------------------------------
//   Returns the node that follows this one.
//----------------------------------------------------------------
public DoubleNode getNext()
{
   return next;
}


//----------------------------------------------------------------
//   Returns the node that precedes this one.
//----------------------------------------------------------------
public DoubleNode getPrevious()
{
   return previous;
}


//----------------------------------------------------------------
//   Sets the node that follows this one.
//----------------------------------------------------------------
public void setNext (DoubleNode dnode)
{
   next = dnode;
}


//----------------------------------------------------------------
//   Sets the node that follows this one.
//----------------------------------------------------------------
public void setPrevious (DoubleNode dnode)
{
   previous = dnode;
}


//----------------------------------------------------------------
//   Returns the element stored in this node.
//----------------------------------------------------------------
public Object getElement()
{
   return element;
}
```

**listing
8.9**   continued

```
//------------------------------------------------------------
//  Sets the element stored in this node.
//------------------------------------------------------------
public void setElement (Object elem)
{
    element = elem;
}
}
```

The remove operation can now be implemented much more elegantly using a doubly linked list. Note that we can now use the find operation to locate the target, and there is no longer a need for us to keep track of a previous reference. In this example, we also make use of the removeFirst and removeLast operations to handle the special cases associated with removing either the first or last element.

```
//------------------------------------------------------------
//  Removes and returns the specified element.
//------------------------------------------------------------
public Object remove (Object element)
{
    Object result;
    DoubleNode nodeptr = find (element);

    if (nodeptr == null)
        throw new ElementNotFoundException ("list");

    result = nodeptr.getElement();

    // check to see if front or rear
    if (nodeptr == front)
        result = this.removeFirst();
```

```
    else
        if (nodeptr == rear)
            result = this.removeLast();
        else
        {
            nodeptr.getNext().setPrevious(nodeptr.getPrevious());
            nodeptr.getPrevious().setNext(nodeptr.getNext());
            count--;
        }

    return result;
}
```

Figure 8.14 illustrates the structure of a doubly linked list. The implementations of the other operations for doubly linked lists are left as exercises.

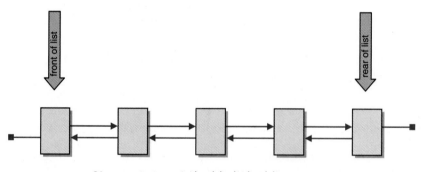

figure 8.14   A doubly linked list

8.6 analysis of list implementations

Because each type of list collection has unique issues related to its implementation, we'll cover the analysis of each type of list collection separately.

analysis of ordered list implementations

The difference in space complexity between the linked and array implementations of an ordered list is much the same as what we have seen with unordered lists, stacks, and queues. The linked implementation requires more space per object to be inserted in the list simply because of the space allocated for the next reference. However, the array implementation must allocate an initial array of references to store the objects in the list, and whatever space is not used within the array is wasted.

The analysis of the time complexity of most of the operations for the implementations of a list is identical to the discussion from Chapter 8. Only the addElement operation is unique.

The addElement operations of the two implementations are nearly identical. One substantial difference between the two algorithms is that once the insertion location is found, the array implementation must shift all of the elements in the array from the current position to the tail, up one position. Very much like the insertAfter operation for unordered lists, the addElement operation for the array implementation of ordered lists will always result in a total of n+1 comparison plus shifts. One potential confusion in the analysis of this algorithm might be that the shift occurs within a while loop, making it appear that this could be an $O(n^2)$ algorithm. However, notice that within the same segment of the algorithm, the found flag is set to true so that the while loop will end after the iteration where the shift has occurred.

analysis of unordered list implementations

The difference in space complexity between the linked and array implementations of an unordered list is much the same as what we have seen with stacks and queues. The linked implementation requires more space per object to be inserted in the list simply because of the space allocated for the next reference. However, the array implementation must allocate an initial array of references to store the objects in the list, and whatever space is not used within the array is wasted.

The analysis of the time complexity of the operations for the various implementations of a list is quite simple. We will address each operation for each of the three implementations.

The `addtoFront` operation for the linked implementation consists of the following steps:

- Create a new node with the `element` reference pointing to the object to be added to the list and with the `next` reference set to null.
- If the list is empty, set the `tail` reference to point to the new object.
- Set the `next` reference of the new object equal to the current head of the list.
- Set the `head` reference to point to the new object.
- Increment the `count` of elements in the list.

All of these steps are O(1), thus the `addtoFront` operation for the linked implementation is O(1).

The `addtoFront` operation for the array implementation consists of the following steps:

- Check to make sure that the array is not full (if it is, throw an exception).
- Set the reference in position [(head–1 + length) % length] of the array to point to the object being added to the list.
- Set head to (head–1 + length) % length.
- Increment the `count`.

All of these steps are O(1), thus the `addtoFront` operation for the array implementation is O(1). There is no substantial difference in time complexity for the `addtoFront` operations.

The `addtoRear` operation for the linked implementation consists of the following steps:

- Create a new node with the `element` reference pointing to the object to be added to the list and with the `next` reference set to null.
- If the list is empty, set the `head` and `tail` references to point to the new object.
- Set the `next` reference of the node at the tail of the list to point to the new object.

▸ Set the `tail` reference equal to the new object.

▸ Increment the number of objects in the list.

All of these steps are O(1), thus the `addtoRear` operation for the linked implementation is O(1).

The `addtoRear` operation for the array implementation consists of the following steps:

▸ Check to make sure that the array is not full (if it is, throw an exception).

▸ Set the reference in position `tail` of the array to point to the object being added to the list.

▸ Set `tail` to `(tail+1) % length` where `length` is the fixed length of the array.

▸ Increment the `count`.

All of these steps are O(1), thus the `addtoRear` operation for the array implementation is O(1). There is no substantial difference in the time complexity of the `addtoRear` operations.

The `insertAfter` operation for the linked implementation consists of the following steps:

▸ Set a boolean flag `found` to false.

▸ Set a temporary reference `current` to point to the head of the list.

▸ If the current node equals the target element, then set `found` to true, else set `current` to `current.next`.

▸ If the target element was not found, throw an exception.

▸ Create a new node storing the element to be inserted.

▸ Set the `next` reference of the new node to point to the same object pointed to by the `next` reference of the current node.

▸ Set the `next` reference of the current node to point to the new object.

▸ If the current object is also the tail, set the `tail` reference to point to the new object.

▸ Increment the number of objects in the list.

All of these steps are O(1) except for the search for the target element, which is O(n). As with any simple linear search, the best case is that the target element is the first element of the list, the worst case is that the target element is the last element, and the expected case is that the target element is in the middle of the list.

The insertAfter operation for the array implementation consists of the following steps:

- If the list is full, throw an exception.
- Set a temporary index value to the head of the list.
- Set a boolean flag found to false.
- Set a boolean flag firstelement to true.
- Set firstelement to false.
- If the current element is the target element, set found to true.
- If the target element was not found, throw an exception.
- Shift all of the reference values in the list from the current (index + 1) to the tail of the list up one position.
- Set the next reference in the (index) position in the array to point to the object to be inserted.
- Set the tail equal to (tail+1)%length.
- Increment the count of objects in the list.

The insertAfter operation for the array implementation requires two O(n) steps, the while loop to find the target element, and the process of shifting all of the elements above the target one position to the right. The best case in terms of the search component is that the target element is found at the head of the list. However, the best case for the shift component is that the target element is found at the tail of the list. The expected case in both cases is n/2, which is O(n). In fact, the combination of the two always results in n total steps between comparisons and shifts, because no matter where we find our target location in the array, we have to shift all of the elements we did not compare. The insertAfter operation is O(n) for both implementations. The array implementation requires two O(n) operations, the search and the shift, as opposed to only one O(n) operation, the search, in the linked implementation.

The removeElement operation for the linked implementation consists of the following steps:

- If the list is empty, throw an exception.
- Initialize found to false, previous to null, and current to the head of the list.

▸ If the current node equals the target element, then set `found` to true, else set `previous` equal to `current` and then set `current` equal to `current.next`.

▸ If the target element was not found, throw an exception.

▸ If there is only one element in the list, set `head` and `tail` to null.

▸ If the target element is at the head of the list, set `head` equal to `head.next`.

▸ If the target element `if` at the tail of the list, set `tail` equal to `previous` and set `tail.next` to null.

▸ Set `previous.next` equal to `current.next`.

▸ Decrement the number of objects in the list.

▸ Return `current.element`.

All of these steps are O(1) except for the search, which is O(n). Thus the `removeElement` operation for the linked implementation is O(n).

The `removeElement` operation for the array implementation consists of the following steps:

▸ If the list is empty, throw an exception.

▸ Set a temporary index value to the head of the list.

▸ Set a boolean flag `found` to false.

▸ Set a boolean flag `firstelement` to true.

▸ Set `firstelement` to false.

▸ If the current element is the target element, set `found` to true.

▸ Increment the index.

▸ If the target element was not found, throw an exception.

▸ Set a temporary object reference equal to the `element` reference of the position `index` of the array.

▸ Shift all of the reference values in the list from the current (`index + 1`) to the tail of the list down one position.

▸ Set the `tail` index equal to `(tail-1+length) % length`.

▸ Decrement the count of objects in the list.

▸ Return the temporary object.

Like the analysis of the `insertAfter` operation for the array implementation, the `removeElement` operation consists of two O(n) steps, the search and the shift, and thus the operation is O(n).

The firstelement and lastelement operations for both implementations are O(1). The removeFirst operation is O(1) for both implementations. The removeLast operation is O(1) for the array implementation, but O(n) for the linked implementation. This is due to the fact that the entire list must be traversed to reach the element before the last element. The isEmpty and size operations are both O(1) for both implementations. The contains and find operations are simple linear searches in both implementations and thus are O(n).

analysis of indexed list implementations

The difference in space complexity between the linked and array implementations of an indexed list is much the same as what we have seen with prior data structures. The linked implementation requires more space per object to be inserted in the list simply because of the space allocated for the references. Keep in mind that the LinkedList class is actually a doubly linked list, thus requiring twice the number of references. The ArrayList class is more efficient at managing space than the array-based implementations we have discussed previously. This is due to the fact that an ArrayList is resizable, and thus can dynamically allocate space as needed. Therefore, there need not be a large amount of wasted space allocated all at once. Rather, the list can grow as needed.

The analysis of the time complexity for the operations for the ArrayList and LinkedList implementations generally falls into one of three categories: access to objects, insertion of objects, and removal of objects.

The concept of access to objects includes operations such as contains, get, and indexof. In the case of an ArrayList, if the index of the object to be accessed is already known, then the access to the object is O(1) since any object in the list can be accessed by index value in equal time. If the index of the object is not already known, then the access to the object is O(n), where n is the number of objects in the list, since the list will have to be traversed comparing for the object (best case is one comparison, worst case is n comparisons, expected case is n/2 comparisons).

Access to objects in a LinkedList tends to be more costly. Regardless of whether or not the index of the object to be accessed is already known, access to the object is O(n). If we know the index, the operations will still have to start at one end or the other, whichever is closer, and traverse their way to the particular index location (best case is no traversal if the index we are looking for is one of our endpoints, worst case is n/2 traversals if the index we are looking for is in the middle of the list, expected case is n/4 traversals). Traversing the list looking for a particular object is O(n) with the same best, worst, and expected cases as the `ArrayList` implementation.

Insertion of objects into an `ArrayList` is done either at the end of the list, which is an O(1) operation, or into a particular index value in the list, which is an O(n) operation. This due to the fact that an insertion into a particular index location requires all of the positions above that in the array to be shifted one position. The best case for this type of insert is one shift if we are inserting into the last index in the array, the worst case is n shifts if we are inserting into the first index in the array, and the expected case is n/2 shifts. One complicating factor for insertion into an `ArrayList` is capacity. The insertion may cause the `ArrayList` to have to be resized. While certainly this could have an effect on the completion time of a particular `insert` operation, it does not affect the analysis of the time complexity. Averaged across all insertions, this time to resize is negligible.

Insertion of an object into a `LinkedList` also falls into one of two categories: insertion at either end of the list, which, because of the doubly linked list, is O(1) in both cases, or insertion into a particular index position within the list, which, like the analysis of the `ArrayList` implementation, is O(n), but for a very different reason. In the `LinkedList` implementation, we do not require all of the elements above the insertion point to be shifted; however, we also do not have direct access to the particular index position in the list without traversing the list from one end or the other. Thus, the best case is no traversal if the insertion point is one of the end points, the worst case is n/2 traversals if the insertion point is in the middle of the list, and the expected case is n/4 traversals.

The analysis of the deletion of objects from the list is similar to that of insertions. For an `ArrayList`, the best case is that we are removing the element at the end of the list and are not required to shift any elements in the list. The worst case is that we are removing the element at the beginning of the list and must shift all of the remaining n–1 elements in the list. The expected case is n/2 shifts. Thus, deletion from an `ArrayList` is an O(n) operation.

Deletion from a `LinkedList` is similar. The best case is that we are deleting one of the two ends of the list and thus do not have to traverse the list at all. The worst case is that we are deleting an element in the middle of the list and must traverse n/2 elements to reach the middle. The expected case is n/4 traversals. Thus, deletion from a `LinkedList` is an O(n) operation. Of course, the `removeFirst` and `removeLast` operations are O(1) since they are always dealing with the ends of the list and require no traversals.

summary of
key concepts

- List collections can be categorized as ordered, unordered, and indexed.
- The elements of an ordered list have an inherent relationship defining their order.
- The elements of an unordered list are kept in whatever order the client chooses.
- An indexed list maintains a contiguous numeric index range for its elements.
- Many common operations can be defined for all list types. The differences between them stem from how elements are added.
- Interfaces can be used to derive other interfaces. The child interface contains all abstract methods of the parent.
- An ordered list is a convenient collection to use when creating a tournament schedule.
- The Josephus problem is a classic computing problem that is appropriately solved with indexed lists.
- Only `Comparable` objects can be stored in an ordered list.
- The Java Collections API contains two implementations of an indexed list.

self-review questions

8.1 What is the difference between an indexed list, an ordered list, and an unordered list?

8.2 What are the basic methods of accessing an indexed list?

8.3 What are the additional operations required of implementations that are part of the Java Collections framework?

8.4 What are the trade-offs in space complexity between an `ArrayList` and a `LinkedList`?

8.5 What are the trade-offs in time complexity between an `ArrayList` and a `LinkedList`?

8.6 What is the time complexity of the `contains` operation and the `find` operation for both implementations?

8.7   What effect would it have if the `LinkedList` implementation were to use a singly linked list instead of a doubly linked list?

8.8   Why is the time to increase the capacity of the array on an `add` operation considered negligible for the `ArrayList` implementation?

exercises

8.1   Hand trace an ordered list X through the following operations:

```
X.add(new Integer(4));

X.add(new Integer(7));

Object Y = X.first();

X.add(new Integer(3));

X.add(new Integer(2));

X.add(new Integer(5));

Object Y = X.removeLast();

Object Y = X.remove(new Integer(7));

X.add(new Integer(9));
```

8.2   Given the resulting list X from Exercise 8.1, what would be the result of each of the following?

   a. `X.last();`

   b. `z = X.contains(new Integer(3));`

       `X.first();`

   c. `Y = X.remove(new Integer(2));`

       `X.first();`

8.3   What would be the time complexity of the `size` operation for each of the implementations if there were not a `count` variable?

8.4   In the array implementation, under what circumstances could the `head` and `tail` references be equal?

8.5   In the linked implementation, under what circumstances could the `head` and `tail` references be equal?

8.6   If there were not a count variable in the array implementation, how could you determine whether or not the list was empty?

8.7   If there were not a count variable in the array implementation, how could you determine whether or not the list was full?

programming projects

8.1   Implement a stack using a LinkedList.

8.2   Implement a stack using an ArrayList.

8.3   Implement a queue using a LinkedList.

8.4   Implement a queue using an ArrayList.

8.5   Implement the Josephus problem using a queue and compare the performance of that algorithm to the ArrayList implementation from this chapter.

8.6   Implement an OrderedList using a LinkedList.

8.7   Implement an OrderedList using an ArrayList.

8.8   Complete the implementation of the ArrayList class.

8.9   Complete the implementation of the ArrayOrderedList class.

8.10 Complete the implementation of the ArrayUnorderedList class.

8.11 Write an implementation of the LinkedList class.

8.12 Write an implementation of the LinkedOrderedList class.

8.13 Write an implementation of the LinkedUnorderedList class.

8.14 Create an implementation of a doubly linked DoubleOrderedList class. You will need to create a DoubleNode class, a DoubleList class, and a DoubleIterator class.

8.15 Create a graphical application that provides a button for add and remove from an ordered list, a text field to accept a string as input for add, and a text area to display the contents of the list after each operation.

8.16 Create a graphical application that provides a button for addToFront, addToRear, addAfter, and remove from an unordered list. Your application must provide a text field to accept a string as input for any of the add operations. The user should be able to select the element to be added after, and select the element to be removed.

answers to self-review questions

8.1 An indexed list is a collection of objects with no inherent order that are ordered by index value. An ordered list is a collection of objects ordered by value. An unordered list is a collection of objects with no inherent order.

8.2 Access to the list is accomplished one of three ways: by accessing a particular index position in the list, by accessing the ends of the list, or by accessing an object in the list by value.

8.3 All Java Collections framework classes implement the Collections interface, the Serializable interface, and the Cloneable interface.

8.4 The linked implementation requires more space per object to be inserted in the list simply because of the space allocated for the references. Keep in mind that the LinkedList class is actually a doubly linked list, thus requiring twice as much space for references. The ArrayList class is more efficient at managing space than the array-based implementations we have discussed previously. This is due to the fact that ArrayList collections are resizable, and thus can dynamically allocate space as needed. Therefore, there need not be a large amount of wasted space allocated all at once. Rather, the list can grow as needed.

8.5 The major difference between the two is access to a particular index position of the list. The ArrayList implementation can access any element of the list in equal time if the index value is known. The LinkedList implementation requires the list to be traversed from one end or the other to reach a particular index position.

8.6 The contains and find operations for both implementations will be O(n) because they are simply linear searches.

8.7 This would change the time complexity for the addLast and removeLast operations because they would now require traversal of the list.

8.8 Averaged over the total number of insertions into the list, the time to enlarge the array has little effect on the total time.

This chapter begins our exploration of
nonlinear collections and data structures.
We discuss the use and implementation of
trees, define the terms associated
with trees, analyze possible tree
implementations, and look at
examples of implementing and
using trees.

9.1 trees

The collections we've examined earlier in the book (stacks, queues, and lists) are all linear data structures, meaning their elements are arranged in order one after another. A *tree* is a nonlinear structure in which elements are organized into a hierarchy. This section describes trees in general and establishes some important terminology.

A tree is composed of a set of *nodes* in which elements are stored, and *edges* that connect one node to another. Each node is at a particular *level* in the tree hierarchy. The *root* of the tree is the only node at the top level of the tree. There is only one root node in a tree. Figure 9.1 shows a tree that helps to illustrate these terms.

The nodes at lower levels of the tree are the *children* of nodes at the previous level. In Figure 9.1, the nodes labeled B, C, D, and E are the children of A. Nodes F and G are the children of B. A node can only have one parent, but a node may have multiple children. Nodes that have the same parent are called *siblings*. Thus, Nodes H, I, and J are siblings because they are all children of D.

The root node is the only node in a tree that does not have a parent. A node that does not have any children is called a *leaf*. A node that is not the root and has at least one child is called an *internal node*. Note that the tree analogy is upside-down. Our trees "grow" from the root at the top of the tree to the leaves toward the bottom of the tree.

The root is the entry point into a tree structure. We can follow a *path* through the tree from parent to child. For example, the path from node A to N in Figure

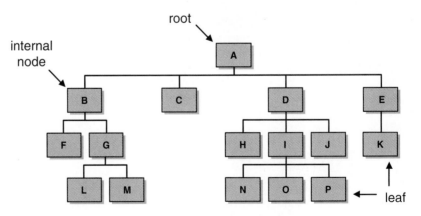

figure 9.1   Tree terminology

9.1 is A, D, I, N. A node is the *ancestor* of another node if it is above it on the path from the root. Thus the root is the ultimate ancestor of all nodes in a tree. Nodes that can be reached by following a path from a particular node are the *descendants* of that node.

> Trees are described by a large set of related terms.

The level of a node is also the length of the path from the root to the node. This *path length* is determined by counting the number of edges that must be followed to get from the root to the node. The root is considered to be level 0, the children of the root are at level 1, the grandchildren of the root are at level 2, and so on. Path length and level are depicted in Figure 9.2.

The *height* of a tree is the length of the longest path from the root to a leaf. Thus the height or order of the tree in Figure 9.2 is 3, because the path length from the root to leaf F is 3. The path length from the root to leaf C is 1.

tree classifications

Trees can be classified in many ways. The most important criterion is the maximum number of children any node in the tree may have. This value is sometimes referred to as the *order* of the tree. A tree that has no limit to the number of children a node may have is called a *general tree*. A tree that limits each node to no more than n children is referred to as an *n-ary tree*.

One n-ary tree is of particular importance. A tree in which nodes may have at most two children is called a *binary tree*. This type of tree is helpful in many situations. Much of our exploration of trees will focus on binary trees.

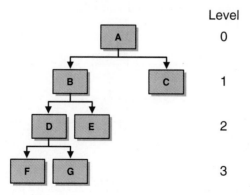

figure 9.2   Path length and level

Another way to classify a tree is whether it is balanced or not. A tree is considered to be *balanced* if all of the leaves of the tree are on the same level or at least within one level of each other. Thus the tree shown on the left in Figure 9.3 is balanced, while the one on the right is not.

The concept of a *complete* tree is related to the balance of a tree. A tree is considered *complete* if it is balanced and all of the leaves at the bottom level are on the left side of the tree. While a seemingly arbitrary concept, this definition has implications for how the tree is stored in certain implementations.

Another related concept is the notion of a *full* tree. An N-ary tree is considered full if all of the leaves of the tree are at the same level and every node is either a leaf or has exactly N children. The balanced tree from Figure 9.3 would not be considered complete while all of the 3-ary (or tertiary) trees shown in Figure 9.4 are complete. Only the third tree in Figure 9.4 is full.

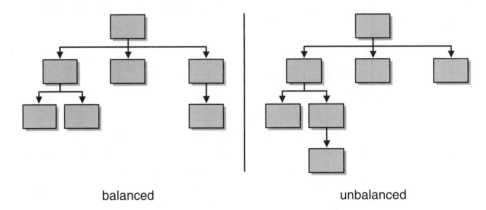

balanced   unbalanced

figure 9.3   Balanced and unbalanced trees

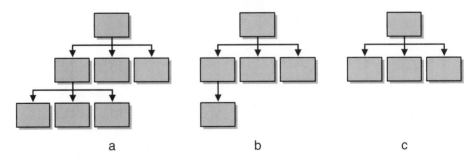

a   b   c

figure 9.4   Some complete trees

9.2 strategies for implementing trees

Let's examine some general strategies for implementing trees. The most obvious implementation of a tree is a linked structure. Each node could be defined as a `TreeNode` class, as we did with the `LinearNode` class for linked lists. Each node would contain a pointer to the element to be stored in that node as well as pointers for each of the possible children of the node. Depending on the implementation, it may also be useful to store in each node a pointer to its parent.

Because a tree is a nonlinear structure, it may not seem reasonable to attempt to implement it using an underlying linear structure such as an array. However, sometimes that approach is useful. The strategies for array implementations of a tree may be less obvious. There are two principle approaches: a computational strategy and a simulated link strategy.

computational strategy for array implementation of trees

For certain types of trees, specifically binary trees, a computational strategy can be used for storing a tree using an array. One possible strategy is as follows: for any element stored in position n of the array, that element's left child will be stored in position $(2 * n + 1)$ and that element's right child will be stored in position $(2 * (n + 1))$. This strategy is very effective and can be managed in terms of capacity in much the same way that we managed capacity for the array implementations of lists, queues, and stacks. However, despite the conceptual elegance of this solution, it is not without drawbacks. For example, if the tree that we are storing is not complete or relatively complete, we may be wasting large amounts of memory allocated in the array for positions of the tree that do not contain data. This strategy is illustrated in Figure 9.5.

> **key concept**
>
> One possible computational strategy places the left child of element n at position $(2*n+1)$ and the right child at position $(2*(n+1))$.

simulated link strategy for array implementation of trees

A second possible array implementation of trees is modeled after the way operating systems manage memory. Instead of assigning elements of the tree to array positions by location in the tree, array positions are allocated contiguously on a first-come first-served basis. Each element of the array will be a node class similar to the `TreeNode` class that we discussed earlier. However, instead of storing

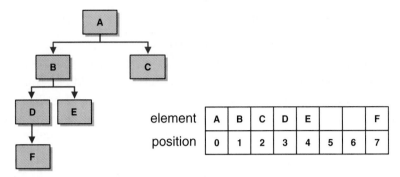

figure 9.5 Computational strategy for array implementation of trees

object reference variables as pointers to its children (and perhaps its parent), each node would store the array index of each child (and perhaps its parent). This approach allows elements to be stored contiguously in the array so that space is not wasted. However, this approach increases the overhead for deleting elements in the tree, since either remaining elements will have to be shifted to maintain contiguity or a freelist will have to be maintained. This strategy is illustrated in Figure 9.6. The order of the elements in the array is determined simply by their entry order into the tree. In this case, the entry order is assumed to have been A, C, B, E, D, F.

> **key concept**
>
> The simulated link strategy allows array positions to be allocated contiguously regardless of the completeness of the tree.

This same strategy may also be used when tree structures need to be stored directly on disk using a direct I/O approach. In this case, rather than using an array index as a pointer, each node will store the relative position in the file of its children so that an offset can be calculated given the base address of the file.

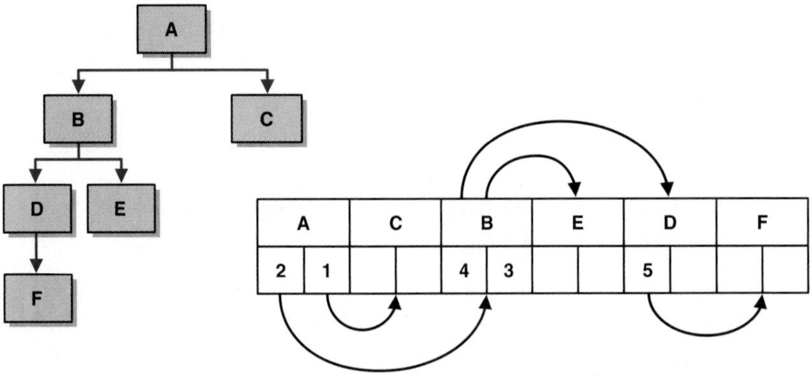

figure 9.6 Simulated link strategy for array implementation of trees

analysis of trees

As we discussed earlier, trees are a useful and efficient way to implement other collections. Let's take an ordered list for example. In our analysis of list implementations in Chapter 8, we described the find operation as expected case n/2 or O(n). However, if we implemented an ordered list using a balanced *binary search tree*—a binary tree with the added property that the left child is always less than the parent, which is always less than or equal to the right child—then we could improve the efficiency of the find operation to O(log n). We will discuss binary search trees in much greater detail in Chapter 10.

This order of complexity is due to the fact that the height or order of such a tree will always be $\log_2 n$, where n is the number of elements in the tree. This is very similar to our discussion of the binary search in Chapter 5. In fact, for any balanced n-ary tree with n elements, the tree's height will be $\log_n n$. With the added ordering property of a binary search tree, you are guaranteed to at worst search one path from the root to a leaf.

> **key concept**
>
> In general, a balanced n-ary tree with n elements will have height $\log_n n$.

9.3 tree traversals

Because a tree is a nonlinear structure, the concept of traversing a tree is generally more interesting than the concept of traversing a linear structure. There are four basic methods for traversing a tree:

- Preorder traversal
- Inorder traversal
- Postorder traversal
- Level-order traversal

Preorder traversal is accomplished by visiting each node, followed by its children, starting with the root. Inorder traversal is accomplished by visiting the left child of the node, then the node, then any remaining nodes, starting with the root. Postorder traversal is accomplished by visiting the children, then the node, starting with the root. Level-order traversal is accomplished by visiting all of the nodes at each level, one level at a time, starting with the root. Each of these definitions applies to all trees. However, as an example, let us examine how each of these definitions would apply to a binary tree (i.e., a tree in which each node has at most two children).

> **key concept**
>
> There are four basic methods for traversing a tree.

preorder traversal

Given the tree shown in Figure 9.7, a preorder traversal would produce the sequence A, B, D, E, C. The definition stated previously says that preorder traversal is accomplished by visiting each node, followed by its children, starting with the root. So, starting with the root, we visit the root, giving us A. Next we traverse to the first child of the root, which is the node containing B. We then use the same algorithm by first visiting the current node, yielding B, and then visiting its children. Next we traverse to the first child of B, which is the node containing D. We then use the same algorithm again by first visiting the current node, yielding D, and then visiting its children. Only this time, there are no children. We then traverse to any other children of B. This yields E, and since E has no children, we then traverse to any other children of A. This brings us to the node containing C, where we again use the same algorithm, first visiting the node, yielding C, and then visiting any children. Since there are no children of C and no more children of A, the traversal is complete.

Stated in pseudocode for a binary tree, the algorithm for a preorder traversal is

```
Visit node

Traverse(left child)

Traverse(right child)
```

inorder traversal

Given the tree shown in Figure 9.7, an inorder traversal would produce the sequence D, B, E, A, C. The definition stated earlier says that inorder traversal is accomplished by visiting the left child of the node, then the node, then any

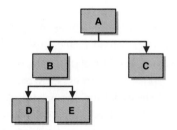

figure 9.7   A complete tree

remaining nodes, starting with the root. So, starting with the root, we traverse to the left child of the root, the node containing B. We then use the same algorithm again and traverse to the left child of B, the node containing D. Note that we have not yet visited any nodes. Using the same algorithm again, we attempt to traverse to the left child of D. Since there is not one, we then visit the current node, yielding D. Continuing the same algorithm, we attempt to traverse to any remaining children of D. Since there are not any, we then visit the previous node, yielding B. We then attempt to traverse to any remaining children of B. This brings us to the node containing E. Since E does not have a left child, we visit the node, yielding E. Since E has no right child, we then visit the previous node, yielding A. We then traverse to any remaining children of A, which takes us to the node containing C. Using the same algorithm, we then attempt to traverse to the left child of C. Since there is not one, we then visit the current node, yielding C. We then attempt to traverse to any remaining children of C. Since there are not any, we return to the previous node, which happens to be the root. Since there are no more children of the root, the traversal is complete.

Stated in pseudocode for a binary tree, the algorithm for an inorder traversal is

```
Traverse(left child)
Visit node
Traverse(right child)
```

postorder traversal

Given the tree shown in Figure 9.7, a postorder traversal would produce the sequence D, E, B, C, A. The definition stated earlier says that postorder traversal is accomplished by visiting the children, then the node, starting with the root. So, starting from the root, we traverse to the left child, the node containing B. Repeating that process, we traverse to the left child again, the node containing D. Since that node does not have any children, we then visit that node, yielding D. Returning to the previous node, we visit the right child, the node containing E. Since this node does not have any children, we visit the node, yielding E, and then return to the previous node and visit it, yielding B. Returning to the previous node, in this case the root, we find that it has a right child, so we traverse to the right child, the node containing C. Since this node does not have any children, we visit it, yielding C. Returning to the previous node (the root), it has no remaining children, so we visit it, yielding A, and the traversal is complete.

Stated in pseudocode for a binary tree, the algorithm for a postorder traversal is

```
Traverse(left child)
Traverse(right child)
Visit node
```

level-order traversal

Given the tree shown in Figure 9.7, a level-order traversal would produce the sequence A, B, C, D, E. The definition stated earlier says that a level-order traversal is accomplished by visiting all of the nodes at each level, one level at a time, starting with the root. Using this definition, we first visit the root, yielding A. Next we visit the left child of the root, yielding B, then the right child of the root, yielding C, and then the child of B, yielding D and E.

Stated in pseudocode for a binary tree, an algorithm for a level-order traversal is

```
Create two queues: nodes and result
Enqueue the root onto the nodes queue
While the nodes queue is not empty
{
  Dequeue the first element from the queue
  If that element is not null
      Enqueue that element on the result queue
      Enqueue the children of the element on the nodes queue
  Else
      Enqueue null on the result queue
}
Return an iterator for the result queue
```

This algorithm for a level-order traversal is only one of many possible solutions. However, it does have some interesting properties. First, note that we are using a collection, namely a queue, to solve a problem within another collection, namely a binary tree. Second, recall that in our earlier discussions of iterators, we talked about their behavior with respect to the collection if the collection is modified while the iterator is in use. In this case, using a queue to store the elements in the proper order and then returning an iterator over the queue, this iterator behaves like a snap-shot of the binary tree and is not affected by any concurrent modifications. This can be both a positive and negative attribute depending upon how the iterator is used.

9.4 implementing binary trees

As an example of possible implementations of trees, let us take a look at a simple binary tree implementation. In Section 9.6, we will illustrate an example using this implementation. As we discussed earlier in this chapter, it is difficult to abstract an interface for all trees. However, once we have narrowed our focus to binary trees, the task becomes more reasonable. One possible set of operations for a binary tree ADT is listed in Figure 9.8. Keep in mind that the definition of a data structure is not universal. You will find variations in the operations defined for specific data structures from one book to another. We've been very careful in this book to define the operations on each data structure so that they are consistent with its purpose.

Operation	Description
removeLeftSubtree	Removes the left subtree of the root.
removeRightSubtree	Removes the right subtree of the root.
removeAllElements	Removes all of the elements from the tree.
isEmpty	Determines if the tree is empty.
size	Determines the number of elements in the tree.
contains	Determines if the specified target is in the tree.
find	Returns a reference to the specified target if it is found.
tostring	Returns a string representation of the tree.
iteratorInOrder	Returns an iterator for an inorder traversal of the tree.
iteratorPreOrder	Returns an iterator for a preorder traversal of the tree.
iteratorPostOrder	Returns an iterator for a postorder traversal of the tree.
iteratorLevelOrder	Returns an iterator for a level-order traversal of the tree.

figure 9.8   The operations on a binary tree

Notice that in all of the operations listed, there are no operations to add elements to the tree. This is due to the fact that until we specify the purpose of the binary tree, there is no way to know how to add an element to the tree other than through a constructor.

It is also interesting to note that, unlike our earlier examples, there is no removeElement method in our BinaryTreeADT. As with adding an element, we do not yet have enough information to know how to remove an element. When we were dealing with bags in Chapters 2 and 3, we could think about the concept of removing an element from a bag and it was easy to conceptualize the state of the bag after the removal of the element. The same can be said of stacks and queues since we could only remove an element from one end of the linear structures. Even with lists, where we could remove an element from the middle of the linear structure, it was easy to conceptualize the state of the resulting list. With a tree, however, upon removing an element, we have many issues to handle that will affect the state of the tree. What happens to the children and other descendants of the element that is removed? Where does the child pointer of the element's parent now point? What if the element we are removing is the root? As we will see in our example using expression trees later in this chapter, there will be applications of trees where there is no concept of the removal of an element from the tree. Once we have specified more detail about the use of the tree, we may then decide that a removeElement method is appropriate. An excellent example of this is binary search trees, as we will see in Chapter 10.

Listing 9.1 shows the BinaryTreeADT interface. Figure 9.9 shows the UML description for the BinaryTreeADT interface.

We will examine how some of these methods might be implemented, while others will be left as exercises. The BinaryTree class implementing the BinaryTreeADT interface will need to keep track of the node that is at the root of the tree and the number of elements on the tree. The BinaryTree instance data could be declared as

```
private int count;
protected BinaryTreeNode root;
```

listing
9.1

```
//**********************************************************************
//  BinaryTreeADT.java        Authors:  Lewis/Chase
//
//  Defines the interface to a binary tree data structure.
//**********************************************************************

package jss2;

import java.util.Iterator;

public interface BinaryTreeADT
{
    public void removeLeftSubtree();
    public void removeRightSubtree();
    public void removeAllElements();
    public boolean isEmpty();
    public int size();
    public boolean contains (Object targetElement);
    public Object find (Object targetElement);
    public String toString();
    public Iterator iteratorInOrder();
    public Iterator iteratorPreOrder();
    public Iterator iteratorPostOrder();
    public Iterator iteratorLevelOrder();
}
```

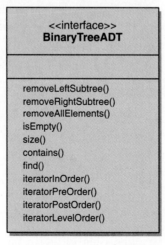

figure 9.9   UML description of the BinaryTreeADT interface

The constructors for the `BinaryTree` class should handle three cases: we want to create a binary tree with nothing in it, we want to create a binary tree with a single element but no children, and we want to create a binary tree with an element and two subtrees. With these goals in mind, the `BinaryTree` class might have the following constructors. Note that each of constructors must account for both the `root` and `count` attributes, and that the last constructor must account for the possibility that either or both of the subtrees might be null.

```
//------------------------------------------------------------------
//  Creates an empty binary tree.
//------------------------------------------------------------------
public BinaryTree()
{
    count = 0;
    root = null;
}


//------------------------------------------------------------------
//  Creates a binary tree with the specified element as its root.
//------------------------------------------------------------------
public BinaryTree (Object element)
{
    count = 1;
    root = new BinaryTreeNode (element);
}


//------------------------------------------------------------------
//  Constructs a binary tree from the two specified binary trees.
//------------------------------------------------------------------
public BinaryTree (Object element, BinaryTree leftSubtree,
                                   BinaryTree rightSubtree)
{
    root = new BinaryTreeNode (element);
    count = 1;
```

```
        if (leftSubtree != null)
        {
            count = count + leftSubtree.size();
            root.left = leftSubtree.root;
        }
        else
            root.left = null;

        if (rightSubtree !=null)
        {
            count = count + rightSubtree.size();
            root.right = rightSubtree.root;
        }
        else
            root.right = null;
    }
```

Note that both the instance data and the constructors make use of an additional class called `BinaryTreeNode`. As discussed earlier, this class keeps track of the element stored at each location as well as pointers to the left and right subtree or children of each node. In this particular implementation, we chose not to include a pointer back to the parent of each node. Listing 9.2 shows the `BinaryTreeNode` class. The `BinaryTreeNode` class also includes a recursive method to return the number of children of the given node.

There are a variety of other possibilities for implementation of a tree node or binary tree node class. For example, methods could be included to test whether the node is a leaf (i.e., does not have any children), to test whether the node is an internal node (i.e., has at least one child), to test the depth of the node from the root, or to calculate the height of the left and right subtrees.

Another alternative would be to use polymorphism such that rather than testing a node to see if it has data, or has children, we would create various implementations, such as an `emptyTreeNode`, `innerTreeNode`, and `leafTreeNode`, that would distinguish the various possibilities.

**listing
  9.2**

```
//********************************************************************
//   BinaryTreeNode.java          Authors: Lewis/Chase
//
//   Represents a node in a binary tree with a left and right child.
//********************************************************************
package jss2;

class BinaryTreeNode
{
   protected Object element;
   protected BinaryTreeNode left, right;

   //-----------------------------------------------------------------
   //   Creates a new tree node with the specified data.
   //-----------------------------------------------------------------
   BinaryTreeNode (Object obj)
   {
      element = obj;
      left = null;
      right = null;
   }


   //-----------------------------------------------------------------
   //   Returns the number of non-null children of this node.
   //   This method may be able to be written more efficiently.
   //-----------------------------------------------------------------
   public int numChildren()
   {
      int children = 0;

      if (left != null)
         children = 1 + left.numChildren();

      if (right != null)
         children = children + 1 + right.numChildren();

      return children;
   }
}
```

the `removeLeftSubtree` method

To remove the left subtree of a binary tree, we must set the left child pointer of the root to null and subtract the total number of nodes in the left subtree from the count:

```
//----------------------------------------------------------------
//   Removes the left subtree of this binary tree.
//----------------------------------------------------------------
public void removeLeftSubtree()
{
   if (root.left != null)
      count = count - root.left.numChildren() - 1;
   root.left = null;
}
```

The other `remove` operations are very similar and are left as exercises. Since we are maintaining a `count` variable, the `isEmpty` and `size` operations are identical to the methods we developed in our earlier collections.

the `find` method

As with our earlier collections, our `find` method traverses the tree using the `equals` method of the class stored in the tree to determine equality. This puts the definition of equality under the control of the class being stored in the tree. The `find` method throws an exception if the target element is not found.

Many methods associated with trees may be written either recursively or iteratively. Often, when written recursively, these methods require the use of a private support method since the signature and/or the behavior of the first call and each successive call may not be the same. The `find` method in our simple implementation is an excellent example of this strategy.

We have chosen to use a recursive `findAgain` method. We know that the first call to `find` will start at the root of the tree, and if that instance of the `find` method completes without finding the target, we need to throw an exception. The private `findAgain` method allows us to distinguish between this first instance of the `find` method and each successive call.

```
//------------------------------------------------------------------
//  Returns a reference to the specified target element if it is
//  found in the binary tree.  Throws a NoSuchElementException if
//  the specified target element is not found in the binary tree.
//------------------------------------------------------------------
public Object find (Object targetElement) throws
                    ElementNotFoundException
{

   BinaryTreeNode current = root;
   BinaryTreeNode temp = current;

   if (!(current.element.equals(targetElement)) &&
        (current.left != null))
   current = findAgain( targetElement, current.left);

   if (!(current.equals(targetElement)))
      current = temp;

   if (!(current.element.equals(targetElement)) &&
        (current.right != null))
      current = findAgain(targetElement, current.right);

   if (!(current.element.equals(targetElement)))
      throw new ElementNotFoundException ("binarytree");

   return current.element;
}

//------------------------------------------------------------------
//  Returns a reference to the specified target element if it is
//  found in the binary tree.
//------------------------------------------------------------------
private BinaryTreeNode findAgain (Object targetElement,
                                  BinaryTreeNode next)
{
   BinaryTreeNode current = next;
   if (!(next.element.equals(targetElement)) && (next.left !=null))
      next = findAgain (targetElement, next.left);
```

```
      if (!(next.equals(targetElement)))
         next = current;

      if (!(next.element.equals(targetElement)) &&
            (next.right != null))
      next = findAgain (targetElement, next.right);

      return next;
   }
```

The contains method, as we did in earlier examples, can make use of the find method and is left as an exercise.

the iteratorInOrder method

Another interesting operation is the iteratorInOrder method. The task is to create an iterator object that will allow a user class to step through the elements of the tree in an inorder traversal. The solution to this problem provides another example of using one collection to build another. We simply traverse the tree using a definition of "visit" from earlier pseudocode that enqueues the contents of the node onto a queue. We then return the queue iterator as the result of the iterator method for our tree. This approach is possible because of the linear nature of a queue and the way that we implemented the iterator method for a queue and the LinkedIterator class. The iterator method for a queue returns a LinkedIterator that starts with the element at the front of the queue and steps through the queue linearly. It is important to understand that this behavior is not a requirement for an iterator associated with a queue. It is simply an artifact of the way that we chose to implement the iterator method for a queue and the LinkedIterator class.

Like the find operation, we use a private helper method in our recursion.

```
//------------------------------------------------------------------
//  Performs an inorder traversal on the binary tree by calling a
//  recursive inorder method that starts with the root.
//------------------------------------------------------------------
public Iterator iteratorInOrder()
{
   LinkedQueue queue = new LinkedQueue();
   inorder (root, queue);
   return queue.iterator();
}


//------------------------------------------------------------------
//  Performs a recursive inorder traversal.
//------------------------------------------------------------------
protected void inorder (BinaryTreeNode node, LinkedQueue queue)
{
   if (node != null)
   {
      inorder (node.left, queue);
      queue.enqueue(node.element);
      inorder (node.right, queue);
   }
}
```

The other iterator operations are similar and are left as exercises.

9.5   using binary trees: expression trees

In Chapter 6, we used a stack algorithm to evaluate postfix expressions. In this section, we modify that algorithm to construct an expression tree using an expression tree class that extends our definition of a binary tree. Figure 9.10 illustrates the concept of an expression tree. Notice that the root and all of the internal nodes of an expression tree contain operations and that all of the leaves contain

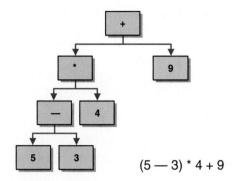

figure 9.10   An example expression tree

operands. An expression tree is evaluated from the bottom up. In this case, the (5–3) term is evaluated first, yielding 2. That result is then multiplied by 4, yielding 8. Finally, the result of that term is added to 9, yielding 17.

Listing 9.3 illustrates our `ExpressionTree` class. This class extends the `BinaryTree` class, providing constructors that reference the constructors for the `BinaryTree` class and providing an `evaluate` method to recursively evaluate an expression tree once it has been constructed.

The `evaluateTree` method calls the recursive `evaluateNode` method. The `evaluateNode` method returns the value if the node contains a number, or it returns the result of the operation using the value of the left and right subtrees if the node contains an operation. The `ExpressionTree` class makes use of the `ExpressionTreeObj` class as the element to store at each node of the tree. The `ExpressionTreeObj` class allows us to keep track of whether the element is a number or an operator, and which operator or what value is stored there. The `ExpressionTreeObj` class is illustrated in Listing 9.4.

The `Postfix` and `PostfixEvaluator` classes are a modification of our solution from Chapter 6. This solution allows the user to enter a postfix expression from the keyboard. As each term is entered, if it is an operand, a new `ExpressionTreeObj` is created with the given value and then an `ExpressionTree` is constructed using that element as the root and with no children. The new `ExpressionTree` is then pushed onto a stack. If the term entered

listing
    9.3

```
//********************************************************************
//   ExpressionTree.java        Authors: Lewis/Chase
//
//   Represents an expression tree of operators and operands.
//********************************************************************

package jss2;

public class ExpressionTree extends BinaryTree
{
   //-----------------------------------------------------------------
   //   Creates an empty expression tree.
   //-----------------------------------------------------------------
   public ExpressionTree()
   {
      super();
   }


   //-----------------------------------------------------------------
   //   Constructs an expression tree from the two specified trees.
   //-----------------------------------------------------------------
   public ExpressionTree (Object element, ExpressionTree leftSubtree,
                          ExpressionTree rightSubtree)
   {
      super(element, leftSubtree, rightSubtree);
   }


   //-----------------------------------------------------------------
   //   Evaluates the expression tree using the recursive evaluateNode
   //   method.
   //-----------------------------------------------------------------
   public int evaluateTree()
   {
      return evaluateNode(root);
   }


   //-----------------------------------------------------------------
   //   Recursively evaluates each node of the tree.
   //-----------------------------------------------------------------
   public int evaluateNode (BinaryTreeNode root)
   {
      int result, operand1, operand2;
      ExpressionTreeObj temp;
```

listing
    9.3   continued

```java
      if (root == null)
         result = 0;
      else
      {
         temp = (ExpressionTreeObj)root.element;
         if (temp.isOperator())
         {
            operand1 = evaluateNode(root.left);
            operand2 = evaluateNode(root.right);
            result = computeTerm(temp.getOperator(), operand1, operand2);
         }
         else
            result = temp.getValue();
      }

      return result;
   }

   //-----------------------------------------------------------------
   //  Evaluates an operator and two operands.
   //-----------------------------------------------------------------
   private static int computeTerm (char operator, int operand1,
                                   int operand2)
   {
      int result = 0;

      if (operator == '+')
         result = operand1 + operand2;
      else if (operator == '-')
         result = operand1 - operand2;
      else if (operator == '*')
         result = operand1 * operand2;
      else
         result = operand1 / operand2;

      return result;
   }
}
```

listing
    9.4

```java
//****************************************************************
//  ExpressionTreeObj.java        Authors: Lewis/Chase
//
//  Represents an element in an expression tree.
//****************************************************************

package jss2;

public class ExpressionTreeObj
{
   private int termtype;
   private char operator;
   private int value;

   //----------------------------------------------------------------
   //  Creates a new expression tree object with the specified data.
   //----------------------------------------------------------------
   public ExpressionTreeObj (int type, char op, int val)
   {
      termtype = type;
      operator = op;
      value = val;
   }

   //----------------------------------------------------------------
   //  Returns true if this object is an operator and false
   //  otherwise.
   //----------------------------------------------------------------
   public boolean isOperator()
   {
      return (termtype == 1);
   }

   //----------------------------------------------------------------
   //  Returns the operator.
   //----------------------------------------------------------------
   public char getOperator()
   {
      return operator;
   }
```

listing 9.4   continued

```
//---------------------------------------------------------------
//  Returns the value.
//---------------------------------------------------------------
public int getValue()
{
    return value;
}
}
```

is an operator, the top two `ExpressionTrees` on the stack are popped off, a new `ExpressionTreeObj` is created with the given operator value, and a new `ExpressionTree` is created with this operator as the root and the two `ExpressionTrees` popped off of the stack as the left and right subtrees. Figure 9.11 illustrates this process for the expression tree from Figure 9.10. Note that the top of the expression tree stack is on the right.

The `Postfix` class is shown in Listing 9.5 and the `PostfixEvaluator` class is shown in Listing 9.6. The UML description of the `Postfix` class is shown in Figure 9.12.

Input in Postfix: 5 3 — 4 * 9 +

Token	Processing Steps	Expression Tree Stack (top at right)
5	push(new ExpressionTree(5, null, null)	5
3	push(new ExpressionTree(3, null, null)	5 3

figure 9.11   Building an expression tree from a postfix
expression, continued on next page

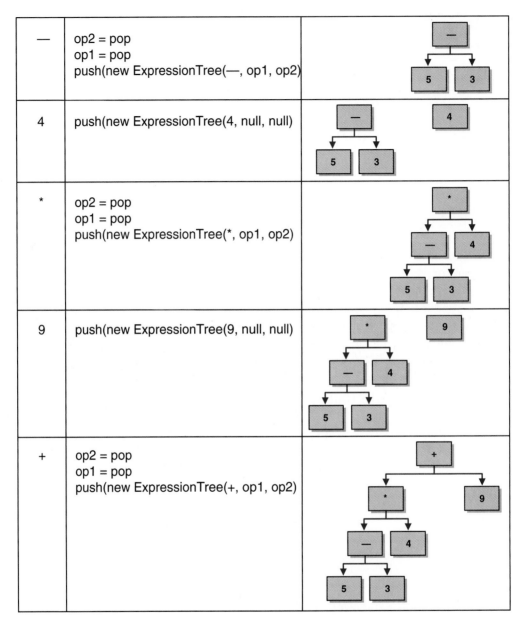

—	op2 = pop op1 = pop push(new ExpressionTree(—, op1, op2))	
4	push(new ExpressionTree(4, null, null))	
*	op2 = pop op1 = pop push(new ExpressionTree(*, op1, op2))	
9	push(new ExpressionTree(9, null, null))	
+	op2 = pop op1 = pop push(new ExpressionTree(+, op1, op2))	

figure 9.11   Building an expression tree from a postfix
expression (continued)

listing
   9.5

```
//*******************************************************************
//   Postfix.java        Authors: Lewis/Chase
//
//   Uses the PostfixEvaluator class to solve a postfix expression.
//*******************************************************************

public class Postfix
{
   public static void main (String[] args)
   {
      PostfixEvaluator temp = new PostfixEvaluator();
      temp.solve();
   }
}
```

output

```
Enter a valid postfix expression one token at a time.
Enter an integer, an operator (+,-,*,/) or ! to quit
3
4
+
5
/
4
5
-
*
!
The result is -1
```

```
listing
  9.6
```

```java
//***********************************************************************
//   PostfixEvaluator.java        Authors:  Lewis/Chase
//
//   This modification of the stack example uses a pair of stacks to
//   create an expression tree from a valid postfix expression and then
//   uses a recursive method from the ExpressionTree class to evaluate
//   the tree.
//***********************************************************************

import jss2.*;
import jss2.exceptions.*;
import java.util.StringTokenizer;
import java.util.Iterator;
import java.io.*;

public class PostfixEvaluator
{
   //-----------------------------------------------------------------
   //   Retrieves and returns the next operand from the tree stack.
   //-----------------------------------------------------------------
   private ExpressionTree getOperand(LinkedStack treeStack)
   {
      ExpressionTree temp;
      temp = (ExpressionTree)treeStack.pop();
      return temp;
   }

   //-----------------------------------------------------------------
   //   Retrieves the next token.
   //-----------------------------------------------------------------
   private String getNextToken()
   {
      String tempToken = "0", instring;
      StringTokenizer tokenizer;

      try
      {
         BufferedReader in = new
         BufferedReader(new InputStreamReader(System.in));
         instring = in.readLine();
         tokenizer = new StringTokenizer(instring);
         tempToken = (tokenizer.nextToken());
      }
```

listing
   9.6   continued

```java
    catch (Exception IOException)
    {
        System.out.println("An I/O exception has occurred");
    }

    return tempToken;
}

//------------------------------------------------------------------
//  Prompts the user for a valid postfix expression then
//  converts it to an expression tree using a two stack method
//  and then calls a recursive method to evaluate the expression.
//------------------------------------------------------------------
public void solve()
{
    ExpressionTree operand1, operand2;
    char operator;
    String tempToken;
    LinkedStack treeStack = new LinkedStack();

    System.out.println("Enter a valid postfix expression " +
                        "one token at a time.");
    System.out.println("Enter an integer, an operator (+,-,*,/) " +
                        "or ! to quit ");

    tempToken = getNextToken();
    operator = tempToken.charAt(0);

    while (!(operator == '!'))
    {
        if ((operator == '+') || (operator == '-') ||
            (operator == '*') || (operator == '/'))
        {
            operand1 = getOperand(treeStack);
            operand2 = getOperand(treeStack);
            treeStack.push (new ExpressionTree(new ExpressionTreeObj
                        (1, operator, 0), operand2, operand1));
        }
        else
            treeStack.push (new ExpressionTree(new ExpressionTreeObj
                (2, ' ', Integer.parseInt(tempToken)), null, null));
```

listing
9.6 continued

```
        tempToken = getNextToken();
        operator = tempToken.charAt(0);
    }

    System.out.print ("The result is ");
    System.out.println (((ExpressionTree) treeStack.peek()
                        ).evaluateTree());
  }
}
```

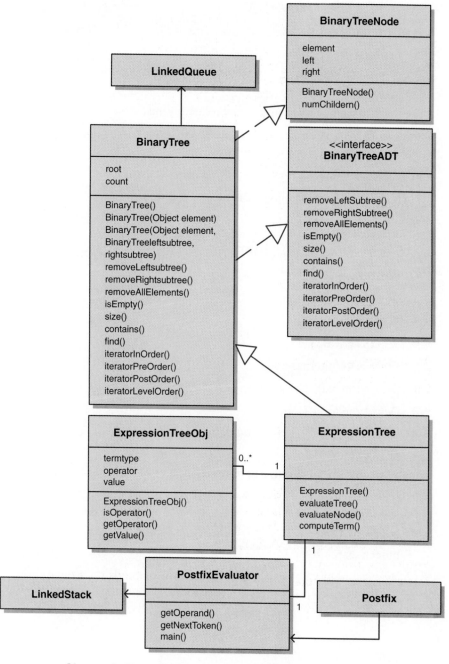

figure 9.12   UML description of the Postfix example

summary of
key concepts

▶ A tree is a nonlinear structure whose elements are organized into a hierarchy.

▶ Trees are described by a large set of related terms.

▶ The simulated link strategy allows array positions to be allocated contiguously regardless of the completeness of the tree.

▶ In general, a balanced n-ary tree with n elements will have height $\log_n n$.

▶ There are four basic methods for traversing a tree.

self-review questions

9.1   What is a tree?

9.2   What is a node?

9.3   What is the root of the tree?

9.4   What is a leaf?

9.5   What is an internal node?

9.6   Define the height of a tree.

9.7   Define the level of a node.

9.8   What are the advantages and disadvantages of the computational strategy?

9.9   What are the advantages and disadvantages of the simulated link strategy?

9.10 What attributes should be stored in the TreeNode class?

9.11 Which method of traversing a tree would result in a sorted list for a binary search tree?

9.12 We used a queue to implement the iterator methods for a binary tree. What must be true for this strategy to be successful?

exercises

9.1 Develop a pseudocode algorithm for a level-order traversal of a binary tree.

9.2 Draw either a matrilineage (following your mother's lineage) or a patri-lineage (following your father's lineage) for a couple of generations. Develop a pseudocode algorithm for inserting a person into their proper place in the tree.

9.3 Develop a pseudocode algorithm to build an expression tree from a prefix expression.

9.4 Develop a pseudocode algorithm to build an expression tree from an infix expression.

9.5 Calculate the time complexity of the `find` method.

9.6 Calculate the time complexity of the `iteratorinorder` method.

9.7 Develop a pseudocode algorithm for the `size` method assuming that there is not a `count` variable.

9.8 Develop a pseudocode algorithm for the `isEmpty` operation assuming that there is not a `count` variable.

9.9 Draw an expression tree for the expression (9 + 4) * 5 + (4 – (6 – 3)).

programming projects

9.1 Complete the implementation of the `removeRightSubtree` and `removeAllElements` operations of a binary tree.

9.2 Complete the implementation of the `size` and `isEmpty` operations of a binary tree assuming that there is not a `count` variable.

9.3 Create boolean methods for our `BinaryTreeNode` class to determine if the node is a leaf or an internal node.

9.4 Create a method called `depth` that will return an `int` representing the level or depth of the given node from the root.

9.5 Complete the implementation of the `contains` method for a binary tree.

9.6 Implement the `contains` method for a binary tree without using the `find` operation.

9.7 Complete the implementation of the iterator methods for a binary tree.

9.8   Implement the iterator methods for a binary tree without using a queue.

9.9   Modify the ExpressionTree class to create a method called draw that will graphically depict the expression tree.

9.10   We use postfix notation in the example in this chapter because it eliminates the need to parse an infix expression by precedence rules and parentheses. Some infix expressions do not need parentheses to modify precedence. Implement a method for the ExpressionTree class that will determine if an integer expression would require parentheses if it were written in infix notation.

9.11   Create an array-based implementation of a binary tree using the computational strategy.

9.12   Create an array-based implementation of a binary tree using the simulated link strategy.

answers to self-review questions

9.1   A tree is a nonlinear structure defined by the concept that each node in the tree, other than the first node or root node, has exactly one parent.

9.2   Node refers to a location in the tree where an element is stored.

9.3   Root refers to the node at the base of the tree or the one node in the tree that does not have a parent.

9.4   A leaf is a node that does not have any children.

9.5   An internal node is any non-root node that has at least one child.

9.6   The height of the tree is the length of the longest path from the root to a leaf.

9.7   The level of a node is measured by the number of links that must be followed to reach that node from the root.

9.8   The computational strategy does not have to store links from parent to child since that relationship is fixed by position. However, this strategy may lead to substantial wasted space for trees that are not balanced and/or not complete.

9.9   The simulated link strategy stores array index values as pointers between parent and child and allows the data to be stored contiguously no matter how balanced and/or complete the tree. However, this strategy increases the overhead in terms of maintaining a freelist or shifting elements in the array.

9.10 The `TreeNode` class must store a pointer to the element stored in that position as well as pointers to each of the children of that node. The class may also contain a pointer to the parent of the node.

9.11 In-order traversal of a binary search tree would result in a sorted list in ascending order.

9.12 For this strategy to be successful, the iterator for a queue must return the elements in the order in which they were enqueued. For this particular implementation of a queue, we know this is indeed the case.

In this chapter, we will explore the concept of binary search trees and options for their implementation. We will examine algorithms for adding and removing elements from binary search trees and for maintaining balanced binary search trees. We will discuss the analysis of these implementations and also explore various uses of binary search trees.

chapter
objectives

▶ Define a binary search tree abstract data structure

▶ Demonstrate how a binary search tree can be used to solve problems

▶ Examine various binary search tree implementations

▶ Compare binary search tree implementations

10.1 a binary search tree

> **key concept** A *binary search tree* is a binary tree with the added property that the left child is less than the parent, which is less than or equal to the right child.

A *binary search tree* is a binary tree with the added property that, for each node, the left child is less than the parent, which is less than or equal to the right child. As we discussed in Chapter 9, it is very difficult to abstract a set of operations for a tree without knowing what type of tree it is and its intended purpose. With the added ordering property that must be maintained, we can now extend our definition to include the operations on a binary search tree listed in Figure 10.1.

> **key concept** The definition of a binary search tree is an extension of the definition of a binary tree.

We must keep in mind that the definition of a binary search tree is an extension of the definition of a binary tree that we discussed in the last chapter. Thus these operations are in addition to the ones defined for a binary tree. We must also keep in mind that while at this point we are simply discussing binary search trees, as we will see shortly, the interface for a balanced binary search tree will be the same. Listing 10.1 and Figure 10.2 describe a `BinarySearchTreeADT`.

Operation	Description
`addElement`	Add an element to the tree.
`removeElement`	Remove an element from the tree.
`removeAllOccurrences`	Remove all occurrences of element from the tree.
`removeMin`	Remove the minimum element in the tree.
`removeMax`	Remove the maximum element in the tree.
`findMin`	Returns a reference to the minimum element in the tree.
`findMax`	Returns a reference to the maximum element in the tree.

figure 10.1 The operations on a binary search tree

listing
   10.1

```
//***********************************************************************
//   BinarySearchTree.java        Authors: Lewis/Chase
//
//   Defines the interface to a binary search tree.
//***********************************************************************
package jss2;
public interface BinarySearchTreeADT extends BinaryTreeADT
{
    public void addElement (Comparable element);
    public Comparable removeElement (Comparable targetElement);
    public void removeAllOccurrences (Comparable targetElement);
    public Comparable removeMin();
    public Comparable removeMax();
    public Comparable findMin();
    public Comparable findMax();
}
```

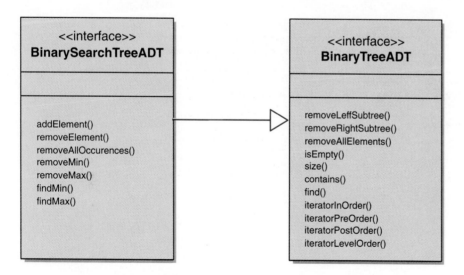

figure 10.2   UML description of the BinarySearchTreeADT

10.2 implementing binary search trees: with links

In Chapter 9, we introduced a simple implementation of a BinaryTree class using a BinaryTreeNode class to represent each node of the tree. Each BinaryTreeNode object maintains a reference to the element stored at that node as well as references to each of the node's children. We can simply extend that definition with a BinarySearchTree class implementing the BinarySearchTreeADT interface. Since we are extending the BinaryTree class from Chapter 9, all of the methods we discussed are still supported, including the various traversals.

Our BinarySearchTree class offers two constructors: one to create an empty BinarySearchTree and the other to create a BinarySearchTree with a particular element at the root. Both of these constructors simply refer to the equivalent constructors of the super class (i.e., the BinaryTree class).

```java
//-----------------------------------------------------------------
//  Creates an empty binary search tree.
//-----------------------------------------------------------------
public BinarySearchTree()
{
    super();
}


//-----------------------------------------------------------------
//  Creates a binary search with the specified element as its
//  root.
//-----------------------------------------------------------------
public BinarySearchTree (Comparable element)
{
    super (element);
}
```

the `addElement` operation

The `addElement` method adds a given `Comparable` element to an appropriate location in the tree, given its value. If the tree is empty, the new element becomes the root. If the tree is not empty, the new element is compared to the element at the root. If it is less than the element stored at the root and the left child of the root is null, then the new element becomes the left child of the root. If the new element is less than the element stored at the root and the left child of the root is not null, then we traverse to the left child of the root and compare again. If the new element is greater than or equal to the element stored at the root and the right child of the root is null, then the new element becomes the right child of the root. If the new element is greater than or equal to the element stored at the root and the right child of the root is not null, then we traverse to the right child of the root and compare again. Figure 10.3 illustrates this process of adding elements to a binary search tree.

```
//------------------------------------------------------------
//  Adds the specified object to the binary search tree in the
//  appropriate position according to its key value.  Note that
//  equal elements are added to the right.
//------------------------------------------------------------
public void addElement (Comparable element)
{
   BinaryTreeNode temp = new BinaryTreeNode (element);

   if (isEmpty())
      root = temp;
   else
   {
      BinaryTreeNode current = root;
      boolean added = false;

      while (!added)
      {
         if (element.compareTo(current.element) < 0)

            if (current.left == null)
            {
               current.left = temp;
               added = true;
            }
```

```
        else
            current = current.left;
        else
            if (current.right == null)
            {
                current.right = temp;
                added = true;
            }
            else
                current = current.right;
    }
}

    count++;
}
```

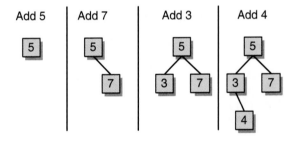

figure 10.3   Adding elements to a binary search tree

the removeElement operation

The removeElement method removes a given Comparable element from a binary search tree or throws an ElementNotFoundException if the given target is not found in the tree. Unlike our earlier study of linear structures, we cannot simply remove the node by making the reference point around the node to be removed.

Instead, another node will have to be *promoted* to replace the one being removed. The protected method replacement returns a reference to a node that will replace the one specified for removal. There are three cases for selecting the replacement node:

- If the node has no children, replacement returns null.

- If the node has only one child, replacement returns that child.

- If the node to be removed has two children, replacement will return the inorder predecessor of the node to be removed.

Listing 10.2 illustrates the replacement method. Figure 10.4 further illustrates the process of removing elements from a binary search tree.

> In removing an element from a binary search tree, another node must be promoted to replace the node being removed.
>
> key concept

```
//-----------------------------------------------------------------
//  Removes the first element that matches the specified target
//  element from the binary search tree and returns a reference to
//  it. Throws an ElementNotFoundException if the specified target
//  element is not found in the binary search tree.
//-----------------------------------------------------------------
public Comparable removeElement (Comparable targetElement) throws
ElementNotFoundException
{
    Comparable result = null;

    if (!isEmpty())

        if (targetElement.equals(root.element))
        {
            result = (Comparable) root.element;
            root = replacement (root);
            count--;
        }
        else
        {
            BinaryTreeNode current, parent = root;
            boolean found = false;

            if (targetElement.compareTo(root.element) < 0)
                current = root.left;
```

```
        else
           current = root.right;

        while (current != null && !found)
        {
           if (targetElement.equals(current.element))
           {
              found = true;
              count--;
              result = (Comparable) current.element;

              if (current == parent.left)
                 parent.left = replacement (current);
              else
                 parent.right = replacement (current);
           }
           else
           {
              parent = current;

              if (targetElement.compareTo(current.element) < 0)
                 current = current.left;
              else
                 current = current.right;
           }
        }
        if (!found)
           throw new ElementNotFoundException("binary tree");
     }

   return result;
}
```

```
//-----------------------------------------------------------------
//  Returns a reference to a node that will replace the one
//  specified for removal.  In the case where the removed
//  node has two children, the inorder predecessor is used
//  as its replacement.
//-----------------------------------------------------------------
protected BinaryTreeNode replacement (BinaryTreeNode node)
{
   BinaryTreeNode result = null;

   if ((node.left == null)&&(node.right==null))
      result = null;
   else
      if ((node.left != null)&&(node.right==null))
         result = node.left;
      else
         if ((node.left == null)&&(node.right != null))
            result = node.right;
         else
         {
            BinaryTreeNode current = node.left;
            BinaryTreeNode parent = node;

            while (current.right != null)
            {
               parent = current;
               current = current.right;
            }

            parent.right = current.left;
            result = current;
         }

   return result;
}
```

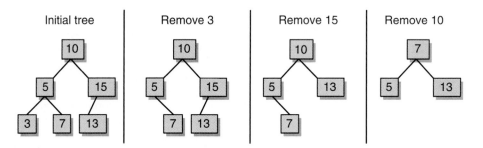

figure 10.4   Removing elements from a binary search tree

the removeAllOccurrences operation

The removeAllOccurrences method removes all occurrences of a given Comparable element from a binary search tree and throws an ElementNotFoundException if the given element is not found in the tree. This method makes use of the removeElement method by calling it once, guaranteeing that the exception will be thrown if there is not at least one occurrence of the element in the tree. The removeElement method is then called again as long as the tree contains the target element.

```
//-----------------------------------------------------------------
//  Removes elements that match the specified target element
//  from the binary search tree. Throws an
//  ElementNotFoundException if the specified target element
//  is not found in the binary search tree.
//-----------------------------------------------------------------
public void removeAllOccurrences (Comparable targetElement) throws
ElementNotFoundException
{
    removeElement(targetElement);

    while (contains(targetElement))
        removeElement(targetElement);
}
```

the removeMin operation

There are three possible cases for the location of the minimum element in a binary search tree:

- If the root has no left child, then the root is the minimum element and the right child of the root becomes the new root.

- If the leftmost node of the tree is a leaf, then it is the minimum element and we simply set its parent's left child reference to null.

- If the leftmost node of the tree is an internal node, then we set its parent's left child reference to point to the right child of the node to be removed.

> **key concept**
>
> The leftmost node in a binary search tree will contain the minimum element while the rightmost node will contain the maximum element.

Figure 10.5 illustrates these possibilities.

```java
//-----------------------------------------------------------------
//  Removes the node with the least value from the binary search
//  tree and returns a reference to its element.  Throws an
//  EmptyBinarySearchTreeException if the binary search tree is
//  empty.
//-----------------------------------------------------------------
public Comparable removeMin() throws EmptyCollectionException
{
    Comparable result = null;

    if (isEmpty())
        throw new EmptyCollectionException ("binary tree");
    else
    {
        if (root.left == null)
        {
            result = (Comparable) root.element;
            root = root.right;
        }
        else
        {
            BinaryTreeNode parent = root;
            BinaryTreeNode current = root.left;
            while (current.left != null)
```

```
            {
                parent = current;
                current = current.left;
            }
            result = (Comparable) current.element;
            parent.left = current.right;
        }

        count--;
    }

    return result;
}
```

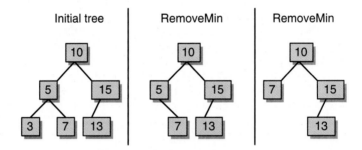

figure 10.5 Removing the minimum element from a binary search tree

The removeMax, findMin, and findMax operations are left as exercises.

10.3 using binary search trees: implementing ordered lists

As we discussed in Chapter 9, one of the principle uses of trees is to provide efficient implementations of other collections. The `OrderedList` collection from Chapter 8 provides an excellent example. Figure 10.6 reminds us of the common operations for lists, and Figure 10.7 reminds us of the operation particular to an ordered list. Using a binary search tree, we can create an implementation called `BinarySearchTreeOrderedList` that is a more efficient implementation than those we discussed in Chapter 8.

Operation	Description
removeFirst	Removes the first element from the list.
removeLast	Removes the last element from the list.
remove	Removes a particular element from the list.
first	Examines the element at the front of the list.
last	Examines the element at the rear of the list.
contains	Determines if the list contains a particular element.
isEmpty	Determines if the list is empty.
size	Determines the number of elements on the list.

figure 10.6   The common operations on a list

Operation	Description
add	Adds an element to the list.

figure 10.7   The operation particular to an ordered list

For simplicity, we have implemented both the ListADT and the OrderedListADT interfaces with the BinarySearchTreeOrderedList class as shown in Listing 10.2. For some of the methods, the same method from either the BinaryTree or BinarySearchTree classes will suffice. This is the case for the contains, isEmpty, and size operations. For the rest of the operations, there is a one-to-one correspondence between methods of the BinaryTree or BinarySearchTree class and the required methods for an OrderedList. Thus, each of these methods is implemented by simply calling the associated method for a BinarySearchTree. This is the case for the add, removeFirst, removeLast, remove, first, last, and iterator methods.

analysis of the BinarySearchTreeOrderedList implementation

We will assume that the BinarySearchTree implementation used in the BinarySearchTreeOrderedList implementation is a balanced binary search tree with the added property that the maximum depth of any node is $\log_2(n)$, where n is the number of elements stored in the tree. This is a tremendously important assumption, as we will see over the next several sections. With that assumption, Figure 10.8 shows a comparison of the order of each operation for a singly linked implementation of an ordered list and our BinarySearchTreeOrderedList implementation.

Note that given our assumption of a balanced binary search tree, both the add and remove operations could cause the tree to need to be rebalanced, which, depending on the algorithm used, could affect the analysis. It is also important to note that while some operations are more efficient in the tree implementation, such as removeLast, last, and contains, others, such as removeFirst and first, are less efficient when implemented using a tree.

listing
   10.2

```
//*******************************************************************
//   BinarySearchTreeOrderedList.java        Authors: Lewis/Chase
//
//   Represents an ordered list implemented using a binary search
//   tree.
//*******************************************************************

package jss2;
import jss2.exceptions.*;
import java.util.Iterator;

public class BinarySearchTreeOrderedList extends BinarySearchTree
implements ListADT, OrderedListADT
{
    //-----------------------------------------------------------------
    //   Creates an empty list.
    //-----------------------------------------------------------------
    public BinarySearchTreeOrderedList()
    {
        super();
    }

    //-----------------------------------------------------------------
    //   Adds the specified element to the list.
    //-----------------------------------------------------------------
    public void add (Comparable element)
    {
        addElement(element);
    }

    //-----------------------------------------------------------------
    //   Removes and returns the first element from this list.
    //-----------------------------------------------------------------
    public Object removeFirst ()
    {
        return removeMin();
    }
```

listing
10.2   continued

```java
//----------------------------------------------------------------
//   Removes and returns the last element from this list.
//----------------------------------------------------------------
public Object removeLast ()
{
   return removeMax();
}

//----------------------------------------------------------------
//   Removes and returns the specified element from this list.
//----------------------------------------------------------------
public Object remove (Object element)
{
   return removeElement((Comparable)element);
}

//----------------------------------------------------------------
//   Returns a reference to the first element on this list.
//----------------------------------------------------------------
public Object first ()
{
   return findMin();
}

//----------------------------------------------------------------
//   Returns a reference to the last element on this list.
//----------------------------------------------------------------
public Object last ()
{
   return findMax();
}

//----------------------------------------------------------------
//   Returns an iterator for the list.
//----------------------------------------------------------------
public Iterator iterator()
{
   return iteratorInOrder();
}
}
```

Operation	LinkedList	BinarySearchTreeOrderedList
removeFirst	O(1)	O(log n)
removeLast	O(n)	O(log n)
remove	O(n)	O(log n)*
first	O(1)	O(log n)
last	O(n)	O(log n)
contains	O(n)	O(log n)
isEmpty	O(1)	O(1)
size	O(1)	O(1)
add	O(n)	O(log n)*
*both the add and remove operations may cause the tree to become unbalanced		

figure 10.8   Analysis of linked list and binary search tree implementations of an ordered list

10.4 balanced binary search trees

Why is our balance assumption important? What would happen to our analysis if the tree were not balanced? As an example, let's assume that we read the following list of integers from a file and added them to a binary search tree:

3   5   9   12   18   20

Figure 10.9 shows the resulting binary search tree. This resulting binary tree, referred to as a *degenerate tree,* looks more like a linked list, and in fact is less efficient than a linked list because of the additional overhead associated with each node.

If this is the tree we are manipulating, then our analysis from the previous section will look far worse. For example, without our balance assumption, the addElement operation would have worst case time complexity of O(n) instead of O(log n) because of the possibility that the root is the smallest element in the tree and the element we are inserting might be the largest element.

> key concept
>
> If a binary search tree is not balanced, it may be less efficient than a linear structure.

Our goal instead is to keep the maximum path length in the tree at or near $\log_2 n$. There are a variety of algorithms available for balancing or maintaining balance in a tree. There are brute-force methods, which are not elegant or efficient, but get the job done. For example, we could write an inorder traversal of

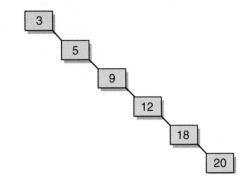

figure 10.9   A degenerate binary tree

the tree to an array and then use a recursive method (much like binary search) to insert the middle element of the array as the root, then build balanced left and right subtrees. Though such an approach would work, there are more elegant solutions, such as AVL trees and red/black trees, which we examine later in this chapter.

However, before we move on to these techniques, we need to understand some additional terminology that is common to many balancing techniques. The methods described here will work for any subtree of a binary search tree as well. We simply replace the reference to root with whatever reference points to the root of the subtree.

right rotation

Figure 10.10 shows a binary search tree that is not balanced and the processing steps necessary to rebalance it. The maximum path length in this tree is 3 while the minimum path length is 1. With only 6 elements in the tree, the maximum path length should be $\log_2 6$ or 2. To get this tree into balance, we need to

▸ Make the left child element of the root the new root element.

▸ Make the former root element the right child element of the new root.

▸ Make the right child of what was the left child of the former root the new left child of the former root.

This is referred to as a *right rotation* and is often referred to as a right rotation of the left child around the parent. The last image in Figure 10.10 shows the same tree after a right rotation. The same kind of rotation can be done at any level of the tree. This single rotation to the right will solve the imbalance if the imbalance is caused by a long path length in the left subtree of the left child of the root.

left rotation

Figure 10.11 shows another binary search tree that is not balanced. Again, the maximum path length in this tree is 3 while the minimum path length is 1. However, this time the larger path length is in the right subtree of the right child of the root. To get this tree into balance, we need to

▸ Make the right child element of the root the new root element.

▸ Make the former root element the left child element of the new root.

▸ Make the left child of what was the right child of the former root the new right child of the former root.

This is referred to as a *left rotation* and is often stated as a left rotation of the right child around the parent. Figure 10.11 shows the same tree through the processing steps of a left rotation. The same kind of rotation can be done at any level

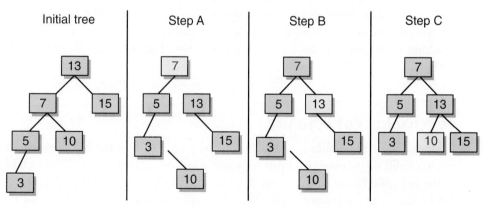

figure 10.10   Unbalanced tree and balanced tree after a right rotation

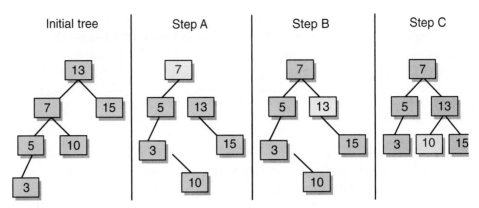

figure 10.11   Unbalanced tree and balanced tree after a left rotation

of the tree. This single rotation to the left will solve the imbalance if the imbalance is caused by a longer path length in the right subtree of the right child of the root.

rightleft rotation

Unfortunately, not all imbalances can be solved by single rotations. If the imbalance is caused by a long path length in the left subtree of the right child of the root, we must first perform a right rotation of the left child of the right child of the root around the right child of the root, and then perform a left rotation of the resulting right child of the root around the root. Figure 10.12 illustrates this process.

leftright rotation

Similarly, if the imbalance is caused by a long path length in the right subtree of the left child of the root, we must first perform a left rotation of the right child of the left child of the root around the left child of the root, and then perform a right rotation of the resulting left child of the root around the root. Figure 10.13 illustrates this process.

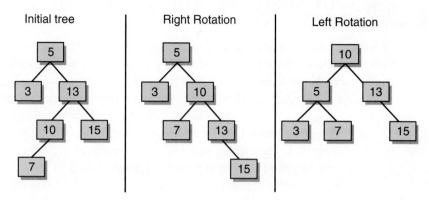

figure 10.12   A rightleft rotation

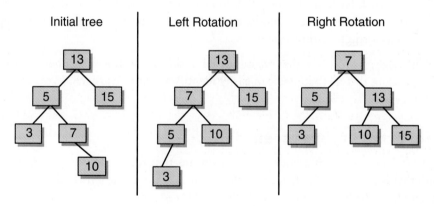

figure 10.13   A leftright rotation

10.5 implementing binary search trees: AVL trees

We have been discussing a generic method for balancing a tree where the maximum path length from the root must be no more than $\log_2 n$ and the minimum path length from the root must be no less than $\log_2 n - 1$. Adel'son-Vel'skii and Landis developed a method called *AVL trees* that is a variation on this theme. For each node in the tree, we will keep track of the height of the left and right subtrees. For any node in the tree, if the *balance factor*, or the difference in the heights of its subtrees (height of the right subtree minus the height of the left subtree), is greater than 1 or less than −1, then the subtree with that node as the root needs to be rebalanced.

> **key concept**
>
> The height of the right subtree minus the height of the left subtree is called the balance factor of a node.

There are only two ways that a tree, or any subtree of a tree, can become unbalanced: through the insertion of a node or through the deletion of a node. Thus, each time one of these operations is performed, the balance factors must be updated and the balance of the tree must be checked starting at the point of insertion or removal of a node and working up toward the root of the tree. Because of this need to work back up the tree, AVL trees are often best implemented by including a parent reference in each node. In the diagrams that follow, all edges are represented as a single bi-directional line.

> **key concept**
>
> There are only two ways that a tree, or any subtree of a tree, can become unbalanced: through the insertion of a node or through the deletion of a node.

The cases for rotation that we discussed in the last section apply here as well, and by using this method, we can easily identify when to use each.

right rotation in an AVL tree

If the balance factor of a node is −2, this means that the node's left subtree has a path that is too long. We then check the balance factor of the left child of the original node. If the balance factor of the left child is −1, this means that the long path is in the left subtree of the left child and therefore a simple right rotation of the left child around the original node will rebalance the tree. Figure 10.14 shows how an insertion of a node could cause an imbalance and how a right rotation would resolve it. Note that we are representing both the values stored at each node and the balance factors, with the balance factors shown in parentheses.

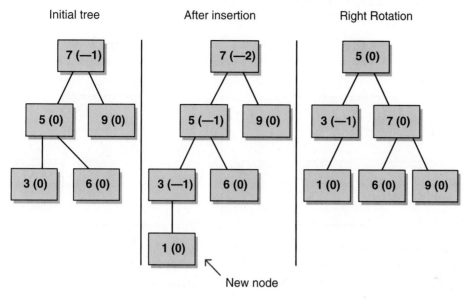

figure 10.14   A right rotation in an AVL tree

left rotation in an AVL tree

If the balance factor of a node is +2, this means that the node's right subtree has a path that is too long. We then check the balance factor of the right child of the original node. If the balance factor of the right child is +1, this means that the long path is in the right subtree of the right child and therefore a simple left rotation of the right child around the original node will rebalance the tree.

rightleft rotation in an AVL tree

If the balance factor of a node is +2, this means that the node's right subtree has a path that is too long. We then check the balance factor of the right child of the original node. If the balance factor of the right child is −1, this means that the long path is in the left subtree of the right child and therefore a rightleft double rotation will rebalance the tree. This is accomplished by first performing a right rotation of the left child of the right child of the original node around the right child of the original node, and then performing a left rotation of the right child of the original node around the original node. Figure 10.15 shows how the

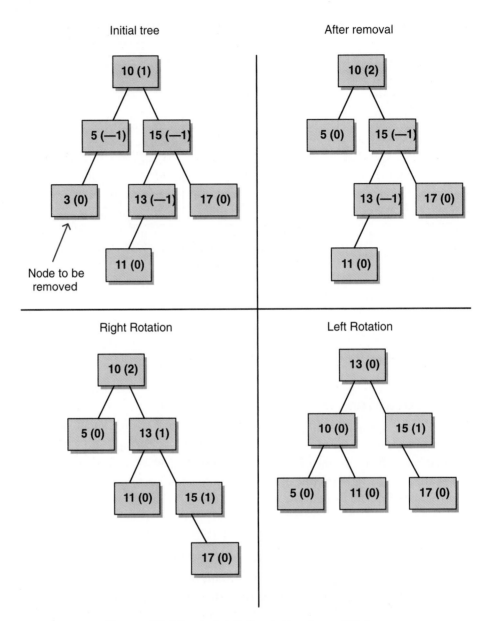

figure 10.15 A rightleft rotation in an AVL tree

removal of an element from the tree could cause an imbalance and how a rightleft rotation would resolve it. Again, note that we are representing both the values stored at each node and the balance factors, with the balance factors shown in parentheses.

leftright rotation in an AVL tree

If the balance factor of a node is –2, this means that the node's left subtree has a path that is too long. We then check the balance factor of the left child of the original node. If the balance factor of the left child is +1, this means that the long path is in the right subtree of the left child and therefore a leftright double rotation will rebalance the tree. This is accomplished by first performing a left rotation of the right child of the left child of the original node around the left child of the original node, then performing a right rotation of the left child of the original node around the original node.

10.6 implementing binary search trees: red/black trees

Another alternative to the implementation of binary search trees is the concept of a red/black tree developed by Bayer and extended by Guibas and Sedgewick. A red/black tree is a balanced binary search tree where we will store a color with each node (either red or black, usually implemented as a boolean value with false being equivalent to red). The following rules govern the color of a node:

- The root is black.
- All children of a red node are black.
- Every path from the root to a leaf contains the same number of black nodes.

Figure 10.16 shows three valid red/black trees (the lighter shade nodes are "red"). Notice that the balance restriction on a red/black tree is somewhat less strict than that for AVL trees or for our earlier theoretical discussion. However, finding an element in both implementations is still an O(log n) operation. Since no red node can have a red child, then at most half of the nodes in a path could be red nodes and

> **key concept**
> The balance restriction on a red/black tree is somewhat less strict than that for AVL trees.

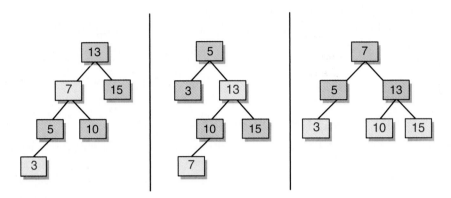

figure 10.16 Valid red/black trees

at least half of the nodes in a path are black. From this we can argue that the maximum height of a red/black tree is roughly 2*log n and thus the traversal of the longest path is still order log n.

As with AVL trees, the only time we need to be concerned about balance is after an insertion or removal of an element in the tree. Unlike AVL trees, the two are handled quite separately.

insertion into a red/black tree

Insertion into a red/black tree will progress much as it did in our earlier `addElement` method. However, we will always begin by setting the color of the new element to red. Once the new element has been inserted, we will then rebalance the tree as needed and change the color of elements as needed to maintain the properties of a red/black tree. As a last step, we will always set the color of the root of the tree to black. For purposes of our discussion, we will simply refer to the color of a node as `node.color`. However, it may be more elegant in an actual implementation to create a method to return the color of a node.

The rebalancing (and recoloring) process after insertion is an iterative one starting at the point of insertion and working up the tree toward the root. Therefore, like AVL trees, red/black trees are often best implemented by including a parent reference in each node. The termination conditions for this process are (current == root), where current is the node we are currently processing, or (current.parent.color == black) (i.e., the color of the parent of the current node is black). The first condition terminates the process because we will always set the root color to black and the root is included in all paths and therefore cannot violate the rule that each path have the same number of black elements. The second condition terminates the process because the node pointed to by current will always be a red node. This means that if the parent of the current node is black then all of the rules are met as well since a red node does not affect the number of black nodes in a path and since we are working from the point of insertion up, we will have already balanced the subtree under the current node.

In each iteration of the rebalancing process, we will focus on the color of the sibling of the parent of the current node. Keep in mind that there are two possibilities for the parent of the current node: current.parent could be a left child or a right child. Assuming that the parent of current is a right child, we can get the color information by using current.parent.parent.left.color, but for purposes of our discussion, we will use the terms leftaunt.color and rightuncle.color. It is also important to keep in mind that the color of a null element is considered to be black.

In the case where the parent of current is a right child, there are two cases, either (leftaunt.color == red) or (leftaunt.color == black). Keep in mind that in either case, we are describing processing steps that are occurring inside of a loop with the termination conditions described earlier. Figure 10.17 shows a red/black tree after insertion with this first case (leftaunt.color==red). The processing steps in this case are

- Set the color of current's parent to black.
- Set the color of leftaunt to black.
- Set the color of current's grandparent to red.
- Set current to point to the grandparent of current.

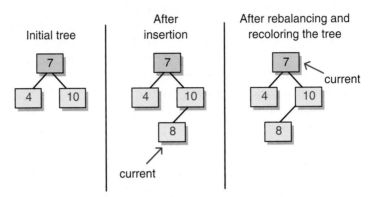

figure 10.17 red/black tree after insertion

In Figure 10.17 we inserted 8 into our tree. Keep in mind that current points to our new node and current.color is set to red. Following the processing steps, we set the parent of current to black, we set the left aunt of current to black, and we set the grandparent of current to red. We then set current to point to the grandparent. Since the grandparent is the root, the loop terminates. Finally, we set the root of the tree to black.

However, if (leftaunt.color == black), then we first need to check to see if current is a left or right child. If current is a left child, then we must set current equal to its parent and then rotate current.left to the right (around current) before continuing. Once this is accomplished, the processing steps are the same as if current were a right child to begin with:

▸ Set the color of current's parent to black.

▸ Set the color of current's grandparent to red.

▸ If current's grandparent does not equal null, then rotate current's parent to the left around current's grandparent.

In the case where the parent of current is a left child, there are two cases, either (rightuncle.color == red) or (rightuncle.color == black). Keep in mind that in either case, we are describing processing steps that are occurring inside of a loop with the termination conditions described earlier. Figure 10.18 shows a red/black tree after insertion with this case (`rightuncle.color==red`). The processing steps in this case are

▸ Set the color of current's parent to black.

▸ Set the color of rightuncle to black.

▸ Set the color of current's grandparent to red.

▸ Set current to point to the grandparent of current.

In Figure 10.18 we inserted 5 into our tree, setting `current` to point to the new node and setting `current.color` to red. Again, following our processing steps, we set the parent of `current` to black, we set the right uncle of `current` to black, and we set the grandparent of `current` to red. We then set `current` to point to its grandparent. Since the parent of the new `current` is black, our loop terminates. Lastly, we set the color of the root to black.

However, if (`rightuncle.color == black`), then we first need to check to see if `current` is a left or right child. If `current` is a right child, then we must set `current` equal to `current.parent` and then rotate `current.right` to the left

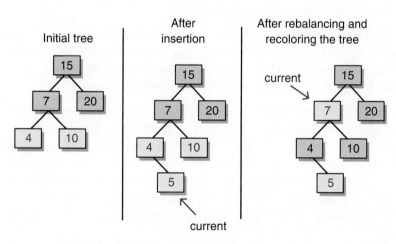

figure 10.18   red/black tree after insertion

(around current) before continuing. Once this is accomplished, the processing steps are the same as if current were a left child to begin with:

- Set the color of current's parent to black.

- Set the color of current's grandparent to red.

- If current's grandparent does not equal null, then rotate current's parent to the right around current's grandparent.

As you can see, the cases, depending on whether or not current's parent is a left or right child, are symmetrical.

element removal from a red/black tree

As with insertion, the removeElement operation behaves much as it did before, only with the additional step of rebalancing (and recoloring) the tree. This rebalancing (and recoloring) process after removal of an element is an iterative one starting at the point of removal and working up the tree toward the root. Therefore, as stated earlier, red/black trees are often best implemented by including a parent reference in each node. The termination conditions for this process are (current == root), where current is the node we are currently processing, or (current.color == red).

As with the cases for insertion, the cases for removal are symmetrical depending upon whether current is a left or right child. We only examine the case where current is a right child. The other cases are easily derived by simply substituting left for right and right for left in the following cases.

In insertion, we were most concerned with the color of the aunt or uncle of the current node. For removal, we will focus on the color of the sibling of current. We could reference this color using current.parent.left.color but we will simply refer to it as sibling.color. We will also look at the color of the children of the sibling. It is important to note that the default for color is black. Therefore, if at any time we are attempting to get the color of a null object, the result will be black. Figure 10.19 shows a red/black tree after the removal of an element.

If the sibling's color is red, then before we do anything else, we must complete the following processing steps:

- Set the color of the sibling to black.
- Set the color of current's parent to red.
- Rotate the sibling right around current's parent.
- Set the sibling equal to the left child of current's parent.

Next, our processing continues regardless of whether the original sibling was red or black. Now our processing is divided into one of two cases based upon the color of the children of the sibling. If both children of the sibling are black (or null), then we do the following:

- Set the color of the sibling to red.
- Set current equal to current's parent.

If the children of the sibling are not both black, then we check to see if the left child of the sibling is black. If it is, we must complete the following steps before continuing:

- Set the color of the sibling's right child to black.
- Set the color of the sibling to red.
- Rotate the sibling's right child left around the sibling.
- Set the sibling equal to the left child of current's parent.

Then to complete the process when both of the sibling's children are not black, we must:

- Set the color of the sibling to the color of current's parent.
- Set the color of current's parent to black.
- Set the color of the sibling's left child to black.
- Rotate the sibling right around current's parent.
- Set current equal to the root.

Once the loop terminates we must always then remove the node and set its parent's child reference to null.

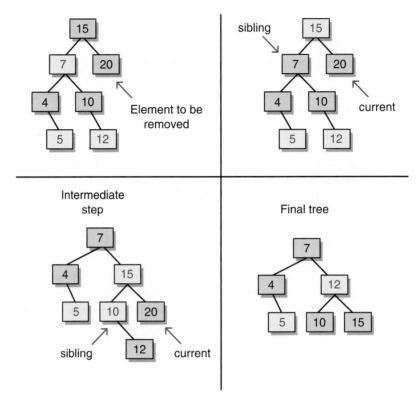

figure 10.19   red/black tree after removal

10.7   implementing binary search trees: the Java Collections API

The Java Collections API provides two implementations of balanced binary search trees: `TreeSet` and `TreeMap`. Both use a red/black tree implementation approach. In order to understand these implementations, we must first discuss the difference between a *set* and a *map* in the Java Collections API.

> **key concept**
>
> The Java Collections API provides two implementations of balanced binary search trees: `TreeSet` and `TreeMap`, both of which use a red/black tree implementation.

In the terminology of the Java Collections API, all of the collections that we have discussed thus far could be considered sets (except that sets do not allow duplicates). This is because the data or element stored in each collection contains all of the data associated with that object.

For example, if we were creating an ordered list of employees, ordered by name, then we would have created an employee object that contained all of the data for each employee, including the name and a compareTo method to test the name, and we would have used our operations for an ordered list to add those employees into the list.

However, in this same scenario, if we wanted to create an ordered list that is a map, we would have created a class to represent the name of each employee and a reference that would point to a second class that contains all of the rest of the employee data. We would have then used our ordered list operations to load the first class into our list, while the objects of the second class could exist anywhere in memory. The first class in this case is sometimes referred to as the *key,* while the second class is often referred to as the *data.* Tables 10.1 and 10.2 show the operations for a TreeSet and TreeMap, respectively. Note that these implementations use (and allow the use of) a Comparator instead of using Comparable as we did in our earlier implementations. The Comparator interface describes a method, compare, that, like compareTo, returns –1, 0, or 1, representing less than, equal, or greater than. However, unlike compareTo, compare takes two arguments and does not need to be implemented within the class be stored in the collection.

In this way, as we manipulate elements of the list, we are only dealing with the key, the name, and the reference, which is a much smaller segment of memory than if we were manipulating all of the data associated with an employee. We also have the advantage that the same employee data could be referenced by multiple maps without having to make multiple copies. Thus if for one application we wanted to represent employees in a bag collection while for another application we needed to represent employees as an ordered list, we could load keys into a bag and load matching keys into an ordered list while only having one instance of the actual data. Like any situation dealing with aliases (i.e., multiple references to the same object) we must be careful that changes to an object through one reference affect the object referenced by all of the other references since there is only one instance of the object.

Operation	Description
TreeSet()	Constructs a new, empty set, sorted according to the elements natural order.
TreeSet(Collection c)	Constructs a new set containing the elements in the specified collection, sorted according to the elements natural order.
TreeSet(Comparator c)	Constructs a new, empty set, sorted according to the given comparator.
TreeSet(SortedSet s)	Constructs a new set containing the same elements as the given sorted set, sorted according to the same ordering.
boolean add(Object o)	Adds the specified element to this set if it is not already present.
boolean addAll(Collection c)	Adds all of the elements in the specified collection to this set.
void clear()	Removes all of the elements from this set.
Object clone()	Returns a shallow copy of this TreeSet instance.
Comparator comparator()	Returns the comparator used to order this sorted set, or null if this TreeSet uses its elements natural ordering.
boolean contains(Object o)	Returns true if this set contains the specified element.
Object first()	Returns the first (lowest) element currently in this sorted set.
SortedSet headSet(Object toElement)	Returns a view of the portion of this set whose elements are strictly less than toElement.
boolean isEmpty()	Returns true if this set contains no elements.
Iterator iterator()	Returns an iterator over the elements in this set.
Object last()	Returns the last (highest) element currently in this sorted set.
boolean remove(Object o)	Removes the given element from this set if it is present.
int size()	Returns the number of elements in this set (its cardinality).
SortedSet subSet(Object fromElement, (Object toElement)	Returns a view of the portion of this set whose elements range from fromElement, inclusive, to toElement, exclusive.
SortedSet tailSet(Object fromElement)	Returns a view of the portion of this set whose elements are greater than or equal to fromElement.

table 10.1   Operations on a TreeSet

Operation	Description
`TreeMap()`	Constructs a new, empty map, sorted according to the keys natural order.
`TreeMap(Comparator c)`	Constructs a new, empty map, sorted according to the given comparator.
`TreeMap(Map m)`	Constructs a new map containing the same mappings as the given map, sorted according to the keys natural order.
`TreeMap(SortedMap m)`	Constructs a new map containing the same mappings as the given `SortedMap`, sorted according to the same ordering.
`void clear()`	Removes all mappings from this `TreeMap`.
`Object clone()`	Returns a shallow copy of this `TreeMap` instance.
`Comparator comparator()`	Returns the comparator used to order this map, or null if this map uses its keys natural order.
`boolean containsKey(Object key)`	Returns true if this map contains a mapping for the specified key.
`boolean containsValue(Object value)`	Returns true if this map maps one or more keys to the specified value.
`Set entrySet()`	Returns a set view of the mappings contained in this map.
`Object firstKey()`	Returns the first (lowest) key currently in this sorted map.
`Object get(Object key)`	Returns the value to which this map maps the specified key.
`SortedMap headMap(Object toKey)`	Returns a view of the portion of this map whose keys are strictly less than `toKey`.
`Set keySet()`	Returns a set view of the keys contained in this map.
`Object lastKey()`	Returns the last (highest) key currently in this sorted map.
`Object put(Object key, Object value)`	Associates the specified value with the specified key in this map.
`void putAll(Map map)`	Copies all of the mappings from the specified map to this map.
`Object remove(Object key)`	Removes the mapping for this key from this `TreeMap` if present.
`int size()`	Returns the number of key-value mappings in this map.
`SortedMap subMap(Object fromKey, Object toKey)`	Returns a view of the portion of this map whose keys range from `fromKey`, inclusive, to `toKey`, exclusive.
`SortedMap tailMap(Object fromKey)`	Returns a view of the portion of this map whose keys are greater than or equal to `fromKey`.
`Collection values()`	Returns a collection view of the values contained in this map.

table 10.2   Operations on a `TreeMap`

summary of key concepts

▸ A binary search tree is a binary tree with the added property that the left child is less than the parent, which is less than or equal to the right child.

▸ The definition of a binary search tree is an extension of the definition of a binary tree.

▸ Each `BinaryTreeNode` object maintains a reference to the element stored at that node as well as references to each of the node's children.

▸ In removing an element from a binary search tree, another node must be promoted to replace the node being removed.

▸ The leftmost node in a binary search tree will contain the minimum element, while the rightmost node will contain the maximum element.

▸ One of the principle uses of trees is to provide efficient implementations of other collections.

▸ If a binary search tree is not balanced, it may be less efficient than a linear structure.

▸ The height of the right subtree minus the height of the left subtree is called the balance factor of a node.

▸ There are only two ways that a tree, or any subtree of a tree, can become unbalanced: through the insertion of a node or through the deletion of a node.

▸ The balance restriction on a red/black tree is somewhat less strict than that for AVL trees. However, in both cases, the find operation is order log n.

▸ The Java Collections API provides two implementations of balanced binary search trees: `TreeSet` and `TreeMap`, both of which use a red/black tree implementation.

self-review questions

10.1   What is the difference between a binary tree and a binary search tree?

10.2   Why are we able to specify `addElement` and `removeElement` operations for a binary search tree but we were unable to do so for a binary tree?

10.3   Assuming that the tree is balanced, what is the time complexity (Order) of the `addElement` operation?

10.4   Without the balance assumption, what is the time complexity (Order) of the `addElement` operation?

10.5   In this chapter we stated that a degenerate tree might actually be less efficient than a linked list. Why?

10.6   Our `removeElement` operation uses the inorder predecessor as the replacement for a node with two children. What would be another reasonable choice for the replacement?

10.7   The `removeAllOccurences` operation makes use of both the `contains` and `removeElement` operations. What is the resulting time complexity (order) for this operation?

10.8   `RemoveFirst` and `first` were O(1) operations for our earlier implementation of an ordered list. Why are they less efficient for our `BinarySearchTreeOrderedList`?

10.9   Why does the `BinarySearchTreeOrderedList` class have to define the `iterator` method? Why can it not just rely on the `iterator` method of its parent class like it does for `size` and `isEmpty`?

10.10 What is the time complexity of the `addElement` operation after modifying to implement an AVL tree?

10.11 What imbalance is fixed by a single right rotation?

10.12 What imbalance is fixed by a leftright rotation?

10.13 What is the balance factor of an AVL tree node?

10.14 In our discussion of the process for rebalancing an AVL tree, we never discussed the possibility of the balance factor of a node being either +2 or −2 and the balance factor of one of its children being either +2 or −2. Why not?

10.15 We noted that the balance restriction for a red/black tree is less strict than that of an AVL tree and yet we still claim that traversing the longest path in a red/black tree is still O(log n). Why?

10.16 What is the difference between a `TreeSet` and a `TreeMap`?

exercises

10.1 Draw the binary search tree that results from adding the following integers (34 45 3 87 65 32 1 12 17). Assume our simple implementation with no balancing mechanism.

10.2 Starting with the resulting tree from Exercise 10.1, draw the tree that results from removing (45 12 1) again using our simple implementation with no balancing mechanism.

10.3 Repeat Exercise 10.1, this time assuming an AVL tree. Include the balance factors in your drawing.

10.4 Repeat Exercise 10.2, this time assuming an AVL tree and using the result of Exercise 10.3 as a starting point. Include the balance factors in your drawing.

10.5 Repeat Exercise 10.1, this time assuming a red/black tree. Label each node with its color.

10.6 Repeat Exercise 10.2, this time assuming a red/black tree and using the result of Exercise 10.5 as a starting point. Label each node with its color.

10.7 Starting with an empty red/black tree, draw the tree after insertion and before rebalancing, and after rebalancing (if necessary) for the following series of inserts and removals:

```
AddElement(40);

AddElement(25):

AddElement(10);

AddElement(5);

AddElement(1);

Addelement(45);

AddElement(50);

RemoveElement(40);

RemoveElement(25);
```

10.8 Repeat Exercise 10.7, this time with an AVL tree.

programming projects

10.1   The `BinarySearchTree` class is currently making use of the `find` and `contains` methods of the `BinaryTree` class. Implement these methods for the `BinarySearchTree` class so that they will be more efficient by making use of the ordering property of a binary search tree.

10.2   Implement the `removeMax`, `findMin`, and `findMax` operations for our binary search tree implementation.

10.3   Implement a balance tree method using the brute-force method described in Section 10.4.

10.4   Develop an array implementation of a binary search tree built upon an array implementation of a binary tree using the simulated link strategy. Each element of the array will need to maintain a reference to the data element stored there as well as maintain the array positions of the left and right child. You will also need to maintain a list of available array positions where elements have been removed in order to reuse those positions.

10.5   Develop an array implementation of a binary search tree built upon an array implementation of a binary tree using the computational strategy.

10.6   Modify the binary search tree implementation to make it an AVL tree.

10.7   Modify the binary search tree implementation to make it a red/black tree.

10.8   Create a binary search tree implementation of a bag.

10.9   Create a binary search tree implementation of a set.

answers to self-review questions

10.1   A binary search tree has the added ordering property that the left child of any node is less than the node, and the node is less than or equal to its right child.

10.2   With the added ordering property of a binary search tree, we are now able to define what the state of the tree should be after an `add` or `remove`. We were unable to define that state for a binary tree.

10.3   If the tree is balanced, it will take at worst log n steps to find the insertion point for the new element, and since inserting the element is simply a matter of setting the value of one reference, the operation is Order(log n).

10.4   Without the balance assumption, the worst case would be a degenerate tree, which is effectively a linked list. Therefore the `addElement` operation would be O(n).

10.5   A degenerate tree will waste space with unused references, and many of the algorithms will check for null references before following the degenerate path, thus adding steps that the linked list implementation does not have.

10.6   The two best choices are the inorder predecessor and the inorder successor, and their is little or no difference between them in this regard.

10.7   With our balance assumption, the `contains` operation uses the `find` operation, which will be rewritten in the binary search tree class to take advantage of the ordering property and will be O(log n). The `removeElement` operation is O(log n). The `while` loop will iterate some constant (k) number of times depending on how many times the given element occurs within the tree. The worst case would be that all n elements of the tree are the element to be removed, which would make the tree degenerate, and in which case the complexity would be $n*2*n$ or $O(n^2)$. However, the expected case would be some small constant (0<=k<n) occurrences of the element in a balanced tree, which would result in a complexity of $k*2*\log n$ or O(log n).

10.8   In our earlier linked implementation of an ordered list, we had a reference that kept track of the first element in the list, which made it quite simple to remove it or return it. With a binary search tree, we have to traverse to get to the leftmost element before knowing that we have the first element in the ordered list.

10.9   Remember that the iterators for a binary tree are all followed by which traversal order to use. That is why the `iterator` method for the `BinarySearchTreeOrderedList` class calls the `iteratorInOrder` method of the `BinaryTree` class.

10.10 Keep in mind that an `addElement` method only affects one path of the tree, which in a balanced AVL tree has a maximum length of log n. As we have discussed previously, finding the position to insert and setting the reference is O(log n). We then have to progress back up the same path, updating the balance factors of each node (if necessary) and rotating if necessary. Updating the balance factors is an O(1) step and rotation is also an O(1) step. Each of these will at most have to be done log n times. Therefore, `addElement` has time complexity 2*log n or O(log n).

10.11 A single right rotation will fix the imbalance if the long path is in the left subtree of the left child of the root.

10.12 A leftright rotation will fix the imbalance if the long path is in the right subtree of the left child of the root.

10.13 The balance factor of an AVL tree node is the height of the right subtree minus the height of the left subtree.

10.14 Rebalancing an AVL tree is done after either an insertion or a deletion and it is done starting at the affected node and working up along a single path to the root. As we progress upward, we update the balance factors and rotate if necessary. We will never encounter a situation where both a child and a parent have balance factors of +/–2 because we would have already fixed the child before we ever reached the parent.

10.15 Since no red node can have a red child, then at most half of the nodes in a path could be red nodes and at least half of the nodes in a path are black. From this we can argue that the maximum height of a red/black tree is roughly 2*log n and thus the traversal of the longest path is O(log n).

10.16 Both are red/black tree implementations of a binary search tree. The difference is that in a `Set`, all of the data are stored with an element, and with a `TreeMap`, a separate key is created and stored in the collection while the data are stored separately.

references

Adel'son-Vel'skii, G.M., and E.M. Landis. "An Algorithm for the Organization of Information." *Soviet Mathematics* 3 (1962): 1259–1263.

Bayer, R. "Symmetric Binary B-trees: Data Structure and Maintenance Algorithms." *Acta Informatica* (1972): 290-306.

Collins, W. J. *Data Structures and the Java Collections Framework*. New York: McGraw-Hill, 2002.

Cormen, T., C. Leierson, and R. Rivest. *Introduction to Algorithms*. New York: McGraw-Hill, 1992.

Guibas, L., and R. Sedgewick. "A Diochromatic Framework for Balanced Trees." *Proceedings of the 19th Annual IEEE Symposium on Foundations of Computer Science* (1978): 8–21.

In this chapter, we will look at another
ordered extension of binary trees.
We will examine heaps, including both linked
and array implementations and
the algorithms for adding and
removing elements from a heap.
We will also examine a couple
uses for heaps.

11.1 a heap

A *heap* is a binary tree with two added properties:

- It is a complete tree, as described in Chapter 9.
- For each node, the node is less than or equal to both the left child and the right child.

key concept: A *heap* is a complete binary tree in which each node is less than or equal to both of its children.

This definition describes a *minheap*. A heap can also be a *maxheap*, in which the node is greater than or equal to its children. We will focus our discussion in this chapter on minheaps. All of the same processes work for maxheaps by reversing the comparisons.

Figure 11.1 describes the operations on a heap. The definition of a heap is an extension of a binary tree and thus inherits all of those operations as well. Listing 11.1 shows the interface definition for a heap. Figure 11.2 shows the UML description of the `HeapADT`.

key concept: A minheap stores its smallest element at the root of the binary tree, and both children of the root of a minheap are also minheaps.

Simply put, a minheap will always store its smallest element at the root of the binary tree, and both children of the root of a minheap are also minheaps. Figure 11.3 illustrates two valid minheaps with the same data. Let's look at the basic operations on a heap and examine generic algorithms for each.

the `addElement` operation

The `addElement` method adds a given `Comparable` element to the appropriate location in the heap, maintaining both the completeness property and the ordering property of the heap. A binary tree is considered *complete* if it is balanced,

Operation	Description
`addElement`	Adds the given element to the heap.
`removeMin`	Removes the minimum element in the heap.
`findMin`	Returns a reference to the minimum element in the heap.

figure 11.1 The operations on a heap

listing
11.1

```
//********************************************************************
//    HeapADT.java         Authors:  Lewis/Chase
//
//    Defines the interface to a heap.
//********************************************************************

package jss2;

public interface HeapADT extends BinaryTreeADT
{
    public void addElement (Comparable obj);

    public Comparable removeMin();

    public Comparable findMin();
}
```

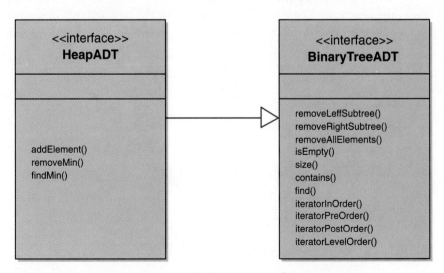

figure 11.2   UML description of the HeapADT

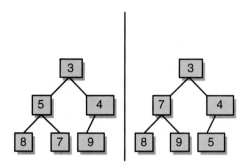

figure 11.3   Two minheaps containing the same data

meaning all of the leaves are at level h or h–1 where h is $\log_2 n$ and n is the number of elements in the tree, and all of the leaves at level h are on the left side of the tree. Since a heap is a complete tree, there is only one correct location for the insertion of a new node. That location is either the next open position from the left at level h or the first position on the left at level h+1 if level h is full. Figure 11.4 illustrates these two possibilities.

Once we have located the new node in the proper position, we then must account for the ordering property. To do this, we simply compare the new value to its parent value and swap the values if the new node is less than its parent. We continue this process up the tree until either the new value is greater than its parent or the new value is in the root of the heap. Figure 11.5 illustrates this process for inserting a new ele-

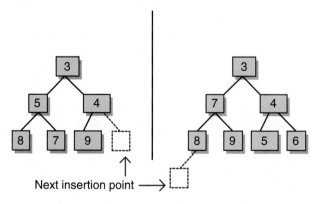

figure 11.4   Insertion points for a heap

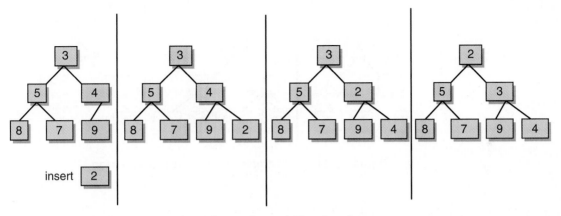

figure 11.5   Insertion and reordering in a heap

ment into a heap. Typically, in heap implementations, we keep track of the position of the last node or, more precisely, the last leaf in the tree. After an `addElement` operation, the last node is set to the node that was inserted.

> **key concept**
> Typically, in heap implementations, we keep track of the position of the last node or, more precisely, the last leaf in the tree.

the `removeMin` operation

The `removeMin` method removes the minimum element from the min-heap and returns it. Since the minimum element is stored in the root of a minheap, we need to return the element stored at the root and replace it with another element in the heap. As with the `addElement` operation, in order to maintain the completeness of the tree, there is only one valid element to replace the root and that is the element stored in the last leaf in the tree. This last leaf will be the rightmost leaf at level h of the tree. Figure 11.6 illustrates this concept of the last leaf under a variety of circumstances.

> **key concept**
> In order to maintain the completeness of the tree, there is only one valid element to replace the root and that is the element stored in the last leaf in the tree.

Once the element stored in the last leaf has been moved to the root, the heap will then have to be reordered to maintain the heap's ordering property. This is accomplished by comparing the new root element to the smaller of its children and then swapping them if the child is smaller. This process is repeated on down the tree until either the element is in a leaf or the element is less than both of its children. Figure 11.7 illustrates the process of removing the minimum element and then reordering the tree.

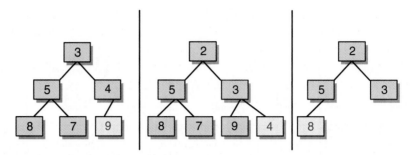

figure 11.6 Examples of the last leaf in a heap

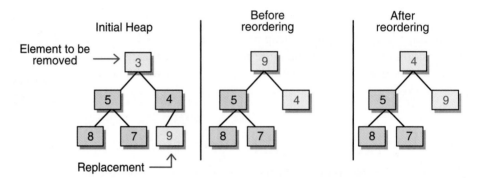

figure 11.7 Removal and reordering in a heap

the findMin operation

The findMin method returns a reference to the smallest element in the minheap. Since that element is always stored in the root of the tree, this method is simply implemented by returning the element stored in the root.

11.2 using heaps: heap sort

In Chapter 5, we introduced a variety of sorting techniques, some of which were sequential sorts (bubble sort, selection sort, and insertion sort) and some of which were logarithmic sorts (merge sort and quick sort). Given the ordering property of a heap, it is natural to think of using a heap to sort a list of numbers. The process is quite simple. Simply add each of the elements of the list to a heap and then remove them one at a time from the root. In the case of a minheap, the result will be the list in ascending order. In the case of a maxheap, the result will be the list in descending order. Insertion into a heap is O(log n) for any given node and thus would be O(n log n) for n nodes.

It is also possible to "build" a heap in place using the current array. Since we know the relative position of each parent and child in the heap, we can simply start with the first non-leaf node in the array, compare it to its children, and swap if necessary. We then work backward in the array until we reach the root. Since, at most, this will require us to make two comparisons for each non-leaf node, this approach is O(n). The implementation of this approach is left as an exercise.

> **key concept**
>
> The `heapSort` method consists of adding each of the elements of the list to a heap and then removing them one at a time.

The `heapSort` method could be added to our class of searching and sorting methods described in Chapter 5. We will discuss the efficiency of the `heapSort` method later in this chapter.

```
//--------------------------------------------------------------------
//   Sorts a given array of Comparable objects using a heap.
//--------------------------------------------------------------------
public static void heapSort(Comparable[] data, int min, int max)
{
   Heap temp = new Heap();

   // Copy the array into a heap
   for (int ct=min; ct <= max; ct++)
      temp.addElement(data[ct]);

   // Place the sorted elements back into the array
   int count = min;
   while (!(temp.isEmpty()))
   {
      data[count] = temp.removeMin();
      count++;
   }
}
```

11.3 using heaps: priority queues

A *priority queue* is a collection that follows two ordering rules. First, items with higher priority go first. Second, items with the same priority use a first in, first out method to determine their ordering. Priority queues have a variety of applications (e.g., task scheduling in an operating system, traffic scheduling on a network, and even job scheduling at your local auto mechanic).

A priority queue could be implemented using a list of queues where each queue represented items of a given priority. Another solution to this problem is to use a minheap. Sorting the heap by priority accomplishes the first ordering (higher priority items go first). However, the first in, first out ordering of items with the same priority is something we will have to manipulate. The solution is to create a PriorityQueueNode object that stores the element to be place on the queue, the priority of the element, and the order in which elements are placed on the queue. Then we simply define the compareTo method for the PriorityQueueNode class to compare priorities first and then compare order if there is a tie. Listing 11.2 shows the PriorityQueueNode class and Listing 11.3 shows the PriorityQueue class. The UML description of the PriorityQueue class is left as an exercise.

> **key concept**
>
> Though not a queue at all, a minheap provides an efficient implementation of a priority queue.

listing 11.2

```
//****************************************************************
//   PriorityQueueNode.java       Authors: Lewis/Chase
//
//   Represents the node in a priority queue.
//****************************************************************
package jss2;

public class PriorityQueueNode implements Comparable
{
    private static int nextorder = 0;
    private int priority;
    private int order;
    private Comparable element;
```

listing
  11.2   continued

```
//-------------------------------------------------------------------
//   Creates a new PriorityQueueNode with the specified data.
//-------------------------------------------------------------------
public PriorityQueueNode (Comparable obj, int prio)
{
   element = obj;
   priority = prio;
   order = nextorder;
   nextorder++;
}

//-------------------------------------------------------------------
//   Returns the element.
//-------------------------------------------------------------------
public Comparable getElement()
{
   return element;
}

//-------------------------------------------------------------------
//   Returns the priority.
//-------------------------------------------------------------------
public int getPriority()
{
   return priority;
}

//-------------------------------------------------------------------
//   Returns the order.
//-------------------------------------------------------------------
public int getOrder()
{
   return order;
}
```

listing
    11.2   continued

```java
//-----------------------------------------------------------------
//  Returns 1 if the current node has higher priority than the
//  specified node, -1 otherwise.
//-----------------------------------------------------------------
public int compareTo(Object obj)
{
    int result;
    PriorityQueueNode temp = (PriorityQueueNode)obj;

    if (priority > temp.getPriority())
        result = 1;
    else if (priority < temp.getPriority())
        result = -1;
    else if (order > temp.getOrder())
        result = 1;
    else
        result = -1;

    return result;
}
}
```

listing
11.3

```java
//*****************************************************************
//  PriorityQueue.java        Authors: Lewis/Chase
//
//  Represents a priority queue implemented using a heap.
//*****************************************************************

package jss2;

public class PriorityQueue extends Heap
{
   //------------------------------------------------------------
   //  Creates an empty priority queue.
   //------------------------------------------------------------
   public PriorityQueue()
   {
      super();
   }


   //------------------------------------------------------------
   //  Adds the given element to the priority queue.
   //------------------------------------------------------------
   public void addElement (Comparable object, int priority)
   {
      PriorityQueueNode node = new PriorityQueueNode (object, priority);
      super.addElement(node);
   }


   //------------------------------------------------------------
   //  Removes the next highest priority element from the priority
   //  queue and returns a reference to it.
   //------------------------------------------------------------
   public Comparable removeNext()
   {
      PriorityQueueNode temp = (PriorityQueueNode)super.removeMin();
      return temp.getElement();
   }
}
```

11.4 implementing heaps: with links

All of our implementations of trees thus far have been illustrated using links. Thus it is natural to extend that discussion to a linked implementation of a heap. Because of the requirement that we be able to traverse up the tree after an insertion, it is necessary for the nodes in a heap to store a pointer to their parent. Since our `BinaryTreeNode` class did not have a parent pointer, we start our linked implementation by creating a `HeapNode` class that extends our `BinaryTreeNode` class and adds a parent pointer. Listing 11.4 shows the `HeapNode` class.

> **key concept**
>
> Because of the requirement that we be able to traverse up the tree after an insertion, it is necessary for the nodes in a heap to store a pointer to their parent.

listing 11.4

```java
//******************************************************************
//   HeapNode.java       Authors: Lewis/Chase
//
//   Represents a node in a heap.
//******************************************************************

package jss2;

public class HeapNode extends BinaryTreeNode
{
   protected HeapNode parent;

   //----------------------------------------------------------------
   //   Creates a new heap node with the specified data.
   //----------------------------------------------------------------
   HeapNode (Comparable obj)
   {
      super(obj);
      parent = null;
   }
}
```

The instance data for a linked implementation will consist of a single reference to a `HeapNode` called `lastNode` so that we can keep track of the last leaf in the heap:

```
public HeapNode lastNode;
```

the `addElement` operation

The `addElement` method must accomplish three tasks: add the new node at the appropriate location, reorder the heap to maintain the ordering property, and then reset the `lastNode` pointer to point to the new last node.

```
//---------------------------------------------------------------
//  Adds the specified element to the heap in the appropriate
//  position according to its key value.  Note that equal elements
//  are added to the right.
//---------------------------------------------------------------
public void addElement (Comparable obj)
{
   HeapNode node = new HeapNode(obj);

   if (root == null)
      root=node;
   else
   {
      HeapNode nextParent = getNextParentAdd();
      if (nextParent.left == null)
         nextParent.left = node;
      else
         nextParent.right = node;
      node.parent = nextParent;
   }

   lastNode = node;
   count++;
   if (count>1)
      heapifyAdd();
}
```

This method also makes use of two private methods: `getNextParentAdd`, which returns a reference to the node that will be the parent of the node to be inserted, and `heapifyAdd`, which accomplishes any necessary reordering of the heap starting with the new leaf and working up toward the root. Both of those methods are shown below.

```
//--------------------------------------------------------------
//  Returns the node that will be the parent of the new node.
//--------------------------------------------------------------
private HeapNode getNextParentAdd()
{
   HeapNode result = lastNode;

   while ((result != root) && (result.parent.left != result))
      result = result.parent;

   if (result != root)
      if (result.parent.right == null)
         result = result.parent;
      else
      {
         result = (HeapNode)result.parent.right;
         while (result.left != null)
            result = (HeapNode)result.left;
      }
   else
      while (result.left != null)
         result = (HeapNode)result.left;

   return result;
}


//--------------------------------------------------------------
//  Reorders the heap after adding a node.
//--------------------------------------------------------------
private void heapifyAdd()
{
   Comparable temp;
```

```
HeapNode next = lastNode;
while ((next != root) &&
    (((Comparable)next.element).compareTo(next.parent.element) < 0))
{
    temp = (Comparable)next.element;
    next.element = next.parent.element;
    next.parent.element = temp;
    next = next.parent;
}
```

the removeMin operation

The removeMin method must accomplish three tasks: replace the element stored in the root with the element stored in the last node, reorder the heap if necessary, and return the original root element. Like the addElement method, the removeMin method makes use of two additional methods: getNewLastNode, which returns a reference to the node that will be the new last node, and heapifyRemove, which will accomplish any necessary reordering of the tree starting from the root down. All three of these methods are shown below.

```
//----------------------------------------------------------
//  Removes the element with the lowest value in the heap and
//  returns a reference to it.  Throws an EmptyCollectionException
//  if the heap is empty.
//----------------------------------------------------------
public Comparable removeMin() throws EmptyCollectionException
{
    if (isEmpty())
        throw new EmptyCollectionException ("Empty Heap");

    Comparable minElement = (Comparable) root.element;

    if (count == 1)
    {
        root = null;
        lastNode = null;
    }
```

```
      else
      {
         HeapNode nextLast = getNewLastNode();
         if (lastNode.parent.left == lastNode)
            lastNode.parent.left = null;
         else
            lastNode.parent.right = null;

         root.element = lastNode.element;
         lastNode = nextLast;
         heapifyRemove();
      }

      count--;
      return minElement;
   }

   //----------------------------------------------------------------
   //  Reorders the heap after removing the root element.
   //----------------------------------------------------------------
   private void heapifyRemove()
   {
      Comparable temp;
      HeapNode node = (HeapNode)root;
      HeapNode left = (HeapNode)node.left;
      HeapNode right = (HeapNode)node.right;
      HeapNode next;

      if ((left == null) && (right == null))
         next = null;
      else if (left == null)
         next = right;
      else if (right == null)
         next = left;
      else if (((Comparable)left.element).compareTo(right.element) < 0)
         next = left;
      else
         next = right;

      while ((next != null) &&
         (((Comparable)next.element).compareTo(node.element) < 0))
      {
         temp = (Comparable)node.element;
         node.element = next.element;
         next.element = temp;
         node = next;
```

```
        left = (HeapNode)node.left;
        right = (HeapNode)node.right;
        if ((left == null) && (right == null))
            next = null;
        else if (left == null)
            next = right;
        else if (right == null)
            next = left;
        else if (((Comparable)left.element).compareTo(right.element) < 0)
            next = left;
        else
            next = right;
    }
}

//------------------------------------------------------------------
//  Returns the node that will be the new last node after a
//  remove.
//------------------------------------------------------------------
private HeapNode getNewLastNode()
{
    HeapNode result = lastNode;

    while ((result != root) && (result.parent.left == result))
        result = result.parent;

    if (result != root)
        result = (HeapNode)result.parent.left;

    while (result.right != null)
        result = (HeapNode)result.right;

    return result;
}
```

the findMin operation

The findMin method simply returns a reference to the element stored at the root
of the heap.

11.5 implementing heaps: with arrays

An array implementation of a heap may provide a simpler alternative than our linked implementation. Many of the intricacies of a the linked implementation have to do with needing to traverse up and down the tree to determine the last leaf of the tree or to determine the parent of the next node to insert. Many of those difficulties do not exist in the array implementation because we are able to determine the last node in the tree by looking at the last one stored in the array.

As we discussed in Chapter 9, a simple array implementation of a binary tree can be created using the notion that the root of the tree is in position 0, and for each node n, n's left child will be in position 2n+1 of the array and n's right child will be in position 2(n+1) of the array. Of course, the inverse is also true. For any node n other than the root, n's parent is in position (n–1)/2. Because of our ability to calculate the location of both parent and child, unlike the linked implementation, the array implementation does not require the creation of a `HeapNode` class. The UML description of the array implementation of a heap is left as an exercise.

> **key concept**
>
> In an array implementation of a binary tree, the root of the tree is in position 0, and for each node n, n's left child is in position 2n+1 and n's right child is in position 2(n+1).

the `addElement` operation

The `addElement` method for the array implementation must accomplish three tasks: add the new node at the appropriate location, reorder the heap to maintain the ordering property, and increment the count by one. Of course, as with all of our array implementations, the method must first check for available space and expand the capacity of the array if necessary. Like the linked implementation, the `addElement` operation of the array implementation makes use of a private method called `heapifyAdd` to reorder the heap if necessary.

```
//----------------------------------------------------------------
//  Adds the specified element to the heap in the appropriate
//  position according to its key value.  Note that equal elements
//  are added to the right.
//----------------------------------------------------------------
public void addElement (Comparable obj)
{
   if (count==size())
      expandCapacity();

   tree[count] = obj;
   count++;

   if (count>1)
      heapifyAdd();
}


//----------------------------------------------------------------
//  Reorders the heap to maintain the ordering property.
//----------------------------------------------------------------
private void heapifyAdd()
{
   Comparable temp;

   int next = count - 1;
   while ((next != 0) &&
      (((Comparable)tree[next]).compareTo(tree[(next-1)/2]) < 0))
   {
      temp = (Comparable)tree[next];
      tree[next] = tree[(next-1)/2];
      tree[(next-1)/2]= temp;
      next = (next-1)/2;
   }
}
```

the removeMin operation

The removeMin method must accomplish three tasks: replace the element stored in the root with the element stored in the last element, reorder the heap if necessary, and return the original root element. In the case of the array implementation, we know the last element of the heap is stored in position count –1 of the array. We then make use of a private method heapifyRemove to reorder the heap as necessary.

```
//------------------------------------------------------------------
//   Removes the element with the lowest value in the heap and
//   returns a reference to it.  Throws an EmptyHeapException if
//   the heap is empty.
//------------------------------------------------------------------
public Comparable removeMin() throws EmptyCollectionException
{
   if (isEmpty())
      throw new EmptyCollectionException ("Empty Heap");

   Comparable maxElement = (Comparable) tree[0];

   tree[0] = tree[count-1];
   heapifyRemove();
   count--;
   return maxElement;
}


//------------------------------------------------------------------
//   Reorders the heap to maintain the ordering property.
//------------------------------------------------------------------
private void heapifyRemove()
{
   Comparable temp;
   int node = 0;
   int left = 1;
   int right = 2;
   int next;

   if ((tree[left] == null) && (tree[right] == null))
      next = count;
   else if (tree[left] == null)
      next = right;
   else if (tree[right] == null)
      next = left;
   else if (((Comparable)tree[left]).compareTo(tree[right]) < 0)
      next = left;
   else
      next = right;
   while ((next < count) &&
      (((Comparable)tree[next]).compareTo(tree[node]) < 0))
```

```
    {
        temp = (Comparable)tree[node];
        tree[node] = tree[next];
        tree[next] = temp;
        node = next;
        left = 2*node+1;
        right = 2*(node+1);
        if ((tree[left] == null) && (tree[right] == null))
            next = count;
        else if (tree[left] == null)
            next = right;
        else if (tree[right] == null)
            next = left;
        else if (((Comparable)tree[left]).compareTo(tree[right]) < 0)
            next = left;
        else
            next = right;
    }
}
```

the findMin operation

Like the linked implementation, the findMin method simply returns a reference to the element stored at the root of the heap or position 0 of the array.

11.6 analysis of heap implementations

Now that we have examined each of the implementations, let's look at the efficiency of each of the operations.

the addElement operation

In the linked implementation, the first step is to determine the parent of the node to be inserted. Since, worst case, this involves traversing from the bottom right node of the heap up to the root and then down to the bottom left node of the heap, this step has time complexity 2*log n. The next step is to insert the new node. Since this involves only simple assignment statements, this step has time complexity 1. The last step is to reorder the path from the inserted leaf to the root if necessary. This process involves at most log n comparisons since that is the length of the path. Thus the addElement operation for the linked implementation has time complexity 2*log n + 1 + log n or O(log n).

The array implementation does not require the first step of determining the parent of the new node. However, both of the other steps are the same. Thus the time complexity for the addElement operation for the array implementation is 1 + log n or O(log n). Granted, the two have the same order, but the array implementation is more efficient.

the removeMin operation

The removeMin method for the linked implementation must remove the root element and replace it with the element from the last node. Since this is simply assignment statements, this step has time complexity 1. Next, this method must reorder the heap if necessary from the root down to a leaf. Since the maximum path length from the root to a leaf is log n, this step has time complexity log n. Finally, like the removeMin method, we must determine the new last node. Like the process for determining the next parent node for the addElement method, the worst case is that we must traverse from a leaf through the root and down to another leaf. Thus the time complexity of this step is 2*log n. The resulting time complexity of the removeMin operation is 2*log n + log n + 1 or O(log n).

Like the addElement method, the array implementation of the removeMin operation looks just like the linked implementation except that it does not have to determine the new last node. Thus the resulting time complexity is log n + 1 or O(log n).

the findMin operation

The findMin method for both implementations is O(1).

heap sort

Now that we have looked at the efficiency of the various implementations, we can determine the efficiency of the heap sort algorithm. It might be tempting, since both the add and remove operations are O(log n), to conclude that heap sort is also O(log n). However, keep in mind that those operations are O(log n) to add or remove a single element in a list of n elements.

With the heap sort algorithm, we are performing both operations, `addElement` and `removeMin`, n times, once for each of the elements in the list. Therefore, the resulting time complexity is 2*n*log n or O(n log n).

> **Heap sort is O(n log n).**
>
> key concept

summary of
key concepts

- A heap is a complete binary tree in which each node is less than or equal to both the left child and the right child.

- A minheap stores its smallest element at the root of the binary tree, and both children of the root of a minheap are also minheaps.

- The addElement method adds a given Comparable element to the appropriate location in the heap, maintaining both the completeness property and the ordering property of the heap.

- Since a heap is a complete tree, there is only one correct location for the insertion of a new node. That location is either the next open position from the left at level h or the first position on the left at level h+1 if level h is full.

- Typically, in heap implementations, we keep track of the position of the last node or, more precisely, the last leaf in the tree.

- In order to maintain the completeness of the tree, there is only one valid element to replace the root and that is the element stored in the last leaf in the tree.

- The heapSort method consists of adding each of the elements of the list to a heap and then removing them one at a time.

- Though not a queue at all, a minheap provides an efficient implementation of a priority queue.

- Because of the requirement that we be able to traverse up the tree after an insertion, it is necessary for the nodes in a heap to store a pointer to their parent.

- In an array implementation of a binary tree, the root of the tree is in position 0, and for each node n, n's left child is in position 2n+1 and n's right child is in position 2(n+1).

- The `addElement` operation for both the linked and array implementations is O(log n).

- The `removeMin` operation for both implementations is O(log n).

- Heap sort is O(n log n).

self-review questions

11.1   What is the difference between a heap (a minheap) and a binary search tree?

11.2   What is the difference between a minheap and a maxheap?

11.3   What does it mean for a heap to be complete?

11.4   Does a heap ever have to be rebalanced?

11.5   The `addElement` operation for the linked implementation must determine the parent of the next node to be inserted. Why?

11.6   Why does the `addElement` operation for the array implementation not have to determine the parent of the next node to be inserted?

11.7   The `removeMin` operation for both implementations replaces the element at the root with the element in the last leaf of the heap. Why is this the proper replacement?

11.8   What is the time complexity of the `addElement` operation?

11.9   What is the time complexity of the `removeMin` operation?

11.10 What is the time complexity of heap sort?

exercises

11.1   Draw the heap that results from adding the following integers (34 45 3 87 65 32 1 12 17).

11.2   Starting with the resulting tree from Exercise 11.1, draw the tree that results from performing a `removeMin` operation.

11.3 Starting with an empty minheap, draw the heap after each of the following operations:

```
addElement(40);

addElement(25):

removeMin();

addElement(10);

removeMin();

addElement(5);

addElement(1);

removeMin();

addElement(45);

addElement(50);
```

11.4 Repeat Exercise 11.3, this time with maxheap.

11.5 Draw the UML description for the `PriorityQueue` class described in the chapter.

11.6 Draw the UML description for the array implementation of heap described in the chapter.

programming projects

11.1 Implement a queue using a heap. Keep in mind that a queue is a first in, first out structure. Thus the comparison in the heap will have to be according to order entry into the queue.

11.2 Implement a stack using a heap. Keep in mind that a stack is a last in, first out structure. Thus the comparison in the heap will have to be according to order entry into the queue.

11.3 Implement a maxheap using an array implementation.

11.4 Implement a maxheap using a linked implementation.

11.5 It is possible to make the heap sort algorithm more efficient by writing a method that will order the entire list at once instead of adding the elements one at a time. Implement such a method and rewrite the heap sort algorithm to make use of it.

11.6 Use a heap to implement a simulator for a process scheduling system. In this system, jobs will be read from a file consisting of the job id (a six character string), the length of the job (an int representing seconds), and the priority of the job (an int where the higher the number the higher the priority). Each job will also be assigned an arrival number (an int representing the order of its arrival). The simulation should output the job id, the priority, the length of the job, and the completion time (relative to a simulation start time of 0).

11.7 Create a birthday reminder system using a minheap such that the ordering on the heap is done each day according to days remaining until the individual's birthday. Keep in mind, when a birthday passes, the heap must be reordered.

11.8 In Section 11.2, we described a more efficient heap sort algorithm that would build the heap within the existing array. Implement this more efficient heap sort algorithm.

answers to self-review questions

11.1 A binary search tree has the ordering property that the left child of any node is less than the node, and the node is less than or equal to its right child. A minheap is complete and has the ordering property that the node is less than both of its children.

11.2 A minheap has the ordering property that the node is less than both of its children. A maxheap has the ordering property that the node is greater than both of its children.

11.3 A heap is considered *complete* if it is balanced, meaning all of the leaves are at level h or h–1 where h is $\log_2 n$ and n is the number of elements in the tree, and all of the leaves at level h are on the left side of the tree.

11.4 No. By definition, a complete heap is balanced and the algorithms for add and remove maintain that balance.

11.5 The addElement operation must determine the parent of the node to be inserted so that a child pointer of that node can be set to the new node.

11.6   The addElement operation for the array implementation does not have to determine the parent of the new node because the new element is inserted in position count of the array and its parent is determined by position in the array.

11.7   In order to maintain the completeness of the tree, the only valid replacement for the element at the root is the element at the last leaf. Then the heap must be reordered as necessary to maintain the ordering property.

11.8   For both implementations, the addElement operation is O(log n). However, despite having the same order, the array implementation is somewhat more efficient since it does not have to determine the parent of the node to be inserted.

11.9   For both implementations, the removeMin operation is O(log n). However, despite having the same order, the array implementation is somewhat more efficient since it does not have to determine the new last leaf.

11.10 The heap sort algorithm is O(n log n).

multi-way search trees

When we first introduced the concept of efficiency of algorithms, we said that we were interested in issues such as processing time and memory. In this chapter, we explore multi-way trees that were specifically designed around the use of space and the effect that a particular use of space could have on the total processing time for an algorithm.

12.1 `combining tree concepts`

In Chapter 9 we established the difference between a general tree, which has a varying number of children per node, and a binary tree, which has at most two children per node. Then in Chapter 10 we discussed the concept of a search tree, which has a specific ordering relationship among the elements in the nodes to allow efficient searching for a target value. In particular, in Chapter 10 we focused on binary search trees. Now we can combine these concepts and extend them further.

In a *multi-way search tree*, each node might have more than two child nodes, and (because it is a search tree) there is a specific ordering relationship among the elements. Furthermore, a single node in a multi-way search tree may store more than one element.

This chapter examines three specific forms of a multi-way search tree:

▸ 2-3 trees

▸ 2-4 trees

▸ B-trees

12.2 `2-3 trees`

A *2-3 tree* is a multi-way search tree in which each node has two children (referred to as a *2-node*) or three children (referred to as a *3-node*). A 2-node contains one element and, like a binary search tree, the left subtree contains elements that are less than that element and the right subtree contains elements that are greater than or equal to that element. However, unlike a binary search tree, a 2-node can have either no children or two children—it cannot have just one child.

A 3-node contains two elements, one designated as the smaller element and one as the larger element. A 3-node has either no children or three children. If a 3-node has children, the left subtree contains elements that are less than the smaller element and the right subtree contains elements that are greater than the larger element. The middle subtree contains elements that are greater than or equal to the smaller element and less than the larger element.

All of the leaves of a 2-3 tree are on the same level. Figure 12.1 illustrates a valid 2-3 tree.

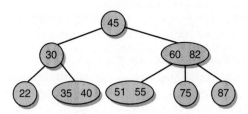

figure 12.1   A 2-3 tree

inserting elements into a 2-3 tree

Similar to a binary search tree, all insertions into a 2-3 tree occur at the leaves of the tree. That is, the tree is searched to determine where the new element will go, then it is inserted. Unlike a binary tree, however, the process of inserting an element into a 2-3 tree can have a ripple effect on the structure of the rest of the tree.

Inserting an element into a 2-3 tree has three cases. The first, and simplest, case is that the tree is empty. In this case, a new node is created containing the new element, and this node is designated as the root of the tree.

The second case occurs when we want to insert a new element at a leaf that is a 2-node. That is, we traverse the tree to the appropriate leaf (which may also be the root) and find that the leaf is a 2-node (containing only one element). In this case, the new element is added to the 2-node, making it a 3-node. Note that the new element may be less than or greater than the existing element. Figure 12.2 illustrates this case by inserting the value 27 into the tree pictured in Figure 12.1. The leaf node containing 22 is a 2-node, therefore 27 is inserted into that node,

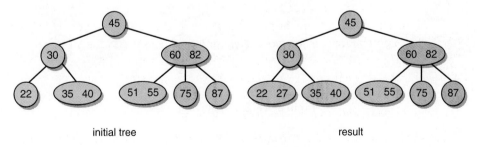

initial tree   result

figure 12.2   Inserting 27

making it a 3-node. Note that neither the number of nodes in the tree nor the height of the tree changed because of this insertion.

The third insertion situation occurs when we want to insert a new element at a leaf that is a 3-node (containing two elements). In this case, because the 3-node cannot hold any more elements, it is *split,* and the middle element is moved up a level in the tree. The middle element that moves up a level could be either of the two elements that already existed in the 3-node, or it could be the new element being inserted. It depends on the relationship among those three elements.

Figure 12.3 shows the result of inserting the element 32 into the tree from Figure 12.2. Searching the tree, we reach the 3-node that contains the elements 35 and 40. That node is split and the middle element (35) is moved up to join its parent node. Thus the internal node that contains 30 becomes a 3-node that contains both 30 and 35. Note that the act of splitting a 3-node results in two 2-nodes at the leaf level. In this example, we are left with one 2-node that contains 32 and another 2-node that contains 40.

Now consider the situation in which we must split a 3-node whose parent is itself a 3-node already. The middle element that is promoted causes the parent to split, moving an element up yet another level in the tree. Figure 12.4 shows the effect of inserting the element 57 into the tree from Figure 12.3. Searching the tree, we reach the 3-node leaf that contains 51 and 55. This node is split, causing the middle element 55 to move up a level. But that node is already a 3-node, containing the values 60 and 82. Therefore we split that node as well, promoting the element 60, which joins the 2-node containing 45 at the root.

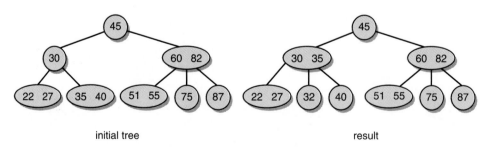

initial tree   result

figure 12.3 Inserting 32

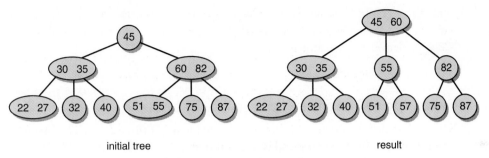

initial tree   result

figure 12.4   Inserting 57

2-node is encountered (which can accommodate the new element). Therefore, inserting an element into a 2-3 tree can cause a ripple effect that changes several nodes in the tree.

> **key concept**
>
> Inserting an element into a 2-3 tree can have a ripple effect up the tree.

If this effect propagates all the way to the root of the entire tree, a new 2-node root is created. For example, inserting the element 25 into the tree from Figure 12.4 results in the tree depicted in Figure 12.5. The 3-node containing 22 and 27 is split, promoting 25. This causes the 3-node containing 30 and 35 to split, promoting 30. This causes the 3-node containing 45 and 60 (which happens to be the root of the entire tree) to split, creating a new 2-node root that contains 45.

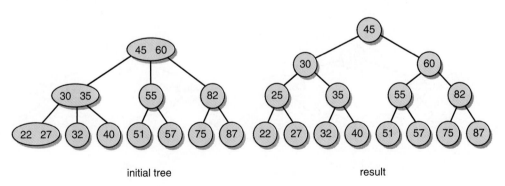

initial tree   result

figure 12.5   Inserting 25

Note that when the root of the tree splits, the height of the tree increases by one. The insertion strategy for a 2-3 tree keeps all of the leaves at the same level.

removing elements from a 2-3 tree

Removal of elements from a 2-3 tree is also made up of three cases. The first case is that the element to be removed is in a leaf that is a 3-node. In this case, removal is simply a matter of removing the element from the node. Figure 12.6 illustrates this process by removing the element 51 from the tree we began with in Figure 12.1. Note that the properties of a 2-3 tree are maintained.

The second case is that the element to be removed is in a leaf that is a 2-node. This condition is called *underflow* and creates a situation in which we must rotate the tree and/or reduce the tree's height in order to maintain the properties of the 2-3 tree. This situation can be broken down into four subordinate cases that we will refer to as cases 2.1, 2.2, 2.3, and 2.4. Figure 12.7 illustrates case 2.1 and shows what happens if we remove the element 22 from our initial tree from Figure 12.1. In this case, since the parent node has a right child that is a 3-node, we can maintain the properties of a 2-3 tree by rotating the smaller element of the 3-node around the parent. The same process will work if the element being removed from a 2-node leaf is the right child, and the left child is a 3-node.

What happens if we now remove the element 30 from the resulting tree in Figure 12.7? We can no longer maintain the properties of a 2-3 tree through a

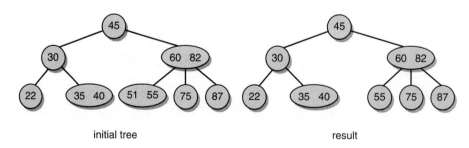

initial tree   result

figure 12.6   Removal from a 2-3 tree (case 1)

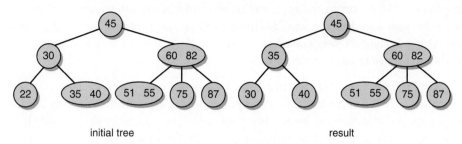

initial tree   result

figure 12.7   Removal from a 2-3 tree (case 2.1)

local rotation. Keep in mind, a node in a 2-3 tree cannot have just one child. Since the leftmost child of the right child of the root is a 3-node, we can rotate the smaller element of that node around the root to maintain the properties of a 2-3 tree. This process is illustrated in Figure 12.8 and represents case 2.2. Notice that

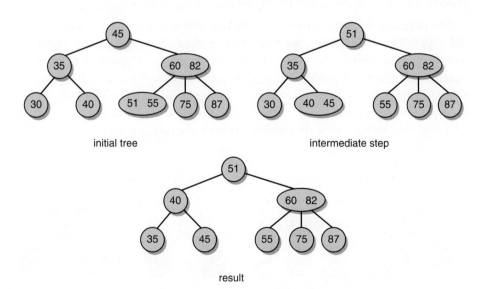

initial tree   intermediate step

result

figure 12.8   Removal from a 2-3 tree (case 2.2)

the element 51 moves to the root, the element 45 becomes the larger element in a 3-node leaf, and then the smaller element of that leaf is rotated around its parent. Once element 51 was moved to the root and element 45 was moved to a 3-node leaf, we were back in the same situation as case 2.1.

Given the resulting 2-3 tree in Figure 12.8, what happens if we now remove element 55? None of the leaves of this tree are 3-nodes. Thus rotation from a leaf, even from a distance, is no longer an option. However, since the parent node is a 3-node, all that is required to maintain the properties of a 2-3 node is to change this 3-node to a 2-node by rotating the smaller element (60) into what will now be the left child of the node. Figure 12.9 illustrates this process.

If we then remove element 60 (using case 1), the resulting tree contains nothing but 2-nodes. Now, if we remove another element, perhaps element 45, rotation is no longer an option. We must instead reduce the height of the tree in order to maintain the properties of a 2-3 tree. This is case 2.4. To accomplish this, we simply combine each of the leaves with their parent and siblings in order. If any of these combinations contain more than two elements, we split them into two 2-nodes and promote or propagate the middle element. Figure 12.10 illustrates this process for reducing the height of the tree.

The third case is that the element to be removed is in an internal node. As we did with binary search trees, we can simply replace the element to be removed with its inorder predecessor. In a 2-3 tree, the inorder predecessor of an internal element will always be a leaf, which, if it is a 2-node, will bring us back to our first case, and if it is a 3-node, requires no further action. Figure 12.11 illustrates these possibilities by removing the element 30 from our original tree from Figure 12.1 and then by removing the element 60 from the resulting tree.

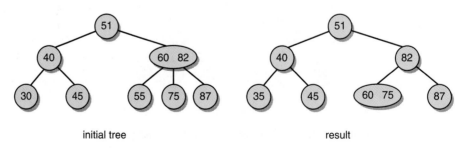

initial tree   result

figure 12.9   Removal from a 2-3 tree (case 2.3)

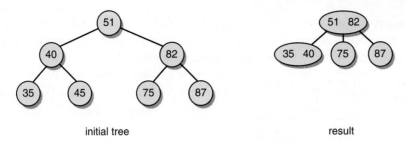

initial tree   result

figure 12.10   Removal from a 2-3 tree (case 2.4)

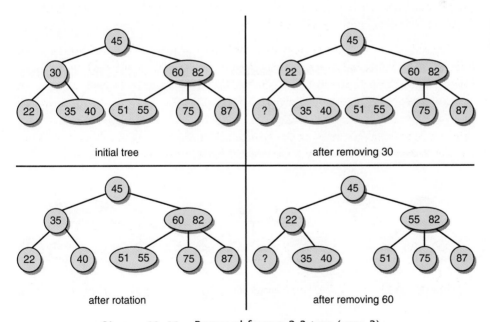

initial tree   after removing 30

after rotation   after removing 60

figure 12.11   Removal from a 2-3 tree (case 3)

12.3 2-4 trees

A *2-4 tree* is similar to a 2-3 tree, adding the characteristic that a node can contain three elements. Expanding on the same principles as a 2-3 tree, a *4-node* contains three elements and has either no children or four children. The same ordering property applies: the left child will be less than the leftmost element of a node, which will be less than or equal to the second child of the node, which will be less than the second element of the node, which will be less than or equal to the third child of the node, which will be less than the third element of the node, which will be less than or equal to the fourth child of the node.

The same cases for insertion and removal of elements apply, with 2-nodes and 3-nodes behaving similarly on insertion and 3-nodes and 4-nodes behaving similarly on removal. Figure 12.12 illustrates a series of insertions into a 2-4 tree. Figure 12.13 illustrates a series of removals from a 2-4 tree.

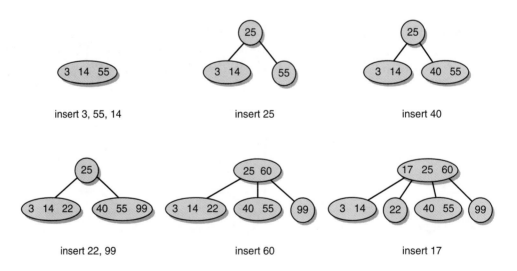

figure 12.12 Insertions into a 2-4 tree

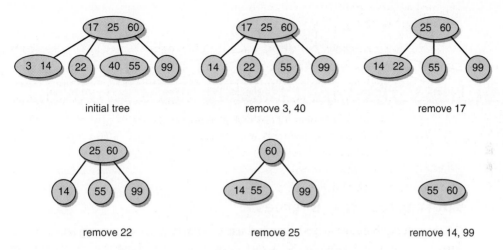

figure 12.13 Removals from a 2-3 tree

12.4 B-trees

Both 2-3 and 2-4 trees are examples of a larger class of multi-way search trees called *B-trees*. We refer to the maximum number of children of each node as the *order* of the B-tree. Thus, 2-3 trees are order 3 B-trees, and 2-4 trees are order 4 B-trees.

> **key concept**
>
> A B-tree extends the concept of 2-3 and 2-4 trees so that nodes can have an arbitrary maximum number of elements.

B-trees of order m have the following properties:

- The root has at least two subtrees unless it is a leaf.
- Each non-root internal node n holds k–1 elements and k children where $\lceil m/2 \rceil \le k \le m$.
- Each leaf n holds k-1 elements where $\lceil m/2 \rceil \le k \le m$.
- All leaves are on the same level.

Figure 12.14 illustrates a B-tree of order 6.

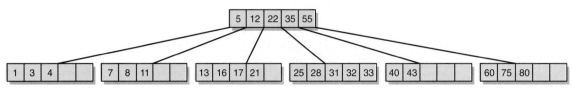

`figure 12.14`   A B-tree of order 6

motivation for B-trees

The reasoning behind the creation and use of B-trees is an interesting study of the effects of algorithm and data structure design. To understand this reasoning, we must understand the context of most all of the collections we have discussed thus far. Our assumption has always been that we were dealing with a collection in primary memory. However, what if the data set that we are manipulating is too large for primary memory? In that case, our data structure would be paged in and out of memory from disk or some other secondary storage device. An interesting thing happens to time complexity once a secondary storage device is involved. No longer is the time to access an element of the collection simply a function of how many comparisons are needed to find the element. Now we must also consider the access time of the secondary storage device and how many separate accesses we will make to that device.

In the case of a disk, this access time consists of seek time (the time it takes to position the read-write head over the appropriate track on the disk), rotational delay (the time it takes to spin the disk to the correct sector), and the transfer time (the time it takes to transfer a block of memory from the disk into primary memory). Adding this "physical" complexity to the access time for a collection can be very costly. Access to secondary storage devices is very slow relative to access to primary storage.

Given this added time complexity, it makes sense to develop a structure that minimizes the number of times the secondary storage device must be accessed. A B-tree can be just such a structure. B-trees are typically tuned so that the size of a node is the same as the size of a block on secondary storage. In this way, we get the maximum amount of data for each disk access. Since B-trees can have many more elements per node than a binary tree, they are much flatter structures than binary trees. This reduces the number of nodes and/or blocks that must be accessed, thus improving performance.

We have already demonstrated the processes of insertion and removal of elements for 2-3 and 2-4 trees, both of which are B-trees. The process for any order m B-tree is similar. Let's now briefly examine some interesting variations of B-trees that were designed to solve specific problems.

B*-trees

One of the potential problems with a B-tree is that while we are attempting to minimize access to secondary storage, we have actually created a data structure that may be half empty. In order to minimize this problem, B*-trees were developed. B*-trees have all of the same properties as B-trees except that instead of each node having k children where $\lceil m/2 \rceil \leq k \leq m$, in a B*-tree, each node has k children where $\lceil (2m-1)/3 \rceil \leq k \leq m$. This means that each non-root node is at least two-thirds full.

This is accomplished by delaying splitting of nodes by rebalancing across siblings. Once siblings are full, instead of splitting one node into two, creating two half-full nodes, we split two nodes into three, creating three two-thirds full nodes.

B+-trees

Another potential problem with B-trees is sequential access. As with any tree, we can use an inorder traversal to look at the elements of the tree sequentially. However, this means that we are no longer taking advantage of the blocking structure of secondary storage. In fact, we have made it much worse because now we will access each block containing an internal node many separate times as we pass through it during the traversal.

B+-trees provide a solution to this problem. In a B-tree, each element appears only once in the tree, regardless of whether it appears in an internal node or in a leaf. In a B+-tree, each element appears in a leaf, regardless of whether or not it appears in an internal node. Elements appearing in an internal node will be listed again as the inorder successor (which is a leaf) of their position in the internal node. Additionally, each leaf node will maintain a pointer to the following leaf node. In this way, a B+-tree provides indexed access through the B-tree structure and sequential access through a linked list of leaves. Figure 12.15 illustrates this strategy.

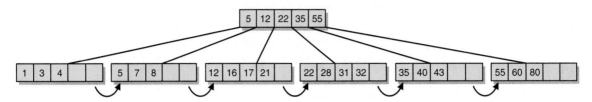

figure 12.15   A B+-tree of order 6

analysis of B-trees

With balanced binary search trees, we were able to say that searching for an element in the tree was $O(\log_2 n)$. This is due to the fact that, at worst, we had to search a single path from the root to a leaf in the tree and that, at worst, the length of that path would be $\log_2 n$. Analysis of B-trees is similar. At worst, searching a B-tree, we will have to search a single path from the root to a leaf, and at worst, that path length will be $\log_m n$, where m is the order of the B-tree and n is the number of elements in the tree. However, finding the appropriate node is only part of the search. The other part of the search is finding the appropriate path from each node, and then finding the target element in a given node. Since there are up to m-1 elements per node, it may take up to m-1 comparisons per node to find the appropriate path and/or to find the appropriate element. Thus the analysis of a search of a B-tree yields $O((m-1)\log_m n)$. Since for any given implementation, m is a constant, we can say that searching a B-tree is $O(\log n)$.

The analysis of insertion and deletion from a B-tree is similar and is left as an exercise.

12.5 implementation strategies for B-trees

Through most of this text, we have provided a variety of implementations for the collections we have discussed. As we have progressed, however, we have gradually transitioned from providing full implementations to providing partial implementations and algorithms. Now that you are much more experienced in the development of collections, we will provide strategies and algorithms but leave the implementations as exercises.

We have already discussed insertion of elements into B-trees, removal of elements from B-trees, and the balancing mechanisms necessary to maintain the properties of a B-tree. What remains is to discuss strategies for storing B-trees. While it might seem natural to think about B-tree nodes being a collection of elements and pointers or object reference variables, this is probably not the best approach. Keep in mind that the B-tree structure was developed specifically to address the issue of a collection that must move in and out of primary memory from secondary storage. If we attempt to use object reference variables, what we are actually doing is storing a primary memory address for an object. Once that object is moved back to secondary storage, that address is no longer valid.

A better solution is to think of each node as a pair of arrays. The first array would be an array of m−1 elements and the second array would be an array of m children. Next, if we think of the tree itself as one large array of nodes, then the elements stored in the array of children in each node would simply be integer indexes into this array of nodes.

> **key concept**
>
> Arrays are a better solution both within a B-tree node and for collecting B-tree nodes because they are effective in both primary memory and secondary storage.

In primary memory, this strategy works because, using an array, as long as we know the index position of the element within the array, it does not matter to us where the array is loaded in primary memory. For secondary memory, this same strategy works because, given that each node is of fixed length, the address in memory of any given node is given by:

The base address of the file + (index of the node − 1) * length of a node.

summary of key concepts

- A multi-way search tree can have more than two children per node and can store more than one element in each node.

- A 2-3 tree contains nodes that contain either one or two elements and have two or three children.

- Inserting an element into a 2-3 tree can have a ripple effect up the tree.

- If the propagation effect of a 2-3 tree insertion causes the root to split, the tree increases in height.

- A 2-4 tree expands on the concept a 2-3 tree to include the use of 4-nodes.

- A B-tree extends the concept of 2-3 and 2-4 trees so that nodes can have an arbitrary maximum number of elements.

- Access to secondary storage is very slow relative to access to primary storage, which is motivation to use structures such as B-trees.

- Arrays are a better solution both within a B-tree node and for collecting B-tree nodes because they are effective in both primary memory and secondary storage.

self-review questions

12.1   Describe the nodes in a 2-3 tree.

12.2   When does a node in a 2-3 tree split?

12.3   How can splitting a node in a 2-3 tree affect the rest of the tree?

12.4   Describe the process of deleting an element from a 2-3 tree.

12.5   Describe the nodes in a 2-4 tree.

12.6   How do insertions and deletions in a 2-4 tree compare to insertions and deletions in a 2-3 tree?

12.7   When is rotation no longer an option for rebalancing a 2-3 tree after a deletion?

exercises

12.1 Draw the 2-3 tree that results from adding the following elements into an initially empty tree:

> 34 45 3 87 65 32 1 12 17

12.2 Using the resulting tree from Exercise 12.1, draw the resulting tree after removing each of the following elements:

> 3 87 12 17 45

12.3 Repeat Exercise 12.1 using a 2-4 tree.

12.4 Repeat Exercise 12.2 using the resulting 2-4 tree from Exercise 12.3.

12.5 Draw the order 8 B-tree that results from adding the following elements into an initially empty tree:

> 34 45 3 87 65 32 1 12 17 33 55 23 67 15 39 11 19 47

12.6 Draw the B-tree that results from removing the following from the resulting tree from Exercise 12.5:

> 1 12 17 33 55 23 19 47

12.7 Describe the complexity (order) of insertion into a B-tree.

12.8 Describe the complexity (order) of deletion from a B-tree.

programming projects

12.1 Create an implementation of a 2-3 tree using the array strategy discussed in Section 12.5.

12.2 Create an implementation of a 2-3 tree using a linked strategy.

12.3 Create an implementation of a 2-4 tree using the array strategy discussed in Section 12.5.

12.4 Create an implementation of a 2-4 tree using a linked strategy.

12.5 Create an implementation of an order 7 B-tree using the array strategy discussed in Section 12.5.

12.6 Create an implementation of an order 9 B^+-tree using the array strategy discussed in Section 12.5.

12.7 Create an implementation of an order 11 B^*-tree using the array strategy discussed in Section 12.5.

12.8   Implement a graphical system to manage employees using an employee id, employee name, and years of service. The system should use an order 7 B-tree to store employees, and must provide the ability to add and remove employees. After each operation, your system must update a sorted list of employees sorted by name on the screen.

answers to self-review questions

12.1   A 2-3 tree node can have either one element or two, and can have no children, two children, or three children. If it has one element, then it is a 2-node and either has no children or two children. If it has two elements, then it is a 3-node and either has no children or three children.

12.2   A 2-3 tree node spits when it has three elements. The smallest element becomes a 2-node, the largest element becomes a 2-node, and the middle element is promoted or propagated to the parent node.

12.3   If the split and resulting propagation forces the root node to split, then it will increase the height of the tree.

12.4   Deletion from a 2-3 tree falls into one of three cases. Case 1, deletion of an element from a 3-node leaf, means simply removing the element and has no impact on the rest of the tree. Case 2, deletion of an element from a 2-node leaf, results in one of four cases. Case 2.1, deletion of an element from a 2-node that has a 3-node sibling, is resolved by rotating either the inorder predecessor or inorder successor of the parent, depending upon whether the 3-node is a left child or a right child, around the parent. Case 2.2, deletion of an element from a 2-node when there is a 3-node leaf elsewhere in the tree, is resolved by rotating an element out of that 3-node and propagating that rotation until a sibling of the node being deleted becomes a 3-node, then this case becomes case 2.1. Case 2.3, deletion of a 2-node where there is a 3-node internal node, can be resolved through rotation as well. Case 2.3, deletion of a 2-node when there are no 3-nodes in the tree, is resolved by reducing the height of the tree.

12.5   Nodes in a 2-4 tree are exactly like those of a 2-3 tree except that 2-4 trees also allow 4-nodes, or nodes containing three elements and having four children.

12.6   Insertions and deletions in a 2-4 tree are exactly like those of a 2-3 tree except that splits occur when there are four elements instead of three as in a 2-3 tree.

12.7   If all of the nodes in 2-3 tree are 2-nodes, then rotation is not an option for rebalancing.

references

Bayer, R. "Symmetric Binary B-trees: Data Structure and Maintenance Algorithms." *Acta Informatica* (1972): 290–306.

Comer, D. "The Ubiquitous B-Tree." *Computing Surveys* 11 (1979): 121–137.

Wedeking, H. "On the Selection of Access Paths in a Data Base System." In *Data Base Management*, edited by J.W. Klimbie and K.L. Koffeman, 385–397. Amsterdam: North-Holland, 1974.

In Chapter 10, we discussed the idea that
a binary search tree is, in effect,
an efficient implementation of
a set or a map. In this chapter,
we examine hashing, an
approach to implementing a set
or map collection that can be
even more efficient than binary
search trees.

chapter
objectives

▶ Define hashing

▶ Examine various hashing functions

▶ Examine the problem of collisions
in hash tables

▶ Explore the Java Collections API
implementations of hashing

13.1 a hashing

In all of our discussions of the implementations of collections, we have proceeded with one of three assumptions about the order of elements in a collection:

- Order is unimportant, as in the case of our bag and unordered list collections.

- Order is determined by the order elements are added and/or removed from our collection, as in the case of stacks, queues, and indexed lists.

- Order is determined by comparing the values of the elements (or some key component of the elements) to be stored in the collection, as in the case of ordered lists and binary search trees.

In this chapter we will explore the concept of *hashing*, which means that the order—and, more specifically, the location of an item within the collection—is determined by some function of the value of the element to be stored, or some function of a key value of the element to be stored. In hashing, elements are stored in a *hash table*, with their location in the table determined by a *hashing function*. Each location in the table may be referred to as a *cell* or a *bucket*. We will discuss hashing functions further in Section 13.2. We will discuss implementation strategies and algorithms, and leave the implementations as programming projects.

> **key concept**
>
> In hashing, elements are stored in a hash table, with their location in the table determined by a hashing function.

Consider a simple example where we create an array that will hold 26 elements. Wishing to store names in our array, we create a hashing function that equates each name to the position in the array associated with the first letter of the name (e.g., a first letter of A would be mapped to position 0 of the array, a first letter of D would be mapped to position 3 of the array). Figure 13.1 illustrates this scenario after several names have been added.

Notice that unlike our earlier implementations of collections, using a hashing approach results in the access time to a particular element being independent of the number of elements in the table. This means that all of the operations on an element of a hash table should be O(1). This is the result of no longer having to do comparisons to find a particular element or to locate the appropriate position for a given element. Using hashing, we simply calculate where a particular element should be.

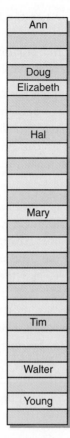

figure 13.1   A simple hashing example

However, this efficiency is only fully realized if each element maps to a unique position in the table. Consider our example from Figure 13.1. What will happen if we attempt to store the name "Ann" and the name "Andrew"? This situation, where two elements or keys map to the same location in the table, is called a *collision*. We will discuss how to resolve collisions in Section 13.3.

A hashing function that maps each element to a unique position in the table is said to be a *perfect hashing function*. While it is possible in some situations to develop a perfect hashing function, a hashing function that does a good job of distributing the elements among the table positions will still result in constant time (O(1)) access to elements in the table and an improvement over our earlier algorithms that were either O(n) in the case of our linear approaches or O(log n) in the case of search trees.

Another issue surrounding hashing is the question of how large the table should be. If the data set is of known size and a perfect hashing function can be used, then we simply make the table the same size as the data set. If a perfect hashing function is not available or practical but the size of the data set is known, a good rule of thumb is to make the table 150 percent the size of the data set.

The third case is very common and far more interesting. What if we do not know the size of the data set? In this case, we depend on *dynamic resizing.* Dynamic resizing of a hash table involves creating a new hash table that is larger than, perhaps even twice as large as, the original, inserting all of the elements of the original table into the new table, and then discarding the original table. Deciding when to resize is also an interesting question. One possibility is to use the same method we used with our earlier array implementations and simply expand the table when it is full. However, it is the nature of hash tables that their performance seriously degrades as they become full. A better approach is to use a *load factor.* The load factor of a hash table is the percentage occupancy of the table at which the table will be resized. For example, if the load factor were set to 0.50, then the table would be resized each time it reached 50 percent capacity.

13.2 hashing functions

While perfect hashing functions are possible if the data set is known, we do not need the hashing function to be perfect to get good performance from the hash table. Our goal is simply to develop a function that does a reasonably good job of distributing our elements in the table such that we avoid collisions. A reasonably good hashing function will still result in constant time access (O(1)) to our data set.

There a variety of approaches to developing a hashing function for a particular data set. The method that we used in our example in the previous section is called *extraction.* Extraction involves using only a part of the element's value or key to compute the location at which to store the element. In our previous example, we simply extracted the first letter of a string and computed its value relative to the letter A.

Other examples of extraction would be to store phone numbers according to the last four digits, or to store information about cars according to the first three characters of the license plate.

the division method

Creating a hashing function by *division* simply means we will use the remainder of the key divided by some positive integer p as the index for the given element. This function could be defined as follows:

```
Hashcode(key) = Math.abs(key)%p
```

This function will yield a result in the range from 0 to p–1. If we use our table size as p, we then have an index that maps directly to a location in the table. Using a prime number p as the table size and the divisor helps provide a better distribution of keys to locations in the table.

For example, if our key value is 79 and our table size is 43, the division method would result in an index value of 36. The division method is very effective when dealing with an unknown set of key values.

> **key concept**
> The division method is very effective when dealing with an unknown set of key values.

the folding method

In the *folding method*, the key is divided into parts that are then combined or folded together to create an index into the table. This is done by first dividing the key into parts where each of the parts of the key will be the same length as the desired index, except possibly the last one. In the *shift folding method*, these parts are then added together to create the index. For example, if our key is the Social Security number 987-65-4321, we might divide this into three parts, 987, 654, and 321. Adding these together yields 1962. Assuming we are looking for a three-digit key, at this point we could use either division or extraction to get our index.

> **key concept**
> In the shift folding method, the parts of the key are added together to create the index.

A second possibility is *boundary folding*. There are a number of variations on this approach. However, generally, they involve reversing some of the parts of the key before adding. One variation on this approach is to imagine that the parts of the key are written side by side on a piece of paper and that the piece of paper is folded along the boundaries of the parts of the key. In this way, if we begin with the same key, 987-65-4321, we first divide it into parts, 987, 654, and 321. We then reverse every other part of the key, yielding 987, 456, and 321. Adding these together yields 1764 and once again we can proceed with either extraction or division to get our index. Other variations on folding use different algorithms to determine which parts of the key to reverse.

Folding may also be a useful method for building a hashing function for a key that is a string. One approach to this is to divide the string into substrings the same length (in bytes) as the desired index and then combine these strings using an exclusive-or function. This is also a useful way to convert a string to a number so that other methods, such as division, may be applied to strings.

the mid-square method

In the *mid-square method*, the key is multiplied by itself and then the extraction method is used to extract the appropriate number of digits from the middle of the squared result to serve as an index. The same "middle" digits must be chosen each time, to provide consistency. For example, if our key is 4321, we would multiply the key by itself, yielding 18671041. Assuming that we need a three-digit key, we might extract 671 or 710, depending upon how we construct our algorithm. It is also possible to extract bits instead of digits and then construct the index from the extracted bits.

The mid-square method may also be effectively used with strings by manipulating the binary representations of the characters in the string.

the radix transformation method

In the *radix transformation method*, the key is transformed into another numeric base. For example, if our key is 23 in base 10, we might convert it to 32 in base 7. We then use the division method and divide the converted key by the table size and use the remainder as our index. Continuing our previous example, if our table size is 17, we would compute the function:

```
Hashcode(23) = Math.abs(32)%17
```

the digit analysis method

In the *digit analysis method*, the index is formed by extracting, and then manipulating, specific digits from the key. For example, if our key is 1234567, we might select the digits in positions 2 through 4, yielding 234, and then manipulate them to form our index. This manipulation can take many forms, including simply reversing the digits (yielding 432), performing a circular shift to the right (yielding 423), performing a circular shift to the left (yielding 342), swapping each pair of digits (yielding 324), or any number of other possibilities including the methods we have already discussed. The goal is simply to provide a function that does a reasonable job of distributing keys to locations in the table.

the length-dependent method

In the *length-dependent method*, the key and the length of the key are combined in some way to form either the index itself or an intermediate value that is then used with one of our other methods to form the index. For example, if our key is 8765, we might multiply the first two digits by the length and then divide by the last digit, yielding 69. If our table size is 43, we would then use the division method, resulting in an index of 26.

> **key concept**
>
> The length-dependent method and the mid-square method may also be effectively used with strings by manipulating the binary representations of the characters in the string.

The length-dependent method may also be effectively used with strings by manipulating the binary representations of the characters in the string.

hashing functions in the Java language

The `java.lang.Object` class defines a method called `hashcode` that returns an integer based on the memory location of the object. This is generally not very useful. Classes that are derived from `Object` often override the inherited definition of `hashcode` to provide their own version. For example, the `String` and `Integer` classes define their own `hashcode` methods. These more specific `hashcode` functions can be very effective for hashing. By having the `hashcode` method defined in the `Object` class, all Java objects can be hashed. However, it is also possible, and often preferable, to define your own `hashcode` method for any class that you intend to store in a hash table.

> **key concept**
>
> Although Java provides a `hashcode` method for all objects, it is often preferable to define a specific hashing function for any particular class.

13.3 resolving collisions

If we are able to develop a perfect hashing function for a particular data set, then we do not need to concern ourselves with collisions: the situation where more than one element or key map to the same location in the table. However, when a perfect hashing function is not possible or practical, there are a number of ways to handle collisions. Similarly, if we are able to develop a perfect hashing function for a particular data set, then we do not need to concern ourselves with the size of the table. In this case, we will simply make the table the exact size of the data set. Otherwise, if the size of the data set is known, it is generally a good idea to set the initial size of the table to about 150 percent of the expected element count. If the size of the data set is not known, then dynamic resizing of the table becomes an issue.

chaining

The *chaining method* for handling collisions simply treats the hash table conceptually as a table of collections rather than as a table of individual cells. Thus each cell is a pointer to the collection associated with that location in the table. Usually this internal collection is either an unordered list or an ordered list. Figure 13.2 illustrates this conceptual approach.

> **key concept**
>
> The chaining method for handling collisions simply treats the hash table conceptually as a table of collections rather than as a table of individual cells.

Chaining can be implemented in a variety of ways. One approach would be to make the array holding the table larger than the number of cells in the table and use the extra space as an overflow area to store the linked lists associated with each table location. In this method, each position in the array could store both an element (or a key) and the array index of the next element in its list. The first element mapped to a particular location in the table would actually be stored in that location. The next element mapped to that location would be stored in a free location in this overflow area and the array index of this second element would be stored with the first element in the table. If a third element is mapped to the same location, the third element would also be stored in this overflow area and the index of third element would be stored with the second element. Figure 13.3 illustrates this strategy.

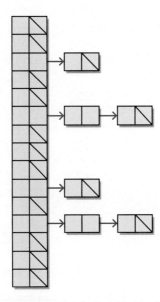

figure 13.2   The chaining method of collision handling

Note that, using this method, the table itself can never be full. However, if the table is implemented as an array, the array can become full, requiring a decision on whether to throw an exception or simply expand capacity. In our earlier collections, we chose to expand the capacity of the array. In this case, expanding the capacity of the array but leaving the embedded table the original size would have disastrous effects on efficiency. A more complete solution is to expand the array and expand the embedded table within the array. This will, however, require that all of the elements in the table be rehashed using the new table size. We will discuss the dynamic resizing of hash tables further in Section 13.5.

Using this method, the worst case is that our hashing function will not do a good job of distributing elements to locations in the table so that we end up with one linked list of n elements, or a small number of linked lists with roughly n/k elements each, where k is some relatively small constant. In this case, hash tables become O(n) for both insertions and searches. Thus you can see how important it is to develop a good hashing function.

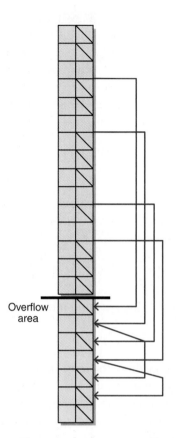

figure 13.3 Chaining using an overflow area

A second method for implementing chaining is to use links. In this method, each cell or bucket in the hash table would be something like the `LinearNode` class used in earlier chapters to construct linked lists. In this way, as a second element is mapped to a particular bucket, we simply create a new `LinearNode`, set the `next` reference of the existing node to point to the new node, set the `element` reference of the new node to the element being inserted, and set the `next` reference of the new node to null. The result is an implementation model that looks exactly like the conceptual model shown in Figure 13.2.

A third method for implementing chaining is to literally make each position in the table a pointer to a collection. In this way, we could represent each position in the table with a list or perhaps even a more efficient collection (e.g., a balanced binary search tree) and this would improve our worst case. Keep in mind, however, that if our hashing function is doing a good job of distributing elements to locations in the table, this approach may incur a great deal of overhead while accomplishing very little improvement.

open addressing

The *open addressing method* for handling collisions looks for another open position in the table other than the one to which the element is originally hashed. There are a variety of methods to find another available location in the table. We will examine three of these methods: linear probing, quadratic probing, and double hashing.

> The open addressing method for handling collisions looks for another open position in the table other than the one to which the element is originally hashed.
>
> key concept

The simplest of these methods is *linear probing*. In linear probing, if an element hashes to position p and position p is already occupied, we simply try position (p+1)%s, where s is the size of the table. If position (p+1)%s is already occupied, we try position (p+2)%s, and so on until either we find an open position or we find ourselves back at the original position. If we find an open position, we insert the new element. What to do if we do not find an open position is a design decision when creating a hash table. As we have discussed previously, one possibility is to throw an exception if the table is full. A second possibility is to expand the capacity of the table and rehash the existing entries.

The problem with linear probing is that it tends to create clusters of filled positions within the table, and these clusters then affect the performance of insertions and searches. Figure 13.4 illustrates the linear probing method and the creation of a cluster using our earlier hashing function of extracting the first character of the string.

In this example, Ann was entered, followed by Andrew. Since Ann already occupied position 0 of the array, Andrew was placed in position 1. Later, Bob was entered. Since Andrew already occupied position 1, Bob was placed in the next open position, which was position 2. Doug and Elizabeth were already in the

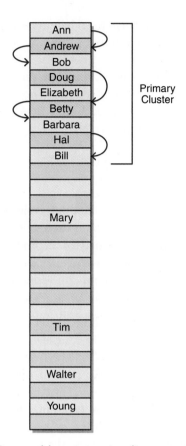

figure 13.4 Open addressing using linear probing

table by the time Betty arrived, thus Betty could not be placed in position 1, 2, 3, or 4 and was placed in the next open position, position 5. After Barbara, Hal, and Bill were added, we find that there is now a nine-location cluster at the front of the table, which will continue to grow as more names are added. Thus we see that linear probing may not be the best approach.

A second form of the open addressing method is *quadratic probing*. Using quadratic probing, instead of using a linear approach, once we have a collision, we follow a formula such as

```
newhashcode(x) = hashcode(x) + (-1)^(i-1)((i+1)/2)^2
```

for i in the range 1 to s-1 where s is the table size.

The result of this formula is the search sequence p, p + 1, p − 1, p + 4, p − 4, p + 9, p − 9, ... Of course, this new hash code is then put through the division method to keep it within the table range. As with linear probing, the same possibility exists that we will eventually get back to the original hash code without having found an open position in which to insert. This "full" condition can be handled in all of the same ways that we described for chaining and linear probing. The benefit of the quadratic probing method is that it does not have as strong a tendency toward clustering as does linear probing. Figure 13.5 illustrates quadratic probing for the same key set and hashing function that we used in Figure 13.4. Notice that after the same data has been entered, we still have a cluster at the front of the table. However, this cluster only occupies six buckets instead of the nine-bucket cluster created by linear probing.

A third form of the open addressing method is *double hashing*. Using the double hashing method, we will resolve collisions by providing a secondary hashing function to be used when the primary hashing function results in a collision. For example, if a key x hashes to a position p that is already occupied, then the next position p' that we will try will be

```
p' = p + secondaryhashcode(x)
```

If this new position is also occupied, then we look to position

```
p" = p + 2 * secondaryhashcode(x)
```

We continue searching this way, of course using the division method to maintain our index within the bounds of the table, until an open position is found. This method, while somewhat more costly because of the introduction of an additional function, tends to further reduce clustering beyond the improvement gained by quadratic probing. Figure 13.6 illustrates this approach, again using the same key set and hashing function from our previous examples. For this

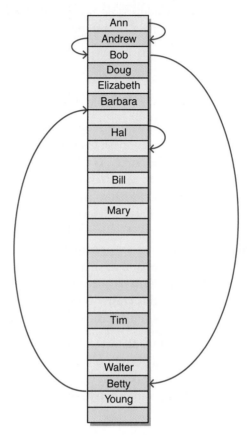

figure 13.5   Open addressing using quadratic probing

example, the secondary hashing function is the length of the string. Notice that with the same data, we no longer have a cluster at the front of the table. However, we have developed a six-bucket cluster from Doug through Barbara. The advantage of double hashing, however, is that even after a cluster has been created, it will tend to grow more slowly than it would if we were using linear probing or even quadratic probing.

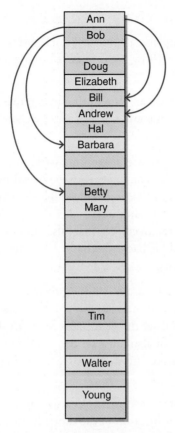

figure 13.6   Open addressing using double hashing

13.4 deleting elements from a hash table

Thus far, our discussion has centered on the efficiency of insertion of and search-ing for elements in a hash table. What happens if we remove an element from a hash table? The answer to this question depends upon which implementation we have chosen.

deleting from a chained implementation

If we have chosen to implement our hash table using a chained implementation and an array with an overflow area, then removing an element falls into one of five cases:

Case 1   The element we are attempting to remove is the only one mapped to the particular location in the table. In this case, we simply remove the element by setting the table position to null.

Case 2   The element we are attempting to remove is stored in the table (not in the overflow area) but has an index into the overflow area for the next element at the same position. In this case, we replace the element and the next index value in the table with the element and next index value of the array position pointed to by the element to be removed. We then also must set the position in the overflow area to null and add it back to whatever mechanism we are using to maintain a list of free positions.

Case 3   The element we are attempting to remove is at the end of the list of elements stored at that location in the table. In this case, we set its position in the overflow area to null, and set the next index value of the previous element in the list to null as well. We then also must set the position in the overflow area to null and add it back to whatever mechanism we are using to maintain a list of free positions.

Case 4   The element we are attempting to remove is in the middle of the list of elements stored at that location in the table. In this case, we set its position in the overflow area to null, and set the next index value of the previous element in the list to the next index value of the element being removed. We then also must add it back to whatever mechanism we are using to maintain a list of free positions.

Case 5   The element we are attempting to remove is not in the list. In this case, we throw an `ElementNotFoundException`.

If we have chosen to implement our hash table using a chained implementation where each element in the table is a collection, then we simply remove the target element from the collection.

deleting from open addressing implementation

If we have chosen to implement our hash table using an open addressing implementation, then deletion creates more of a challenge. Consider the example in Figure 13.7. Notice that elements "Ann," "Andrew," and "Amy" all mapped to the same location in the table and the collision was resolved using linear probing. What happens if we now remove "Andrew"? If we then search for "Amy" we will not find that element because the search will find "Ann" and then follow the linear probing rule to look in the next position, find it null, and return an exception.

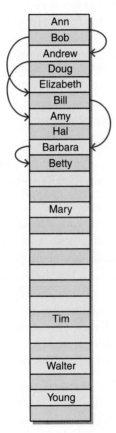

figure 13.7   Open addressing and deletion

The solution to this problem is to mark items as deleted but not actually remove them from the table until some future point when the deleted element is overwritten by a new inserted element or the entire table is rehashed, either because it is being expanded or because we have reached some predetermined threshold for the percentage of deleted records in the table. This means that we will need to add a `boolean` flag to each node in the table and modify all of our algorithms to test and/or manipulate that flag.

13.5 hash tables in the Java Collections API

The Java Collections API provides seven implementations of hashing: `Hashtable`, `HashMap`, `HashSet`, `IdentityHashMap`, `LinkedHashSet`, `LinkedHashMap`, and `WeakHashMap`. To understand these different solutions we must first remind ourselves of the distinction between a *set* and a *map* in the Java Collections API as well as some of our other pertinent definitions.

A *set* is a collection of objects where in order to find an object, we must have an exact copy of the object for which we are looking. A *map*, on the other hand, is a collection that stores key-value pairs so that, given the key, we can find the associated value.

Another definition that will be useful to us as we explore the Java Collections implementations of hashing is the concept of a *load factor* that we discussed earlier. The load factor is the maximum percentage occupancy allowed in the hash table before it is resized. For the implementations that we are going to discuss here, the default is 0.75. Thus, using this default, when one of these implementations becomes 75 percent full, a new hash table is created that is twice the size of the current one, and then all of the elements from the current table are inserted into the new table. The load factor of these implementations can be altered when the table is created.

> **key concept**
>
> The load factor is the maximum percentage occupancy allowed in the hash table before it is resized.

All of these implementations rely on the `hashcode` method of the object being stored to return an integer. This integer is then processed using the division method (using the table size) to produce an index within the bounds of the table. As stated earlier, the best practice is to define your own `hashcode` method for any class that you intend to store in a hash table.

Let's look at each of these implementations.

Hashtable

The `Hashtable` implementation of hashing is the oldest of the implementations in the Java Collections API. In fact, it predates the Collections API and was modified in version 1.2 to implement the `Map` interface so that it would become a part of the Collections API. Unlike the newer Java Collections implementations, `Hashtable` is synchronized. Table 13.1 shows the operations for the `Hashtable` class.

Return Value	Method	Description
	`Hashtable()`	Constructs a new, empty hash table with a default initial capacity (11) and load factor, which is 0.75.
	`Hashtable(int initialCapacity)`	Constructs a new, empty hash table with the specified initial capacity and default load factor, which is 0.75.
	`Hashtable(int initialCapacity, float loadFactor)`	Constructs a new, empty hash table with the specified initial capacity and the specified load factor.
	`Hastable (Map t)`	Constructs a new hash table with the same mappings as the given `Map`.
`void`	`clear()`	Clears this hash table so that it contains no keys.
`Object`	`clone()`	Creates a shallow copy of this hash table.
`boolean`	`contains(Object value)`	Tests if some key maps into the specified value in this hash table.
`boolean`	`containsKey(Object key)`	Tests if the specified object is a key in this hash table.
`boolean`	`containsValue (Object value)`	Returns true if this hash table maps one or more keys to this value.
`Enumeration`	`elements()`	Returns an enumeration of the values in this hash table.
`Set`	`entrySet()`	Returns a `Set` view of the entries contained in this hash table.
`boolean`	`equals(Object o)`	Compares the specified `Object` with this `Map` for equality, as per the definition in the `Map` interface.
`Object`	`get(Object key)`	Returns the value to which the specified key is mapped in this hash table.
`int`	`hashCode()`	Returns the hash code value for this `Map` as per the definition in the `Map` interface.
`boolean`	`isEmpty()`	Tests if this hash table maps no keys to values.
`Enumeration`	`keys()`	Returns an enumeration of the keys in this hash table.
`Set`	`keysSet)`	Returns a `Set` view of the keys contained in this hash table.

table 13.1   Operations on the `Hashtable` class

Object	put(Object key Object value)	Maps the specified key to the specified value in this hash table.
void	putAll(Map t)	Copies all of the mappings from the specified Map to this hash table. These mappings will replace any mappings that this hash table had for any of the keys currently in the specified Map.
protected void	rehash()	Increases the capacity of and internally reorganizes this hash table, in order to accommodate and access its entries more efficiently.
Object	remove(Object key)	Removes the key (and its corresponding value) from this hash table.
int	size()	Returns the number of keys in this hash table.
String	toString()	Returns a string representation of this hash table object in the form of a set of entries, enclosed in braces and separated by the ASCII characters comma and space.
Collection	values()	Returns a Collection view of the values contained in this hash table.

table 13.1   Operations on the Hashtable class

Creation of a Hashtable requires two parameters: initial capacity (with a default of 11) and load factor (with a default of 0.75). Capacity refers to the number of cells or locations in the initial table. Load factor is, as we described earlier, the maximum percentage occupancy allowed in the hash table before it is resized. Hashtable uses the chaining method for resolving collisions.

The Hashtable class is a legacy class that will be most useful if you are connecting to legacy code or require synchronization. Otherwise, it is preferable to use the HashMap class.

HashSet

The HashSet class implements the Set interface using a hash table. The HashSet class, like most of the Java Collections API implementations of hashing, uses chaining to resolve collisions (each table position effectively being a linked list). The HashSet implementation does not guarantee the order of the set on iteration and does not guarantee that the order will remain constant over time. This is due to the fact that the iterator simply steps through the table in order. Since the hashing function will somewhat randomly distribute the elements to table positions, order cannot be guaranteed. Further, if the table is expanded, all of the elements are rehashed relative to the new table size, and the order may change.

Like the `Hashtable` class, the `HashSet` class also requires two parameters: initial capacity and load factor. The default for the load factor is the same as it is for `Hashtable` (0.75). The default for initial capacity is currently unspecified (originally it was 101). Table 13.2 shows the operations for the `HashSet` class. The `HashSet` class is not synchronized and permits null values.

Return Value	Method	Description
	`HashSet()`	Constructs a new, empty set; the backing `HashMap` instance has the default capacity and load factor, which is 0.75.
	`HashSet(Collection c)`	Constructs a new set containing the elements in the specified collection.
	`HashSet(int initialCapacity)`	Constructs a new, empty set; the backing `HashMap` instance has the specified initial capacity and default load factor, which is 0.75.
	`HashSet(int initial Capacity, float loadFactor)`	Constructs a new, empty set; the backing hashmap instance has the specified initial capacity and the specified load factor.
`boolean`	`add(Object o)`	Adds the specified element to this set if it is not already present.
`void`	`clear()`	Removes all of the elements from this set.
`Object`	`clone()`	Returns a shallow copy of this `HashSet` instance: the elements themselves are not cloned.
`boolean`	`contains(Object o)`	Returns true if this set contains the specified element.
`boolean`	`isEmpty()`	Returns true if this set contains no elements.
`iterator()`	`iterator()`	Returns an iterator over the elements in this set.
`boolean`	`remove(Object o)`	Removes the given element from this set if it is present.
`int`	`size()`	Returns the number of elements in this set (its cardinality).

table 13.2   Operations on the `HashSet` class

the `HashMap` class

The `HashMap` class implements the `Map` interface using a hash table. The `HashMap` class also uses a chaining method to resolve collisions. Like the `HashSet` class, the `HashMap` class is not synchronized and allows null values. Also like the previous implementations, the default load factor is 0.75. Like the `HashSet` class, the current default initial capacity is unspecified though it was also originally 101.

Table 13.3 shows the operations on the `HashMap` class.

the `IdentityHashMap` class

The `IdentityHashMap` class implements the `Map` interface using a hash table. The difference between this and the `HashMap` class is that the `IdentityHashMap` class uses reference-equality instead of object-equality when comparing both keys and values. This is the difference between using `key1==key2` and using `key1.equals(key2)`.

This class has one parameter: expected maximum size. This is the maximum number of key-value pairs that the table is expected to hold. If the table exceeds this maximum, then the table size will be increased and the table entries rehashed.

Table 13.4 shows the operations on the `IdentityHashMap` class.

the `WeakHashMap` class

The `WeakHashMap` class implements the `Map` interface using a hash table. This class is specifically designed with weak keys so that an entry in a `WeakHashMap` will automatically be removed when its key is no longer in use. In other words, if the use of the key in a mapping in the `WeakHashMap` is the only remaining use of the key, the garbage collector will collect it anyway.

The `WeakHashMap` class allows both null values and null keys, and has the same tuning parameters as the `HashMap` class: initial capacity and load factor.

Table 13.5 shows the operations on the `WeakHashMap` class.

Return Value	Method	Description
	HashMap()	Constructs a new, empty map with a default capacity and load factor, which is 0.75.
	HashMap(int initial Capacity)	Constructs a new, empty map with the specified initial capacity and default load factor, which is 0.75.
	HashMap(int initial Capacity, float loadFactor)	Constructs a new, empty map with the specified initial capacity and the specified load factor.
	HashMap(Map t)	Constructs a new map with the same mappings as the given map.
void	clear()	Removes all mappings from this map.
Object	clone()	Returns a shallow copy of this HashMap instance: the keys and values themselves are not cloned.
boolean	containsKey(Object key)	Returns true if this map contains a mapping for the specified key.
boolean	containsValue (Object value)	Returns true if this map maps one or more keys to the specified value.
set	entrySet()	Returns a collection view of the mappings contained in this map.
Object	get(Object key)	Returns the value to which this map maps the specified key.
boolean	isEmpty()	Returns true if this map contains no key-value mappings.
Set	keySet()	Returns a set view of the keys contained in this map.
Object	put(Object key, Object value)	Associates the specified value with the specified key in this map.
void	putAll(Map t)	Copies all of the mappings from the specified map to this one.
Object	remove(Object key)	Removes the mapping for this key from this map if present.
int	size()	Returns the number of key-value mappings in this map.
Collection	values()	Returns a collection view of the values contained in this map.

table 13.3   Operations on the HashMap class

Return Value	Method	Description
	IdentityHashMap()	Constructs a new, empty identity hash map with a default expected maximum size (21).
	IdentityHashMap(int expectedMaxSize)	Constructs a new, empty map with the specified expected maximum size.
	IdentityHashMap(Map m)	Constructs a new identity hash map containing the keys-value mappings in the specified map.
void	clear()	Removes all mappings from this map.
Object	clone()	Returns a shallow copy of this identity hash map: the keys and values themselves are not cloned.
boolean	containsKey(Object key)	Tests whether the specified object reference is a key in this identity hash map.
boolean	containsValue (Object value)	Tests whether the specified object reference is a value in this identity hash map.
Set	entrySet()	Returns a set view of the mappings contained in this map.
boolean	equals(Object o)	Compares the specified object with this map for equality.
Object	get(Object key)	Returns the value to which the specified key is mapped in this identity hash map, or null if the map contains no mapping for this key.
int	hashCode()	Returns the hash code value for this map.
boolean	isEmpty()	Returns true if this identity hash map contains no key-value mappings.
Set	keySet()	Returns an identity-based set view of the keys contained in this map.
Object	put(Object key, Object value)	Associates the specified value with the specified key in this identity hash map.
void	putAll(Map t)	Copies all of the mappings from the specified map to this map. These mappings will replace any mappings that this map had for any of the keys currently in the specified map.
Object	remove(Object key)	Removes the mapping for this key from this map if present.
int	size()	Returns the number of key-value mappings in this identity hash map.
Collection	values()	Returns a collection view of the values contained in this map.

table 13.4   Operations on the IdentityHashMap class

Return Value	Method	Description
	`WeakHashMap()`	Constructs a new, empty `WeakHashMap` with the default initial capacity and the default load factor, which is 0.75.
	`WeakHashMap(int initialCapacity)`	Constructs a new, empty `WeakHashMap` with the given initial capacity and the default load factor, which is 0.75.
	`WeakHashMap(int initial Capacity, float loadFactor)`	Constructs a new, empty `WeakHashMap` with the given initial capacity and the given load factor.
	`WeakHashMap(Map t)`	Constructs a new `WeakHashMap` with the same mappings as the specified map.
`void`	`clear()`	Removes all mappings from this map.
`boolean`	`containsKey(Object key)`	Returns true if this map contains a mapping for the specified key.
`Set`	`entrySet()`	Returns a set view of the mappings in this map.
`Object`	`get(Object key)`	Returns the value to which this map maps the specified key.
`boolean`	`isEmpty()`	Returns true if this map contains no key-value mappings.
`Set`	`keySet()`	Returns a set view of the keys contained in this map.
`Object`	`put(Object key, Object value)`	Associates the specified value with the specified key in this map.
`void`	`putAll(Map t)`	Copies all of the mappings from the specified map to this map. These mappings will replace any mappings that this map had for any of the keys currently in the specified map.
`Object`	`remove(Object key)`	Removes the mapping for the given key from this map, if present.
`int`	`size()`	Returns the number of key-value mappings in this map.
`Collection`	`values()`	Returns a collection view of the values contained in this map.

table 13.5   Operations on a `WeakHashMap`

LinkedHashSet and LinkedHashMap

The two remaining hashing implementations are extensions of previous classes. The `LinkedHashSet` class extends the `HashSet` class, and the `LinkedHashMap` class extends the `HashMap` class. Both of them are designed to solve the problem of iterator order. These implementations maintain a doubly linked list running through the entries in order to maintain the insertion order of the elements. Thus the iterator order for these implementations is the order in which the elements were inserted.

Table 13.6 shows the additional operations for the LinkedHashSet class. Table 13.7 shows the additional operations for the LinkedHashMap class.

Return Value	Method	Description
	LinkedHashSet()	Constructs a new, empty linked hash set with the default initial capacity (16) and load factor (0.75).
	LinkedHashSet (Collection c)	Constructs a new linked hash set with the same elements as the specified collection.
	LinkedHashSet (int initialCapacity)	Constructs a new, empty linked hash set with the specified initial capacity and the default load factor (0.75).
	LinkedHashSet(int initialCapacity, float loadFactor)	Constructs a new, empty linked hash set with the specified initial capacity and load factor.

table 13.6   Additional operations on the LinkedHashSet class

Return Value	Method	Description
	LinkedHashMap()	Constructs an empty insertion-ordered LinkedHashMap instance with a default capacity (16) and load factor (0.75).
	LinkedHashMap (int initialCapacity)	Constructs an empty insertion-ordered LinkedHashMap instance with the specified initial capacity and a default load factor (0.75).
	LinkedHashMap (int initialCapacity, float loadFactor)	Constructs an empty insertion-ordered LinkedHashMap instance with the specified initial capacity and load factor.
	LinkedHashMap (int initialCapacity, float loadFactor, boolean accessOrder)	Constructs an empty Linkedhashmap instance with the specified initial capacity, load factor, and ordering mode.
	LinkedHashMap(Map m)	Constructs an insertion-ordered LinkedHashMap instance with the same mappings as the specified map.
void	clear()	Removes all mappings from this map.
boolean	containsValue (Object value)	Returns true if this map maps one or more keys to the specified value.
Object	get(Object key)	Returns the value to which this map maps the specified key.
protected boolean	removeEldestEntry (Map.Entry eldest)	Returns true if this map should remove its eldest entry.

table 13.7   Additional operations on the LinkedHashMap class

summary of key concepts

▸ In hashing, elements are stored in a *hash table,* with their location in the table determined by a *hashing function.*

▸ The situation where two elements or keys map to the same location in the table is called a *collision.*

▸ A hashing function that maps each element to a unique position in the table is said to be a *perfect hashing function.*

▸ Extraction involves using only a part of the element's value or key to compute the location at which to store the element.

▸ The division method is very effective when dealing with an unknown set of key values.

▸ In the shift folding method, the parts of the key are added together to create the index.

▸ The length-dependent method and the mid-square method may also be effectively used with strings by manipulating the binary representations of the characters in the string.

▸ Although Java provides a `hashcode` method for all objects, it is often preferable to define a specific hashing function for any particular class.

▸ The chaining method for handling collisions simply treats the hash table conceptually as a table of collections rather than as a table of individual cells.

▸ The open addressing method for handling collisions looks for another open position in the table other than the one to which the element is originally hashed.

▸ The load factor is the maximum percentage occupancy allowed in the hash table before it is resized.

self-review questions

13.1   What is the difference between a hash table and the other collections we have discussed?

13.2   What is a collision in a hash table?

13.3   What is a perfect hashing function?

13.4   What is our goal for a hashing function?

13.5   What is the consequence of not having a good hashing function?

13.6   What is the extraction method?

13.7   What is the division method?

13.8   What is the shift folding method?

13.9   What is the boundary folding method?

13.10 What is the mid-square method?

13.11 What is the radix transformation method?

13.12 What is the digit analysis method?

13.13 What is the length-dependent method?

13.14 What is chaining?

13.15 What is open addressing?

13.16 What are linear probing, quadratic probing, and double hashing?

13.17 Why is deletion from an open addressing implementation a problem?

13.18 What is the load factor and how does it affect table size?

exercises

13.1   Draw the hash table that results from adding the following integers (34 45 3 87 65 32 1 12 17) to a hash table of size 11 using the division method and linked chaining.

13.2   Draw the hash table from Exercise 13.1 using a hash table of size 11 using array chaining with a total array size of 20.

13.3   Draw the hash table from Exercise 13.1 using a table size of 17 and open addressing using linear probing.

13.4   Draw the hash table from Exercise 13.1 using a table size of 17 and open addressing using quadratic probing.

13.5   Draw the hash table from Exercise 13.1 using a table size of 17 and double hashing using extraction of the first digit as the secondary hashing function.

13.6   Draw the hash table that results from adding the following integers (1983, 2312, 6543, 2134, 3498, 7654, 1234, 5678, 6789) to a hash table using shift folding of the first two digits with the last two digits. Use a table size of 13.

13.7 Draw the hash table from Exercise 13.6 using boundary folding.

13.8 Draw a UML diagram that shows how all of the various implementations of hashing within the Java Collections API are constructed.

programming projects

13.1 Implement the hash table illustrated in Figure 13.1 using the array version of chaining.

13.2 Implement the hash table illustrated in Figure 13.1 using the linked version of chaining.

13.3 Implement the hash table illustrated in Figure 13.1 using open addressing with linear probing.

13.4 Implement a dynamically resizable hash table to store people's names and Social Security numbers. Use the extraction method with division using the last four digits of the Social Security number. Use an initial table size of 31 and a load factor of 0.80. Use open addressing with double hashing using an extraction method on the first three digits of the Social Security number.

13.5 Implement the problem from Programming Project 13.4 using linked chaining.

13.6 Implement the problem from Programming Project 13.4 using the HashMap class of the Java Collections API.

13.7 Create a new implementation of the bag collection called HashtableBag using a hash table.

13.8 Implement the problem from Programming Project 13.4 using shift folding with the Social Security number divided into three equal three-digit parts.

13.9 Create a graphical system that will allow a user to add and remove employees where each employee has an employee id (six-digit number), employee name, and years of service. Use the hashcode method of the Integer class as your hashing function and use one of the Java Collections API implementations of hashing.

13.10 Complete Programming Project 13.9 using your own hashcode function. Use extraction of the first three digits of the employee id as the hashing function and use one of the Java Collections API implementations of hashing.

13.11   Complete Programming Project 13.9 using your own `hashcode` function and your own implementation of a hash table.

13.12   Create a system that will allow a user to add and remove vehicles from an inventory system. Vehicles will be represented by license number (an eight-character string), make, model, and color. Use your own array-based implementation of a hash table using chaining.

13.13   Complete Programming Project 13.12 using a linked implementation with open addressing and double hashing.

answers to self-review questions

13.1   Elements are placed into a hash table at an index produced by a function of the value of the element or a key of the element. This is unique from other collections where the position/location of an element in the collection was determined either by comparison with the other values in the collection or by the order in which the elements were added or removed from the collection.

13.2   The situation where two elements or keys map to the same location in the table is called a collision.

13.3   A hashing function that maps each element to a unique position in the table is said to be a perfect hashing function.

13.4   We need a hashing function that will do a good job of distributing elements into positions in the table.

13.5   If we do not have a good hashing function, the result will be too many elements mapped to the same location in the table. This will result in poor performance.

13.6   Extraction involves using only a part of the element's value or key to compute the location at which to store the element.

13.7   The division method involves dividing the key by some positive integer p (usually the table size and usually prime) and then using the remainder as the index.

13.8   Shift folding involves dividing the key into parts (usually the same length as the desired index) and then adding the parts. Extraction or division is then used to get an index within the bounds of the table.

13.9   Like shift folding, boundary folding involves dividing the key into parts (usually the same length as the desired index). However, some of the parts are then reversed before adding. One example is to imagine that the parts are written side by side on a piece of paper, which is then folded on the boundaries between parts. In this way, every other part is reversed.

13.10 The mid-square method involves multiplying the key by itself and then extracting some number of digits or bytes from the middle of the result. Division can then be used to guarantee an index within the bounds of the table.

13.11 The radix transformation method is a variation on the division method where the key is first converted to another numeric base and then divided by the table size with the remainder used as the index.

13.12 In the digit analysis method, the index is formed by extracting, and then manipulating, specific digits from the key.

13.13 In the length-dependent method, the key and the length of the key are combined in some way to form either the index itself or an intermediate value that is then used with one of our other methods to form the index.

13.14 The chaining method for handling collisions simply treats the hash table conceptually as a table of collections rather than as a table of individual cells. Thus each cell is a pointer to the collection associated with that location in the table. Usually this internal collection is either an unordered list or an ordered list.

13.15 The open addressing method for handling collisions looks for another open position in the table other than the one to which the element is originally hashed.

13.16 Linear probing, quadratic probing, and double hashing are methods for determining the next table position to try if the original hash causes a collision.

13.17 Because of the way that a path is formed in open addressing, deleting an element from the middle of that path can cause elements beyond that on the path to be unreachable.

13.18 The load factor is the maximum percentage occupancy allowed in the hash table before it is resized. Once the load factor has been reached, a new table is created that is twice the size of the current table, and then all of the elements in the current table are inserted into the new table.

In Chapter 9, we introduced the concept
of a tree, a nonlinear structure defined
by the concept that each node in the tree,
other than the root node, has
exactly one parent. If we were to
violate that premise and allow
each node in the tree to be connected to a variety of other
nodes with no notion of parent
or child, the result would be the
concept of a graph, which we
explore in this chapter. Graphs
and graph theory make up entire
subdisciplines of both mathematics and computer science. In
this chapter we introduce the
basic concepts of graphs and
their implementation.

14.1   undirected graphs

Like trees, a graph is made up of nodes and the connections between those nodes. In graph terminology, we refer to the nodes as *vertices* and refer to the connections among them as *edges*. Vertices are typically referenced by a name or a label. For example, we might label vertices A, B, C, and D. Edges are referenced by a pairing of the vertices that they connect. For example, we might have an edge (A, B), which means there is and edge from vertex A to vertex B.

> **key concept**
> An undirected graph is a graph where the pairings representing the edges are unordered.

An *undirected graph* is a graph where the pairings representing the edges are unordered. Thus, listing an edge as (A, B) means that there is a connection between A and B that can be traversed in either direction. Thus, in an undirected graph, listing an edge as (A, B) means exactly the same thing as listing the edge as (B, A). Figure 14.1 illustrates an undirected graph.

> **key concept**
> Two vertices in a graph are adjacent if there is an edge connecting them.

Two vertices in a graph are *adjacent* if there is an edge connecting them. For example, in the graph of Figure 14.1, vertices A and B are adjacent while vertices A and D are not. Adjacent vertices are sometimes referred to as *neighbors*. An edge of a graph that connects a vertex to itself is called a *self-loop* or a *sling*.

> **key concept**
> An undirected graph is considered complete if it has the maximum number of edges connecting vertices.

An undirected graph is considered *complete* if it has the maximum number of edges connecting vertices. For the first vertex, it requires (n–1) edges to connect it to the other vertices. For the second vertex, it requires only (n–2) edges since it is already connected to the first vertex. For the third vertex, it requires (n–3) edges. This sequence contin-

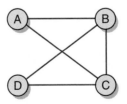

figure 14.1   An example undirected graph

ues until the final vertex requires no additional edges because all the other vertices have already been connected to it. Mathematically, this is the summation:

$$\sum_{i=1}^{n-1} i = \frac{n(n-1)}{2}$$

A *path* is a sequence of edges that connects two vertices in a graph. For example, in our graph from Figure 14.1, A, B, D is a path from A to D. Notice that each sequential pair, (A, B) and then (B, D), is an edge. A path in an undirected graph is bi-directional. For example, A, B, D is the path from A to D but since the edges are undirected, the inverse, D, B, A, is also the path from D to A. The *length* of a path is the number of edges in the path (or the number of vertices − 1). So for our previous example, the path length is 2. Notice that this definition of path length is identical to the definition that we used in discussing trees. In fact, trees are graphs.

An undirected graph is considered *connected* if for any two vertices in the graph, there is a path between them. Our graph from Figure 14.1 is connected. The same graph with a minor modification is not connected, as illustrated in Figure 14.2.

A *cycle* is a path in which the first and last vertices are the same and none of the edges are repeated. In Figure 14.2, we would say that the path A, B, C, A is a cycle. A graph that has no cycles is called *acyclic*. Earlier we mentioned the relationship between graphs and trees. Now that we have introduced these definitions, we can formalize that relationship. An undirected tree is a connected, acyclic, undirected graph with one element designated as the root.

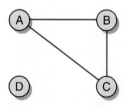

figure 14.2   An example undirected graph that is not connected

14.2 directed graphs

A *directed graph*, sometimes referred to as a *digraph*, is a graph where the edges are ordered pairs of vertices. This means that the edges (A, B) and (B, A) are separate, directional edges in a directed graph. In our previous example we had the following description for an undirected graph:

Vertices: A, B, C, D

Edges: (A, B), (A, C), (B, C), (B, D)

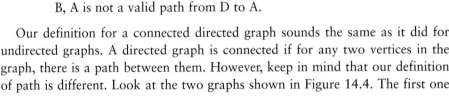

> **key concept**
> A directed graph, sometimes referred as a digraph, is a graph where the edges are ordered pairs of vertices.

Figure 14.3 shows what happens if we interpret this earlier description as a directed graph. We represent each of the edges now with the direction of traversal specified by the ordering of the vertices. For example, the edge (A, B) allows traversal from A to B but not the other direction.

> **key concept**
> A path in a directed graph is a sequence of directed edges that connects two vertices in a graph.

Our previous definitions change slightly for directed graphs. For example, a path in a directed graph is a sequence of directed edges that connects two vertices in a graph. In our undirected graph we listed the path A, B, D, as the path from A to D, and that is still true in our directed interpretation of the graph description. However, paths in a directed graph are not bi-directional, so the inverse is no longer true: D, B, A is not a valid path from D to A.

Our definition for a connected directed graph sounds the same as it did for undirected graphs. A directed graph is connected if for any two vertices in the graph, there is a path between them. However, keep in mind that our definition of path is different. Look at the two graphs shown in Figure 14.4. The first one

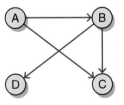

figure 14.3   An example directed graph

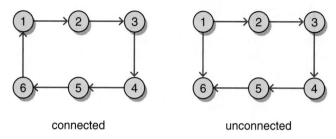

connected   unconnected

figure 14.4   A connected and an unconnected directional graph

is connected. The second one, however, is not connected because there is no path from any other vertex to vertex 1.

If a directed graph has no cycles, it is possible to arrange the vertices such that vertex A precedes vertex B if an edge exists from A to B. The order of vertices resulting from this arrangement is called *topological order* and is very useful for examples such as course prerequisites.

As we discussed earlier, trees are graphs. In fact, most of our previous work with trees actually focused on directed trees. A directed tree is a directed graph that has an element designated as the root and has the following properties:

▸ There are no connections from other vertices to the root.

▸ Every non-root element has exactly one connection to it.

▸ There is a path from the root to every other vertex.

14.3 networks

A *network,* or a *weighted graph,* is a graph with weights or costs associated with each edge. Figure 14.5 shows an undirected network of the connections and the airfares between cities. This weighted graph or network could then be used to determine the cheapest path from one city to another. The weight of a path in a weighted graph is the sum of the weights of the edges in the path.

> **key concept**
>
> A network, or a weighted graph, is a graph with weights or costs associated with each edge.

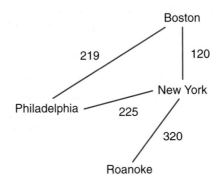

figure 14.5   An undirected network

Networks may be either undirected or directed depending upon the need. Take our airfare example from Figure 14.5. What if the airfare to fly from New York to Boston is one price but the airfare to fly from Boston to New York is a different price? This would be an excellent application of a directed network, as illustrated in Figure 14.6.

For networks, we represent each edge with a triple including the starting vertex, ending vertex, and the weight. Keep in mind, for undirected networks, the starting and ending vertices could be swapped with no impact. However, for

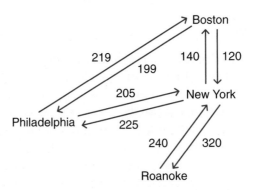

figure 14.6   A directed network

directed graphs, a triple must be included for every directional connection. For example, the network of Figure 14.6 would be represented as follows:

Vertices: Boston, New York, Philadelphia, Roanoke

Edges: (Boston, New York, 120), (Boston, Philadelphia, 199),
      (New York, Boston, 140), (New York, Philadelphia, 225),
      (New York, Roanoke, 320), (Philadelphia, Boston, 219),
      (Philadelphia, New York, 205), (Roanoke, New York, 240)

14.4 common graph algorithms

There are a number of common graph algorithms that may apply to undirected graphs, directed graphs, and/or networks. These include various traversal algorithms (or iterators) similar to what we explored with trees, as well as algorithms for finding the shortest path, algorithms for finding the least costly path in a network, and algorithms to answer simple questions about the graph such as whether or not the graph is connected or the shortest path between two vertices.

traversals

In our discussion of trees in Chapter 9, we defined four types of traversals or iterators: pre-order traversal, in-order traversal, post-order traversal, and level-order traversal. Since we know that a tree is a graph, we know that for certain types of graphs these traversals would still apply. Generally, however, we divide graph traversal into two categories: breadth-first traversal, which behaves very much like the level-order traversal of a tree, and depth-first traversal, which behaves very much like the pre-order traversal of a tree. One difference here is that there is not a root node. Thus our traversal may start at any vertex in the graph.

We can construct a breadth-first traversal for a graph using two queues. We will use one queue (traversal-queue) to manage the traversal and the other (result-queue) to build our result. The first step is to enqueue the starting vertex into the traversal-queue and mark the starting vertex as visited. We then begin a loop that will continue until the traversal-queue is empty. Within this loop we will take the first vertex off of the traversal-queue and enqueue that vertex into the result-queue. Next, we will enqueue each of the vertices that are adjacent to the current one, and have not already been marked as visited, into the traversal-queue, mark each of them as visited, and then repeat the loop. We simply repeat this process for each of the visited vertices until the traversal-queue is empty, meaning we can no longer reach any new vertices. The result-queue now contains the vertices in breadth-first order from the given starting point. Very similar logic can be used to construct a breadth-first iterator. Listing 14.1 shows this algorithm in pseudocode form. The determination of vertices that are adjacent to the current one depends upon the implementation we choose to represent edges in a graph. We will discuss this further in Section 14.5.

listing
14.1

```
create a queue called traversal-queue
create a queue called result-queue
enqueue the starting vertex on the traversal-queue
mark the starting-vertex as visited
while the traversal-queue is not empty
{
    x = traversal-queue.dequeue()
    result-queue.enqueue(x)
    for all vertices y adjacent to x
        if y has not been visited
        {
            traversal-queue.enqueue(y)
            mark y as visited
        }
}
```

key concept

The only difference between a depth-first traversal of a graph and a breadth-first traversal is the use of a stack instead of a queue to manage the traversal.

A depth-first traversal for a graph can be constructed using virtually the same logic by simply replacing the traversal-queue with a traversal-stack.

Let's look at an example. Figure 14.7 shows a sample undirected graph where each vertex is labeled with an integer. For a breadth-first traversal starting from vertex 9, we do the following:

1. Add 9 to the traversal-queue and mark it as visited.

2. Dequeue 9 from the traversal-queue.

3. Enqueue 9 on the result-queue.

4. Add 6, 7, and 8 to the traversal-queue, marking each of them as visited.

5. Dequeue 6 from the traversal-queue.

6. Enqueue 6 on the result-queue.

7. Add 3 and 4 to the traversal-queue, marking them both as visited.

8. Dequeue 7 from the traversal-queue and add it to the result-queue.

9. Add 5 to the traversal-queue, marking it as visited.

10. Dequeue 8 from the traversal-queue and add it to the result-queue. (We do not add any new vertices to the traversal-queue since there are no neighbors of 8 that have not already been visited.)

11. Dequeue 3 from the traversal-queue and add it to the result-queue.

12. Add 1 to the traversal-queue, marking it as visited.

13. Dequeue 4 from the traversal-queue and add it to the result-queue.

14. Add 2 to the traversal-queue, marking it as visited.

15. Dequeue 5 from the traversal-queue and add it to the result-queue. (Since there are no unvisited neighbors, we continue without adding anything to the traversal-queue.)

16. Dequeue 1 from the traversal-queue and add it to the result-queue. (Since there are no unvisited neighbors, we continue without adding anything to the traversal-queue.)

17. Dequeue 2 from the traversal-queue and add it to the result-queue.

Thus the result-queue now contains the breadth-first order starting at vertex 9: 9, 6, 7, 8, 3, 4, 5, 1, and 2.

Now let us look at a depth-first traversal using the same graph and the same starting point. Keep in mind, we are using a stack to manage the traversal now instead of a queue. As with the breadth-first example, we begin with our starting vertex and do the following:

1. Add 9 to the result-queue and mark it as visited.

2. Push the neighbors of 9 onto the stack, pushing 6, then 7, then 8, and mark each of them as visited.

3. Pop the top vertex off of the stack, vertex 8, add it to the result-queue.

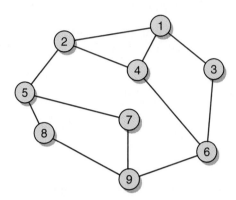

figure 14.7   A traversal example

4. Push its unvisited neighbor(s), vertex 5, onto the stack and mark it as visited.

5. Pop the top vertex off of the stack, vertex 5, add it to the queue, and then push its unvisited neighbor(s), vertex 2, onto the stack, marking it as visited.

6. Pop 2 off of the stack and add it to the queue.

7. Push its unvisited neighbor(s), vertices 4 and 1, onto the stack, marking them as visited.

8. Pop vertex 1 off of the stack and add it to the queue.

9. Push its unvisited neighbor(s), vertex 3, onto the stack.

10. Pop 3 off of the stack and add it to the queue.

11. Push its unvisited neighbors onto the stack (it has none since 1 and 6 have both already been marked as visited).

12. Pop 4 off of the stack, add it to the queue, and check for unvisited neighbors.

13. Pop 7 off of the stack, add it to the queue, and check for unvisited neighbors.

14. Pop 6 off of the stack, add it to the queue, and check for unvisited neighbors.

Since the stack is now empty, we know that the queue now contains our result: 9, 8, 5, 2, 1, 3, 4, 7, 6.

testing for connectivity

In our earlier discussion, we defined a graph as *connected* if for any two vertices in the graph, there is a path between them. This definition holds true for both undirected and directed graphs. Given our algorithm we just discussed, there is a simple solution to the question of whether or not a graph is connected: The graph is connected if and only if for each vertex v in a graph containing n vertices, the size of the result of a breadth-first traversal starting at v is n.

> **key concept**
>
> A graph is connected if and only if the number of vertices in the breadth-first traversal is the same as the number of vertices in the graph regardless of the starting vertex.

Let's look at the example undirected graphs in Figure 14.8. We stated earlier that the graph on the left is connected and that the graph on the right is not. Let's confirm that by following our algorithm. Table 14.1 shows the breadth-first traversals for the graph on the left using each of the vertices as a starting point. As you can see, all of the traversals yield n = 4 vertices, thus the graph is connected. Table 14.2 shows the breadth-first traversals for the graph on the right using each of the vertices as a starting point. Notice that not only do none of the traversals contain n = 4 vertices, but the one starting at vertex D has only the one vertex. Thus the graph is not connected.

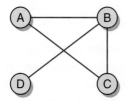 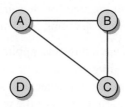

figure 14.8   Connectivity in an undirected graph

Starting Vertex	Breadth-First Traversal
A	A, B, C, D
B	B, A, D, C
C	C, B, A, D
D	D, B, A, C

table 14.1   Breadth-first traversals for a connected undirected graph

Starting Vertex	Breadth-First Traversal
A	A, B, C
B	B, A, C
C	C, B, A
D	D

table 14.2   Breadth-first traversals for an unconnected undirected graph

minimum spanning trees

A *spanning tree* is a tree that includes all of the vertices of a graph and some, but possibly not all, of the edges. Since trees are also graphs, for some graphs, the graph itself will be a spanning tree, and thus the only spanning tree for that graph will include all of the edges. Figure 14.9 shows a spanning tree for our graph from Figure 14.7.

One interesting application of spanning trees is to find a *minimum spanning tree* for a weighted graph. A *minimum spanning tree* is a spanning tree where the sum of the weights of the edges is less than or equal to the sum of the weights for any other spanning tree for the same graph.

> **key concept**
>
> A spanning tree is a tree that includes all of the vertices of a graph and some, but possibly not all, of the edges.

> **key concept**
>
> A minimum spanning tree is a spanning tree where the sum of the weights of the edges is less than or equal to the sum of the weights for any other spanning tree for the same graph.

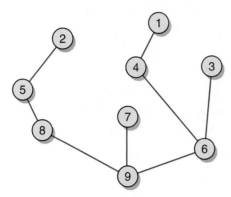

figure 14.9   A spanning tree

The algorithm for developing a minimum spanning tree was developed by Prim (1957) and is quite elegant. As we discussed earlier, each edge is represented by a triple including the starting vertex, ending vertex, and the weight. We then pick an arbitrary starting vertex (it does not matter which one) and add it to our minimum spanning tree (MST). Next we add all of the edges that include our starting vertex to a minheap ordered by weight. Keep in mind that if we are dealing with a directed network, we will only add edges that start at the given vertex.

Next we remove the minimum edge from the minheap, and add the edge and the new vertex to our MST. Next we add to our minheap all of the edges that include this new vertex and whose other vertex is not already in our MST. We continue this process until either our MST includes all of the vertices in our original graph or the minheap is empty. Figure 14.10 shows a weighted network and its associated minimum spanning tree. Listing 14.2 illustrates this algorithm.

determining the shortest path

There are two possibilities for determining the "shortest" path in a graph. The first, and perhaps simplest, possibility is to determine the literal shortest path between a starting vertex and a target vertex, meaning the least number of edges between the two vertices. This turns out to be a simple variation of our earlier

listing
   14.2

```
create a traversal-minheap
add the starting-vertex to the MST
mark the starting-vertex as visited
for all vertices y adjacent to starting-vertex
   if y has not been visited
   {
      traversal-minheap.add(starting-vertex, y, weight)
   }


while ((number vertices in MST < number of vertices in original graph) &&
       (traversal-minheap not empty))
{
   (x, y) = traversal-minheap.remove()
   add vertex y and edge (x, y) to the MST
   mark vertex y as visited
   for all vertices z adjacent to y
      if z has not been visited
      {
         traversal-minheap.add(y, z, weight)
      }
}
```

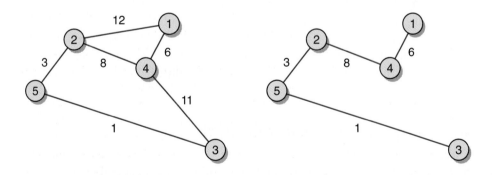

Network   Minimum Spanning Tree

figure 14.10   A minimum spanning tree

breadth-first traversal algorithm. To refresh our memory, let's look at that algorithm again:

```
create a queue called traversal-queue
create a queue called result-queue
enqueue the starting-vertex on the traversal-queue
mark the starting-vertex as visited
while the traversal-queue is not empty
{
    x = traversal-queue.dequeue()
    result-queue.enqueue(x)
    for all vertices y adjacent to x
        if y has not been visited
        {
            traversal-queue.enqueue(y)
            mark y as visited
        }
}
```

To convert this algorithm to find the shortest path, we simply store two additional pieces of information for each vertex during our traversal: the path length from the starting vertex to this vertex, and the vertex that is the predecessor of this vertex in that path. Then we modify our loop to terminate when we reach our target vertex. The path length for the shortest path is simply the path length to the predecessor of the target + 1, and if we wish to output the vertices along the shortest path, we can simply backtrack along the chain of predecessors. Listing 14.3 shows the algorithm with these modifications.

The second possibility for determining the shortest path is to look for the cheapest path in a weighted graph. Dijkstra (1959) developed an algorithm for this possibility that is similar to our previous algorithm. However, instead of using a queue of vertices that causes us to progress through the graph in the order we encounter vertices, we use a minheap or a priority queue storing vertex, weight pairs based upon total weight (the sum of the weights from the starting vertex to this vertex) so that we always traverse through the graph following the cheapest path first. For each vertex, we must store the label of the vertex, the weight of the cheapest path (thus far) to that vertex from our starting point, and the predecessor of that vertex along that path. On the minheap, we will store vertex, weight pairs for each possible path that we have encountered but not yet traversed. As we remove a vertex, weight pair from the minheap, if we encounter a vertex with a weight less than the one already stored with the vertex, we update the cost. Listing 14.4 illustrates this algorithm.

listing
14.3

```
create a queue called traversal-queue
create a queue called result-queue
enqueue the starting-vertex on the traversal-queue
mark the starting-vertex as visited
set starting-vertex.predecessor = null
set starting-vertex.pathlength = 0
int count = 0
vertex x = null
while ((x not equal target-vertex) && (traversal-queue not empty))
{
    x = traversal-queue.dequeue()
    result-queue.enqueue(x)
    count = count + 1
    for all vertices y adjacent to x
        if y has not been visited
        {
            set y.pathlength = count
            set y.predecessor = x
            traversal-queue.enqueue(y)
            mark y as visited
        }
}
```

listing
14.4

```
create a minheap called traversal-minheap
add (starting-vertex, 0) on the traversal-minheap
mark the starting-vertex as visited
set predecessor of all vertices to null
set starting-vertex.weight = 0
set weight of all other vertices to a very large initial value (maxint)
vertex x = starting-vertex
while ((x not equal target-vertex) && (traversal-minheap not empty))
{
    (x, weight) = traversal-minheap.remove()
    for all vertices y adjacent to x
        if  (weight + weight(x, y)) < y.weight)
            {
                set y.weight = weight + weight(x, y)
                set y.predecessor = x
                add (y, y.weight) on the traversal-minheap
            }
}
```

14.5 strategies for implementing graphs

As we have done in the previous two chapters, we will present algorithms and strategies for the implementation of graphs but leave the implementations as programming projects. Let us begin our discussion of implementation strategies by examining what operations would need to be available for a graph. Of course, we would need to be able to add and remove vertices, and add and remove edges from the graph. There will need to be traversals (perhaps breadth first and depth first) beginning with a particular vertex, and these might be implemented as iterators as we did for binary trees. Other operations like size, isEmpty, toString, and find will be useful as well. In addition to these, operations to determine the shortest path from a particular vertex to a particular target vertex, to determine the adjacency of two vertices, to construct a minimum spanning tree, and to test for connectivity would all likely need to be implemented.

Whatever storage mechanism we use for vertices must allow us to mark vertices as visited during traversals and other algorithms. This can be accomplished by simply adding a Boolean variable to the class representing the vertices.

adjacency lists

Since trees are graphs, perhaps the best introduction to how we might implement graphs is to consider the discussions and examples that we have already seen concerning the implementation of trees. One might immediately think of using a set of nodes where each node contains an element and perhaps a linked list of up to n–1 links to other nodes. When we used this strategy with trees, the number of connections from any given node was limited by the order of the tree (e.g., a maximum of two directed edges starting at any particular node in a binary tree). Because of this limitation, we were able to specify, for example, that a binary-node had a left and a right child pointer. Even if the binary-node was a leaf, the pointer still existed. It was simply set to null.

In the case of a *graph-node*, since each node could have up to n–1 edges connecting it to other nodes, it would be better to use a dynamic structure such as a linked list to store the edges within each node. This list is called an *adjacency list*. In the case of a network or weighted graph, each edge would be stored as a triple including the weight. In the case of an undirected graph, an edge (A, B) would appear in the adjacency list of both vertex A and vertex B.

adjacency matrices

Keep in mind that we must somehow efficiently (both in terms of space and access time) store both vertices and edges. Since vertices are just elements, we can use any of our collections to store the vertices. In fact we often talk about a set of vertices, the term *set* implying an implementation strategy. However, another solution for storing edges is motivated by our use of array implementations of trees, but instead of using a one-dimensional array, we will use a two-dimensional array that we call an *adjacency matrix*. In an adjacency matrix, each position of the two-dimensional array represents an intersection between two vertices in the graph. Each of these intersections is represented by a Boolean value indicating whether or not the two vertices are connected. Figure 14.11 shows the undirected graph that we began with at the beginning of this chapter. Figure 14.12 shows the adjacency matrix for this graph.

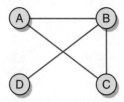

figure 14.11   An undirected graph

For any position (row, column) in the matrix, that position is true if and only if the edge (v_{row}, v_{column}) is in the graph. Since edges in an undirected graph are bi-directional, if (A, B) is an edge in the graph, then (B, A) is also in the graph.

Notice that this matrix is symmetrical—that is, each side of the diagonal is a mirror image of the other. The reason for this is that we are representing an undirected graph. For undirected graphs, it may not be necessary to represent the entire matrix but simply one side or the other of the diagonal.

However, for directed graphs, since all of the edges are directional, the result can be quite different. Figure 14.13 shows a directed graph and Figure 14.14 shows the adjacency matrix for this graph.

Adjacency matrices may also be used with networks or weighted graphs by simply storing an object at each position of the matrix to represent the weight of the edge. Positions in the matrix where edges do not exist would simply be set to null.

	A	B	C	D
A	F	T	T	F
B	T	F	T	T
C	T	T	F	F
D	F	T	F	F

figure 14.12   An adjacency matrix for an undirected graph

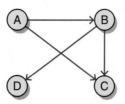

figure 14.13   A directed graph

	A	B	C	D
A	F	T	T	F
B	F	F	T	T
C	F	F	F	F
D	F	F	F	F

figure 14.14   An adjacency matrix for a directed graph

summary of key concepts

▸ An undirected graph is a graph where the pairings representing the edges are unordered.

▸ Two vertices in a graph are adjacent if there is an edge connecting them.

▸ An undirected graph is considered complete if it has the maximum number of edges connecting vertices.

▸ A path is a sequence of edges that connects two vertices in a graph.

▸ A cycle is a path in which the first and last vertices are the same and none of the edges are repeated.

▸ A directed graph, sometimes referred as a digraph, is a graph where the edges are ordered pairs of vertices.

▸ A path in a directed graph is a sequence of directed edges that connects two vertices in a graph.

▸ A network, or a weighted graph, is a graph with weights or costs associated with each edge.

▸ The only difference between a depth-first traversal of a graph and a breadth-first traversal is the use of a stack instead of a queue to manage the traversal.

▸ A graph is connected if and only if the number of vertices in the breadth-first traversal is the same as the number of vertices in the graph regardless of the starting vertex.

▸ A spanning tree is a tree that includes all of the vertices of a graph and some, but possibly not all, of the edges.

▸ A minimum spanning tree is a spanning tree where the sum of the weights of the edges is less than or equal to the sum of the weights for any other spanning tree for the same graph.

self-review questions

14.1   What is the difference between a graph and a tree?

14.2   What is an undirected graph?

14.3   What is a directed graph?

14.4   What does it mean to say that a graph is complete?

14.5   What is the maximum number of edges for an undirected graph? A directed graph?

14.6   What is the definition of path? Of cycle?

14.7   What is the difference between a network and a graph?

14.8   What is a spanning tree? A minimum spanning tree?

exercises

14.1   Draw the undirected graph that is represented by the following:

vertices: 1, 2, 3, 4, 5, 6, 7

edges: (1, 2), (1, 4), (2, 3), (2, 4), (3, 7), (4, 7), (4, 6), (5, 6), (5, 7), (6, 7)

14.2   Is the graph from Exercise 14.1 connected? Complete?

14.3   List all of the cycles in the graph from Exercise 14.1.

14.4   Draw a spanning tree for the graph of Exercise 14.1.

14.5   Using the same data from Exercise 14.1, draw the resulting directed graph.

14.6   Is the directed graph of Exercise 14.5 connected? Complete?

14.7   List all of the cycles in the graph of Exercise 14.5.

14.8   Draw a spanning tree for the graph of Exercise 14.5.

14.9   Consider the weighted graph shown in Figure 14.10. List all of the possible paths from vertex 2 to vertex 3 along with the total weight of each path.

programming projects

14.1   Implement an undirected graph using whatever underlying data structure you prefer. Keep in mind that you must store both vertices and edges. Your implementation should include methods for adding and removing vertices, adding and removing edges, size (which should return the number of vertices), isEmpty, a breadth-first iterator, and a depth-first iterator.

14.2   Repeat Programming Project 14.1 for a directed graph.

14.3   Implement a shortest path method to go along with your implementation for Programming Project 14.1 that will either return the length of the shortest path or return −1 if no path is found.

14.4   Repeat Programming Project 14.3 for the directed graph implementation of Exercise 14.2.

14.5   Extend your implementation from Programming Project 14.1 to create a weighted, undirected graph and add a method to return a minimum spanning tree.

14.6   Extend your implementation from Programming Project 14.2 to create a weighted, directed graph and add a method to return a minimum spanning tree.

14.7   Create a limited airline scheduling system that will allow a user to enter city to city connections and their prices. Your system should then allow a user to enter two cities and should return the shortest path and the cheapest path between the two cities. Your system should report if there is no connection between two cities. Assume an undirected network.

14.8   Repeat Programming Project 14.7 assuming a directed network.

14.9   Create a simple graphical application that will produce a textual representation of the shortest path and the cheapest path between two vertices in a network.

14.10   Create a network routing system that given the point to point connections in the network, and the costs of utilizing each, will produce cheapest path connections from each point to each point in the network, pointing out any disconnected locations.

answers to self-review questions

14.1   A graph is the more general concept without the restriction that each node have one and only one parent except for the root, which does not have a parent. In the case of a graph, there is no root, and each vertex can be connected to up to n−1 other vertices.

14.2   An undirected graph is a graph where the pairings representing the edges are unordered.

14.3   A directed graph, sometimes referred as a digraph, is a graph where the edges are ordered pairs of vertices.

14.4   An graph is considered complete if it has the maximum number of edges connecting vertices.

14.5   The maximum number of edges for an undirected graph is n(n–1)/2. For a directed graph, it is n(n–1).

14.6   A path is a sequence of edges that connects two vertices in a graph. A cycle is a path in which the first and last vertices are the same and none of the edges are repeated.

14.7   A network is a graph, either directed or undirected, with weights or costs associated with each edge.

14.8   A spanning tree is a tree that includes all of the vertices of a graph and some, but possibly not all, of the edges. A minimum spanning tree is a spanning tree where the sum of the weights of the edges is less than or equal to the sum of the weights for any other spanning tree for the same graph.

references

Collins, W. J. *Data Structures: An Object-Oriented Approach*. Reading, Mass.: Addison-Wesley, 1992.

Dijkstra, E. W. " A Note on Two Problems in Connection with Graphs." *Numerische Mathematik*, vol. 1 (1959): 269–271.

Drosdek, A., *Data Structures and Algorithms in Java*, Pacific Grove, CA, Brooks/Cole, 2001.

Prim, R. C. "Shortest Connection Networks and Some Generalizations." *Bell System Technical Journal*, vol. 36 (1957): 1389–1401.

This appendix serves as an overview of object-oriented concepts and discusses how these concepts are realized in the Java programming language. It can serve as a review for students who've seen this material before and help them fill in any holes in that background. It can also serve students who learned object-oriented concepts using a different language and need to see how those concepts are accomplished in Java. Most of the material in this appendix is based on the book *Java Software Solutions: Foundations of Program Design*, by John Lewis and William Loftus.

A.1 an overview of object-orientation

Java is an object-oriented language. As the name implies, an *object* is a fundamental entity in a Java program. In addition to objects, a Java program also manages primitive data. *Primitive data* includes common, fundamental values such as numbers and characters. An object usually represents something more specialized or complex, such as a bank account. An object often contains primitive values, and is in part defined by them. For example, an object that represents a bank account might contain the account balance, which is stored as a primitive numeric value.

An object is defined by a *class*, which can be thought of as the data type of the object. The operations that can be performed on the object are defined by the methods in the class.

Once a class has been defined, multiple objects can be created from that class. For example, once we define a class to represent the concept of a bank account, we can create multiple objects that represent specific, individual bank accounts. Each bank account object would keep track of its own balance. This is an example of *encapsulation*, meaning that each object protects and manages its own information. The methods defined in the bank account class would allow us to perform operations on individual bank account objects. For instance, we might withdraw money from a particular account. We can think of these operations as services that the object performs. The act of invoking a method on an object sometimes is referred to as sending a *message* to the object, requesting that the service be performed.

Classes can be created from other classes using *inheritance*. That is, the definition of one class can be based on another class that already exists. Inheritance is a form of software *reuse*, capitalizing on the similarities between various kinds of classes that we may want to create. One class can be used to derive several new classes. Derived classes can then be used to derive even more classes. This creates a hierarchy of classes, where characteristics defined in one class are inherited by its children, which in turn pass them on to their children, and so on. For example, we might create a hierarchy of classes that represent various types of accounts. Common characteristics are defined in high-level classes, and specific differences are defined in derived classes.

Classes, objects, encapsulation, and inheritance are the primary ideas that make up the world of object-oriented software. They are depicted in Figure A.1, and are explored in more detail throughout this appendix.

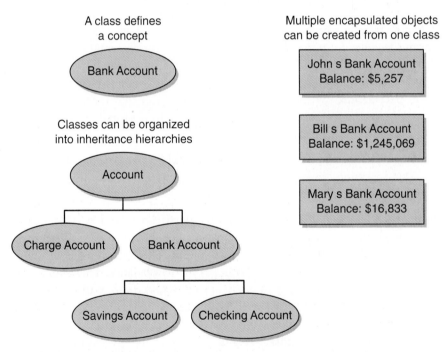

figure A.1   Various aspects of object-oriented software

A.2 using objects

The following `println` statement illustrates the process of using an object for the services it provides:

```
System.out.println ("Whatever you are, be a good one.");
```

The `System.out` object represents an output device or file, which by default is the monitor screen. To be more precise, the object's name is `out` and it is stored in the `System` class.

The `println` method represents a service that the `System.out` object performs for us. Whenever we request it, the object will print a string of characters to the screen. We can say that we send the `println` message to the `System.out` object to request that some text be printed.

abstraction

An object is an *abstraction*, meaning that the precise details of how it works are irrelevant from the point of view of the user of the object. We don't really need to know how the `println` method prints characters to the screen, as long as we can count on it to do its job. Of course, there are times when it is helpful to understand such information, but it is not necessary in order to *use* the object.

Sometimes it is important to hide or ignore certain details. A human being is capable of mentally managing around seven (plus or minus two) pieces of information in short-term memory. Beyond that, we start to lose track of some of the pieces. However, if we group pieces of information together, then those pieces can be managed as one "chunk" in our minds. We don't actively deal with all of the details in the chunk but we can still manage it as a single entity. Therefore, we can deal with large quantities of information by organizing it into chunks. An object is a construct that organizes information and allows us to hide the details inside. An object is therefore a wonderful abstraction.

We use abstractions every day. Think about a car for a moment. You don't necessarily need to know how a four-cycle combustion engine works in order to drive a car. You just need to know some basic operations: how to turn it on, how to put it in gear, how to make it move with the pedals and steering wheel, and how to stop it. These operations define the way a person interacts with the car.

They mask the details of what is happening inside the car that allow it to function. When you're driving a car, you're not usually thinking about the spark plugs igniting the gasoline that drives the piston that turns the crankshaft that turns the axle that turns the wheels. If we had to worry about all of these underlying details, we'd never be able to operate something as complicated as a car.

Initially, all cars had manual transmissions. The driver had to understand and deal with the details of changing gears with the stick shift. Eventually, automatic transmissions were developed, and the driver no longer had to worry about shifting gears. Those details were hidden by raising the *level of abstraction*.

Of course, someone has to deal with the details. The car manufacturer has to know the details in order to design and build the car in the first place. A car mechanic relies on the fact that most people don't have the expertise or tools necessary to fix a car when it breaks.

The level of abstraction must be appropriate for each situation. Some people prefer to drive a manual transmission car. A race car driver, for instance, needs to control the shifting manually for optimum performance.

Likewise, someone has to create the code for the objects we use. Later in this appendix we explore how to define objects by creating classes. For now, we can create and use objects from classes that have been defined for us already. Abstraction makes that possible.

creating objects

A Java variable can hold either a primitive value or a *reference to an object*. Like variables that hold primitive types, a variable that serves as an object reference must be declared. A class is used to define an object, and the class name can be thought of as the type of an object. The declarations of object references have a similar structure to the declarations of primitive variables.

The following declaration creates a reference to a `String` object:

```
String name;
```

That declaration is like the declaration of an integer, in that the type is followed by the variable name we want to use. However, no `String` object actually exists yet. To create an object, we use the `new` operator:

```
name = new String ("James Gosling");
```

The act of creating an object using the `new` operator is called *instantiation*. An object is said to be an *instance* of a particular class. After the new operator creates the object, a *constructor* is invoked to help set it up initially. A constructor has the same name as the class, and is similar to a method. In this example, the parameter to the constructor is a string literal that specifies the characters that the `String` object will hold.

> **key concept**
> The new operator returns a reference to a newly created object.

The act of declaring the object reference variable and creating the object itself can be combined into one step by initializing the variable in the declaration, just as we do with primitive types:

```
String name = new String ("James Gosling");
```

After an object has been instantiated, we use the *dot operator* to access its methods. The dot operator is appended directly after the object reference, followed by the method being invoked. For example, to invoke the `length` method defined in the `String` class, we use the dot operator on the `name` reference variable:

```
count = name.length();
```

An object reference variable (such as `name`) actually stores the address where the object is stored in memory. However, we don't usually care about the actual address value. We just want to access the object, wherever it is.

Even though they are not primitive types, strings are so fundamental and frequently used that Java defines string literals delimited by double quotation marks, as we've seen in various examples. This is a shortcut notation. Whenever a string literal appears, a `String` object is created. Therefore, the following declaration is valid:

```
String name = "James Gosling";
```

That is, for `String` objects, the explicit use of the `new` operator and the call to the constructor can be eliminated. In most cases, this simplified syntax for strings is used.

A.3 class libraries and packages

A *class library* is a set of classes that support the development of programs. A compiler often comes with a class library. Class libraries can also be obtained separately through third-party vendors. The classes in a class library contain methods that are often valuable to a programmer because of the special functionality they offer. In fact, programmers often become dependent on the methods in a class library and begin to think of them as part of the language. But, technically, they are not in the language definition.

The String class, for instance, is not an inherent part of the Java language. It is part of the Java *standard class library* that can be found in any Java development environment. The classes that make up the library were created by employees at Sun Microsystems, the company that created the Java language.

The class library is made up of several clusters of related classes, which are sometimes called Java APIs. API stands for *application programmer interface*. For example, we may refer to the Java Database API when we're talking about the set of classes that help us write programs that interact with a database. Another example of an API is the Java Swing API, which refers to a set of classes that define special graphical components used in a graphical user interface. Sometimes the entire standard library is referred to generically as the Java API.

The classes of the Java standard class library are also grouped into *packages*, which, like the APIs, let us group related classes by one name. Each class is part of a particular package. The String class and the System class, for example, are both part of the java.lang package.

The package organization is more fundamental and language-based than the API names. Though there is a general correspondence between package and API names, the groups of classes that make up a given API might cross packages. We primarily refer to classes in terms of their package organization in this text.

Appendix B serves as a general reference for many of the classes in the Java class library.

the `import` declaration

The classes of the package `java.lang` are automatically available for use when writing a program. To use classes from any other package, however, we must either *fully qualify* the reference or use an `import` *declaration*.

When you want to use a class from a class library in a program, you could use its fully qualified name, including the package name, every time it is referenced. For example, every time you want to refer to the `Random` class that is defined in the `java.util` package, you can write `java.util.Random`. However, completely specifying the package and class name every time it is needed quickly becomes tiring. Java provides the `import` declaration to simplify these references.

The `import` declaration identifies the packages and classes that will be used in a program, so that the fully qualified name is not necessary with each reference. The following is an example of an `import` declaration:

```
import java.util.Random;
```

This declaration asserts that the `Random` class of the `java.util` package may be used in the program. Once this `import` declaration is made, it is sufficient to use the simple name `Random` when referring to that class in the program.

Another form of the `import` declaration uses an asterisk (*) to indicate that any class inside the package might be used in the program. Therefore, the declaration

```
import java.util.*;
```

allows all classes in the `java.util` package to be referenced in the program without the explicit package name. If only one class of a particular package will be used in a program, it is usually better to name the class specifically in the `import` declaration. However, if two or more classes will be used, the * notation is fine. Once a class is imported, it is as if its code has been brought into the program. The code is not actually moved, but that is the effect.

The classes of the `java.lang` package are automatically imported because they are fundamental and can be thought of as basic extensions to the language. Therefore, any class in the `java.lang` package, such as `String`, can be used without an explicit `import` declaration. It is as if all programs automatically contain the following declaration:

```
import java.lang.*;
```

A.4 object state and behavior

Think about objects in the world around you. How would you describe them? Let's use a ball as an example. A ball has particular characteristics such as its diameter, color, and elasticity. Formally, we say the properties that describe an object, called *attributes*, define the object's *state of being*. We also describe a ball by what it does, such as the fact that it can be thrown, bounced, or rolled. These activities define the object's *behavior*.

All objects have a state and a set of behaviors. We can represent these characteristics in software objects as well. The values of an object's variables describe the object's state, and the methods that can be invoked using the object define the object's behaviors.

Consider a computer game that uses a ball. The ball could be represented as an object. It could have variables to store its size and location, and methods that draw it on the screen and calculate how it moves when thrown, bounced, or rolled. The variables and methods defined in the ball object establish the state and behavior that are relevant to the ball's use in the computerized ball game.

Each object has its own state. Each ball object has a particular location, for instance, which typically is different from the location of all other balls. Behaviors, though, tend to apply to all objects of a particular type. For instance, in general, any ball can be thrown, bounced, or rolled. The act of rolling a ball is generally the same for all balls.

The state of an object and that object's behaviors work together. How high a ball bounces depends on its elasticity. The action is the same, but the specific result depends on that particular object's state. An object's behavior often modifies its state. For example, when a ball is rolled, its location changes.

Any object can be described in terms of its state and behavior. Let's consider another example. In software that is used to manage a university, a student could be represented as an object. The collection of all such objects represents the entire student body at the university. Each student has a state. That is, each student object would contain the variables that store information about a particular student, such as name, address, major, courses taken, grades, and grade point average. A student object also has behaviors. For example, the class of the student object may contain a method to add a new course.

Although software objects often represent tangible items, they don't have to. For example, an error message can be an object, with its state being the text of the message, and behaviors including the process of issuing (perhaps printing) the error. A common mistake made by new programmers to the world of object-orientation is to limit the possibilities to tangible entities.

A.5 classes

An object is defined by a class. A class is the model, pattern, or blueprint from which an object is created. Consider the blueprint created by an architect when designing a house. The blueprint defines the important characteristics of the house: walls, windows, doors, electrical outlets, and so forth. Once the blueprint is created, several houses can be built using it.

In one sense, the houses built from the blueprint are different. They are in different locations, have different addresses, contain different furniture, and different people live in them. Yet, in many ways they are the "same" house. The layout of the rooms and other crucial characteristics are the same in each. To create a different house, we would need a different blueprint.

A class is a blueprint of an object. But a class is not an object any more than a blueprint is a house. In general, no space to store data values is reserved in a class. To allocate space to store data values, we have to instantiate one or more objects from the class (the exception to this rule is discussed in Section A.10 of this appendix). Each object is an instance of a class. Each object has space for its own data, which is why each object can have its own state.

> **key concept**
>
> A class is a blueprint for an object; it reserves no memory space for data. Each object has its own data space, thus its own state.

A class contains the declarations of the data that will be stored in each instantiated object, and the declarations of the methods that can be invoked using an object. Collectively these are called the *members* of the class. See Figure A.2.

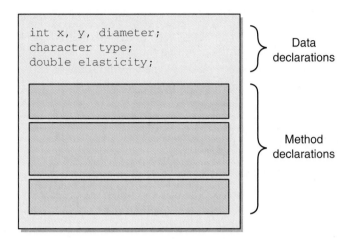

figure A.2   The members of a class: data and method declarations

Consider the following class, called `Coin`, that represents a coin that can be flipped and that at any point in time shows a face of either heads or tails.

```
//***************************************************************
//  Coin.java          Authors: Lewis/Loftus
//
//  Represents a coin with two sides that can be flipped.
//***************************************************************

import java.util.Random;

public class Coin
{
    private final int HEADS = 0;
    private final int TAILS = 1;

    private int face;

    //--------------------------------------------------------------
    //  Sets up the coin by flipping it initially.
    //--------------------------------------------------------------
    public Coin ()
    {
        flip();
    }
```

```java
//-----------------------------------------------------------
//  Flips the coin by randomly choosing a face value.
//-----------------------------------------------------------
public void flip ()
{
    face = (int) (Math.random() * 2);
}

//-----------------------------------------------------------
//  Returns true if the current face of the coin is heads.
//-----------------------------------------------------------
public boolean isHeads ()
{
    return (face == HEADS);
}

//-----------------------------------------------------------
//  Returns the current face of the coin as a string.
//-----------------------------------------------------------
public String toString()
{
    String faceName;

    if (face == HEADS)
        faceName = "Heads";
    else
        faceName = "Tails";

    return faceName;
}
}
```

In the Coin class, we have two integer constants, HEADS and TAILS, and one integer variable, face. The rest of the Coin class is composed of the Coin constructor and three regular methods: flip, isHeads, and toString.

Constructors are special methods that have the same name as the class. The Coin constructor gets called when the new operator is used to create a new instance of the Coin class. The rest of the methods in the Coin class define the various services provided by Coin objects.

A class we define can be used in multiple programs. This is no different from using the String class in whatever program we need it. When designing a class, it is always good to look to the future to try to give the class behaviors that may be beneficial in other programs, not just fit the specific purpose for which you are creating it at the moment.

instance data

Note that in the Coin class, the constants HEADS and TAILS and the variable face are declared inside the class, but not inside any method. The location at which a variable is declared defines its *scope*, which is the area within a program in which that variable can be referenced. By being declared at the class level (not within a method), these variables and constants can be referenced in any method of the class.

> **key concept**
>
> The scope of a variable, which determines where it can be referenced, depends on where it is declared.

Attributes declared at the class level are also called *instance data*, because memory space for the data is reserved for each instance of the class that is created. Each Coin object, for example, has its own face variable with its own data space. Therefore, at any point in time two Coin objects can have their own states: one can be showing heads and the other can be showing tails, perhaps.

Java automatically initializes any variables declared at the class level. For example, all variables of numeric types such as int and double are initialized to zero. However, despite the fact that the language performs this automatic initialization, it is good practice to initialize variables explicitly (usually in a constructor) so that anyone reading the code will clearly understand the intent.

A.6 encapsulation

We can think about an object in one of two ways. The view we take depends on what we are trying to accomplish at the moment. First, when we are designing and implementing an object, we need to think about the details of how an object works. That is, we have to design the class; we have to define the variables that will be held in the object and define the methods that make the object useful.

However, when we are designing a solution to a larger problem, we have to think in terms of how the objects in the program interact. At that level, we have to think only about the services that an object provides, not about the details of how those services are provided. As we discussed earlier in this appendix, an object provides a level of abstraction that allows us to focus on the larger picture when we need to.

This abstraction works only if we are careful to respect its boundaries. An object should be *self-governing,* which means that the variables contained in an object should be modified only within the object. Only the methods within an object should have access to the variables in that object. We should make it difficult, if not impossible, for code outside of a class to "reach in" and change the value of a variable that is declared inside the class.

The object-oriented term for this characteristic is *encapsulation.* An object should be encapsulated from the rest of the system. It should interact with other parts of a program only through the specific set of methods that define the services that that object provides. These methods define the *interface* between that object and the program that uses it.

> **key concept**
>
> Objects should be encapsulated. The rest of a program should interact with an object only through a well-defined interface.

The code that uses an object, sometimes called the *client* of an object, should not be allowed to access variables directly. The client should interact with the object's methods, which in turn interact on behalf of the client with the data encapsulated within the object.

visibility modifiers

In Java, we accomplish object encapsulation using *modifiers.* A modifier is a Java reserved word that is used to specify particular characteristics of a programming language construct. For example, the `final` modifier is used to declare a constant. Java has several modifiers that can be used in various ways. Some modifiers can be used together, but some combinations are invalid.

Some Java modifiers are called *visibility modifiers* because they control access to the members of a class. The reserved words `public` and `private` are visibility modifiers that can be applied to the variables and methods of a class. If a member of a class has *public visibility,* then it can be directly referenced from outside of the object. If a member of a class has *private visibility,* it can be used anywhere inside the class definition but cannot be referenced externally. A third visibility modifier, `protected`, is relevant only in the context of inheritance and is discussed in Section A.13 of this appendix.

Public variables violate encapsulation. They allow code external to the class in which the data is defined to reach in and access or modify the value of the data. Therefore instance data should be defined with private visibility. Data that is declared as private can be accessed only by the methods of the class, which makes the objects created from that class self-governing.

> **key concept**
>
> Instance variables should be declared with private visibility to promote encapsulation.

The visibility we apply to a method depends on the purpose of that method. Methods that provide services to the client of the class must be declared with public visibility so that they can be invoked by the client. These methods are sometimes referred to as *service methods*. A private method cannot be invoked from outside the class. The only purpose of a private method is to help the other methods of the class do their job. Therefore they are sometimes referred to as *support methods*.

The table in Figure A.3 summarizes the effects of public and private visibility on both variables and methods.

Note that a client can still access or modify `private` data by invoking service methods that change the data. A class must provide service methods for valid client operations. The code of those methods must be carefully designed to permit only appropriate access and valid changes.

Giving constants public visibility is generally considered acceptable: although their values can be accessed directly, they cannot be changed because they were declared using the `final` modifier. Keep in mind that encapsulation means that data values should not be able to be *changed* directly by another part of the code. Because constants, by definition, cannot be changed, the encapsulation issue is largely moot.

UML diagrams reflect the visibility of a class member with special notations. A member with public visibility is preceded by a plus sign (+), and a member with private visibility is preceded by a minus sign (-).

	public	private
Variables	Violate encapsulation	Enforce encapsulation
Methods	Provide services to clients	Support other methods in the class

figure A.3   The effects of public and private visibility

local data

As we defined earlier, the scope of a variable or constant is the part of a program in which a valid reference to that variable can be made. A variable can be declared inside a method, making it *local data* as opposed to instance data. Recall that instance data is declared in a class but not inside any particular method. Local data has scope limited to only the method in which it is declared. Any reference to local data of one method in any other method would cause the compiler to issue an error message. A local variable simply does not exist outside of the method in which it is declared. Instance data, declared at the class level, has a scope of the entire class. Any method of the class can refer to it.

> **key concept**
> A variable declared in a method is local to that method and cannot be used outside of it.

Because local data and instance data operate at different levels of scope, it's possible to declare a local variable inside a method using the same name as an instance variable declared at the class level. Referring to that name in the method will reference the local version of the variable. This naming practice obviously has the potential to confuse anyone reading the code, so it should be avoided.

The formal parameter names in a method header serve as local data for that method. They don't exist until the method is called, and cease to exist when the method is exited.

A.7   constructors

A constructor is similar to a method that is invoked when an object is instantiated. When we define a class, we usually define a constructor to help us set up the class. In particular, we often use a constructor to initialize the variables associated with each object.

A constructor differs from a regular method in two ways. First, the name of a constructor is the same name as the class. Therefore, the name of the constructor in the `Coin` class is `Coin`, and the name of the constructor in the `Account` class is `Account`. Second, a constructor cannot return a value and does not have a return type specified in the method header.

A common mistake made by programmers is to put a `void` return type on a constructor. As far as the compiler is concerned, putting any return type on a constructor, even `void`, turns it into a regular method that happens to have the same name as the class. As such, it cannot be invoked as a constructor. This leads to error messages that are sometimes difficult to decipher.

> **key concept**
> A constructor cannot have any return type, even `void`.

A constructor is generally used to initialize the newly instantiated object. We don't have to define a constructor for every class. Each class has a *default constructor* that takes no parameters and is used if we don't provide our own. This default constructor generally has no effect on the newly created object.

A.8 method overloading

When a method is invoked, the flow of control transfers to the code that defines the method. After the method has been executed, control returns to the location of the call and processing continues.

Often the method name is sufficient to indicate which method is being called by a specific invocation. But in Java, as in other object-oriented languages, you can use the same method name with different parameter lists for multiple methods. This technique is called *method overloading*. It is useful when you need to perform similar methods on different types of data.

> **key concept**
>
> The versions of an overloaded method are distinguished by their signatures. The number, type, or order of their parameters must be distinct.

The compiler must still be able to associate each invocation to a specific method declaration. If the method name for two or more methods is the same, then additional information is used to uniquely identify the version that is being invoked. In Java, a method name can be used for multiple methods as long as the number of parameters, the types of those parameters, or the order of the types of parameters is distinct. A method's name along with the number, type, and order of its parameters is called the method's *signature*. The compiler uses the complete method signature to *bind* a method invocation to the appropriate definition.

The compiler must be able to examine a method invocation, including the parameter list, to determine which specific method is being invoked. If you attempt to specify two method names with the same signature, the compiler will issue an appropriate error message and will not create an executable program. There can be no ambiguity.

Note that the return type of a method is not part of the method signature. That is, two overloaded methods cannot differ only by their return type. The reason is that the value returned by a method can be ignored by the invocation. The compiler would not be able to distinguish which version of an overloaded method is being referenced in such situations.

The `println` method is an example of a method that is overloaded several times, each accepting a single type. Here is a partial list of its various signatures:

- `println (String s)`
- `println (int i)`
- `println (double d)`
- `println (char c)`
- `println (boolean b)`

The following two lines of code actually invoke different methods that have the same name:

```
System.out.println ("The total is: ");
System.out.println (count);
```

The first line invokes the `println` that accepts a string, and the second line, assuming `count` is an integer variable, invokes the version of `println` that accepts an integer. We often use a `println` statement that prints several distinct types, such as:

```
System.out.println ("The total is: " + count);
```

In this case, the plus sign is the string concatenation operator. First, the value in the variable `count` is converted to a string representation, then the two strings are concatenated into one longer string, and the definition of `println` that accepts a single string is invoked.

Constructors are a primary candidate for overloading. By providing multiple versions of a constructor, we provide several ways to set up an object.

A.9 references revisited

In previous examples, we've declared *object reference variables* through which we access particular objects. Let's examine this relationship in more detail.

An object reference variable and an object are two separate things. Remember that the declaration of the reference variable and the creation of the object that it refers to are separate steps. We often declare the reference variable and create an object for it to refer to on the same line, but keep in mind that we don't have to do so. In fact, in many cases, we won't want to.

The reference variable holds the address of an object even though the address never is disclosed to us. When we use the dot operator to invoke an object's method, we are actually using the address in the reference variable to locate the representation of the object in memory, look up the appropriate method, and invoke it.

null reference

A reference variable that does not currently point to an object is called a *null reference*. When a reference variable is initially declared as an instance variable, it is a null reference. If we try to follow a null reference, a `NullPointerException` is thrown, indicating that there is no object to reference. For example, consider the following situation:

```java
class NameIsNull
{
    String name; // not initialized, therefore null

    void printName()
    {
        System.out.println (name.length()); // causes an exception
    }
}
```

The declaration of the instance variable `name` asserts it to be a reference to a `String` object, but doesn't create any `String` object for it to refer to. The variable `name`, therefore, contains a null reference. When the method attempts to invoke the `length` method of the object to which `name` refers, an exception is thrown because no object exists to execute the method.

Note that this situation can arise only in the case of instance variables. Suppose, for instance, the following two lines of code were in a method:

```java
String name;
System.out.println (name.length());
```

In this case, the variable `name` is local to whatever method it is declared in. The compiler would complain that we were using the `name` variable before it had been initialized. In the case of instance variables, however, the compiler can't determine whether a variable had been initialized or not. Therefore, the danger of attempting to follow a null reference is a problem.

The identifier null is a reserved word in Java and represents a null reference. We can explicitly set a reference to null to ensure that it doesn't point to any object. We can also use it to check whether a particular reference currently points to an object. For example, we could have used the following code in the printName method to keep us from following a null reference:

```
if (name == null)
    System.out.println ("Invalid Name");
else
    System.out.println (name.length());
```

the this reference

Another special reference for Java objects is called the this reference. The word this is a reserved word in Java. It allows an object to refer to itself. As we have discussed, a method is always invoked through a particular object or class. Inside that method, the this reference can be used to refer to the currently executing object.

> **key concept**
>
> The this reference always refers to the currently executing object.

For example, in the ChessPiece class there could be a method called move, which could contain the following line:

```
if (this.position == piece2.position)
    result = false;
```

In this situation, the this reference is being used to clarify which position is being referenced. The this reference refers to the object through which the method was invoked. So when the following line is used to invoke the method, the this reference refers to bishop1:

```
bishop1.move();
```

But when another object is used to invoke the method, the this reference refers to it. Therefore, when the following invocation is used, the this reference in the move method refers to bishop2:

```
bishop2.move();
```

The `this` reference can also be used to distinguish the parameters of a constructor from their corresponding instance variables with the same names. For example, the constructor of a class called `Account` could be defined as follows:

```
public Account (String owner, long account, double initial)
{
    name = owner;
    acctNumber = account;
    balance = initial;
}
```

In this constructor, we deliberately came up with different names for the parameters to distinguish them from the instance variables `name`, `acctNumber`, and `balance`. This distinction is arbitrary. The constructor could have been written as follows using the `this` reference:

```
public Account (String name, long acctNumber, double balance)
{
    this.name = name;
    this.acctNumber = acctNumber;
    this.balance = balance;
}
```

In this version of the constructor, the `this` reference specifically refers to the instance variables of the object. The variables on the right-hand side of the assignment statements refer to the formal parameters. This approach eliminates the need to come up with different yet equivalent names. This situation sometimes occurs in other methods, but comes up often in constructors.

aliases

Because an object reference variable stores an address, programmers must be careful when managing objects. In particular, the semantics of an assignment statement for objects must be carefully understood. First, let's review the concept of assignment for primitive types. Consider the following declarations of primitive data:

```
int num1 = 5;
int num2 = 12;
```

In the following assignment statement, a copy of the value that is stored in num1 is stored in num2:

```
num2 = num1;
```

The original value of 12 in num2 is overwritten by the value 5. The variables num1 and num2 still refer to different locations in memory, and both of those locations now contain the value 5.

Now consider the following object declarations:

```
ChessPiece bishop1 = new ChessPiece();
ChessPiece bishop2 = new ChessPiece();
```

Initially, the references bishop1 and bishop2 refer to two different ChessPiece objects. The following assignment statement copies the value in bishop1 into bishop2:

```
bishop2 = bishop1;
```

The key issue is that when an assignment like this is made, the address stored in bishop1 is copied into bishop2. Originally the two references referred to different objects. After the assignment, both bishop1 and bishop2 contain the same address, and therefore refer to the same object.

The bishop1 and bishop2 references are now *aliases* of each other, because they are two names that refer to the same object. All references to the object that was originally referenced by bishop2 are now gone; that object cannot be used again in the program.

> **key concept**
> Several references can refer to the same object. These references are aliases of each other.

One important implication of aliases is that when we use one reference to change the state of the object, it is also changed for the other, because there is really only one object. If you change the state of bishop1, for instance, you change the state of bishop2, because they both refer to the same object. Aliases can produce undesirable effects unless they are managed carefully.

Another important aspect of references is the way they affect how we determine if two objects are equal. The == operator that we use for primitive data can be used with object references, but it returns true only if the two references being compared are aliases of each other. It does not "look inside" the objects to see if they contain the same data.

> **key concept**
> The == operator compares object references for equality, returning true if the references are aliases of each other.

That is, the following expression is true only if `bishop1` and `bishop2` currently refer to the same object:

```
bishop1 == bishop2
```

A method called `equals` is defined for all objects, but unless we replace it with a specific definition when we write a class, it has the same semantics as the `==` operator. That is, the `equals` method returns a `boolean` value that, by default, will be true if the two objects being compared are aliases of each other. The `equals` method is invoked through one object, and takes the other one as a parameter. Therefore, the expression

```
bishop1.equals(bishop2)
```

> **key concept**
>
> The `equals` method can be defined to determine equality between objects in any way we consider appropriate.

returns true if both references refer to the same object. However, we could define the `equals` method in the `ChessPiece` class to define equality for `ChessPiece` objects any way we would like. That is, we could define the `equals` method to return true under whatever conditions we think are appropriate to mean that one `ChessPiece` is equal to another.

The `equals` method has been given an appropriate definition in the `String` class. When comparing two `String` objects, the `equals` method returns true only if both strings contain the same characters. A common mistake is to use the `==` operator to compare strings, which compares the references for equality, when most of the time we want to compare the characters in the strings for equality. The `equals` method is discussed in more detail in Section A.14 of this appendix.

garbage collection

All interaction with an object occurs through a reference variable, so we can use an object only if we have a reference to it. When all references to an object are lost (perhaps by reassignment), that object can no longer participate in the program. The program can no longer invoke its methods or use its variables. At this point the object is called *garbage* because it serves no useful purpose.

> **key concept**
>
> If an object has no references to it, a program cannot use it. Java performs automatic garbage collection by periodically reclaiming the memory space occupied by these objects.

Java performs *automatic garbage collection*. When the last reference to an object is lost, the object becomes a candidate for garbage collection. Occasionally, the Java run time executes a method that "collects" all of the objects marked for garbage collection and returns their allocated memory to the system for future use. The programmer does not have to worry about explicitly returning memory that has become garbage.

If there is an activity that a programmer wants to accomplish in conjunction with the object being destroyed, the programmer can define a method called `finalize` in the object's class. The `finalize` method takes no parameters and has a `void` return type. It will be executed by the Java run time after the object is marked for garbage collection and before it is actually destroyed. The `finalize` method is not often used because the garbage collector performs most normal cleanup operations. However, it is useful for performing activities that the garbage collector does not address, such as closing files.

passing objects as parameters

Another important issue related to object references comes up when we want to pass an object to a method. Java passes all parameters to a method *by value*. That is, the current value of the actual parameter (in the invocation) is copied into the formal parameter in the method header. Essentially, parameter passing is like an assignment statement, assigning to the formal parameter a copy of the value stored in the actual parameter.

This issue must be considered when making changes to a formal parameter inside a method. The formal parameter is a separate copy of the value that is passed in, so any changes made to it have no effect on the actual parameter. After control returns to the calling method, the actual parameter will have the same value as it did before the method was called.

However, when an object is passed to a method, we are actually passing a reference to that object. The value that gets copied is the address of the object. Therefore, the formal parameter and the actual parameter become aliases of each other. If we change the state of the object through the formal parameter reference inside the method, we are changing the object referenced by the actual parameter, because they refer to the same object. On the other hand, if we change the formal parameter reference itself (to make it point to a new object, for instance), we have not changed the fact that the actual parameter still refers to the original object.

> **key concept**
>
> When an object is passed to a method, the actual and formal parameters become aliases of each other.

A.10 the static modifier

We've seen how visibility modifiers allow us to specify the encapsulation characteristics of variables and methods in a class. Java has several other modifiers that determine other characteristics. For example, the static modifier associates a variable or method with its class rather than with an object of the class.

static variables

So far, we've seen two categories of variables: local variables that are declared inside a method, and instance variables that are declared in a class but not inside a method. The term *instance variable* is used because an instance variable is accessed through a particular instance (an object) of a class. In general, each object has distinct memory space for each variable, so that each object can have a distinct value for that variable.

Another kind of variable, called a *static variable* or *class variable,* is shared among all instances of a class. There is only one copy of a static variable for all objects of a class. Therefore, changing the value of a static variable in one object changes it for all of the others. The reserved word static is used as a modifier to declare a static variable:

```
private static int count = 0;
```

> **key concept**
>
> A static variable is shared among all instances of a class.

Memory space for a static variable is established when the class that contains it is referenced for the first time in a program. A local variable declared within a method cannot be static.

Constants, which are declared using the final modifier, are also often declared using the static modifier as well. Because the value of constants cannot be changed, there might as well be only one copy of the value across all objects of the class.

static methods

A *static method* (also called a *class method*) can be invoked through the class name (all of the methods of the Math class are static methods, for example). You don't have to instantiate an object of the class to invoke a static method. For example, the sqrt method is called through the Math class as follows:

```
System.out.println ("Square root of 27: " + Math.sqrt(27));
```

A method is made static by using the `static` modifier in the method declaration. As we've seen, the `main` method of a Java program must be declared with the `static` modifier; this is so that `main` can be executed by the interpreter without instantiating an object from the class that contains `main`.

Because static methods do not operate in the context of a particular object, they cannot reference instance variables, which exist only in an instance of a class. The compiler will issue an error if a static method attempts to use a nonstatic variable. A static method can, however, reference static variables, because static variables exist independent of specific objects. Therefore, the `main` method can access only static or local variables.

The methods in the `Math` class perform basic computations based on values passed as parameters. There is no object state to maintain in these situations; therefore there is no good reason to force us to create an object in order to request these services.

A.11 wrapper classes

In some object-oriented programming languages, everything is represented using classes and the objects that are instantiated from them. In Java there are primitive types (such as `int`, `double`, `char`, and `boolean`) in addition to classes and objects.

Having two categories of data to manage (primitive values and object references) can present a challenge in some circumstances. For example, we might create an object that serves as a collection to hold various types of other objects. But in a specific situation you may want the collection to hold simple integer values. In these cases we need to "wrap" a primitive type into a class so that it can be treated as an object.

A *wrapper class* represents a particular primitive type. For instance, the `Integer` class represents a simple integer value. An object created from the `Integer` class stores a single `int` value. The constructors of the wrapper classes accept the primitive value to store. For example:

```
Integer ageObj = new Integer(45);
```

Once this declaration and instantiation are performed, the ageObj object effectively represents the integer 45 as an object. It can be used wherever an object is called for in a program instead of a primitive type.

For each primitive type in Java there exists a corresponding wrapper class in the Java class library. All wrapper classes are defined in the java.lang package. There is even a wrapper class that represents the type void. However, unlike the other wrapper classes, the Void class cannot be instantiated. It simply represents the concept of a void reference.

The wrapper classes also provide various methods related to the management of the associated primitive type. For example, the Integer class contains methods that return the int value stored in the object, and that convert the stored value to other primitive types. Details of all wrapper classes can be found in Appendix B.

Wrapper classes also contain static methods that can be invoked independent of any instantiated object. For example, the Integer class contains a static method called parseInt to convert an integer that is stored in a String to its corresponding int value. If the String object str holds the string "987", then the following line of code converts and stores the integer value 987 into the int variable num:

```
num = Integer.parseInt(str);
```

The Java wrapper classes often contain static constants that are helpful as well. For example, the Integer class contains two constants, MIN_VALUE and MAX_VALUE, which hold the smallest and largest int values, respectively. The other wrapper classes contain similar constants for their types.

A.12 interfaces

We've used the term interface to mean the public methods through which we can interact with an object. That definition is consistent with our use of it in this section, but now we are going to formalize this concept using a particular language construct in Java.

A Java *interface* is a collection of constants and abstract methods. An *abstract method* is a method that does not have an implementation. That is, there is no body of code defined for an abstract method. The header of the method, including its parameter list, is simply followed by a semicolon. An interface cannot be instantiated.

An interface called Complexity is shown below. It contains two abstract methods: setComplexity and getComplexity.

```
interface Complexity
{
    void setComplexity (int complexity);
    int getComplexity ();
}
```

An abstract method can be preceded by the reserved word abstract, though in interfaces it usually is not. Methods in interfaces have public visibility by default.

A class *implements* an interface by providing method implementations for each of the abstract methods defined in the interface. A class that implements an interface uses the reserved word implements followed by the interface name in the class header. If a class asserts that it implements a particular interface, it must provide a definition for all methods in the interface. The compiler will produce errors if any of the methods in the interface are not given a definition in the class.

For example, a class called Question could be defined that represents a question that a teacher may ask on a test. If the Question class implements the Complexity interface, it must explicitly say so in the header and must define both methods from the Complexity interface:

```
class Questions implements Complexity
{
    int difficulty;

    // whatever else

    void setComplexity (int complexity)
    {
        difficulty = complexity;
    }

    int getComplexity ()
    {
        return difficulty;
    }
}
```

Multiple classes can implement the same interface, providing alternative definitions for the methods. For example, we could implement a class called `Task` that also implements the `Complexity` interface. In it we could choose to manage the complexity of a task in a different way (though it would still have to implement all the methods of the interface).

A class can implement more than one interface. In these cases, the class must provide an implementation for all methods in all interfaces listed. To show that a class implements multiple interfaces, they are listed in the `implements` clause, separated by commas. For example:

```
class ManyThings implements interface1, interface2, interface3
{
  // all methods of all interfaces
}
```

In addition to, or instead of, abstract methods, an interface can also contain constants, defined using the `final` modifier. When a class implements an interface, it gains access to all of the constants defined in it. This mechanism allows multiple classes to share a set of constants that are defined in a single location.

the `Comparable` interface

The Java standard class library contains interfaces as well as classes. The `Comparable` interface, for example, is defined in the `java.lang` package. It contains only one method, `compareTo`, which takes an object as a parameter and returns an integer.

The intention of this interface is to provide a common mechanism for comparing one object to another. One object calls the method, and passes another as a parameter:

```
if (obj1.compareTo(obj2) < 0)
    System.out.println ("obj1 is less than obj2");
```

As specified by the documentation for the interface, the integer that is returned from the `compareTo` method should be negative if `obj1` is less than `obj2`, 0 if they are equal, and positive if `obj1` is greater than `obj2`. It is up to the designer of each class to decide what it means for one object of that class to be less than, equal to, or greater than another.

The String class contains a compareTo method that operates in this manner. Now we can clarify that the String class has this method because it implements the Comparable interface. The String class implementation of this method bases the comparison on the lexicographic ordering defined by the Unicode character set.

the Iterator interface

The Iterator interface is another interface defined as part of the Java standard class library. It is used by classes that represent a collection of objects, providing a means to move through the collection one object at a time.

The two primary methods in the Iterator interface are hasNext, which returns a boolean result, and next, which returns an object. Neither of these methods takes any parameters. The hasNext method returns true if there are items left to process, and next returns the next object. It is up to the designer of the class that implements the Iterator interface to decide the order in which objects will be delivered by the next method.

We should note that, according to the spirit of the interface, the next method does not remove the object from the underlying collection; it simply returns a reference to it. The Iterator interface also has a method called remove, which takes no parameters and has a void return type. A call to the remove method removes the object that was most recently returned by the next method from the underlying collection.

The Iterator interface is an improved version of an older interface called Enumeration, which is still part of the Java standard class library. The Enumeration interface does not have a remove method. Generally, the Iterator interface is the preferred choice between the two.

A.13 inheritance

A class establishes the characteristics and behaviors of an object, but reserves no memory space for variables (unless those variables are declared as static). Classes are the plan, and objects are the embodiment of that plan.

Many houses can be created from the same blueprint. They are essentially the same house in different locations with different people living in them. But suppose you want a house that is similar to another, but with some different or additional features. You want to start with the same basic blueprint but modify it to suit your needs and desires. Many housing developments are created this way. The houses in the development have the same core layout, but they can have unique features. For instance, they might all be split-level homes with the same bedroom, kitchen, and living-room configuration, but some have a fireplace or full basement while others do not, or an attached garage instead of a carport.

It's likely that the housing developer commissioned a master architect to create a single blueprint to establish the basic design of all houses in the development, then a series of new blueprints that include variations designed to appeal to different buyers. The act of creating the series of blueprints was simplified since they all begin with the same underlying structure, while the variations give them unique characteristics that may be very important to the prospective owners.

Creating a new blueprint that is based on an existing blueprint is analogous to the object-oriented concept of *inheritance,* which allows a software designer to define a new class in terms of an existing one. It is a powerful software development technique and a defining characteristic of object-oriented programming.

derived classes

Inheritance is the process in which a new class is derived from an existing one. The new class automatically contains some or all of the variables and methods in the original class. Then, to tailor the class as needed, the programmer can add new variables and methods to the derived class, or modify the inherited ones.

> **key concept**
> Inheritance is the process of deriving a new class from an existing one.

In general, new classes can be created via inheritance faster, easier, and cheaper than by writing them from scratch. At the heart of inheritance is the idea of *software reuse.* By using existing software components to create new ones, we capitalize on all of the effort that went into the design, implementation, and testing of the existing software.

> **key concept**
> One purpose of inheritance is to reuse existing software.

Keep in mind that the word *class* comes from the idea of classifying groups of objects with similar characteristics. Classification schemes often use levels of classes that relate to each other. For example, all mammals share certain characteristics: they are warm-blooded, have hair, and bear live offspring. Now consider a subset of mammals, such as horses. All horses are mammals, and have all of the characteristics of mammals. But they also have unique features that make them different from other mammals.

If we map this idea into software terms, an existing class called `Mammal` would have certain variables and methods that describe the state and behavior of mammals. A `Horse` class could be derived from the existing `Mammal` class, automatically inheriting the variables and methods contained in `Mammal`. The `Horse` class can refer to the inherited variables and methods as if they had been declared locally in that class. New variables and methods can then be added to the derived class, to distinguish a horse from other mammals. Inheritance nicely models many situations found in the natural world.

> **key concept**
> Inherited variables and methods can be used in the derived class as if they had been declared locally.

The original class that is used to derive a new one is called the *parent class, superclass,* or *base class.* The derived class is called a *child class,* or *subclass.* Java uses the reserved word `extends` to indicate that a new class is being derived from an existing class.

The derivation process should establish a specific kind of relationship between two classes: an *is-a relationship.* This type of relationship means that the derived class should be a more specific version of the original. For example, a horse is a mammal. Not all mammals are horses, but all horses are mammals.

> **key concept**
> Inheritance creates an is-a relationship between all parent and child classes.

Let's look at an example. The following class can be used to define a book:

```java
class Book
{
   protected int numPages;

   protected void pages()
   {
      System.out.println ("Number of pages: " + numPages);
   }
}
```

To derive a child class that is based on the Book class, we use the reserved word extends in the header of the child class. For example, a Dictionary class can be derived from Book as follows:

```
class Dictionary extends Book
{
    private int numDefs;

    public void info()
    {
        System.out.println ("Number of definitions: " + numDefs);
        System.out.println ("Definitions per page: "
                            + numDefs/numPages);
    }
}
```

By saying that the Dictionary class extends the Book class, the Dictionary class automatically inherits the numPages variable and the pages method. Note that the info method uses the numPages variable explicitly.

Inheritance is a one-way street. The Book class cannot use variables or methods that are declared explicitly in the Dictionary class. For instance, if we created an object from the Book class, it could not be used to invoke the info method. This restriction makes sense because a child class is a more specific version of the parent. A dictionary has pages, because all books have pages; but although a dictionary has definitions, not all books do.

Inheritance relationships are represented in UML class diagrams using an arrow with an open arrowhead pointing from the child class to the parent class.

the protected modifier

Not all variables and methods are inherited in a derivation. The visibility modifiers used to declare the members of a class determine which ones are inherited and which are not. Specifically, the child class inherits variables and methods that are declared public, and does not inherit those that are declared private.

However, if we declare a variable with public visibility so that a derived class can inherit it, we violate the principle of encapsulation. Therefore, Java provides a third visibility modifier: protected. When a variable or method is declared with protected visibility, a derived class will inherit it, retaining some of its encapsulation properties. The encapsulation with protected visibility is not as tight as it would be if the variable or method were declared private, but it is better than if it were declared public. Specifically, a variable or method declared with protected visibility may be accessed by any class in the same package.

> **key concept**
>
> Visibility modifiers determine which variables and methods are inherited. Protected visibility provides the best possible encapsulation that permits inheritance.

Each inherited variable or method retains the effect of its original visibility modifier. For example, if a method is public in the parent, it is public in the child.

Constructors are not inherited in a derived class, even though they have public visibility. This is an exception to the rule about public members being inherited. Constructors are special methods that are used to set up a particular type of object, so it wouldn't make sense for a class called `Dictionary` to have a constructor called `Book`.

the `super` reference

The reserved word `super` can be used in a class to refer to its parent class. Using the `super` reference, we can access a parent's members, even if they aren't inherited. Like the `this` reference, what the word `super` refers to depends on the class in which it is used. However, unlike the `this` reference, which refers to a particular instance of a class, `super` is a general reference to the members of the parent class.

One use of the `super` reference is to invoke a parent's constructor. If the following invocation is performed at the beginning of a constructor, the parent's constructor is invoked, passing any appropriate parameters:

> **key concept**
>
> A parent's constructor can be invoked using the `super` reference.

```
super (x, y, z);
```

A child's constructor is responsible for calling its parent's constructor. Generally, the first line of a constructor should use the `super` reference call to a constructor of the parent class. If no such call exists, Java will automatically make a call to `super()` at the beginning of the constructor. This rule ensures that a parent class initializes its variables before the child class constructor begins to execute. Using the `super` reference to invoke a parent's constructor can be done in only the child's constructor, and if included it must be the first line of the constructor.

The `super` reference can also be used to reference other variables and methods defined in the parent's class.

overriding methods

When a child class defines a method with the same name and signature as a method in the parent, we say that the child's version *overrides* the parent's version in favor of its own. The need for overriding occurs often in inheritance situations.

The object that is used to invoke a method determines which version of the method is actually executed. If it is an object of the parent type, the parent's version of the method is invoked. If it is an object of the child type, the child's version is invoked. This flexibility allows two objects that are related by inheritance to use the same naming conventions for methods that accomplish the same general task in different ways.

A method can be defined with the `final` modifier. A child class cannot override a final method. This technique is used to ensure that a derived class uses a particular definition for a method.

The concept of method overriding is important to several issues related to inheritance. These issues are explored in later sections of this appendix.

shadowing variables

It is possible for a child class to declare a variable with the same name as one that is inherited from the parent. This technique is called *shadowing variables*. It is similar to the process of overriding methods, but creates some confusing subtleties. Note the distinction between redeclaring a variable and simply giving an inherited variable a particular value.

Because an inherited variable is already available to the child class, there is usually no good reason to redeclare it. Someone reading code with a shadowed variable will find two different declarations that seem to apply to a variable used in the child class. That confusion causes problems and serves no purpose. A redeclaration of a particular variable name could change its type, though that is usually unnecessary. In general, shadowing variables should be avoided.

A.14 class hierarchies

A child class derived from one parent can be the parent of its own child class. Furthermore, multiple classes can be derived from a single parent. Therefore, inheritance relationships often develop into *class hierarchies*. The UML class diagram in Figure A.4 shows a class hierarchy that incorporates the inheritance relationship between classes `Mammal` and `Horse`.

The child of one class can be the parent of one or more other classes, creating a class hierarchy.

key concept

There is no limit to the number of children a class can have, or to the number of levels to which a class hierarchy can extend. Two children of the same parent are called *siblings*. Although siblings share the characteristics passed on by their common parent, they are not related by inheritance, because one is not used to derive the other.

In class hierarchies, common features should be kept as high in the hierarchy as reasonably possible. That way, the only characteristics explicitly established in a child class are those that make the class distinct from its parent and from its siblings. This approach maximizes the ability to reuse classes. It also facilitates maintenance activities, because when changes are made to the parent, they are automatically reflected in the descendants. Always remember to maintain the is-a relationship when building class hierarchies.

Common features should be located as high in a class hierarchy as is reasonable, minimizing maintenance efforts.

key concept

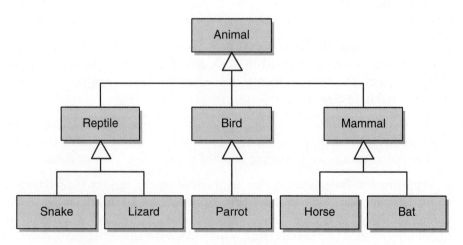

figure A.4   A UML class diagram showing a class hierarchy

The inheritance mechanism is transitive. That is, a parent passes along a trait to a child class, and that child class passes it along to its children, and so on. An inherited feature might have originated in the immediate parent, or possibly from several levels higher in a more distant ancestor class.

There is no single best hierarchy organization for all situations. The decisions made when designing a class hierarchy restrict and guide more detailed design decisions and implementation options, and they must be made carefully.

the `Object` class

In Java, all classes are derived ultimately from the `Object` class. If a class definition doesn't use the `extends` clause to derive itself explicitly from another class, then that class is automatically derived from the `Object` class by default. Therefore, the following two class definitions are equivalent:

```
class Thing
{
    // whatever
}
```

and

```
class Thing extends Object
{
    // whatever
}
```

> **key concept**
>
> All Java classes are derived, directly or indirectly, from the `Object` class.

Because all classes are derived from `Object`, any public method of `Object` can be invoked through any object created in any Java program. The `Object` class is defined in the `java.lang` package of the standard class library.

The `toString` method, for instance, is defined in the `Object` class, so the `toString` method can be called on any object. When a `println` method is called with an object parameter, `toString` is called to determine what to print.

The definition for `toString` that is provided by the `Object` class returns a string containing the object's class name followed by a numeric value that is unique for that object. Usually, we override the `Object` version of `toString` to fit our own needs. The `String` class has overridden the `toString` method so that it returns its stored string value.

The `equals` method of the `Object` class is also useful. Its purpose is to determine if two objects are equal. The definition of the `equals` method provided by the `Object` class returns true if the two object references actually refer to the same object (that is, if they are aliases). Classes often override the inherited definition of the `equals` method in favor of a more appropriate definition. For instance, the `String` class overrides `equals` so that it returns true only if both strings contain the same characters in the same order.

> **key concept**
>
> The `toString` and `equals` methods are defined in the `Object` class and therefore are inherited by every class in every Java program.

abstract classes

An *abstract class* represents a generic concept in a class hierarchy. An abstract class cannot be instantiated, and usually contains one or more abstract methods, which have no definition. In this sense, an abstract class is similar to an interface. Unlike interfaces, however, an abstract class can contain methods that are not abstract, and can contain data declarations other than constants.

A class is declared as abstract by including the `abstract` modifier in the class header. Any class that contains one or more abstract methods must be declared as abstract. In abstract classes (unlike interfaces), the `abstract` modifier must be applied to each abstract method. A class declared as abstract does not have to contain abstract methods.

Abstract classes serve as placeholders in a class hierarchy. As the name implies, an abstract class represents an abstract entity that is usually insufficiently defined to be useful by itself. Instead, an abstract class may contain a partial description that is inherited by all of its descendants in the class hierarchy. Its children, which are more specific, fill in the gaps.

> **key concept**
>
> An abstract class cannot be instantiated. It represents a concept on which other classes can build their definitions.

Consider the class hierarchy shown in Figure A.5. The `Vehicle` class at the top of the hierarchy may be too generic for a particular application. Therefore, we may choose to implement it as an abstract class. Concepts that apply to all vehicles can be represented in the `Vehicle` class and are inherited by its descendants. That way, each of its descendants doesn't have to define the same concept redundantly, and perhaps inconsistently.

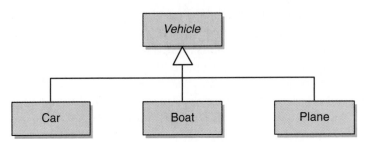

figure A.5   A vehicle class hierarchy

For example, we may say that all vehicles have a particular speed. Therefore, we declare a speed variable in the Vehicle class, and all specific vehicles below it in the hierarchy automatically have that variable via inheritance. Any change we make to the representation of the speed of a vehicle is automatically reflected in all descendant classes. Similarly, we may declare an abstract method called fuelConsumption, whose purpose is to calculate how quickly fuel is being consumed by a particular vehicle. The details of the fuelConsumption method must be defined by each type of vehicle, but the Vehicle class establishes that all vehicles consume fuel and provides a consistent way to compute that value.

Some concepts don't apply to all vehicles, so we wouldn't represent those concepts at the Vehicle level. For instance, we wouldn't include a variable called numberOfWheels in the Vehicle class, because not all vehicles have wheels. The child classes for which wheels are appropriate can add that concept at the appropriate level in the hierarchy.

There are no restrictions as to where in a class hierarchy an abstract class can be defined. Usually they are located at the upper levels of a class hierarchy. However, it is possible to derive an abstract class from a nonabstract parent.

> **key concept**
>
> A class derived from an abstract parent must override all of its parent's abstract methods, or the derived class will also be considered abstract.

Usually, a child of an abstract class will provide a specific definition for an abstract method inherited from its parent. Note that this is just a specific case of overriding a method, giving a different definition than the one the parent provides. If a child of an abstract class does not give a definition for every abstract method that it inherits from its parent, then the child class is also considered to be abstract.

Note that it would be a contradiction for an abstract method to be modified as final or static. Because a final method cannot be overridden in subclasses, an abstract final method would have no way of being given a definition in subclasses. A static method can be invoked using the class name without declaring an object of the class. Because abstract methods have no implementation, an abstract static method would make no sense.

Choosing which classes and methods to make abstract is an important part of the design process. Such choices should be made only after careful consideration. By using abstract classes wisely, we can create flexible, extensible software designs.

interface hierarchies

The concept of inheritance can be applied to interfaces as well as classes. That is, one interface can be derived from another interface. These relationships can form an *interface hierarchy,* which is similar to a class hierarchy. Inheritance relationships between interfaces are shown in UML using the same connection (an arrow with an open arrowhead) as they are with classes.

When a parent interface is used to derive a child interface, the child inherits all abstract methods and constants of the parent. Any class that implements the child interface must implement all of the methods. There are no restrictions on the inheritance between interfaces, as there are with protected and private members of a class, because all members of an interface are public.

> **key concept**
>
> Inheritance can be applied to interfaces, so that one interface can be derived from another interface.

Class hierarchies and interface hierarchies do not overlap. That is, an interface cannot be used to derive a class, and a class cannot be used to derive an interface. A class and an interface interact only when a class is designed to implement a particular interface.

A.15 polymorphism

Usually, the type of a reference variable matches the class of the object it refers to exactly. That is, if we declare a reference as follows:

```
ChessPiece bishop;
```

the bishop reference is used to refer to an object created by instantiating the ChessPiece class. However, the relationship between a reference variable and the object it refers to is more flexible than that.

A polymorphic reference can refer to different types of objects over time.

The term *polymorphism* can be defined as "having many forms." A *polymorphic reference* is a reference variable that can refer to different types of objects at different points in time. The specific method invoked through a polymorphic reference can change from one invocation to the next.

Consider the following line of code:

```
obj.doIt();
```

If the reference obj is polymorphic, it can refer to different types of objects at different times. If that line of code is in a loop or in a method that is called more than once, that line of code might call a different version of the doIt method each time it is invoked.

At some point, the commitment is made to execute certain code to carry out a method invocation. This commitment is referred to as *binding* a method invocation to a method definition. In most situations, the binding of a method invocation to a method definition can occur at compile time. For polymorphic references, however, the decision cannot be made until run time. The method definition that is used is based on the object that is being referred to by the reference variable at that moment. This deferred commitment is called *late binding* or *dynamic binding*. It is less efficient than binding at compile time because the decision has to be made during the execution of the program. This overhead is generally acceptable in light of the flexibility that a polymorphic reference provides.

There are two ways to create a polymorphic reference in Java: using inheritance and using interfaces. The following sections describe these approaches.

references and class hierarchies

A reference variable can refer to any object created from any class related to it by inheritance.

In Java, a reference that is declared to refer to an object of a particular class also can be used to refer to an object of any class related to it by inheritance. For example, if the class Mammal is used to derive the class Horse, then a Mammal reference can be used to refer to an object of class Horse. This ability is shown in the code segment below:

```
Mammal pet;
Horse secretariat = new Horse();
pet = secretariat;  // a valid assignment
```

The reverse operation, assigning the `Mammal` object to a `Horse` reference, is also valid, but requires an explicit cast. Assigning a reference in this direction is generally less useful and more likely to cause problems, because although a horse has all the functionality of a mammal (because a horse *is-a* mammal), the reverse is not necessarily true.

This relationship works throughout a class hierarchy. If the `Mammal` class were derived from a class called `Animal`, then the following assignment would also be valid:

```
Animal creature = new Horse();
```

Carrying this to the extreme, an `Object` reference can be used to refer to any object, because ultimately all classes are descendants of the `Object` class. An `ArrayList`, for example, uses polymorphism in that it is designed to hold `Object` references. That's why an `ArrayList` can be used to store any kind of object. In fact, a particular `ArrayList` can be used to hold several different types of objects at one time, because, in essence, they are all `Object` objects.

polymorphism via inheritance

The reference variable `creature`, as defined in the previous section, can be polymorphic, because at any point in time it could refer to an `Animal` object, a `Mammal` object, or a `Horse` object. Suppose that all three of these classes have a method called `move` that are implemented in different ways (because the child class overrode the definition it inherited). The following invocation calls the `move` method, but the particular version of the method it calls is determined at run time:

```
creature.move();
```

At the point when this line is executed, if `creature` currently refers to an `Animal` object, the `move` method of the `Animal` class is invoked. Likewise, if creature currently refers to a `Mammal` or `Horse` object, the `Mammal` or `Horse` version of `move` is invoked, respectively.

> **key concept**
> A polymorphic reference uses the type of the object, not the type of the reference, to determine which version of a method to invoke.

Of course, since `Animal` and `Mammal` represent general concepts, they may be defined as abstract classes. This situation does not eliminate the ability to have polymorphic references. Suppose the `move` method in the `Mammal` class is abstract, and is given unique definitions in the `Horse`, `Dog`, and `Whale` classes (all derived from `Mammal`). A `Mammal` reference variable can be used to refer to any objects created from any of the `Horse`, `Dog`, and `Whale` classes, and can be used to execute the `move` method on any of them.

Let's consider another situation. The class hierarchy shown in Figure A.6 contains classes that represent various types of employees that might work at a particular company.

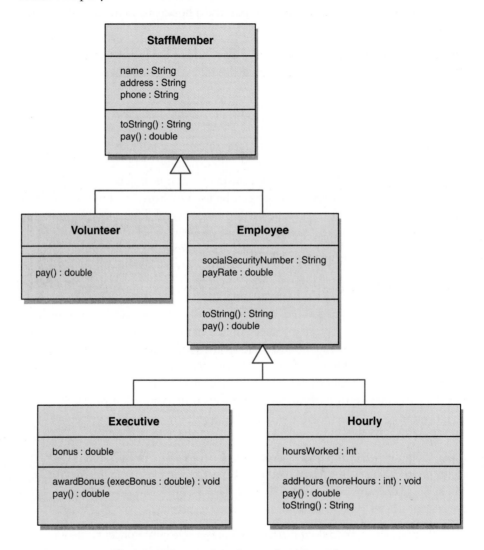

figure A.6 A class hierarchy of employees

Polymorphism could be used in this situation to pay various employees in different ways. One list of employees (of whatever type) could be payed using a single loop that invokes each employee's pay method. But the pay method that is invoked each time will depend on the specific type of employee that is executing the pay method during that iteration of the loop.

This is a classic example of polymorphism—allowing different types of objects to handle a similar operation in different ways.

polymorphism via interfaces

As we've seen, a class name is used to declare the type of an object reference variable. Similarly, an interface name can be used as the type of a reference variable as well. An interface reference variable can be used to refer to any object of any class that implements that interface.

Suppose we declare an interface called Speaker as follows:

> An interface name can be used to declare an object reference variable. An interface reference can refer to any object of any class that implements the interface.
>
> key concept

```java
public interface Speaker
{
    public void speak();
    public void announce (String str);
}
```

The interface name, Speaker, can now be used to declare an object reference variable:

```java
Speaker current;
```

The reference variable current can be used to refer to any object of any class that implements the Speaker interface. For example, if we define a class called Philosopher such that it implements the Speaker interface, we could then assign a Philosopher object to a Speaker reference:

```java
current = new Philosopher();
```

This assignment is valid because a Philosopher is, in fact, a Speaker.

The flexibility of an interface reference allows us to create polymorphic references. As we saw earlier in this appendix, using inheritance, we can create a polymorphic reference that can refer to any one of a set of objects related by inheritance. Using interfaces, we can create similar polymorphic references, except that the objects being referenced, instead of being related by inheritance, are related by implementing the same interface.

For example, if we create a class called `Dog` that also implements the `Speaker` interface, it too could be assigned to a `Speaker` reference variable. The same reference, in fact, could at one point refer to a `Philosopher` object, and then later refer to a `Dog` object. The following lines of code illustrate this:

```
Speaker guest;
guest = new Philosopher();
guest.speak();
guest = new Dog();
guest.speak();
```

In this code, the first time the `speak` method is called, it invokes the `speak` method defined in the `Philosopher` class. The second time it is called, it invokes the `speak` method of the `Dog` class. As with polymorphic references via inheritance, it is not the type of the reference that determines which method gets invoked; it depends on the type of the object that the reference points to at the moment of invocation.

Note that when we are using an interface reference variable, we can invoke only the methods defined in the interface, even if the object it refers to has other methods to which it can respond. For example, suppose the `Philosopher` class also defined a public method called `pontificate`. The second line of the following code would generate a compiler error, even though the object can in fact respond to the `pontificate` method:

```
Speaker special = new Philosopher();
special.pontificate();  // generates a compiler error
```

The problem is that the compiler can determine only that the object is a `Speaker`, and therefore can guarantee only that the object can respond to the `speak` and `announce` methods. Because the reference variable `special` could refer to a `Dog` object (which cannot pontificate), it does not allow the reference. If we know in a particular situation that such an invocation is valid, we can cast the object into the appropriate reference so that the compiler will accept it:

```
((Philosopher) special).pontificate();
```

Similar to polymorphic references based in inheritance, an interface name can be used as the type of a method parameter. In such situations, any object of any class that implements the interface can be passed into the method. For example, the following method takes a `Speaker` object as a parameter. Therefore, both a `Dog` object and a `Philosopher` object can be passed into it in separate invocations.

```
public void sayIt (Speaker current)
{
   current.speak();
}
```

A.16 exceptions

Problems that arise in a Java program may generate exceptions or errors. An *exception* is an object that defines an unusual or erroneous situation. An exception is thrown by a program or the run time environment, and can be caught and handled appropriately if desired. An *error* is similar to an exception, except that an error generally represents an unrecoverable situation, and should not be caught. Java has a predefined set of exceptions and errors that may occur during the execution of a program.

> **key concept**
>
> Errors and exceptions represent unusual or invalid processing.

A program can be designed to process an exception in one of three ways. It can:

- Not handle the exception at all.
- Handle the exception where it occurs.
- Handle the exception at another point in the program.

We explore each of these approaches in the following sections.

exception messages

If an exception is not handled at all by the program, the program will terminate (abnormally) and produce a message that describes what exception occurred and where in the program it was produced. The information associated with an exception is often helpful in tracking down the cause of a problem.

Let's look at the output of an exception. An `ArithmeticException` is thrown when an invalid arithmetic operation is attempted, such as dividing by zero. When that exception is thrown, if there is no code in the program to handle the exception explicitly, the program terminates and prints a message similar to the following:

```
Exception in thread "main" java.lang.ArithmeticException: / by zero
        at Zero.main (Zero.java:17)
```

The first line of the exception output indicates which exception was thrown and provides some information about why it was thrown. The remaining lines are the *call stack trace,* which indicates where the exception occurred. In this case, there is only one line in the call stack trace, but there may be several, depending on where the exception originated in the program. The first line of the trace indicates the method, file, and line number where the exception occurred. The other lines in the trace, if present, indicate the methods that were called to get to the method that produced the exception. In this program, there is only one method, and it produced the exception; therefore, there is only one line in the trace.

key concept

The messages printed by a thrown exception indicate the nature of the problem and provide a method call stack trace.

The call stack trace information is also available by calling methods of the exception object that is being thrown. The method `getMessage` returns a string explaining the reason the exception was thrown. The method `printStackTrace` prints the call stack trace.

the `try` statement

Let's now examine how we catch and handle an exception when it is thrown. A *try statement* consists of a `try` block followed by one or more `catch` clauses. The `try` block is a group of statements that may throw an exception. A `catch` clause defines how a particular kind of exception is handled. A `try` block can have several `catch` clauses associated with it, each dealing with a particular kind of exception. A `catch` clause is sometimes called an *exception handler.*

Here is the general format of a `try` statement:

```
try
{
   // statements in the try block
}
catch (IOException exception)
{
   // statements that handle the I/O problem
}
catch (NumberFormatException exception)
{
   // statements that handle the number format problem
}
```

When a `try` statement is executed, the statements in the `try` block are executed. If no exception is thrown during the execution of the `try` block, processing continues with the statement following the `try` statement (after all of the `catch` clauses). This situation is the normal execution flow and should occur most of the time.

> **key concept**
>
> Each `catch` clause on a `try` statement handles a particular kind of exception that may be thrown within the `try` block.

If an exception is thrown at any point during the execution of the `try` block, control is immediately transferred to the appropriate exception handler if it is present. That is, control transfers to the first `catch` clause whose specified exception corresponds to the class of the exception that was thrown. After executing the statements in the `catch` clause, control transfers to the statement after the entire `try` statement.

exception propagation

If an exception is not caught and handled where it occurs, control is immediately returned to the method that invoked the method that produced the exception. We can design our software so that the exception is caught and handled at this outer level. If it isn't caught there, control returns to the method that called it. This process is called *propagating the exception.*

> **key concept**
>
> If an exception is not caught and handled where it occurs, it is propagated to the calling method.

Exception propagation continues until the exception is caught and handled, or until it is propagates out of the `main` method, which terminates the program and produces an exception message. To catch an exception at an outer level, the method that produces the exception must be invoked inside a `try` block that has an appropriate `catch` clause to handle it.

A programmer must pick the most appropriate level at which to catch and handle an exception. There is no single best answer. It depends on the situation and the design of the system. Sometimes the right approach will be not to catch an exception at all and let the program terminate.

the exception class hierarchy

The classes that define various exceptions are related by inheritance, creating a class hierarchy that is shown in part in Figure A.7.

The `Throwable` class is the parent of both the `Error` class and the `Exception class`. Many types of exceptions are derived from the `Exception` class, and these classes also have many children. Though these high-level classes are defined in the `java.lang` package, many child classes that define specific exceptions are part of several other packages. Inheritance relationships can span package boundaries.

We can define our own exceptions by deriving a new class from `Exception` or one of its descendants. The class we choose as the parent depends on what situation or condition the new exception represents.

After creating the class that defines the exception, an object of that type can be created as needed. The `throw` statement is used to throw the exception. For example:

```
throw new MyException();
```

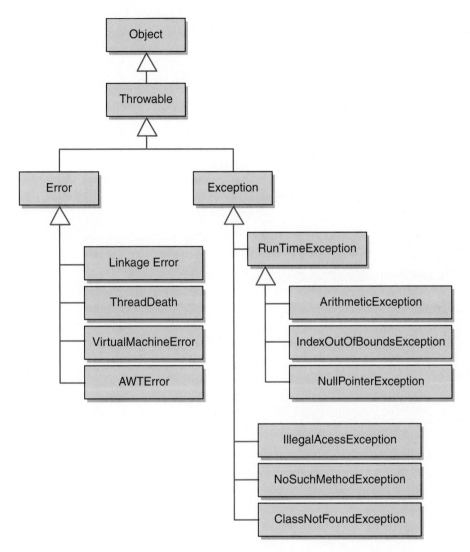

figure A.7   Part of the Error and Exception class hierarchy

This appendix is a reference for many of the classes in the Java standard class library. We list the variables, constants, constructors, and methods of each class. Items within a class are grouped according to their purpose. The classes are listed in alphabetical order. The package each class is contained in is given in parentheses after the class name.

AbstractButton (javax.swing)

A public abstract class, derived from `JComponent` and implementing `ItemSelectable` and `SwingConstants`, that represents the common behaviors for buttons and menu items.

methods

```
public void addActionListener(ActionListener listener)
public void addChangeListener(ChangeListener listener)
public void addItemListener(ItemListener listener)
```
Adds a specific type of listener to this button.

```
public void doClick()
public void doClick(int pressTime)
```
Performs a button click programmatically (as if the user had used the mouse). The button stays visually "pressed" for `pressTime` milliseconds if specified.

```
public Icon getDisabledIcon()
public void setDisabledIcon(Icon disabledIcon)
```
Gets or sets the icon used by this button when it is disabled.

```
public Icon getDisabledSelectedIcon()
public void setDisabledSelectedIcon(Icon disabledSelectedIcon)
```
Gets or sets the icon used by this button when it is disabled and selected.

```
public int getHorizontalAlignment()
public void setHorizontalAlignment(int alignment)
public int getVerticalAlignment()
public void setVerticalAlignment(int alignment)
```
Gets or sets the horizontal or vertical alignment of the icon and text.

```
public int getHorizontalTextPosition()
public void setHorizontalTextPosition(int position)
public int getVerticalTextPosition()
public void setVerticalTextPosition(int position)
```
Gets or sets the horizontal or vertical position of the text relative to the icon.

```
public Icon getIcon()
public void setIcon(Icon icon)
```
Gets or sets the default icon for this button.
```
public Insets getMargin()
public void setMargin(Insets insets)
```
Gets or sets the margin between this button's border and the label.
```
public int getMnemonic()
public void setMnemonic(int mnemonic)
```
Gets or sets this button's keyboard mnemonic.
```
public Icon getPressedIcon()
public void setPressedIcon(Icon icon)
```
Gets or sets the icon used by this button when it is pressed.
```
public Icon getRolloverIcon()
public void setRolloverIcon(Icon icon)
```
Gets or sets the icon used by this button when the mouse rolls over it.
```
public Icon getSelectedIcon()
public void setSelectedIcon(Icon icon)
```
Gets or sets the icon used by this button when it is selected.
```
public String getText()
public void setText(String text)
```
Gets or sets the text displayed on this button.
```
public void setEnabled(boolean flag)
```
Enables or disables this button.
```
public void setRolloverEnabled(boolean flag)
```
Enables or disables the rollover property for this button. Rollover effects will not occur if this property is disabled.
```
public isRolloverEnabled()
```
Returns true if this button currently has its rollover property enabled.
```
public void setSelected(boolean flag)
```
Selects or deselects ths button.
```
public boolean isSelected()
```
Returns true if this button is currently selected.

ActionEvent (java.awt.event)

A public class, derived from `AWTEvent`, that represents an AWT action event.

variables and constants

```
public static final int ALT_MASK
public static final int CTRL_MASK
public static final int META_MASK
public static final int SHIFT_MASK
```
Constant values which represent masks for the Alt, Control, Meta, and Shift keys being pressed during an action event.

```
public static final int ACTION_FIRST
public static final int ACTION_LAST
```
Constant values that represent the index of the first and last action event ids.

```
public static final int ACTION_PERFORMED
```
A constant value that represents an action performed AWT event type.

constructors

```
public ActionEvent(Object src, int type, String cmd)
public ActionEvent(Object src, int type, String cmd, int keys)
```
Creates a new instance of an `ActionEvent` from the specified source object, event type, and command string. Additionally, a mask value can be set that defines the types of keys depressed during the event.

methods

```
public String getActionCommand()
```
Returns the command string associated with this action.

```
public int getModifiers()
```
Returns the mask of the modifiers (special keys) depressed during this event.

```
public String paramString()
```
Returns a string containing the parameters of this `ActionEvent`.

AdjustmentEvent (java.awt.event)

A public class, derived from AWTEvent, that represents an AWT adjustment event.

variables and constructs

```
public static final int ADJUSTMENT_FIRST
public static final int ADJUSTMENT_LAST
```
Constant values that represent the index of the first and last adjustment event ids.

```
public static final int ADJUSTMENT_VALUE_CHANGED
```
A constant value that represents an adjustment value change event.

```
public static final int BLOCK_DECREMENT
public static final int BLOCK_INCREMENT
```
Constant values that represent block decrement and increment events.

```
public static final int TRACK
```
A constant value which represents an absolute tracking adjustment event.

```
public static final int UNIT_DECREMENT
public static final int UNIT_INCREMENT
```
Constant values which represent unit decrement and increment events.

constructors

```
public AdjustmentEvent(Adjustable source, int id, int type, int val)
```
Creates a new instance of an AdjustmentEvent from a specified source and having a specified id, type, and value.

methods

```
public Adjustable getAdjustable()
```
Returns the adjustable object that originated this AWT AdjustmentEvent.

```
public int getAdjustmentType()
```
Returns the type of adjustment for this event.

```
public int getValue()
```
Returns the current value of this AdjustmentEvent.

```
public String paramString()
```
Returns a string containing the parameters of this event.

Applet (java.applet)

A public class, derived from `Panel`, that is intended to be used as a program running inside a Web page.

constructors

`public Applet()`

Creates a new instance of an applet for inclusion on a Web page.

methods

`public void destroy()`

Destroys the applet and all of its resources. This method contains no functionality and should be overridden by subclasses.

`public AppletContext getAppletContext()`

Returns this applet's context (the environment in which it is running).

`public String getAppletInfo()`

Returns a string representation of information regarding this applet. This method contains no functionality and should be overridden by subclasses.

`public AudioClip getAudioClip(URL audio)`

`public AudioClip getAudioClip(URL base, String filename)`

Returns the `AudioClip` requested. The location of the audio clip can be given by the base URL and the filename relative to that base.

`public URL getCodeBase()`

`public URL getDocumentBase()`

`public Locale getLocale()`

Returns the URL of this applet, the document that contains this applet, or the locale of this applet.

`public Image getImage(URL image)`

`public Image getImage(URL base, String filename)`

Returns the image requested. The location of the image can be given by the base URL and the filename relative to that base.

`public String getParameter(String param)`

`public String[][] getParameterInfo()`

Returns the value of the specified parameter for this applet. An array of string elements containing information about each parameter for this applet can also be obtained. Each element of the returned array should be comprised of three strings (parameter name, type, and description). This method contains no functionality and should be overridden by subclasses.

```
public void init()
```
This method provides initialization functionality to the applet prior to the first time that the applet is started. It is automatically called by the browser or the appletviewer program. This method contains no functionality and should be overridden by subclasses.

```
public boolean isActive()
```
Returns a true value if this applet is currently active. An applet is considered active just prior to execution of its start method and is no longer active just after execution of its stop method.

```
public void play(URL source)
```
```
public void play(URL base, String filename)
```
Plays the audio clip located at source. The location of the audio clip can be given as a base URL and the filename relative to that base.

```
public void resize(Dimension dim)
```
```
public void resize(int w, int h)
```
Resizes this applet according to the specified dimension.

```
public final void setStub(AppletStub stub)
```
Sets the interface between this applet and the browser or appletviewer program.

```
public void showStatus(String message)
```
Prints the specified message in the browser's status window.

```
public void start()
```
This method generally contains functionality relevant to the starting of this applet. It is called after the applet has been initialized (with the init method) and every time the applet is reloaded in the browser or appletviewer program. This method contains no functionality and should be overridden by subclasses.

```
public void stop()
```
This method generally contains functionality relevant to the stopping of this applet. It is called by the browser (when the containing Web page is replaced) or appletviewer program. This method contains no functionality and should be overridden by subclasses.

ArrayList (java.util)

A public class, derived from `AbstractList`, that represents a resizable array implementation of a list. Similar to `Vector`, but unsynchronized.

constructors

`public ArrayList()`

`public ArrayList(int initialCapacity)`
   Creates a new list with the specified initial capacity (ten by default).

`public ArrayList(Collection col)`
   Creates a new list containing the elements of the specified collection.

methods

`public void add(int index, Object element)`
   Inserts the specified element into this list at the specified index.

`public boolean add(Object obj)`
   Appends the specified element to the end of this list.

`public boolean addAll(Collection col)`

`public boolean addAll(int index, Collection col)`
   Inserts all of the elements in the specified collection into the list at the specified index, or appends them to the end of the list if no index is specified.

`public void clear()`
   Removes all of the elements from this list.

`public boolean contains(Object obj)`
   Returns true if this list contains the specified object.

`public void ensureCapacity(int minimumCapacity)`
   Increases the capacity of this list to the specified value if necessary.

`public Object get(int index)`
   Returns the element at the specified index. Throws `IndexOutOfBoundsException` if the index is out of range.

`public int indexOf(Object obj)`
   Returns the index of the first occurrence of the specified object (based on the `equals` method) or −1 if it is not found.

`public boolean isEmpty()`
   Returns true if this list contains no elements.

```
public int lastIndexOf(Object obj)
```
Returns the index of the last occurrence of the specified object (based on the equals method) or –1 if it is not found.

```
public Object remove(int index)
```
Removes and returns the object at the specified index in this list. Throws IndexOutOfBoundsException if the index is out of range.

```
protected void removeRange(int fromIndex, int toIndex)
```
Removes the elements at the indexes in the specified range, exclusive.

```
public Object set(int index, Object obj)
```
Replaces the element at the specified index with the specified object.

```
public int size()
```
Returns the number of elements in this list.

```
public Object[] toArray()
```
Returns an array containing the elements in this list.

```
public void trimToSize()
```
Trims the capacity of this list to the current size.

AWTEvent (java.awt)

A public class, derived from EventObject, that is the root class for all of the AWT event classes.

variables and constants

```
public final static long ACTION_EVENT_MASK
public final static long ADJUSTMENT_EVENT_MASK
public final static long COMPONENT_EVENT_MASK
public final static long CONTAINER_EVENT_MASK
public final static long FOCUS_EVENT_MASK
public final static long ITEM_EVENT_MASK
public final static long KEY_EVENT_MASK
public final static long MOUSE_EVENT_MASK
public final static long MOUSE_MOTION_EVENT_MASK
public final static long TEXT_EVENT_MASK
public final static long WINDOW_EVENT_MASK
```
Constant values representing the AWT event masks for various events.

`protected boolean consumed`
> A variable representing the state of the event. A true value means that it has not been sent to the appropriate peer, false indicates that it has.

`protected int id`
> The numeric identification for this event.

constructors

`public AWTEvent(Event evt)`
> Creates a new AWTEvent from the specified event.

`public AWTEvent(Object src, int type)`
> Creates a new AWTEvent from a specified source, and having a defined type.

methods

`protected void consume()`
> Targets this AWTEvent to be sent to the appropriate peer.

`public int getID()`
> Returns this event's type.

`protected boolean isConsumed()`
> Returns a true value if this AWTEvent has been sent to the appropriate peer.

`public String paramString()`
> Returns the parameter string for this AWTEvent.

`public String toString()`
> Returns a string representation of this AWTEvent.

BigDecimal (java.math)

A public class, derived from Number, which can be used to represent a decimal number with a definable precision.

variables and constants

`ROUND_CEILING`
> A constant that represents a rounding mode in which the value of the BigDecimal is rounded up (away from zero) if the number is positive, and down (closer to zero) if the number is negative.

`ROUND_DOWN`
> A constant that represents a rounding mode in which the value of the BigDecimal is rounded closer to zero (decreasing a positive number and increasing a negative number).

ROUND_FLOOR

A constant that represents a rounding mode in which the value of the BigDecimal is rounded down (closer to zero) if the number is positive, and up (away from zero) if the number is negative.

ROUND_HALF_DOWN

A constant that represents a rounding mode in which the value of the BigDecimal is rounded as in ROUND_UP if the fraction of the number is greater than 0.5 and as ROUND_DOWN in all other cases.

ROUND_HALF_EVEN

A constant that represents a rounding mode in which the value of the BigDecimal is rounded as in ROUND_HALF_UP if the number to the left of the decimal is odd and as ROUND_HALF_DOWN when the number is even.

ROUND_HALF_UP

A constant that represents a rounding mode in which the value of the BigDecimal is rounded as in ROUND_UP if the fraction of the number is greater than or equal to 0.5 and as in ROUND_DOWN in all other cases.

ROUND_UNNECESSARY

A constant that represents a rounding mode in which the value of the BigDecimal is not rounded (if possible) and an exact result be returned.

ROUND_UP

A constant that represents a rounding mode in which the value of the BigDecimal is rounded away from zero (increasing a positive number, and decreasing a negative number).

constructors

```
public BigDecimal(BigInteger arg)
public BigDecimal(BigInteger arg, int scale) throws
NumberFormatException
public BigDecimal(double arg) throws NumberFormatException
public BigDecimal(String arg) throws NumberFormatException
```
Creates an instance of a BigDecimal from arg. The string argument may contain a preceding minus sign indicating a negative number. The resulting BigDecimal's scale will be the number of integers to the right of the decimal point in the string, a specified value, or 0 (zero) if none are present.

methods

```
public double doubleValue()
public float floatValue()
public int intValue()
```

```
public long longValue()
public BigInteger toBigInteger()
public String toString()
```
Converts this `BigDecimal` to either a Java primitive type or a `BigInteger`.

```
public BigDecimal abs()
```
Returns the absolute value of this `BigDecimal` with the same scale as this `BigDecimal`.

```
public BigDecimal add(BigDecimal arg)
public BigDecimal subtract(BigDecimal arg)
```
Returns the result of `arg` added to or subtracted from this `BigDecimal`, with the resulting scale equal to the larger of the two `BigDecimals`' scales.

```
public int compareTo(BigDecimal arg)
```
This method compares this `BigDecimal` to `arg` and will return a −1 if this `BigDecimal` is less than `arg`, 0 if equal to `arg` or a 1 if greater than `arg`. If the values of the two `BigDecimals` are identical and the scales are different, they are considered equal.

```
public BigDecimal divide(BigDecimal arg, int mode) throws
ArithmeticException, IllegalArgumentException
public BigDecimal divide(BigDecimal arg, int scale, int mode)
throws ArithmeticException, IllegalArgumentException
```
Returns the result of this `BigDecimal` divided by `arg`. If required the rounding mode is used. The resulting `BigDecimal`'s scale is identical to this `BigDecimal`'s scale or a specified value.

```
public boolean equals(Object arg)
```
Returns a true value if this `BigDecimal`'s value and scale are equal to `arg`'s value and scale.

```
public int hashCode()
```
Returns the hash code of this `BigDecimal`.

```
public BigDecimal max(BigDecimal arg)
public BigDecimal min(BigDecimal arg)
```
Returns the greater or lesser of this `BigDecimal` and `arg`.

```
public BigDecimal movePointLeft(int num)
public BigDecimal movePointRight(int num)
```
Returns this `BigDecimal` with the decimal point moved num positions.

```
public BigDecimal multiply(BigDecimal arg)
```
Returns the result of this `BigDecimal` multiplied with the value of `arg`. The scale of the resulting `BigDecimal` is the result of the addition of the two `BigDecimals`' scales.

```
public BigDecimal negate()
```
Returns the negation of this BigDecimal's value with the same scale.

```
public int scale()
```
Returns the scale of this BigDecimal.

```
public BigDecimal setScale(int val) throws ArithmeticException,
IllegalArgumentException
```

```
public BigDecimal setScale(int val, int mode) throws
ArithmeticException, IllegalArgumentException
```
Returns a BigDecimal whose value is the same as this BigDecimal's and has a new scale specified by val. If rounding is necessary, a rounding mode can be specified.

```
public int signum()
```
Returns a –1 if this BigDecimal is negative, 0 if zero, and 1 if positive.

```
public static BigDecimal valueOf(long value)
```

```
public static BigDecimal valueOf(long value, int scale) throws
NumberFormatException
```
Returns a BigDecimal with a defined value. The scale of the returned number is specified or it defaults to 0 (zero).

BigInteger (java.math)

A public class, derived from Number, that can be used to represent an integer in a two's complement format of any precision.

constructors

```
public BigInteger(byte[] arg) throws NumberFormatException
```

```
public BigInteger(int signum, byte[] magnitude) throws
NumberFormatException
```
Creates an instance of a BigInteger from the specified byte array. The sign of the number can be placed in signum (where –1 is negative, 0 is zero, and 1 is positive).

```
public BigInteger(String arg) throws NumberFormatException
```

```
public BigInteger(String arg, int radix) throws
NumberFormatException
```
Creates an instance of a BigInteger from the string arg, which can contain decimal numbers preceded by an optional minus sign. The argument radix specifies the base of the arg value.

```
public BigInteger(int size, Random rand) throws
IllegalArgumentException
public BigInteger(int size, int prob, Random rand)
```
Creates a (generally) prime instance of a `BigInteger` from a random integer, `rand`, of a specified length, `size`. The certainty parameter (`prob`) represents the amount of probability that the generated number is a prime.

methods

```
public double doubleValue()
public float floatValue()
public int intValue()
public long longValue()
public String toString()
public String toString(int base)
```
Converts this `BigDecimal` to either a Java primitive type or a `BigInteger`. The base can specify the radix of the number value returned.

```
public BigInteger abs()
```
Returns the absolute value of this `BigInteger`.

```
public BigInteger add(BigInteger arg) throws ArithmeticException
public BigInteger subtract(BigInteger arg)
```
Adds the argument to, or subtracts `arg` from this `BigInteger` and returns the result.

```
public BigInteger and(BigInteger arg)
public BigInteger andNot(BigInteger arg)
public BigInteger not()
public BigInteger or(BigInteger arg)
public BigInteger xor(BigInteger arg)
```
Returns the result of a logical operation of this `BigInteger` and the value of `arg`. The not method returns the logical not of this `BigInteger`.

```
public int bitCount()
```
Returns the number of bits from this `BigInteger` that are different from the sign bit.

```
public int bitLength()
```
Returns the number of bits from this `BigInteger`, excluding the sign bit.

```
public BigInteger clearBit(int index) throws ArithmeticException
```
Returns the modified representation of this `BigInteger` with the bit at position `index` cleared.

public int compareTo(BigInteger arg)

Compares this BigInteger to the parameter arg. If this BigInteger is less than arg, a -1 is returned, if equal to arg a 0 (zero) is returned, and if greater than arg, a 1 is returned.

public BigInteger divide(BigInteger arg) throws ArithmeticException

public BigInteger[] divideAndRemainder(BigInteger arg) throws ArithmeticException

Returns the result of this BigInteger divided by arg. The divideAndRemainder method returns as the first element ([0]) the quotient, and the second element ([1]) the remainder.

public boolean equals(Object arg)

Returns a true value if this BigInteger is equal to the parameter arg.

public BigInteger flipBit(int index) throws ArithmeticException

Returns the modified representation of this BigInteger with the bit at position index flipped.

public BigInteger gcd(BigInteger arg)

Returns the greatest common denominator of the absolute value of this BigInteger and the absolute value of the parameter arg.

public int getLowestSetBit()

Returns the index of the rightmost bit that is equal to one from this BigInteger.

public int hashCode()

Returns the hash code of this BigInteger.

public boolean isProbablePrime(int prob)

Returns a true value if this BigInteger is probably a prime number. The parameter prob represents the certainty of the decision.

public BigInteger max(BigInteger arg)

public BigInteger min(BigInteger arg)

Returns the larger or smaller of this BigInteger or arg.

public BigInteger mod(BigInteger arg)

public BigInteger modInverse(BigInteger arg) throws ArithmeticException

public BigInteger modPow(BigInteger exp, BigInteger arg)

Returns the result of this BigInteger mod arg. The modInverse returns the modular multiplicative inverse. modPow returns the result of this (BigInteger ^^ exp) mod arg.

public BigInteger multiply(BigInteger arg)
   Returns the result of this BigInteger multiplied by arg.

public BigInteger negate()
   Returns this BigInteger negated (this BigInteger * −1).

public BigInteger pow(int exp) throws ArithmeticException
   Returns the result of this BigInteger ^^ exp.

public BigInteger remainder(BigInteger arg) throws
ArithmeticException
   Returns the result of this BigInteger mod arg.

public BigInteger setBit(int index) throws ArithmeticException
   Returns the result of this BigInteger with the bit at the specified index set.

public BigInteger shiftLeft(int num)

public BigInteger shiftRight(int num)
   Returns the result of this BigInteger shifted num bits.

public int signum()
   Returns a −1 if the value of this BigInteger is negative, 0 if zero, and 1 if positive.

public boolean testBit(int index) throws ArithmeticException
   Returns a true value if the bit at the specified index is set.

public byte[] toByteArray()
   Returns the two's complement of this BigInteger in an array of bytes.

public static BigInteger valueOf(long arg)
   Returns a BigInteger from the value of arg.

BitSet (java.util)

A public final class, derived from Object and implementing Cloneable and Serializable, that allows for the manipulation of a vectored array of bits.

constructors

public BitSet()

public BitSet(int size)
   Creates a new instance of a bit sequence of size bits (the default is 64). Each of the initial bits are set to false.

methods

public void and(BitSet arg)

public void or(BitSet arg)

```
public void xor(BitSet arg)
```
Places all of the bits from both this BitSet AND/OR/XORed with the bits of arg into this BitSet.

```
public void clear(int index)
```
```
public void set(int index)
```
Clears or sets the bit (sets it to false) at location index.

```
public Object clone()
```
Returns a clone of this BitSet.

```
public boolean equals(Object arg)
```
Returns a true if arg is not null and all bits are equal to this BitSet.

```
public boolean get(int index)
```
Returns the boolean value of the bit at location index.

```
public int hashCode()
```
Returns the hash code of this BitSet.

```
public int size()
```
Returns the size of this BitSet.

```
public String toString()
```
Returns a string representation of this BitSet in set notation (i.e., {1, 2, 5}).

Boolean (java.lang)

A public final class, derived from Object and implementing Serializable, that contains boolean logic operations, constants, and methods as a wrapper around the Java primitive type boolean.

variables and constructs

```
public final static Boolean TRUE
```
```
public final static Boolean FALSE
```
Boolean constant values of true or false.

```
public final static Class TYPE
```
The Boolean constant value of the boolean type class.

constructors

```
public Boolean(boolean arg)
```
```
public Boolean(String arg)
```
Creates an instance of the Boolean class from the parameter arg.

methods

public boolean booleanValue()

The boolean value of the current object.

public boolean equals(Object arg)

Returns the result of an equality comparison against arg. Here arg must be a boolean object with the same value as this Boolean for a resulting true value.

public static boolean getBoolean(String str)

Returns a Boolean representation of the system property named in str.

public int hashCode()

Returns the hash code for this object.

public String toString()

Returns the string representation of the state of the current object (i.e., "true" or "false").

public static Boolean valueOf(String str)

Returns a new Boolean initialized to the value of str.

BorderFactory (javax.swing)

A public class, derived from Object, that represents a factory for creating GUI borders.

methods

public static Border createBevelBorder(int type)

public static Border createBevelBorder(int type, Color highlight, Color shadow)

public static Border createBevelBorder(int type, Color outerHighlight, Color innerHighlight, Color outerShadow, Color innerShadow)

Returns a bevel border with the specified type (BevelBorder.LOWERED or BevelBorder.RAISED) and shading.

public static CompoudBorder createCompoundBorder(Border outside, Border inside)

Returns a border composed of the two other specified borders.

public static Border createEmptyBorder()

public static Border createEmptyBorder(int top, int left, int bottom, int right)

Returns an empty (invisible) border with the specified dimensions, which default to 0.

```
public static Border createEtchedBorder()
public static Border createEtchedBorder(Color highlight, Color
shadow)
public static Border createEtchedBorder(int type)
public static Border createEtchedBorder(int type, Color
highlight, Color shadow)
```
Returns an etched border with the specified type (EtchedBorder.RAISED or
EtchedBorder.LOWERED) and shading.

```
public static Border createLineBorder(Color color)
public static Border createLineBorder(Color color, int
thickness)
```
Returns a line border with the specified color and thickness. If unspecified, the
thickness defaults to one pixel.

```
public static Border createLoweredBevelBorder()
public static Border createRaisedBevelBorder()
```
Returns a border with a lowered or raised beveled edge.

```
public static MatteBorder createMatteBorder(int top, int left,
int bottom, int right, Color color)
public static MatteBorder createMatteBorder(int top, int left,
int bottom, int right, Icon icon)
```
Returns a matte border with the specified edge sizes. The border is made up
either of the specified color or the specified icon.

```
public static TitledBorder createTitledBorder(Border border)
public static TitledBorder createTitledBorder(String title)
public static TitledBorder createTitledBorder(Border border,
String title)
public static TitledBorder createTitledBorder(Border border,
String title, int justification, int position)
public static TitledBorder createTitledBorder(Border border,
String title, int justification, int position, Font font)
public static TitledBorder createTitledBorder(Border border,
String title, int justification, int position, Font font, Color
color)
```
Returns a titled border with the specified border and the specified title text,
justification, position, font, and color. Justification and position are defined by
constants in the TitledBorder class. Justification can be: LEFT, CENTER,
RIGHT, LEADING, or TRAILING (default is LEADING). position specifies the
title's vertical position in relation to the border and can be: TOP, BELOW_TOP,
ABOVE_BOTTOM, BOTTOM, or BELOW_BOTTOM (default is TOP).

BorderLayout (java.awt)

A public class, derived from `Object` and implementing `LayoutManager2` and `Serializable`, that lays out a container using five distinct areas (North, South, East, West, and Center).

variables and constructs

```
public final static String CENTER
public final static String EAST
public final static String NORTH
public final static String SOUTH
public final static String WEST
```
Constant values indicating areas of the border layout manager.

constructors

```
public BorderLayout()
public BorderLayout(int hgap, int vgap)
```
Creates a new instance of a `BorderLayout`. If no initial horizontal and vertical gaps are specified, they default to zero.

methods

```
public void addLayoutComponent(Component item, Object
constraints)
public void removeLayoutComponent(Component item)
```
Adds or removes a component to this layout manager. When adding a component, it is possible to restrict the component to the specified constraints.

```
public int getHgap()
public int getVgap()
```
Returns the horizontal or vertical gap of components laid out by this layout manager.

```
public float getLayoutAlignmentX(Container cont)
public float getLayoutAlignmentY(Container cont)
```
Returns the horizontal or vertical alignment value of the specified container.

```
public void invalidateLayout(Container cont)
```
Forces this layout manager to discard any cached layout information about the specified container.

```
public void layoutContainer(Container cont)
```
Lays out the specified container with this layout manager.

```
public Dimension maximumLayoutSize(Container cont)
public Dimension minimumLayoutSize(Container cont)
public Dimension preferredLayoutSize(Container cont)
```
Returns the maximum, minimum or preferred size of the specified container when laid out by this layout manager.

```
public void setHgap(int hgap)
public void setVgap(int vgap)
```
Sets the horizontal or vertical gap in pixels of components laid out by this layout manager.

Box (javax.swing)

A public class, derived from `JComponent` and implementing `Accessible`, that represents a lightweight container that uses a box layout.

constructors

```
public Box(int axis)
```
Creates a box that displays its components along the specified axis (`BoxLayout.X_AXIS` or `BoxLayout.Y_AXIS`).

methods

```
public static Box createHorizontalBox()
public static Box createVerticalBox()
```
Returns a box that displays its components horizontally (from left to right) or vertically (from top to bottom).

```
public static Component createGlue()
public static Component createHorizontalGlue()
public static Component createVerticalGlue()
```
Returns an invisible glue component that expands as much as necessary to fill the space between neighboring components.

```
public static Component createRigidArea(Dimension dim)
```
Returns an invisible component with the specified size.

```
public static Component createHorizontalStrut(int width)
public static Component createVerticalStrut(int height)
```
Returns an invisible component with a fixed width or height.

BoxLayout (javax.swing)

A public class, derived from `Object` and implementing `LayoutManager2` and `Serializable`, that lays out components either vertically or horizontally.

variables and constructs

`public static final int X_AXIS`

`public static final int Y_AXIS`
   Specifies that components should be laid out left to right or top to bottom.

constructors

`public BoxLayout(Container target, int axis)`
   Creates a box layout for the specified target container along the specified axis.

methods

`public float getLayoutAlignmentX(Container cont)`

`public float getLayoutAlignmentY(Container cont)`
   Returns the horizontal or vertical alignment value of the specified container.

`public void invalidateLayout(Container cont)`
   Forces this layout manager to discard any cached layout information about the specified container.

`public void layoutContainer(Container cont)`
   Lays out the specified container with this layout manager.

`public Dimension maximumLayoutSize(Container cont)`

`public Dimension minimumLayoutSize(Container cont)`

`public Dimension preferredLayoutSize(Container cont)`
   Returns the maximum, minimum, or preferred size of the specified container when laid out by this layout manager.

BufferedReader (java.io)

A public class, derived from `Reader`, that provides a buffered stream of character-based input.

constructors

```
public BufferedReader(Reader rdr)
public BufferedReader(Reader rdr, int size)
```
Creates a `BufferedReader` from the specified `Reader`, by using a specified size (in characters). The default size is 8192 characters.

methods

```
public void close() throws IOException
```
Closes this `BufferedReader`.

```
public void mark(int readAheadLimit) throws IOException
```
Sets a mark in the stream where attempts to reset this `BufferedReader` will return to. The `readAheadLimit` determines how far ahead the stream can be read before the mark expires.

```
public boolean markSupported()
```
An overridden method from `Reader` that determines if this stream supports the setting of a mark.

```
public int read() throws IOException
public String readLine() throws IOException
```
Reads a single character or an entire line from this `BufferedReader` stream. The character is returned as an `int`, the line as a string. A line of text is considered to be a series of characters ending in a carriage return (\r), a line feed (\n), or a carriage return followed by a line (\r\n).

```
public int read(char[] dest, int offset, int size) throws
IOException
```
Reads `size` characters from this `BufferedReader` stream. Reading will skip `offset` characters into the current location in the stream, and place them in the destination array. This method will return the number of characters read from the stream or a -1 if the end of the stream was reached.

```
public boolean ready() throws IOException
```
Returns a true value if this `BufferedReader` is capable of being read from. This state can only be true if the buffer is not empty.

```
public void reset() throws IOException
```
Resets this `BufferedReader` to the last mark.

```
public long skip(long num) throws IOException
```
Skips forward num characters in the stream and returns the actual number of characters skipped.

BufferedWriter (java.io)

A public class, derived from `Writer`, that represents a character output stream that buffers characters for efficiency.

constructors

```
public BufferedWriter(Writer out)
public BufferedWriter(Writer out, int size)
```
Creates a buffered output stream using the specified `Writer` stream and a buffer of the specified size.

methods

```
public void close()
```
Closes this stream.

```
public void flush()
```
Flushes this stream.

```
public void newLine()
```
Writes a line separator to this stream.

```
public void write(int ch)
public void write(String str)
public void write(String str, int offset, int length)
public void write(char[] buffer)
public void write(char[] buffer, int offset, int length)
```
Writes a single character, string, or character array to this stream. A portion of the string or character array can be specified.

ButtonGroup (javax.swing)

A public class, derived from `Object` and implementing `Serializable`, that represents a set of mutually exclusive buttons.

constructors

```
public ButtonGroup()
```
Creates an empty button group.

methods

```
public void add(AbstractButton button)
public void remove(AbstractButton button)
```
Adds or removes the specified button to this group.

```
public int getButtonCount()
```
Returns the number of buttons in this group.

Byte (java.lang)

A public final class, derived from Number, that contains byte logic operations, constants, and methods as a wrapper around the Java primitive type byte.

variables and constructs

```
public final static byte MAX_VALUE
public final static byte MIN_VALUE
```
A constant value that holds the maximum (127) and minimum (–128) values a byte can contain.

```
public final static Class TYPE
```
The Byte constant value of the byte type class.

constructors

```
public Byte(byte arg)
public Byte(String arg) throws NumberFormatException
```
Creates a new instance of a Byte from arg.

methods

```
public byte byteValue()
public double doubleValue()
public float floatValue()
public int intValue()
public long longValue()
public short shortValue()
```
Returns the value of this Byte as a Java primitive type.

```
public static Byte decode(String str) throws
NumberFormatException
```
Returns the given string (str) as a Byte. The parameter string may be encoded as an octal, hexadecimal, or binary number.

```
public boolean equals(Object arg)
```
Returns a true value if this Byte is equal to the parameter object arg.

```
public int hashCode()
```
Returns the hash code of this Byte.

```
public static byte parseByte(String str) throws
NumberFormatException
```

```
public static byte parseByte(String str, int base) throws
NumberFormatException
```
Returns the value of the parsed string (str) as a byte. The radix of the string can be specified in base.

```
public String toString()
```

```
public static String toString(byte prim)
```
Returns a string representation of this Byte or the specified primitive byte (prim), whose radix is assumed to be 10.

```
public static Byte valueOf(String str) throws
NumberFormatException
```

```
public static Byte valueOf(String str, int base) throws
NumberFormatException
```
Returns a Byte object whose initial value is the result of the parsed parameter (str). The parameter is assumed to be the text representation of a byte and its radix 10 (unless specified in base).

Calendar (java.util)

A public abstract class, derived from Object and implementing Cloneable and Serializable, that allows for the manipulation of a Date object.

variables and constructs

```
public static final int AM
```
```
public static final int PM
```
Constant values that represent ante and post meridian.

```
public static final int ERA
```
```
public static final int YEAR
```
```
public static final int MONTH
```
```
public static final int WEEK_OF_YEAR
```
```
public static final int WEEK_OF_MONTH
```
```
public static final int DATE
```
```
public static final int DAY_OF_MONTH
```
```
public static final int DAY_OF_YEAR
```

```
public static final int DAY_OF_WEEK
public static final int DAY_OF_WEEK_IN_MONTH
public static final int AM_PM
public static final int HOUR
public static final int HOUR_OF_DAY
public static final int MINUTE
public static final int SECOND
public static final int MILLISECOND
public static final int ZONE_OFFSET
public static final int DST_OFFSET
```
Constant values that represent the index to the field where particular data is stored representing an instance of time (to millisecond precision). The combination of all of these fields yields a full representation of a moment of time with respect to a particular calendar (i.e., GregorianCalendar).

```
public static final int JANUARY
public static final int FEBRUARY
public static final int MARCH
public static final int APRIL
public static final int MAY
public static final int JUNE
public static final int JULY
public static final int AUGUST
public static final int SEPTEMBER
public static final int OCTOBER
public static final int NOVEMBER
public static final int DECEMBER
public static final int UNDECIMBER
```
Constant values representing various calendar months. UNDECIMBER represents the 13th month of a Gregorian calendar (lunar month).

```
public static final int SUNDAY
public static final int MONDAY
public static final int TUESDAY
public static final int WEDNESDAY
public static final int THURSDAY
public static final int FRIDAY
public static final int SATURDAY
```
Constant values representing the days of a week.

protected boolean areFieldsSet
A boolean flag that indicates if the time fields have been set for this `Calendar`.

public static final int FIELD_COUNT
A constant value that represents the number of date/time fields stored by a `Calendar`.

protected int fields[]
The integer array that contains the values that make up the information about this `Calendar`.

protected boolean isSet[]
The boolean array that contains status values used to indicate if a corresponding time field has been set.

protected boolean isTimeSet
A boolean flag field that is used to indicate if the time is set for this `Calendar`.

protected long time
A `long int` field that contains the time set for this `Calendar`.

methods

public abstract void add(int field, int val)
Adds (or subtracts in the case of a negative `val`) an amount of days or time from the specified `field`.

public abstract boolean after(Object arg)

public abstract boolean before(Object arg)
Returns a true value if this `Calendar` date is after or before the date specified by `arg`.

public final void clear()

public final void clear(int field)
Clears the value from the specified time `field` from this `Calendar`. The `clear` method will clear all of the values from this `Calendar`.

public Object clone()
Returns a clone of this `Calendar`.

protected void complete()
Attempts to complete any empty date/time fields by calling the `completeTime()` and `completeFields()` methods of this `Calendar`.

protected abstract void computeFields()

protected abstract void computeTime()
Computes the values of the time fields based on the currently set time (`computeFields()`) or computes the time based on the currently set time fields (`computeTime()`) for this `Calendar`.

```
public abstract boolean equals(Object arg)
```
Returns a true value if this Calendar is equal to the value of arg.

```
public final int get(int fld)
```
Returns the value of the specified time field from this Calendar.

```
public static synchronized Locale[] getAvailableLocales()
```
Returns the list of locales that are available.

```
public int getFirstDayOfWeek()
```
```
public void setFirstDayOfWeek(int val)
```
Returns or sets the first day of the week to val for this Calendar.

```
public abstract int getGreatestMinimum(int fld)
```
Returns the largest allowable minimum value for the specified field.

```
public static synchronized Calendar getInstance()
```
```
public static synchronized Calendar getInstance(Locale locale)
```
```
public static synchronized Calendar getInstance(TimeZone tz)
```
```
public static synchronized Calendar getInstance(TimeZone tz,
Locale locale)
```
Returns an instance of a Calendar based on the default time zone and locale,
or from a specified time zone and/or locale.

```
public abstract int getLeastMaximum(int fld)
```
Returns the smallest allowable maximum value for the specified field.

```
public abstract int getMaximum(int fld)
```
```
public abstract int getMinimum(int fld)
```
Returns the largest or smallest allowable value for the specified field.

```
public int getMinimalDaysInFirstWeek()
```
```
public void setMinimalDaysInFirstWeek(int val)
```
Returns or sets the smallest allowable number of days in the first week of the
year, based on the locale.

```
public final Date getTime()
```
```
public final void setTime(Date dt)
```
Returns or sets the time for this Calendar.

```
protected long getTimeInMillis()
```
```
protected void setTimeInMillis(long ms)
```
Returns or sets the time in milliseconds for this Calendar.

```
public TimeZone getTimeZone()
```
```
public void setTimeZone(TimeZone val)
```
Returns or sets the time zone for this Calendar.

```
protected final int internalGet(int fld)
```
An internal method used to obtain field values to be used by subclasses of `Calendar`.

```
public boolean isLenient()
```

```
public void setLenient(boolean flag)
```
Returns or sets the flag indicating leniency for date/time input.

```
public final boolean isSet(int fld)
```
Returns a true value if a value is set for the specified field.

```
public abstract void roll(int fld, boolean direction)
```
Adds one single unit of time to the specified date/time field. A true value specified for `direction` increases the field's value, false decreases it.

```
public final void set(int fld, int val)
```
Sets a single specified field to a value.

```
public final void set(int year, int month, int date)
```

```
public final void set(int year, int month, int date, int hour,
int min)
```

```
public final void set(int year, int month, int date, int hour,
int min, int sec)
```
Sets the year, month, date, hour, minute, and seconds of the time fields for this `Calendar`.

CardLayout (java.awt)

A public class, derived from `Object` and implementing `LayoutManager2` and `Serializable`, that lays out components in a series of separate cards, only one of which is visible at any time. The visibility of the cards can be changed, essentially providing the ability to sequence through the cards.

constructors

```
public CardLayout()
```

```
public CardLayout(int hg, int vg)
```
Creates a new instance of a card layout with a specified horizontal and vertical gap (or no gap in the case of the first constructor).

methods

```
public void addLayoutComponent(Component item, Object constr)
public void removeLayoutComponent(Component item)
```
Adds or removes a component to this layout manager. While adding, it is possible to restrict the component to the specified constraints (`constr`).

```
public void first(Container cont)
public void last(Container cont)
```
Moves to the first or last card in the layout. `cont` is the container that is laid out by this layout manager.

```
public int getHgap()
public int getVgap()
```
Returns the horizontal or vertical gap between the components laid out by this layout manager.

```
public float getLayoutAlignmentX(Container parent)
public float getLayoutAlignmentY(Container parent)
```
Returns the horizontal or vertical alignment value of the specified container.

```
public void invalidateLayout(Container cont)
```
Forces this layout manager to discard any cached layout information about the specified container.

```
public void layoutContainer(Container cont)
```
Lays out the specified container with this layout manager.

```
public Dimension maximumLayoutSize(Container cont)
public Dimension minimumLayoutSize(Container cont)
public Dimension preferredLayoutSize(Container cont)
```
Returns the maximum, minimum, or preferred size of the specified container when laid out by this layout manager.

```
public void next(Container cont)
public void previous(Container cont)
```
Cycles to the next or previous card. `cont` is the container that is laid out by this layout manager.

```
public void setHgap(int hg)
public void setVgap(int vg)
```
Sets the horizontal or vertical gap in pixels of components laid out by this layout manager.

```
public void show(Container cont, String str)
```
Cycles to the card that contains the component with the name str. When found, the specified container is laid out with this layout manager.

```
public String toString()
```
Returns a string representation of this layout manager.

Character (java.lang)

A public class, derived from Object and implementing Serializable, that contains character constants and methods to convert and identify characters.

variables and constructs

```
public final static byte COMBINING_SPACING_MARK
public final static byte CONNECTOR_PUNCTUATION
public final static byte CONTROL
public final static byte CURRENCY_SYMBOL
public final static byte DASH_PUNCTUATION
public final static byte DECIMAL_DIGIT_NUMBER
public final static byte ENCLOSING_MARK
public final static byte END_PUNCTUATION
public final static byte FORMAT
public final static byte LETTER_NUMBER
public final static byte LINE_SEPARATOR
public final static byte LOWERCASE_LETTER
public final static byte MATH_SYMBOL
public final static byte MODIFIER_LETTER
public final static byte MODIFIER_SYMBOL
public final static byte NON_SPACING_MARK
public final static byte OTHER_LETTER
public final static byte OTHER_NUMBER
public final static byte OTHER_PUNCTUATION
public final static byte OTHER_SYMBOL
public final static byte PARAGRAPH_SEPARATOR
public final static byte PRIVATE_USE
public final static byte SPACE_SEPARATOR
public final static byte START_PUNCTUATION
public final static byte SURROGATE
```

```
public final static byte TITLECASE_LETTER
public final static byte UNASSIGNED
public final static byte UPPERCASE_LETTER
```
Constant values representing various character symbols and types.
```
public final static int MAX_RADIX
```
A constant value that represents the largest possible value of a radix (base).
```
public final static char MAX_VALUE
```
A constant value that represents the largest possible value of a character in Java = '\uffff'.
```
public final static int MIN_RADIX
```
A constant value that represents that smallest possible value of a radix (base).
```
public final static char MIN_VALUE
```
A constant value that represents the smallest possible value of a character in Java = '\u0000'.
```
public final static Class TYPE
```
The `Character` constant value of the character type class.

constructors

```
public Character(char prim)
```
Creates an instance of the `Character` class from the primitive parameter `prim`.

methods

```
public char charValue()
```
Returns the value of this `Character` as a primitive character.
```
public static int digit(char c, int base)
public static char forDigit(int c, int base)
```
Returns the numeric value or the character depiction of the parameter `c` in radix base.
```
public boolean equals(Object arg)
```
Returns a true value if this `Character` is equal to the parameter `arg`.
```
public static int getNumericValue(char c)
```
Returns the Unicode representation of the character parameter (c) as a non-negative integer. If the character has no numeric representation, a –1 is returned. If the character cannot be represented as a nonnegative number, –2 will be returned.
```
public static int getType(char c)
```
Returns an integer value that represents the type of character the parameter c is.

```
public int hashCode()
```
Returns a hash code for this `Character`.
```
public static boolean isDefined(char c)
public static boolean isISOControl(char c)
```
Returns a true value if the parameter c has a defined meaning in Unicode or is an ISO control character.
```
public static boolean isIdentifierIgnorable(char c)
```
Returns a true value if the parameter c is a character that can be ignored in a Java identifier (such as control characters).
```
public static boolean isJavaIdentifierPart(char c)
public static boolean isJavaIdentifierStart(char c)
```
Returns a true value if the parameter c can be used in a valid Java identifier in any but the leading character. `isJavaIdentifierStart` returns a true value if the parameter c can be used as the leading character in a valid Java identifier.
```
public static boolean isDigit(char c)
public static boolean isLetter(char c)
public static boolean isLetterOrDigit(char c)
public static boolean isLowerCase(char c)
public static boolean isSpaceChar(char c)
public static boolean isTitleCase(char c)
public static boolean isUnicodeIdentifierPart(char c)
public static boolean isWhitespace(char c)
public static boolean isUnicodeIdentifierStart(char c)
public static boolean isUpperCase(char c)
```
Returns a true value if the parameter c is a digit; letter; letter or a digit; lowercase character; space character; titlecase character; can be used in a valid Unicode identifier in any but the leading character; a white space character; can be used as the leading character in a valid Unicode identifier or an uppercase character (respectively).
```
public static char toLowerCase(char c)
public String toString()
public static char toTitleCase(char c)
public static char toUpperCase(char c)
```
Returns a lowercase character, string representation, titlecase, or uppercase character of the parameter c.

Class (java.lang)

A public final class, derived from `Object` and implementing `Serializable`, that describes both interfaces and classes in the currently running Java program.

methods

public static Class forName(String class) throws ClassNotFoundException

Returns a `Class` object that corresponds with the named `class`. The name of the specified class must be a fully qualified class name (as in `java.io.Reader`).

public Class[] getClasses()

public Class[] getDeclaredClasses() throws SecurityException

Returns an array of `Classes` that contains all of the interfaces and classes that are members of this `Class` (excluding superclasses). `getClasses` returns only the list of public interfaces and classes.

public ClassLoader getClassLoader()

Returns the `ClassLoader` for this `Class`.

public Class getComponentType()

Returns the `Component` type of the array that is represented by this `Class`.

public Constructor getConstructor(Class[] types) throws NoSuchMethodException, SecurityException

public Constructor[] getConstructors() throws SecurityException

Returns the `Constructor` object or an array containing the public constructors for this class. The signature of the public constructor that is returned must match exactly the types and sequence of the parameters specified by the `types` array.

public Constructor getDeclaredConstructor(Class[] types) throws NoSuchMethodException, SecurityException

public Constructor[] getDeclaredConstructors() throws SecurityException

Returns the `Constructor` object or an array containing the constructors for this class. The signature of the public constructor that is returned must match exactly the types and sequence of the parameters specified by the `types` array parameter.

public Field getDeclaredField(String field) throws NoSuchFieldException, SecurityException

public Field[] getDeclaredFields() throws SecurityException

Returns the `Field` object or an array containing all of the fields for the specified matching `field` name for this `Class`.

```
public Method getDeclaredMethod(String method, Class[] types)
throws NoSuchMethodException, SecurityException
```

```
public Method[] getDeclaredMethods() throws SecurityException
```
Returns a `Method` object or an array containing all of the methods for the specified `method` of this `Class`. The requested method's parameter list must match identically the types and sequence of the elements of the `types` array.

```
public Class getDeclaringClass()
```
Returns the declaring class of this `Class`, provided that this `Class` is a member of another class.

```
public Field getField(String field) throws NoSuchFieldException,
SecurityException
```

```
public Field[] getFields() throws SecurityException
```
Returns a `Field` object or an array containing all of the fields of a specified matching `field` name for this `Class`.

```
public Class[] getInterfaces()
```
Returns an array containing all of the interfaces of this `Class`.

```
public Method getMethod(String method, Class[] types) throws
NoSuchMethodException, SecurityException
```

```
public Method[] getMethods() throws SecurityException
```
Returns a `Method` object or an array containing all of the public methods for the specified public `method` of this `Class`. The requested method's parameter list must match identically the types and sequence of the elements of the `types` array.

```
public int getModifiers()
```
Returns the encoded integer visibility modifiers for this `Class`. The values can be decoded using the `Modifier` class.

```
public String getName()
```
Returns the string representation of the name of the type that this `Class` represents.

```
public URL getResource(String arg)
```
Returns a URL representing the system resource for the class loader of this `Class`.

```
public InputStream getResourceAsStream(String arg)
```
Returns an input stream representing the system resource `arg` from the class loader of this `Class`.

```
public Object[] getSigners()
```
Returns an array of Objects that contains the signers of this Class.
```
public Class getSuperclass()
```
Returns the superclass of this Class, or null if this Class is an interface or of type Object.
```
public boolean isArray()
```
Returns a true value if this Class represents an array type.
```
public boolean isAssignableFrom(Class other)
```
Returns a true value if this Class is the same as a superclass or superinterface of the other class.
```
public boolean isInstance(Object target)
```
Returns a true value if the specified target object is an instance of this Class.
```
public boolean isInterface()
```
```
public boolean isPrimitive()
```
Returns a true value if this Class represents an interface class or a primitive type in Java.
```
public Object newInstance() throws InstantiationException,
IllegalAccessException
```
Creates a new instance of this Class.
```
public String toString()
```
Returns a string representation of this Class in the form of the word class or interface, followed by the fully qualified name of this Class.

Color (java.awt)

A public final class, derived from Object and implementing Serializable, that is used to represent colors. A color is defined by three components, red, blue, and green, that each have a value ranging from 0 to 255.

variables and constructs

```
public final static Color black
public final static Color blue
public final static Color cyan
public final static Color darkGray
public final static Color gray
```

```
public final static Color green
public final static Color lightGray
public final static Color magenta
public final static Color orange
public final static Color pink
public final static Color red
public final static Color white
public final static Color yellow
```
A constant value that describes the colors black (0, 0, 0), blue (0, 0, 255), cyan (0, 255, 255), darkGray (64, 64, 64), gray (128, 128, 128), green (0, 255, 0), lightGray (192, 192, 192), magenta (255, 0, 255), orange (255, 200, 0), pink (255, 175, 175), red (255, 0, 0), white (255, 255, 255) and yellow (255, 255, 0) as a set of RGB values.

constructors

```
public Color(float r, float g, float b)
public Color(int rgb)
public Color(int r, int g, int b)
```
Creates a new instance of the color described by the rgb value. When passed as a single integer value, the red component is represented in bits 16 to 23, green in 15 to 8, and blue in 0 to 7.

methods

```
public Color brighter()
public Color darker()
```
Returns a brighter or darker version of this color.
```
public static Color decode(String str) throws
NumberFormatException
```
Returns the color specified by str.
```
public boolean equals(Object arg)
```
Returns a true value if this color is equal to arg.
```
public int getBlue()
public int getGreen()
public int getRed()
```
Returns the blue, green, or red component value for this color.
```
public static Color getColor(String str)
public static Color getColor(String str, Color default)
```

```
public static Color getColor(String str, int default)
```
Returns the color represented in the string str (where its value is an integer). If the value is not determined, the color default is returned.

```
public static Color getHSBColor(float h, float s, float b)
```
Returns a color specified by the Hue-Saturation-Brightness model for colors, where h is the hue, s is the saturation, and b is the brightness of the desired color.

```
public int getRGB()
```
Returns an integer representation of the RGB value for this color.

```
public int hashCode()
```
Returns the hash code for this color.

```
public static int HSBtoRGB(float hue, float saturation, float brightness)
```
Converts a hue, saturation, and brightness representation of a color to an RGB value.

```
public static float[] RGBtoHSB(int r, int g, int b, float[] hsbvals)
```
Converts an RGB representation of a color to an HSB value, placing the converted values into the hsbvals array. The RGB value is represented via a red (r), green (g), and blue (b) value.

```
public String toString()
```
Returns a string representation of this color.

Component (java.awt)

A public abstract class, derived from Object and implementing ImageObserver, MenuContainer, and Serializable, that is the superclass to every AWT item that is represented on screen with a specific size and position.

variables and constructs

```
public final static float BOTTOM_ALIGNMENT
public final static float LEFT_ALIGNMENT
public final static float RIGHT_ALIGNMENT
public final static float TOP_ALIGNMENT
```
Constant values that represent specified alignments within the component.

```
protected Locale locale
```
Holds the locale for this component.

constructors

```
protected Component()
```
   Creates a new instance of a component.

methods

```
public synchronized void add(PopupMenu popmenu)
```
```
public synchronized void remove(MenuComponent popmenu)
```
   Adds or removes the specified popup menu to this component.
```
public synchronized void addComponentListener(ComponentListener
listener)
```
```
public synchronized void addFocusListener(FocusListener
listener)
```
```
public synchronized void addKeyListener(KeyListener listener)
```
```
public synchronized void addMouseListener(MouseListener
listener)
```
```
public synchronized void
addMouseMotionListener(MouseMotionListener listener)
```
```
public synchronized void
removeComponentListener(ComponentListener listener)
```
```
public synchronized void removeFocusListener(FocusListener
listener)
```
```
public synchronized void removeKeyListener(KeyListener listener)
```
```
public synchronized void removeMouseListener(MouseListener
listener)
```
```
public synchronized void
removeMouseMotionListener(MouseMotionListener listener)
```
   Adds or removes the specified `listener` to this component.
```
public void addNotify()
```
```
public void removeNotify()
```
   Notifies the component that a peer must be created or destroyed.
```
public int checkImage(Image img, ImageObserver obs)
```
```
public int checkImage(Image img, int width, int height,
ImageObserver obs)
```
   Returns the status of the construction of a scaled image `img`. The image created can be scaled to a `width` and `height`. The image `obs` will be informed of the status of the image.
```
public boolean contains(int x, int y)
```
```
public boolean contains(Point pt)
```
   Returns a true value if this component contains the specified position.

```
public Image createImage(ImageProducer prod)
public Image createImage(int width, int height)
```
Returns a new image created from prod. The second method creates another image which is generally offscreen (having width and height), used for double-buffering drawings.

```
protected final void disableEvents(long mask)
protected final void enableEvents(long mask)
```
Disables or enables all events specified by the mask for this component.

```
public final void dispatchEvent(AWTEvent event)
```
Dispatches an AWTEvent to this component or one of its subcomponents.

```
public void doLayout()
```
Lays out this component.

```
public float getAlignmentX()
public float getAlignmentY()
```
Returns the horizontal or vertical alignment for this component.

```
public Color getBackground()
public Color getForeground()
public void setBackground(Color clr)
public void setForeground(Color clr)
```
Returns or sets the background or foreground color for this component.

```
public Rectangle getBounds()
public void setBounds(int x, int y, int width, int height)
```
Returns or sets the bounds of this component. Setting the bounds resizes and reshapes this component to the bounding box of <x, y> to <x+width, y+height>.

```
public ColorModel getColorModel()
```
Returns the color model of this component.

```
public Component getComponentAt(int x, int y)
public Component getComponentAt(Point pt)
```
Returns the component located at the specified point.

```
public Cursor getCursor()
public synchronized void setCursor(Cursor csr)
```
Returns or sets the cursor set for this component.

```
public Font getFont()
public void setFont(Font ft)
```
Returns or sets the font of this component.

```
public FontMetrics getFontMetrics(Font ft)
```
Returns the font metrics of the specified font.

```
public Graphics getGraphics()
```
Returns the graphics context for this component.
```
public Locale getLocale()
public void setLocale(Locale locale)
```
Returns or sets the locale for this component.
```
public Point getLocation()
public Point getLocationOnScreen()
```
Returns the location of this component relative to the containing or screen space.
```
public Dimension getMaximumSize()
public Dimension getMinimumSize()
public Dimension getPreferredSize()
```
Returns the maximum, minimum, or preferred size of this component.
```
public String getName()
public void setName(String str)
```
Returns or sets the name of this component.
```
public Container getParent()
```
Returns the parent container of this component.
```
public Dimension getSize()
public void setSize(Dimension dim)
public void setSize(int width, int height)
```
Returns the size of or resizes this component to the specified dimension(s).
```
public Toolkit getToolkit()
```
Returns the toolkit of this component.
```
public final Object getTreeLock()
```
Returns the AWT object that is used as the base of the component tree and layout operations for this component.
```
public boolean imageUpdate(Image src, int flags, int x, int y,
int width, int height)
```
Draws more of an image (src) as its information becomes available. The exact value of the x, y, width, and height variables is dependent on the value of the flags variable.
```
public void invalidate()
```
Forces this component to be laid out again by making it "invalid."
```
public boolean isEnabled()
public void setEnabled(boolean toggle)
```
Returns or sets the enabled state of this component.

```
public boolean isFocusTraversable()
```
Returns a true value if this component can be traversed using Tab or Shift-Tab sequences.

```
public boolean isShowing()
public boolean isValid()
```
Returns a true value if this component does not need to be laid out.

```
public boolean isVisible()
public void setVisible(boolean toggle)
```
Returns or sets the state of this component's visibility.

```
public void list()
public void list(PrintStream outstrm)
public void list(PrintStream outstrm, int spc)
public void list(PrintWriter outstrm)
public void list(PrintWriter outstrm, int spc)
```
Prints a listing of this component's parameters to the print writer stream outstrm (default of System.out), indenting spc spaces (default of 0).

```
public void paint(Graphics gc)
public void print(Graphics gc)
```
Paints or prints this component with the graphics context gc.

```
public void paintAll(Graphics gc)
public void printAll(Graphics gc)
```
Paints or prints this component and all of its subcomponents with the graphics context gc.

```
protected String paramString()
```
Returns a string describing the parameters of this component.

```
public boolean prepareImage(Image src, ImageObserver obs)
public prepareImage(Image src, int width, int height,
ImageObserver obs)
```
Downloads the src for display. The image can be scaled to a width and height. The obs is informed of the status of the image.

```
protected void processComponentEvent(ComponentEvent event)
protected void processFocusEvent(FocusEvent event)
protected void processKeyEvent(KeyEvent event)
protected void processMouseEvent(MouseEvent event)
protected void processMouseMotionEvent(MouseEvent event)
```
Processes the specified event for this component, sending the event to a registered event listener.

`protected void processEvent(AWTEvent event)`

Processes an AWT event for this component, sending it to the appropriate processing routine (i.e., `processComponentEvent` method) for further handling.

`public void repaint()`

`public void repaint(int x, int y, int width, int height)`

Repaints a rectangular portion of this component from `<x, y>` to `<x+width, y+height>`.

`public void repaint(long msec)`

`public void repaint(long msec, int x, int y, int width, int height)`

Repaints a rectangular portion of this component from `<x, y>` to `<x+width, y+height>` after a delay of `msec` milliseconds.

`public void requestFocus()`

Requests that this component get the input focus.

`public void setLocation(int x, int y)`

`public void setLocation(Point pt)`

Moves this component to the specified point in the containing space.

`public String toString()`

Returns a string representation of this component.

`public void transferFocus()`

Transfers focus from this component to the next component.

`public void update(Graphics gc)`

Updates this component using graphics context `gc`.

`public void validate()`

Validates this component if needed.

ComponentAdapter (java.awt.event)

A public abstract class, derived from `Object` and implementing `ComponentListener`, that permits a derived class to override the predefined no-op component events.

constructors

`public ComponentAdapter()`

Creates a new instance of a `ComponentAdapter`.

methods

```
public void componentHidden(ComponentEvent event)
public void componentMoved(ComponentEvent event)
public void componentResized(ComponentEvent event)
public void componentShown(ComponentEvent event)
```
Empty methods that should be overridden in order to implement event handling for AWT components.

ComponentEvent (java.awt.event)

A public class, derived from `AWTEvent`, that represents an AWT component event.

variables and constructs

```
public static final int COMPONENT_FIRST
public static final int COMPONENT_LAST
```
Constant values that represent the index of the first and last component event ids.
```
public static final int COMPONENT_MOVED
public static final int COMPONENT_RESIZED
public static final int COMPONENT_SHOWN
public static final int COMPONENT_HIDDEN
```
Constant values that represent AWT component event ids.

constructors

```
public ComponentEvent(Component src, int type)
```
Creates a new instance of a `ComponentEvent` from the specified source and of a specific type.

methods

```
public Component getComponent()
```
Returns the AWT component that triggered this event.
```
public String paramString()
```
Returns a string containing the parameters of this event.

Container (java.awt)

A public abstract class, derived from `Component`, that is the superclass to any AWT component that can contain one or more AWT components.

constructors

```
protected Container()
```
Creates a new instance of a container.

methods

```
public Component add(Component item)
public Component add(Component item, int idx)
public void add(Component item, Object constr)
public void add(Component item, Object constr, int idx)
public Component add(String str, Component item)
```
Adds component `item` to this container at index `idx` (or to the end by default). The new item can have constraints (`constr`) applied to it. A string name can be associated with the added component in the case of the last constructor.

```
public void addContainerListener(ContainerListener listener)
public void removeContainerListener(ContainerListener listener)
```
Adds or removes the specified `listener` to this container.

```
protected void addImpl(Component item, Object constr, int idx)
```
Adds component `item` to this container at index `idx`, and passes the constraints for the new item (`constr`) to the layout manager for this container.

```
public void addNotify()
public void removeNotify()
```
Creates or destroys this container's peer.

```
public void doLayout()
```
Lays out the components of this container.

```
public float getAlignmentX()
public float getAlignmentY()
```
Returns the horizontal or vertical alignment value of this container.

```
public Component getComponent(int idx) throws
ArrayIndexOutOfBoundsException
public Component getComponentAt(int x, int y)
public Component getComponentAt(Point pt)
```
Returns the component that is located at the specified point or index.

```
public int getComponentCount()
```
Returns the number of components in this container.
```
public Component[] getComponents()
```
Returns an array of all of the components in this container.
```
public Insets getInsets()
```
Returns the insets of this container.
```
public LayoutManager getLayout()
public void setLayout(LayoutManager layout)
```
Returns or sets the layout manager of this container.
```
public Dimension getMaximumSize()
public Dimension getMinimumSize()
public Dimension getPreferredSize()
```
Returns the maximum, minimum, or preferred size of this container.
```
public void invalidate()
```
Marks the layout of this container as invalid, forcing the need to lay out the components again.
```
public boolean isAncestorOf(Component comp)
```
Returns a true value if the specified component (comp) is contained in the component hierarchy of this container.
```
public void list(PrintStream outstream, int spaces)
public void list(PrintWriter outstream, int spaces)
```
Prints a listing of all of the components of this container to print stream outstream, indented a specified number of spaces (default of 0).
```
public void paint(Graphics gwin)
public void print(Graphics gwin)
```
Paints or prints this container with graphics context gwin.
```
public void paintComponents(Graphics gwin)
public void printComponents(Graphics gwin)
```
Repaints or prints all of the components in this container with graphics context gwin.
```
protected String paramString()
```
Returns a string representation of this container's parameters.
```
protected void processContainerEvent(ContainerEvent event)
```
Processes any container event, passing the event to a registered container listener.
```
protected void processEvent(AWTEvent event)
```
Handles any AWTEvent, invoking processContainerEvent for container events, and passing the event to the superclass's processEvent otherwise.

```
public void remove(Component comp)
```
```
public void remove(int idx)
```
Removes the specified component (or the component at the specified index) from this container.

```
public void removeAll()
```
Removes all components from this container.

```
public void validate()
```
Validates this container and all of the subcomponents in it.

```
protected void validateTree()
```
Validates this container and all subcontainers in it.

ContainerAdapter (java.awt.event)

A public abstract class, derived from `Object` and implementing `ContainerListener`, that permits a derived class to override the predefined no-op container events.

constructors

```
public ContainerAdapter()
```
Creates a new instance of a `ContainerAdapter`.

methods

```
public void componentAdded(ContainerEvent event)
```
```
public void componentRemoved(ContainerEvent event)
```
Empty methods that should be overridden in order to implement event handling for AWT containers.

ContainerEvent (java.awt.event)

A public class, derived from `ComponentEvent`, that describes a particular AWT container event.

variables and constructs

```
public static final int COMPONENT_ADDED
```
```
public static final int COMPONENT_REMOVED
```
Constant values that represent various container events (a component being added or removed to this container).

```
public static final int CONTAINER_FIRST
public static final int CONTAINER_LAST
```
Constant values that represent the index of the first and last component event ids.

constructors

```
public ContainerEvent(Component src, int type, Component comp)
```
Creates a new instance of a `ContainerEvent` with a specified source component, event type, and a defined component (which is being added or removed).

methods

```
public Component getChild()
```
Returns the child component that was added or removed, triggering this event.

```
public Container getContainer()
```
Returns the container in which this event was triggered.

```
public String paramString()
```
Returns a string containing the parameters of this `ComponentEvent`.

Cursor (java.awt)

A public class, derived from `Object` and implementing `Serializable`, that represents the different states and images of the mouse cursor in a graphical application or applet.

variables and constructs

```
public final static int CROSSHAIR_CURSOR
public final static int DEFAULT_CURSOR
public final static int E_RESIZE_CURSOR
public final static int HAND_CURSOR
public final static int MOVE_CURSOR
public final static int N_RESIZE_CURSOR
public final static int NE_RESIZE_CURSOR
public final static int NW_RESIZE_CURSOR
public final static int S_RESIZE_CURSOR
public final static int SE_RESIZE_CURSOR
public final static int SW_RESIZE_CURSOR
public final static int TEXT_CURSOR
```

```
public final static int W_RESIZE_CURSOR
public final static int WAIT_CURSOR
```
Constant values that represent various cursors.

```
protected static Cursor predefined[]
```
An array used to hold the cursors as they are defined and implemented.

constructors

```
public Cursor(int cursortype)
```
Creates a new instance of a cursor of the specified type (cursortype).

methods

```
public static Cursor getDefaultCursor()
```
Returns the default cursor.

```
public static Cursor getPredefinedCursor(int cursortype)
```
Returns the cursor of the specified type (cursortype).

```
public int getType()
```
Returns the type of this cursor.

Date (java.util)

A public class, derived from Object and implementing Serializable and Cloneable, that creates and manipulates a single moment of time.

constructors

```
public Date()
public Date(long date)
```
Creates a new instance of a Date from a specified date (time in milliseconds since midnight, January 1, 1970 GMT) or by using the current time.

methods

```
public boolean after(Date arg)
public boolean before(Date arg)
```
Returns a true value if this Date is after/before the date specified in arg.

```
public boolean equals(Object arg)
```
Returns a true value if this Date is equal to arg.

```
public long getTime()
```

```
public void setTime(long tm)
```
Returns or sets the time specified by this Date. The time is represented as a long integer equal to the number of seconds since midnight, January 1, 1970 UTC.

```
public int hashCode()
```
Returns the hash code for this Date.

```
public String toString()
```
Returns a string representation of this Date.

DateFormat (java.text)

A public abstract class, derived from Cloneable, that is used to convert date/time objects to locale-specific strings, and vice versa.

variables and constructs

```
public static final int DEFAULT
public static final int FULL
public static final int LONG
public static final int MEDIUM
public static final int SHORT
```
Constant values that represent formatting styles.

```
public static final int AM_PM_FIELD
public static final int DATE_FIELD
public static final int DAY_OF_WEEK_FIELD
public static final int DAY_OF_WEEK_IN_MONTH_FIELD
public static final int DAY_OF_YEAR_FIELD
public static final int ERA_FIELD
public static final int HOUR0_FIELD
public static final int HOUR1_FIELD
public static final int HOUR_OF_DAY0_FIELD
public static final int HOUR_OF_DAY1_FIELD
public static final int MILLISECOND_FIELD
public static final int MINUTE_FIELD
public static final int MONTH_FIELD
public static final int SECOND_FIELD
public static final int TIMEZONE_FIELD
public static final int WEEK_OF_MONTH_FIELD
```

```
public static final int WEEK_OF_YEAR_FIELD
public static final int YEAR_FIELD
```
Constant values that represent various fields for date/time formatting.

```
protected Calendar calendar
```
Holds the calendar that this `DateFormat` uses to produce its date/time formatting.

```
protected NumberFormat numberFormat
```
Holds the number format that this `DateFormat` uses to produce its number formatting.

constructors

```
protected DateFormat()
```
Creates a new instance of a `DateFormat`.

methods

```
public Object clone()
```
Returns a copy of this `DateFormat`.

```
public boolean equals(Object arg)
```
Returns a true value is this `DateFormat` is equal to `arg`.

```
public final String format(Date src)
```
Formats the specified `Date` object into a string.

```
public abstract StringBuffer format(Date src, StringBuffer dest,
FieldPosition pos)
public final StringBuffer format(Object src, StringBuffer dest,
FieldPosition pos)
```
Formats the source object into the specified destination, starting at field `pos`. This method returns the same value as the destination buffer.

```
public static Locale[] getAvailableLocales()
```
Returns the set of available locales for this `DateFormat`.

```
public Calendar getCalendar()
public void setCalendar(Calendar cal)
```
Returns or sets the calendar associated with this `DateFormat`.

```
public static final DateFormat getDateInstance()
public static final DateFormat getDateInstance(int style)
public static final DateFormat getDateInstance(int style, Locale
locale)
```
Returns the `DateFormat` for the specified or default locale (using the default or specified date formatting style).

```
public static final DateFormat getDateTimeInstance()
public static final DateFormat getDateTimeInstance(int dstyle,
int tstyle)
public static final DateFormat getDateTimeInstance(int dstyle,
int tstyle, Locale locale)
```
Returns the DateFormat for the specified or default locale (using the default or specified date and time formatting styles).

```
public static final DateFormat getInstance()
```
Returns the DateFormat for the default locale using the short formatting style.

```
public NumberFormat getNumberFormat()
public void setNumberFormat(NumberFormat format)
```
Returns or sets the NumberFormat for this DateFormat.

```
public static final DateFormat getTimeInstance()
public static final DateFormat getTimeInstance(int style)
public static final DateFormat getTimeInstance(int style, Locale
locale)
```
Returns the DateFormat for the specified or default locale (using the default or specified time formatting style).

```
public TimeZone getTimeZone()
public void setTimeZone(TimeZone tz)
```
Returns or sets the time zone for this DateFormat.

```
public int hashCode()
```
Returns the hash code for this DateFormat.

```
public boolean isLenient()
public void setLenient(boolean lenient)
```
Returns or sets the state of the leniency for this DateFormat.

```
public Date parse(String src) throws ParseException
```
Parses the specified source to a Date object.

```
public abstract Date parse(String src, ParsePosition pos)
public Object parseObject(String src, ParsePosition pos)
```
Parses the specified source string to a Date or Object, starting at the specified position.

DateFormatSymbols (java.text)

A public class, derived from `Object` and implementing `Serializable` and `Cloneable`, that contains functionality for formatting both date and time values. This class is usually utilized as part of a `DateFormat` class (or subclass).

constructors

```
public DateFormatSymbols()
```

```
public DateFormatSymbols(Locale locale)
```
Creates a new instance of `DateFormatSymbols` using the specified or default locale.

methods

```
public Object clone()
```
Returns a clone of this `DateFormatSymbols`.

```
public boolean equals(Object arg)
```
Returns a true value if this `DateFormatSymbols` is equal to `arg`.

```
public String[] getAmPmStrings()
```

```
public void setAmPmStrings(String[] newstr)
```
Returns or sets the AM/PM strings for this set of symbols.

```
public String[] getEras()
```

```
public void setEras(String[] newstr)
```
Returns or sets the eras for this set of symbols.

```
public String getLocalPatternChars()
```

```
public void setLocalPatternChars(String newchars)
```
Returns or sets the local pattern characters for date and time for this set of symbols.

```
public String[] getMonths()
```

```
public void setMonths(String[] newmon)
```
Returns or sets the full names of months for this set of symbols.

```
public String[] getShortMonths()
```

```
public void setShortMonths(String[] newmon)
```
Returns or sets the short names of months for this set of symbols.

```
public String[] getShortWeekdays()
```

```
public void setShortWeekdays(String[] newdays)
```
Returns or sets the short names of weekdays for this set of symbols.

```
public String[] getWeekdays()
public void setWeekdays(String[] newdays)
```
Returns or sets the full names of weekdays for this set of symbols.
```
public String[][] getZoneStrings()
public void setZoneStrings(String[][] newzone)
```
Returns or sets the time zone strings for this set of symbols.
```
public int hashCode()
```
Returns the hash code for this set of symbols.

DecimalFormat (java.text)

A public class, derived from `NumberFormat`, that is used to format decimal numbers to locale-based strings, and vice versa.

constructors

```
public DecimalFormat()
public DecimalFormat(String str)
public DecimalFormat(String str, DecimalFormatSymbols sym)
```
Creates a new instance of a `DecimalFormat` from the specified or default pattern, specified or default symbols and using the default locale.

methods

```
public void applyLocalizedPattern(String str)
public String toLocalizedPattern()
```
Sets or returns the pattern of this `DecimalFormat`. The specified pattern is in a locale-specific format.
```
public void applyPattern(String str)
public String toPattern()
```
Sets or returns the pattern of this `DecimalFormat`.
```
public Object clone()
```
Returns a copy of this `DecimalFormat`.
```
public boolean equals(Object arg)
```
Returns a true value if this `DecimalFormat` is equal to arg.
```
public StringBuffer format(double num, StringBuffer dest,
FieldPosition pos)
```

```
public StringBuffer format(long num, StringBuffer dest,
FieldPosition pos)
```
Formats the specified Java primitive type starting at pos, according to this DecimalFormat, placing the resulting string in the specified destination buffer. This method returns the value of the string buffer.

```
public DecimalFormatSymbols getDecimalFormatSymbols()
```
```
public void setDecimalFormatSymbols(DecimalFormatSymbols
symbols)
```
Returns or sets the decimal number format symbols for this DecimalFormat.

```
public int getGroupingSize()
```
```
public void setGroupingSize(int val)
```
Returns or sets the size of groupings for this DecimalFormat.

```
public int getMultiplier()
```
```
public void setMultiplier(int val)
```
Returns or sets the value of the multiplier for use in percent calculations.

```
public String getNegativePrefix()
```
```
public void setNegativePrefix(String val)
```
Returns or sets the prefix for negative numbers for this DecimalFormat.

```
public String getNegativeSuffix()
```
```
public void setNegativeSuffix(String val)
```
Returns or sets the suffix for negative numbers for this DecimalFormat.

```
public String getPositivePrefix()
```
```
public void setPositivePrefix(String val)
```
Returns or sets the prefix for positive numbers for this DecimalFormat.

```
public String getPositiveSuffix()
```
```
public void setPositiveSuffix(String val)
```
Returns or sets the suffix for positive numbers for this DecimalFormat.

```
public int hashCode()
```
Returns the hash code for this DecimalFormat.

```
public boolean isDecimalSeparatorAlwaysShown()
```
```
public void setDecimalSeparatorAlwaysShown(boolean toggle)
```
Returns or sets the state value that allows/prevents the display of the decimal point when formatting integers.

```
public Number parse(String src, ParsePosition pos)
```
Parses the specified string as a long (if possible) or double, starting a position pos, and returns a Number.

DecimalFormatSymbols (java.text)

A public class, derived from Object and implementing Serializable and Cloneable, that contains functionality for formatting decimal values. This class is usually utilized as part of a DecimalFormat class (or subclass).

constructors

public DecimalFormatSymbols()

public DecimalFormatSymbols(Locale locale)
    Creates a new instance of DecimalFormatSymbols using the specified or default locale.

methods

public Object clone()
    Returns a clone of this DecimalFormatSymbols.

public boolean equals(Object arg)
    Returns a true value if this DecimalFormatSymbols is equal to arg.

public char getDecimalSeparator()

public void setDecimalSeparator(char separator)
    Returns or sets the character used to separate decimal numbers in this set of symbols.

public char getDigit()

public void setDigit(char num)
    Returns or sets the character used as a digit placeholder in a pattern for this set of symbols.

public char getGroupingSeparator()

public void setGroupingSeparator(char separator)
    Returns or sets the character used to separate groups of thousands for this set of symbols.

public String getInfinity()

public void setInfinity(String str)
    Returns or sets the string used to represent the value of infinity for this set of symbols.

public char getMinusSign()

public void setMinusSign(char minus)
    Returns or sets the character used to represent the minus sign for this set of symbols.

```
public String getNaN()
```
```
public void setNaN(String str)
```
Returns or sets the character used to represent a NAN value for this set of symbols.

```
public char getPatternSeparator()
```
```
public void setPatternSeparator(char separator)
```
Returns or sets the character used to separate positive and negative numbers in a pattern from this set of symbols.

```
public char getPercent()
```
```
public void setPercent(char percent)
```
Returns or sets the character used as a percent sign for this set of symbols.

```
public char getPerMill()
```
```
public void setPerMill(char perMill)
```
Returns or sets the character used as a mille percent sign for this set of symbols.

```
public char getZeroDigit()
```
```
public void setZeroDigit(char zero)
```
Returns or sets the character used to represent zero for this set of symbols.

```
public int hashCode()
```
Returns the hash code for this set of symbols.

Dimension (java.awt)

A public class, derived from `Object` and implementing `Serializable`, that is used to encapsulate an object's dimensions (height and width).

variables and constructs

```
public int height
```
```
public int width
```
Variables that contain the height and width of an object.

constructors

```
public Dimension()
```
```
public Dimension(Dimension dim)
```
```
public Dimension(int width, int height)
```
Creates a new instance of a dimension from specified dimensions (or 0 width and 0 height by default).

methods

```
public boolean equals(Object arg)
```
Returns a true value if this dimension is equal to arg.

```
public Dimension getSize()
public void setSize(Dimension dim)
public void setSize(int width, int height)
```
Returns or sets the size of this dimension.

```
public String toString()
```
Returns the string representation of this dimension.

Double (java.lang)

A public final class, derived from Number, that contains floating point math operations, constants, and methods to compute minimum and maximum numbers, and string manipulation routines related to the double primitive type.

variables and constructs

```
public final static double MAX_VALUE
public final static double MIN_VALUE
```
Constant values that contain the maximum (1.79769313486231570e+308d) and minimum (4.94065645841246544e2324d) possible values of an integer in Java.

```
public final static double NaN
```
A constant value that contains the representation of the Not-A-Number double (0.0d).

```
public final static double NEGATIVE_INFINITY
public final static double POSITIVE_INFINITY
```
Constant values that contain the negative (–1.0d / 0.0d) and positive (1.0d / 0.0d) infinity double.

```
public final static Class TYPE
```
A constant value of the Double type class.

constructors

```
public Double(double arg)
public Double(String arg) throws NumberFormatException
```
Creates an instance of the Double class from the parameter arg.

methods

```
public byte byteValue()
public double doubleValue()
public float floatValue()
public int intValue()
public long longValue()
public short shortValue()
```
Returns the value of the current object as a Java primitive type.
```
public static long doubleToLongBits(double num)
public static double longBitsToDouble(long num)
```
Returns a long bit stream or a double representation of parameter num. Bit 63 of the returned long is the sign bit, bits 52 to 62 are the exponent, and bits 0 to 51 are the mantissa.
```
public boolean equals(Object param)
```
Returns a true value if this Double is equal to the specified parameter (param).
```
public int hashCode()
```
Returns a hash code for this Double.
```
public boolean isInfinite()
public static boolean isInfinite(double num)
```
Returns true if the current object or num is positive or negative infinity, false in all other cases.
```
public boolean isNaN()
public static boolean isNaN(double num)
```
Returns true if the current object or num is Not-A-Number, false in all other cases.
```
public static double parseDouble(String str) throws
NumberFormatException
```
Returns the double value represented by str.
```
public String toString()
public static String toString(double num)
```
Returns the string representation of the current object or num in base 10 (decimal).
```
public static Double valueOf(String str) throws
NumberFormatException
```
Returns a Double initialized to the value of str.

Error (java.lang)

A public class, derived from `Throwable`, that is used to signify program-terminating errors that should not be caught.

constructors

```
public Error()
public Error(String str)
```
Creates a new instance of an error. A message can be provided via `str`.

Event (java.awt)

A public class, derived from `Object`, that represents an event obtained from a graphical user interface.

variables and constructs

```
public final static int ACTION_EVENT
```
A constant that represents that the user desires an action.

```
public final static int ALT_MASK
public final static int CTRL_MASK
public final static int META_MASK
public final static int SHIFT_MASK
```
Constant values that represent the mask for Alt, Control, Meta, and Shift keys modifying events.

```
public Object arg
```
An optional argument used by some events.

```
public final static int BACK_SPACE
public final static int CAPS_LOCK
public final static int DELETE
public final static int DOWN
public final static int END
public final static int ENTER
public final static int ESCAPE
public final static int F1
public final static int F2
public final static int F3
```

```
public final static int F4
public final static int F5
public final static int F6
public final static int F7
public final static int F8
public final static int F9
public final static int F10
public final static int F11
public final static int F12
public final static int HOME
public final static int INSERT
public final static int LEFT
public final static int NUM_LOCK
public final static int PAUSE
public final static int PGDN
public final static int PGUP
public final static int PRINT_SCREEN
public final static int RIGHT
public final static int SCROLL_LOCK
public final static int TAB
public final static int UP
```
   Constant values that represent keyboard keys.

```
public int clickCount
```
   The number of consecutive clicks during a MOUSE_DOWN event.

```
public Event evt
```
   The next event to take place, as in a linked list.

```
public final static int GOT_FOCUS
```
   An id field constant that represents when an AWT component gets the focus.

```
public int id
```
   The numeric identification for this event.

```
public int key
```
   The keyboard key that was pressed during this event.

```
public final static int KEY_ACTION
public final static int KEY_ACTION_RELEASE
```
   Constant values that represent when the user presses or releases a function key.

```
public final static int KEY_PRESS
```

`public final static int KEY_RELEASE`
Constant values that represent when the user presses or releases a keyboard key.

`public final static int LIST_DESELECT`

`public final static int LIST_SELECT`
Constant values that represent when the user deselects or selects a list item.

`public final static int LOAD_FILE`

`public final static int SAVE_FILE`
Constant values that represent when a file load or save event occurs.

`public final static int LOST_FOCUS`
An id field constant that represents when an AWT component loses the focus.

`public int modifiers`
Value of any key modifiers for this event.

`public final static int MOUSE_DOWN`

`public final static int MOUSE_DRAG`

`public final static int MOUSE_ENTER`

`public final static int MOUSE_EXIT`

`public final static int MOUSE_MOVE`

`public final static int MOUSE_UP`
Constant values that represent mouse events.

`public final static int SCROLL_ABSOLUTE`
An id field constant that represents when the user has moved the bubble in a scrollbar.

`public final static int SCROLL_BEGIN`

`public final static int SCROLL_END`
Constant values that represent the scroll begin or ending event.

`public final static int SCROLL_LINE_DOWN`

`public final static int SCROLL_LINE_UP`
Constant values that represent when the user has clicked in the line down or up area of the scrollbar.

`public final static int SCROLL_PAGE_DOWN`

`public final static int SCROLL_PAGE_UP`
Constant values that represent when the user has clicked in the page down or up area of the scrollbar.

`public Object target`
The object that this event was created from or took place over.

`public long when`

The time stamp of this event. Represented as the number of milliseconds since midnight, January 1, 1970 UTC.

```
public final static int WINDOW_DEICONIFY
```

```
public final static int WINDOW_DESTROY
```

```
public final static int WINDOW_EXPOSE
```

```
public final static int WINDOW_ICONIFY
```

```
public final static int WINDOW_MOVED
```

Constant values that represent various window events.

```
public int x
```

```
public int y
```

The horizontal or vertical coordinate location of this event.

constructors

```
public Event(Object obj, int id, Object arg)
```

```
public Event(Object obj, long ts, int id, int x, int y, int key,
int state)
```

```
public Event(Object obj, long ts, int id, int x, int y, int key,
int state, Object arg)
```

Creates a new instance of an event with an initial target Object (obj), id, x location, y location, key, modifier state, time stamp (ts), and argument (arg).

methods

```
public boolean controlDown()
```

```
public boolean metaDown()
```

```
public boolean shiftDown()
```

Returns a true value if the Control, Meta, or Shift key is down for this event.

```
protected String paramString()
```

Returns the parameter string for this event.

```
public String toString()
```

Returns a string representation of this event.

```
public void translate(int xval, int yval)
```

Translates this event, modifying the x and y coordinates for this event by adjusting the x location by xval and the y location by yval.

Exception (`java.lang`)

A public class, derived from `Throwable`, that catches conditions that are thrown by methods.

constructors

```
public Exception()
public Exception(String str)
```
Creates a new instance of an exception. A message can be provided via `str`.

Float (`java.lang`)

A public final class, derived from `Number`, that contains floating point math operations, constants, and methods to compute minimum and maximum numbers, and string manipulation routines related to the primitive `float` type.

variables and constructs

```
public final static float MAX_VALUE
public final static float MIN_VALUE
```
Constant values that contain the maximum possible value (3.40282346638528860e+38f) or the minimum possible value (1.40129846432481707e245f) of a float in Java.

```
public final static float NaN
```
A constant value that contains the representation of the Not-A-Number float (0.0f).

```
public final static float NEGATIVE_INFINITY
public final static float POSITIVE_INFINITY
```
Constant values that contain the representation of the negative (−1.0f / 0.0f) or positive (1.0f / 0.0f) infinity float.

```
public final static Class TYPE
```
The `Float` constant value of the float type class.

constructors

```
public Float(double arg)
public Float(float arg) throws NumberFormatException
public Float(String arg)
```
Creates an instance of the `Float` class from the parameter `arg`.

methods

```
public byte byteValue()
public float floatValue()
public double doubleValue()
public int intValue()
public long longValue()
public short shortValue()
```
Returns the value of the current object as a Java primitive type.

```
public boolean equals(Object arg)
```
Returns the result of an equality comparison against arg.

```
public static int floatToIntBits(float num)
public static float intBitsToFloat(int num)
```
Returns the bit stream or float equivalent of the parameter num as an int. Bit 31 of the int returned value is the sign bit, bits 23 to 30 are the exponent, while bits 0 to 22 are the mantissa.

```
public int hashCode()
```
Returns a hash code for this object.

```
public boolean isInfinite()
public static boolean isInfinite(float num)
```
Returns true if the current object or num is positive or negative infinity, false in all other cases.

```
public boolean isNaN()
public static boolean isNaN(float num)
```
Returns true if the current object or num is Not-A-Number, false in all other cases.

```
public static float parseFloat(String str) throws
NumberFormatException
```
Returns the float value represented by str.

```
public String toString()
public static String toString(float num)
```
Returns the string representation of the current object or num.

```
public static Float valueOf(String str) throws
NumberFormatException
```
Returns a Float initialized to the value of str.

FlowLayout (java.awt)

A public class, derived from `Object` implementing `LayoutManager` and `Serializable`, that lays out components in a sequential horizontal order using their preferred size.

variables and constructs

```
public final static int CENTER
public final static int LEFT
public final static int RIGHT
```
Constant values indicating areas of the flow layout manager.

constructors

```
public FlowLayout()
public FlowLayout(int al)
public FlowLayout(int al, int hg, int vg)
```
Creates a new instance of a flow layout and gives it `al` alignment (default of centered) with a `vg` vertical and `hg` horizontal gap (default of 0).

methods

```
public void addLayoutComponent(String str, Component cpnt)
public void removeLayoutComponent(Component cpnt)
```
Adds or removes a component to/from this layout manager. When adding a component, a name may be specified.

```
public int getAlignment()
public void setAlignment(int alg)
```
Returns or sets the alignment value for this layout manager.

```
public int getHgap()
public int getVgap()
```
Returns the value of the horizontal or vertical gap between components laid out by this layout manager.

```
public void layoutContainer(Container cont)
```
Lays out the specified container with this layout manager.

```
public Dimension minimumLayoutSize(Container cont)
public Dimension preferredLayoutSize(Container cont)
```
Returns the minimum or preferred size of the specified container when laid out by this layout manager.

```
public void setHgap(int hg)
```

```
public void setVgap(int vg)
```
Sets the horizontal or vertical gap for this layout manager.

```
public String toString()
```
Returns a string representation of this layout manager.

FocusAdapter (java.awt.event)

A public abstract class, derived from `Object` and implementing `FocusListener`, that permits derived classes to override the predefined no-op focus events.

constructors

```
public FocusAdapter()
```
Creates a new instance of a `FocusAdapter`.

methods

```
public void focusGained(FocusEvent event)
```

```
public void focusLost(FocusEvent event)
```
Empty methods that should be overridden in order to implement event handling for AWT focus-based events.

FocusEvent (java.awt.event)

A public class, derived from `ComponentEvent`, that describes a particular AWT focus event.

variables and constructs

```
public static final int FOCUS_FIRST
```

```
public static final int FOCUS_LAST
```
Constant values that represent the index of the first and last focus event ids.

```
public static final int FOCUS_GAINED
```

```
public static final int FOCUS_LOST
```
Constant values that represent the gain and loss of focus events.

constructors

```
public FocusEvent(Component src, int type)
public FocusEvent(Component src, int type, boolean toggle)
```
Creates a new instance of a `FocusEvent` from the specified source, having a defined event type and toggling this event as a temporary change of focus (false by default).

methods

```
public boolean isTemporary()
```
Returns the status value of the temporary focus toggle.

```
public String paramString()
```
Returns a string containing the parameters of this `FocusEvent`.

Font (java.awt)

A public class, derived from `Object` and implementing `Serializable`, that represents a GUI font.

variables and constructs

```
public final static int BOLD
public final static int ITALIC
public final static int PLAIN
```
Constant values that indicate the style of the font.

```
protected String name
```
The name of the font.

```
protected int size
```
The size of the font in pixels.

```
protected int style
```
The style of the font.

constructors

```
public Font(String str, int st, int sz)
```
Creates a new font with an initial name (`str`), style (`st`), and size (`sz`).

methods

`public static Font decode(String arg)`

Returns the requested font from a specified string.

`public boolean equals(Object obj)`

Returns a true value if this font is equal to `obj`.

`public String getFamily()`

Returns the name of the family this font belongs to.

`public static Font getFont(String str)`

`public static Font getFont(String str, Font ft)`

Returns the font named `str`. If the font cannot be located, the second method returns `ft` as the default.

`public String getName()`

Returns the name of this font.

`public FontPeer getPeer()`

Returns the peer of this font.

`public int getSize()`

`public int getStyle()`

Returns the size or style of this font.

`public int hashCode()`

Returns the hash code for this font.

`public boolean isBold()`

`public boolean isItalic()`

`public boolean isPlain()`

Returns a true value if this font is bolded, italicized, or plain.

`public String toString()`

Returns a string representation of this font.

FontMetrics (java.awt)

A public class, derived from `Object` and implementing `Serializable`, that provides detailed information about a particular font.

variables and constructs

`protected Font font`

The font upon which the metrics are generated.

constructors

```
protected FontMetrics(Font f)
```
Creates a new instance of metrics from a given font f.

methods

```
public int bytesWidth(byte[] src, int offset, int size)
public int charsWidth(char[] src, int offset, int size)
```
Returns the advance width for displaying the subarray of src, starting at index offset, and having a length of size.

```
public int charWidth(char c)
public int charWidth(int c)
```
Returns the advance width of the character c for the font in this font metric.

```
public int getAscent()
public int getDescent()
```
Returns the amount of ascent or descent for the font in this font metric.

```
public Font getFont()
```
Returns the font in this font metric.

```
public int getHeight()
```
Returns the standard height of the font in this font metric.

```
public int getLeading()
```
Returns the standard leading of the font in this font metric.

```
public int getMaxAdvance()
```
Returns the maximum amount of advance for the font in this font metric.

```
public int getMaxAscent()
public int getMaxDescent()
```
Returns the maximum amount of ascent or descent for the font in this font metric.

```
public int[] getWidths()
```
Returns an int array containing the advance widths of the first 256 characters of the font.

```
public int stringWidth(String str)
```
Returns the advance width of the string str as represented by the font in this font metric.

```
public String toString()
```
Returns a string representation of the font metrics.

Format (java.text)

A public abstract class, derived from `Object` and implementing `Cloneable` and `Serializable`, which is used to format locale-based values into strings, and vice versa.

constructors

`public Format()`

Creates a new instance of a `Format`.

methods

`public Object clone()`

Returns a copy of this `Format`.

`public final String format(Object arg)`

Returns a formatted string from `arg`.

`public abstract StringBuffer format(Object arg, StringBuffer dest, FieldPosition pos)`

Formats the specified argument (starting at field `pos`) into a string, and appends it to the specified `StringBuffer`. This method returns the same value as the destination buffer.

`public Object parseObject(String src) throws ParseException`

Parses the specified source string into a formatted object.

`public abstract Object parseObject(String src, ParsePosition pos)`

Parses the specified source string into a formatted object starting at the specified `ParsePosition`.

Graphics (java.awt)

A public abstract class, derived from `Object`, that provides many useful drawing methods and tools for the manipulation of graphics. A `Graphics` object defines a context in which the user draws.

constructors

`protected Graphics()`

Creates a new `Graphics` instance. This constructor cannot be called directly.

methods

`public abstract void clearRect(int x, int y, int width, int height)`

Draws a rectangle (with no fill pattern) in the current background color at position <x, y>, and having a `width` and `height`.

`public abstract void clipRect(int x, int y, int width, int height)`

Sets a clipping rectangle at position <x, y> and having a `width` and `height`.

`public abstract void copyArea(int x, int y, int width, int height, int xoffset, int yoffset)`

Copies a graphic rectangular area at position <x, y> and having a `width` and `height`, to position newx and newy.

`public abstract Graphics create()`

`public Graphics create(int x, int y, int width, int height)`

Returns a copy of this graphics context from position <x, y>, and having a `width` and `height`. In the case of the first method, the entire area is copied.

`public abstract void dispose()`

Disposes this graphics context.

`public void draw3DRect(int x, int y, int width, int height, boolean toggle)`

Draws a 3D rectangle at position <x, y> and having a `width` and `height`. If `toggle` is true, the rectangle will appear raised; otherwise, it will appear indented.

`public abstract void drawArc(int x, int y, int width, int height, int sAngle, int aAngle)`

Draws an arc with a starting position <x, y> and having a `width` and `height`. The start angle (`sAngle`) and arc angle (`aAngle`) are both measured in degrees and describe the starting and ending angle of the arc.

`public void drawBytes(byte[] src, int index, int ln, int x, int y)`

`public void drawChars(char[] src, int index, int ln, int x, int y)`

Draws `ln` bytes or characters of array `src` (starting at the offset `index`) at position <x, y>.

`public abstract boolean drawImage(Image src, int x, int y, Color bgc, ImageObserver obsv)`

`public abstract boolean drawImage(Image src, int x, int y, ImageObserver obsv)`

Draws a graphic image (`src`) at position <x, y>. Any transparent color pixels are drawn as `bgc`, and the `obsv` monitors the progress of the image.

`public abstract boolean drawImage(Image src, int x, int y, int width, int height, Color bgc, ImageObserver obsv)` `public abstract boolean drawImage(Image src, int x, int y, int width, int height, ImageObserver obsv)`

Draws a graphic image (src) at position <x, y> and having a width and height. Any transparent color pixels are drawn as bgc, and the obsv monitors the progress of the image.

`public abstract boolean drawImage(Image src, int xsrc1, int ysrc1, int xsrc1, int ysrc2, int xdest1, int ydest1, int xdest1, int ydest2, Color bgc, ImageObserver obsv)`

`public abstract boolean drawImage(Image src, int xsrc1, int ysrc1, int xsrc1, int ysrc2, int xdest1, int ydest1, int xdest1, int ydest2, ImageObserver obsv)`

Draws a graphic image (src) from the area defined by the bounding rectangle <xsrc1, ysrc1> to <xsrc2, ysrc2> in the area defined by the bounding rectangle <xdest1, ydest1> to <xdest2, ydest2>. Any transparent color pixels are drawn as bgc, and the obsv monitors the progress of the image.

`public abstract void drawLine(int xsrc, int ysrc, int xdest, int ydest)`

Draws a line from position <xsrc, ysrc> to <xdest, ydest>.

`public abstract void drawOval(int xsrc, int ysrc, int width, int height)`

Draws an oval starting at position <xsrc, ysrc> and having a width and height.

`public abstract void drawPolygon(int[] x, int[] y, int num)`

`public void drawPolygon(Polygon poly)`

Draws a polygon constructed from poly or an array of x points, y points and a number of points in the polygon (num).

`public void drawRect(int xsrc, int ysrc, int width, int height)`

`public abstract void drawRoundRect(int xsrc, int ysrc, int width, int height, int awd, int aht)`

Draws a rectangle with or without rounded corners at position <xsrc, ysrc> and having a width and height. The shape of the rounded corners are determined by the width of the arc (awd) and the height of the arc (aht).

`public abstract void drawString(String str, int x, int y)`

Draws the string str at position <x, y> in this Graphic's current font and color.

`public void fill3DRect(int x, int y, int width, int height, boolean toggle)`

Draws a filled 3D rectangle at position <x, y> and having a width and height. The rectangle is filled with this Graphic's current color, and if toggle is true, the rectangle is drawn raised. (Otherwise it is drawn indented.)

`public abstract void fillArc(int x, int y, int width, int height, int sAngle, int aAngle)`

Draws a filled arc at position <x, y> and having a `width` and `height`. The arc has a starting angle of `sAngle` and an ending angle of `aAngle`.

`public abstract void fillOval(int x, int y, int width, int height)`

Draws a filled oval at position <x, y> and having a `width` and `height`.

`public abstract void fillPolygon(int[] x, int[] y, int num)`

`public void fillPolygon(Polygon poly)`

Draws a filled polygon defined by `poly` or the arrays x, y and the number of points in the polygon, num.

`public abstract void fillRect(int x, int y, int width, int height)`

`public abstract void fillRoundRect(int x, int y, int width, int height, int aWidth, int aHeight)`

Draws a filled rectangle with or without rounded corners at position <x, y> and having a `width` and `height`. The shape of the rounded corners are determined by the width of the arc (`aWidth`) and the height of the arc (`aHeight`).

`public void finalize()`

Disposes of the current graphics context.

`public abstract Shape getClip()`

Returns a shape object of the current clipping area for this graphics context.

`public abstract Rectangle getClipBounds()`

Returns a rectangle describing the bounds of the current clipping area for this graphics context.

`public abstract Color getColor()`

`public abstract void setColor(Color clr)`

Returns or sets the current color for this graphics context.

`public abstract Font getFont()`

`public abstract void setFont(Font ft)`

Returns or sets the current font of this graphics context.

`public FontMetrics getFontMetrics()`

`public abstract FontMetrics getFontMetrics(Font fn)`

Returns the font metrics associated with this graphics context or font `fn`.

`public abstract void setClip(int x, int y, int width, int height)`

`public abstract void setClip(Shape shp)`

Sets the clipping area for this graphics context to be at position <x, y> and having a `width` and `height` or to be of a specified shape (`shp`).

```
public abstract void setPaintMode()
```
Sets the current graphics context's paint mode to overwrite any subsequent destinations with the current color.

```
public abstract void setXORMode(Color clr)
```
Sets the current graphics context's paint mode to overwrite any subsequent destinations with the alternating current color and `clr` color.

```
public String toString()
```
Returns a string representation of this graphics context.

```
public abstract void translate(int x, int y)
```
Modifies the origin of this graphics context to be relocated to <x, y>.

GregorianCalendar (java.util)

A public class, derived from `Calendar`, that represents the standard world Gregorian calendar.

variables and constructs

AD

BC

Constant values representing periods of an era.

constructors

```
public GregorianCalendar()
```
```
public GregorianCalendar(Locale locale)
```
```
public GregorianCalendar(TimeZone zone)
```
```
public GregorianCalendar(TimeZone zone, Locale locale)
```
Creates a new `GregorianCalendar` from the current time in the specified time zone (or the default) and the specified locale (or the default).

```
public GregorianCalendar(int year, int month, int date)
```
```
public GregorianCalendar(int year, int month, int date, int
hour, int min)
```
```
public GregorianCalendar(int year, int month, int date, int
hour, int min, int sec)
```
Creates a new `GregorianCalendar`, setting the year, month, date, hour, minute, and seconds of the time fields.

methods

`public void add(int field, int val)`
  Adds (or subtracts in the case of a negative `val`) an amount of days or time from the specified `field`.

`public boolean after(Object arg)`

`public boolean before(Object arg)`
  Returns a true value if this `GregorianCalendar` date is after or before the date specified by `arg`.

`public Object clone()`
  Returns a clone of this `GregorianCalendar`.

`protected void computeFields()`

`protected void computeTime()`
  Computes the values of the time fields based on the currently set time (`computeFields()`) or computes the time based on the currently set time fields (`computeTime()`) for this `GregorianCalendar`.

`public boolean equals(Object arg)`
  Returns a true value if this `GregorianCalendar` is equal to the value of `arg`.

`public int getGreatestMinimum(int fld)`

`public int getLeastMaximum(int fld)`
  Returns the largest allowable minimum or smallest allowable maximum value for the specified field.

`public final Date getGregorianChange()`

`public void setGregorianChange(Date dt)`
  Returns or sets the date of the change from Julian to Gregorian calendars for this calendar. The default value is October 15, 1582 (midnight local time).

`public int getMaximum(int fld)`

`public int getMinimum(int fld)`
  Returns the largest or smallest allowable value for the specified field.

`public synchronized int hashCode()`
  Returns the hash code for this `GregorianCalendar`.

`public boolean isLeapYear(int year)`
  Returns a true value if the specified year is a leap year.

`public void roll(int fld, boolean direction)`
  Adds one single unit of time to the specified date/time field. A true value specified for `direction` increases the field's value, false decreases it.

GridBagConstraints (java.awt)

A public class, derived from `Object` and implementing `Cloneable`, that specifies the layout constraints for each component laid out with a `GridBagLayout`.

variables and constructs

`public int anchor`

   Determines where to place a component that is smaller in size than its display area in the gridbag.

`public final static int BOTH`

`public final static int HORIZONTAL`

`public final static int NONE`

`public final static int VERTICAL`

   Constant values that indicate the direction(s) that the component should grow.

`public final static int CENTER`

`public final static int EAST`

`public final static int NORTH`

`public final static int NORTHEAST`

`public final static int NORTHWEST`

`public final static int SOUTH`

`public final static int SOUTHEAST`

`public final static int SOUTHWEST`

`public final static int WEST`

   Constant values that indicate where the component should be placed in its display area.

`public int fill`

   Determines how to resize a component that is smaller than its display area in the gridbag.

`public int gridheight`

`public int gridwidth`

   Specifies the number of vertical and horizontal cells the component shall occupy.

`public int gridx`

`public int gridy`

   Describes horizontal and vertical cell locations (indices) in the gridbag, where `gridx=0` is the leftmost cell and `gridy=0` is the topmost cell.

`public Insets insets`
Defines the amount of space (in pixels) around the component in its display area.

`public int ipadx`

`public int ipady`
Defines the amount of space (in pixels) to add to the minimum horizontal and vertical size of the component.

`public final static int RELATIVE`
A constant that specifies that this component is the next to last item in its gridbag row or that it should be placed next to the last item added to the gridbag.

`public final static int REMAINDER`
A constant that specifies that this component is the last item in its gridbag row.

`public double weightx`

`public double weighty`
Specifies the weight of horizontal and vertical growth of this component relative to other components during a resizing event. A larger value indicates a higher percentage of growth for this component.

constructors

`public GridBagConstraints()`
Creates a new instance of `GridBagConstraints`.

methods

`public Object clone()`
Creates a copy of these gridbag constraints.

GridBagLayout (java.awt)

A public class, derived from `Object` and implementing `Serializable` and `LayoutManager`, that creates a gridlike area for component layout. Unlike `GridLayout`, `GridBagLayout` does not force the components to be the same size or to be constrained to one cell.

variables and constructs

`public double columnWeights[]`

`public int columnWidths[]`
Holds the weights and widths of each column of this `GridBagLayout`.

`protected Hashtable comptable`
A hashtable of the components managed by this layout manager.

`protected GridBagConstraints defaultConstraints`
Holds the default constraints for any component laid out by this layout manager.

`protected GridBagLayoutInfo layoutInfo`
Holds specific layout information (such as the list of components or the constraints of this manager) for this `GridBagLayout`.

`protected final static int MAXGRIDSIZE`
A constant value that contains the maximum (512) number of grid cells that can be laid out by this `GridBagLayout`.

`protected final static int MINSIZE`
A constant value that contains the minimum (1) number of cells contained within this `GridBagLayout`.

`protected final static int PREFERREDSIZE`
A constant value that contains the preferred (2) number of cells contained within this `GridBagLayout`.

`public int rowHeights[]`

`public double rowWeights[]`
Holds the heights and weights of each row of this `GridBagLayout`.

constructors

`public GridBagLayout()`
Creates a new instance of a `GridBagLayout`.

methods

`public void addLayoutComponent(Component item, Object constraints)`
Adds the component `item` to this layout manager using the specified constraints on the item.

`public void addLayoutComponent(String str, Component item)`
Adds the component `item` to this layout manager and names it `str`.

`protected void AdjustForGravity(GridBagConstraints constraints, Rectangle rect)`
Sets the characteristics of `rect` based on the specified constraints.

`protected void ArrangeGrid(Container parent)`
Arranges the entire grid on the parent.

`public GridBagConstraints getConstraints(Component item)`
Returns a copy of the constraints for the `item` component.

```
public float getLayoutAlignmentX(Container parent)
```
```
public float getLayoutAlignmentY(Container parent)
```
Returns the horizontal and vertical alignment values for the specified container.

```
public int[][] getLayoutDimensions()
```
Returns a two-dimensional array in which the zero index of the first dimension holds the minimum width of each column and the one index of the first dimension holds the minimum height of each column.

```
protected GridBagLayoutInfo GetLayoutInfo(Container parent, int
sizeflag)
```
Computes and returns a `GridBagLayoutInfo` object for components associated with the specified parent container.

```
public Point getLayoutOrigin()
```
Returns this layout's point of origin.

```
public double[][] getLayoutWeights()
```
Returns a two-dimensional array in which the zero index of the first dimension holds the weight in the x direction of each column and the one index of the first dimension holds the weight in the y direction of each column.

```
protected Dimension GetMinSize(Container parent,
GridBagLayoutInfo info)
```
Returns the minimum size for the specified parent container based on laying out the container using the specified `GridBagLayoutInfo`.

```
public void invalidateLayout(Container cont)
```
Forces this layout manager to discard any cached layout information about the specified container.

```
public void layoutContainer(Container cont)
```
Lays out the specified container with this layout manager.

```
public Point location(int x, int y)
```
Returns the upper right corner of the cell in this `GridBagLayout` with dimensions greater than the specified <x, y> coordinate.

```
protected GridBagConstraints lookupConstraints(Component item)
```
Returns the actual constraints for the specified component.

```
public Dimension maximumLayoutSize(Container cont)
```
```
public Dimension minimumLayoutSize(Container cont)
```
```
public Dimension preferredLayoutSize(Container cont)
```
Returns the maximum, minimum, or preferred size of the specified container when laid out by this layout manager.

```
public void removeLayoutComponent(Component comp)
```
   Removes the specified component from this layout manager.

```
public void setConstraints(Component item, GridBagConstraints
constraints)
```
   Sets the `constraints` for the `item` component in this layout manager.

GridLayout (java.awt)

A public class, derived from `Object` and implementing `Serializable` and `LayoutManager`, that creates a grid area of equal sized rectangles to lay out components in.

constructors

```
public GridLayout()
```

```
public GridLayout(int r, int c)
```
   Creates a new instance of a `GridLayout` with a dimension of r rows and c columns (default of 1 by any).

```
public GridLayout(int r, int c, int hg, int vg)
```
   Creates a new instance of a `GridLayout` with a dimension of r rows and c columns. The grid cells have a hg pixel horizontal gap and a vg pixel vertical gap.

methods

```
public void addLayoutComponent(String str, Component comp)
```

```
public void removeLayoutComponent(Component comp)
```
   Adds or removes the specified component. When adding, the component can be given a name (`str`).

```
public int getColumns()
```

```
public void setColumns(int val)
```
   Returns or sets the number of columns of this layout manager.

```
public int getHgap()
```

```
public int getVgap()
```
   Returns the value of the horizontal or vertical gap for this layout manager.

```
public int getRows()
```

```
public void setRows(int val)
```
   Returns or sets the number of rows of this layout manager.

```
public void layoutContainer(Container cont)
```
Lays out the specified container with this layout manager.

```
public Dimension minimumLayoutSize(Container cont)
```

```
public Dimension preferredLayoutSize(Container cont)
```
Returns the minimum or preferred size of the specified container when laid out with this layout manager.

```
public void setHgap(int val)
```

```
public void setVgap(int val)
```
Sets the horizontal or vertical gap for this layout manager to `val`.

Hashtable (java.util)

A public class, derived from `Dictionary` and implementing `Serializable` and `Cloneable`, that allows for the storing of objects that have a relationship with a key. You can then use this key to access the object stored.

constructors

```
public Hashtable()
```

```
public Hashtable(int size)
```

```
public Hashtable(int size, float load) throws
IllegalArgumentException
```
Creates a new instance of a hashtable, setting the initial capacity (or using the default size of 101) and a load factor (default of 0.75). The initial capacity sets the number of objects the table can store, and the load factor value is the percentage filled the table may become before being resized.

methods

```
public void clear()
```
Removes all keys and elements from this `Hashtable`.

```
public Object clone()
```
Returns a clone of this `Hashtable` (the keys and values are not cloned).

```
public boolean contains(Object arg) throws NullPointerException
```
Returns a true value if this `Hashtable` contains a key that is related to the element `arg`.

```
public boolean containsKey(Object obj)
```
Returns a true value if this `Hashtable` contains an entry for the key at `obj`.

```
public Enumeration elements()
```
```
public Enumeration keys()
```
Returns an enumerated list of all of the elements or keys of this `Hashtable`.

```
public Object get(Object obj)
```
```
public Object put(Object obj, Object arg) throws
NullPointerException
```
```
public Object remove(Object obj)
```
Returns, inserts, or removes the element `arg` that corresponds to the key `obj`.

```
public boolean isEmpty()
```
Returns a true value if the `Hashtable` is empty.

```
protected void rehash()
```
Resizes this `Hashtable`. The method is invoked automatically when the number of keys exceeds the capacity and load factor.

```
public int size()
```
Returns the number of elements in this `Hashtable`.

```
public String toString()
```
Returns a string representation of this `Hashtable`'s key-element pairings.

Image (java.awt)

A public abstract class, derived from `Object`, that is used to manage graphic images.

variables and constructs

```
public final static int SCALE_AREA_AVERAGING
```
```
public final static int SCALE_DEFAULT
```
```
public final static int SCALE_FAST
```
```
public final static int SCALE_REPLICATE
```
```
public final static int SCALE_SMOOTH
```
Constant values used to indicate specific scaling algorithms.

```
public final static Object UndefinedProperty
```
A constant value that is returned whenever an undefined property for an image is attempted to be obtained.

constructors

```
public Image()
```
Creates a new instance of an image.

methods

`public abstract void flush()`
Frees the cache memory containing this image.

`public abstract Graphics getGraphics()`
Returns a newly created graphics context for drawing off-screen images.

`public abstract int getHeight(ImageObserver obs)`

`public abstract int getWidth(ImageObserver obs)`
Returns the height or width of this image. If the height is not known, a –1 is returned and the obs is informed later.

`public abstract Object getProperty(String property,`
`ImageObserver obs)`
Returns the value of the property for this image. If the value is not known, a null is returned and obs is informed later.

`public Image getScaledInstance(int width, int height, int algo)`
Returns a scaled version of this image. The new image is scaled to width pixels by height pixels using the specified scaling algorithm (algo). If either of the new width or height values are –1, then the new image will maintain the aspect ratios of the old image.

`public abstract ImageProducer getSource()`
Returns the source image producer for this image.

ImageIcon `(javax.swing)`

A public class, derived from `Object` and implementing `Accessible`, `Icon`, and `Serializable`, that represents an icon based on an image.

constructors

`public ImageIcon()`
`public ImageIcon(byte[] imageData)`
`public ImageIcon(byte[] imageData, String description)`
`public ImageIcon(Image image)`
`public ImageIcon(Image image, String description)`
`public ImageIcon(String filename)`
`public ImageIcon(String filename, String description)`
`public ImageIcon(URL location)`

`public ImageIcon(URL location, String description)`
Creates an icon using an image described by raw image data (in a supported format such as GIF or JPEG), and `Image` object, a file, or a URL. An optional description can be specified as well.

methods

`public String getDescription()`
Returns the description of this image icon.

`public int getIconHeight()`

`public int getIconWidth()`
Returns this icon's height or width.

`public Image getImage()`
Returns this icon's image.

`public void paintIcon(Component observer, Graphics page, int x, int y)`
Paints this icon on the specified graphics context at the specified location using the specified image observer.

`public setDescription(String description)`

`public setImage(Image image)`
Sets the description or the image for this icon.

InputEvent (java.awt.event)

A public abstract class, derived from `ComponentEvent`, that describes a particular AWT input event.

variables and constructs

`public static final int ALT_MASK`
`public static final int BUTTON1_MASK`
`public static final int BUTTON2_MASK`
`public static final int BUTTON3_MASK`
`public static final int CTRL_MASK`
`public static final int META_MASK`
`public static final int SHIFT_MASK`
Constant values that represent various keyboard and mouse masks.

methods

`public void consume()`
Consumes this event, preventing it from being passed to its peer component.

`public int getModifiers()`
Returns the modifiers for this event.

`public long getWhen()`
Returns the timestamp of this event.

`public boolean isConsumed()`
Returns a true value if this event is consumed.

`public boolean isAltDown()`

`public boolean isControlDown()`

`public boolean isMetaDown()`

`public boolean isShiftDown()`
Returns a true value if the Alt, Control, Meta, or Shift key is depressed during this event.

InputStream (java.io)

A public abstract class, derived from `Object`, that is the parent class of any type of input stream that reads bytes.

constructors

`public InputStream()`
Generally called only by subclasses, this constructor creates a new instance of an `InputStream`.

methods

`public int available() throws IOException`
Returns the number of available bytes that can be read. This method returns a 0 (zero) value and should be overridden by a subclass implementation.

`public void close() throws IOException`
Closes the input stream. This method has no functionality and should be overridden by a subclass implementation.

```
public void mark(int size)
```
Sets a mark in the input stream, allowing a rereading of the stream data to occur if the `reset` method is invoked. The `size` parameter indicates how many bytes may be read following the mark being set, before the mark is considered invalid.

```
public boolean markSupported()
```
Returns a true value if this `InputStream` object supports the mark and reset methods. This method always returns a false value and should be overridden by a subclass implementation.

```
public abstract int read() throws IOException
```
Reads the next byte of data from this `InputStream` and returns it as an `int`. This method has no functionality and should be implemented in a subclass. Execution of this method will block until data is available to be read, the end of the input stream occurs, or an exception is thrown.

```
public int read(byte[] dest) throws IOException
```
```
public int read(byte[] dest, int offset, int size) throws
IOException
```
Reads from this `InputStream` into the array `dest`, and returns the number of bytes read. `size` specifies the maximum number of bytes read from this `InputStream` into the array `dest[]` starting at index `offset`. This method returns the actual number of bytes read or –1, indicating that the end of the stream was reached. To read `size` bytes and throw them away, call this method with `dest[]` set to null.

```
public synchronized void reset() throws IOException
```
Resets the read point of this `InputStream` to the location of the last mark set.

```
public long skip(long offset) throws IOException
```
Skips over `offset` bytes from this `InputStream`. Returns the actual number of bytes skipped, as it is possible to skip over less than `offset` bytes.

InputStreamReader (java.io)

A public class, derived from `Reader`, that is an input stream of characters.

constructors

```
public InputStreamReader(InputStream input)
```
```
public InputStreamReader(InputStream input, String encoding)
throws UnsupportedEncodingException
```
Creates an instance of `InputStreamReader` from the `InputStream` input with a specified encoding.

methods

`public void close() throws IOException`
Closes this `InputStreamReader`.

`public String getEncoding()`
Returns the string representation of this `InputStreamReader`'s encoding.

`public int read() throws IOException`
Reads a single character from this `InputStreamReader`. The character read is returned as an `int`, or a –1 is returned if the end of this `InputStreamReader` was encountered.

`public int read(char[] dest, int offset, int size) throws IOException`
Reads no more than `size` bytes from this `InputStreamReader` into the array `dest[]` starting at index `offset`. This method returns the actual number of bytes read or –1, indicating that the end of the stream was reached. To read `size` bytes and throw them away, call this method with `dest[]` set to null.

`public boolean ready() throws IOException`
Returns a true value if this `InputStreamReader` is capable of being read from. This state can only be true if the buffer is not empty.

Insets (java.awt)

A public class, derived from `Object` and implementing `Serializable` and `Cloneable`, that specifies the margins of a container.

variables and constructs

`public int bottom`
`public int left`
`public int right`
`public int top`
Contains the value of the inset for a particular margin.

constructors

`public Insets(int t, int l, int b, int r)`
Creates an instance of insets with initial top (`t`), bottom (`b`), left (`l`), and right (`r`) inset values.

methods

`public Object clone()`
Creates a copy of this group of inset values.

`public boolean equals(Object arg)`
Returns a true value if this inset is equal to the object `arg`.

`public String toString()`
Returns a string representation of this group of inset values.

Integer (java.lang)

A public final class, derived from `Number`, that contains integer math operations, constants, and methods to compute minimum and maximum numbers, and string manipulation routines related to the primitive `int` type.

variables and constructs

`public final static int MAX_VALUE`

`public final static int MIN_VALUE`
Constant values that contain the maximum possible value (2147483647) or minimum possible value (–2174783648) of an integer in Java.

`public final static Class TYPE`
The `Integer` constant value of the integer type class.

constructors

`public Integer(int num)`

`public Integer(String num) throws NumberFormatException`
Creates an instance of the `Integer` class from the parameter num.

methods

`public byte byteValue()`
`public double doubleValue()`
`public float floatValue()`
`public int intValue()`
`public long longValue()`
`public short shortValue()`
Returns the value of this integer as a Java primitive type.

```
public static Integer decode(String str) throws
NumberFormatException
```
Decodes the given string (str) and returns it as an Integer. The decode method can handle octal, hexadecimal, and decimal input values.

```
public boolean equals(Object num)
```
Returns the result of an equality comparison against num.

```
public static Integer getInteger(String str)
```
```
public static Integer getInteger(String str, int num)
```
```
public static Integer getInteger(String str, Integer num)
```
Returns an Integer representation of the system property named in str. If there is no property corresponding to num, or the format of its value is incorrect, then the default num is returned as an Integer object.

```
public int hashCode()
```
Returns a hash code for this object.

```
public static int parseInt(String str) throws
NumberFormatException
```
```
public static int parseInt(String str, int base) throws
NumberFormatException
```
Evaluates the string str and returns the int equivalent in radix base.

```
public static String toBinaryString(int num)
```
```
public static String toHexString(int num)
```
```
public static String toOctalString(int num)
```
Returns the string representation of parameter num in base 2 (binary), 8 (octal), or 16 (hexadecimal).

```
public String toString()
```
```
public static String toString(int num)
```
```
public static String toString(int num, int base)
```
Returns the string representation of this integer or num. The radix of num can be specified in base.

```
public static Integer valueOf(String str) throws
NumberFormatException
```
```
public static Integer valueOf(String str, int base) throws
NumberFormatException
```
Returns an Integer initialized to the value of str in radix base.

ItemEvent (java.awt.event)

A public class, derived from `AWTEvent`, that represents an AWT item event (from a component such as a `Checkbox`, `CheckboxMenuItem`, `Choice`, or `List`).

variables and constructs

`public static final int DESELECTED`

`public static final int SELECTED`

Constant values representing the deselection or selection of an AWT item component.

`public static final int ITEM_FIRST`

`public static final int ITEM_LAST`

Constant values that represent the index of the first and last item event ids.

`public static final int ITEM_STATE_CHANGED`

A constant value that represents the event of the change of state for an AWT item.

constructors

`public ItemEvent(ItemSelectable src, int type, Object obj, int change)`

Creates a new instance of an `ItemEvent` from the specified source, having a specific `type`, item `object`, and state `change`.

methods

`public Object getItem()`

Returns the specific item that triggered this event.

`public ItemSelectable getItemSelectable()`

Returns the `ItemSelectable` object that triggered this event.

`public int getStateChange()`

Returns the state change type (deselection or selection) that triggered this event.

`public String paramString()`

Returns a parameter string containing the values of the parameters for this event.

JApplet (`javax.swing`)

A public class, derived from `Applet` and implementing `Accessible` and `RootPaneContainer`, that represents a primary applet container.

constructors

`public JApplet()`
    Creates an applet container.

methods

`public Container getContentPane()`
`public Component getGlassPane()`
`public JLayeredPane getLayeredPane()`
`public JRootPane getRootPane()`
    Returns the content pane, glass pane, layered pane, or root pane for this applet.

`public void setContentPane(Container contenetPane)`
`public void setGlassPane(Component glassPane)`
`public void setLayeredPane(JLayeredPane layeredPane)`
`public void setRootPane(JRootPane rootPane)`
    Sets the content pane, glass pane, layered pane, or root pane for this applet.

`public void remove(Component comp)`
    Removes the specified component from this applet.

`public JMenuBar getJMenuBar()`
`public void setJMenuBar setJMenuBar(JMenuBar menuBar)`
    Gets or sets the menu bar for this applet.

JButton (`javax.swing`)

A public class, derived from `AbstractButton` and implementing `Accessible`, that represents a GUI push button.

constructors

`public JButton()`
`public JButton(Icon icon)`
`public JButton(String text)`
`public JButton(String text, Icon icon)`
    Creates a button with the specified text and icon.

methods

```
public boolean isDefaultButton()
```
Returns true if this button is the current default button for its root pane.

```
public boolean isDefaultCapable()
```

```
public void setDefaultCapable(boolean capable)
```
Gets or sets the property that determines if this button can be the default button for its root pane.

JCheckBox (javax.swing)

A public class, derived from JToggleButton and implementing Accessible, that represents a GUI component that can be selected or deselected (displaying its state to the user).

constructors

```
public JCheckBox()
```

```
public JCheckBox(Icon icon)
```

```
public JCheckBox(Icon icon, boolean selected)
```

```
public JCheckBox(String text)
```

```
public JCheckBox(String text, boolean selected)
```

```
public JCheckBox(String text, Icon icon)
```

```
public JCheckBox(String text, Icon icon, boolean selected)
```
Creates a check box with the specified text, icon, and selected state (which defaults to unselected).

JCheckBoxMenuItem (javax.swing)

A public class, derived from JMenuItem and implementing Accessible and SwingConstants, that represents a menu item that can be selected or deselected.

constructors

```
public JCheckBoxMenuItem()
```

```
public JCheckBoxMenuItem(Icon icon)
```

```
public JCheckBoxMenuItem(String text)
```

```
public JCheckBoxMenuItem(String text, boolean selected)
```

```
public JCheckBoxMenuItem(String text, Icon icon)
public JCheckBoxMenuItem(String text, Icon icon, boolean
selected)
```
   Creates a menu check box with the specified text, icon, and selected state (which defaults to unselected).

JColorChooser (javax.swing)

A public class, derived from JComponent and implementing Accessible, that represents a pane of controls that allows a user to define and select a color. A color chooser can be displayed as a dialog box or within any container.

constructors

```
public JColorChooser()
public JColorChooser(Color initialColor)
```
   Creates a color chooser with the specified initial color (white by default).

methods

```
public Color getColor()
public void setColor(Color color)
public void setColor(int color)
public void setColor(int red, int green, int blue)
```
   Gets or sets the current color for this color chooser.
```
public static Color showDialog(Component parent, String title,
Color initialColor)
```
   Shows a color chooser dialog box, returning the selected color when the user presses the OK button.

JComboBox (javax.swing)

A public class, derived from JComponent and implementing ItemSelectable, ListDataListener, ActionListener, and Accessible, that represents a GUI component that combines a button (or editable field) and a drop-down list.

constructors

```
public JComboBox()
public JComboBox(Object[] items)
public JComboBox(Vector items)
```
Creates a combo box containing the specified items.

methods

```
public addActionListener(ActionListener listener)
public addItemListener(ItemListener listener)
```
Adds a specific type of listener to this combo box.

```
public void addItem(Object item)
public insertItemAt(Object item, int index)
```
Adds the specified item to the end of the item list or inserts it at the specified index.

```
public Object getItemAt(int index)
```
Returns the item at the specified index.

```
public int getItemCount()
```
Returns the number of items in the list.

```
public Object getSelectedItem()
```
Returns the currently selected item.

```
public void setEditable(boolean flag)
```
Sets whether this combo box is editable.

```
public boolean isEditable()
```
Returns true if this combo box is editable.

```
public void setEnabled(boolean flag)
```
Enables or disables this combo box. When disabled, items cannot be selected.

```
public void removeAllItems()
public void removeItem(Object item)
public void removeItemAt(int index)
```
Removes all items, a specific item, or the item at a specific index, from the list.

JComponent (javax.swing)

A public abstract class, derived from Component and implementing Serializable, that represents the base class for all Swing components (except top-level containers).

methods

```
public float getAlignmentX()
public void setAlignmentX(float alignment)
public float getAlignmentY()
public void setAlignmentY(float alignment)
```
Gets or sets the horizontal or vertical alignment for this component.

```
public Border getBorder()
public void setBorder(Border border)
```
Gets or sets the border for this component.

```
public Graphics getGraphics()
```
Returns the graphics context for this component.

```
public int getHeight()
public int getWidth()
```
Returns the height or width of this component.

```
public Dimension getMaximumSize()
public void setMaximumSize(Dimension size)
public Dimension getMinimumSize()
public void setMinimumSize(Dimension size)
public Dimension getPreferredSize()
public void setPreferredSize(Dimension size)
```
Gets or sets the maximum, minimum, or preferred size for this component.

```
public JRootPane getRootPane()
```
Returns the root pane ancestor for this component.

```
public String getToolTipText()
public void setToolTipText(String text)
```
Gets or sets the text for this component's tool tip.

```
public int getX()
public int getY()
```
Returns the x or y coordinate of this component.

```
public void setEnabled(boolean enabled)
```
Enables or disables this component.

```
public void setFont(Font font)
```
Sets the font for this component.

```
public void setBackground(Color color)
public void setForeground(Color color)
```
Sets the background or foreground color for this component.

```
public setVisible(boolean flag)
```
Makes this component visible or invisible.

JFileChooser (javax.swing)

A public class, derived from JComponent and implementing Accessible, that represents a GUI component that allows the user to select a file from a file system.

variables and constructs

public static final int APPROVE_OPTION
   Return value if approval (Yes, Ok) is chosen.
public static final int CANCEL_OPTION
   Return value if Cancel is chosen.
public static final int ERROR_OPTION
   Return value if an error occured.

constructors

public JFileChooser()
public JFileChooser(File directory)
public JFileChooser(FileSystemView view)
public JFileChooser(String path)
public JFileChooser(File directory, FileSystemView view)
public JFileChooser(String path, FileSystemView view)
   Creates a file chooser with the specified directory or path and optional file system view.

methods

public File getCurrentDirectory()
public void setCurrentDirectory(File directory)
   Gets or sets the current directory for this file chooser.
public String getDescription(File file)
public String getName(File file)
   Returns the description or name of the specified file.
public boolen getDraggedEnabled()
public void setDraggedEnabled(boolean flag)
   Gets or sets the property that determines whether the user can drag to select files.
public File getSelectedFile()
public File[] getSelectedFiles()
   Gets the currently selected file or files.

```
public boolean isMultiSelectionEnabled()
```
   Returns true if multiple files can be selected.
```
public void setDialogTitle(String title)
```
   Sets the title of the dialog box.
```
public void setFileFilter(FileFilter filter)
```
   Sets the current file filter.
```
public void setSelectedFile(File file)
```
```
public void setSelectedFiles(File[] files)
```
   Sets the selected file or files.
```
public int showDialog(Component parent, String
approveButtonText)
```
   Displays a custom file chooser dialog with the specified approve button text.
```
public int showOpenDialog(Component parent)
```
   Displays an "open file" file chooser dialog.
```
public int showSaveDialog(Component parent)
```
   Displays a "save file" file chooser dialog.

JFrame (javax.swing)

A public class, derived from `Frame` and implementing `WindowConstants`, `Accessible`, and `RootPaneContainer`, that represents a primary GUI window.

variables and constructs

```
public static final int EXIT_ON_CLOSE
```
   Represents the exit application default window close operation.

constructors

```
public JFrame()
```
```
public JFrame(String title)
```
   Creates a frame with the specified title.

methods

```
public Container getContentPane()
```
```
public Component getGlassPane()
```
```
public JLayeredPane getLayeredPane()
```
```
public JRootPane getRootPane()
```
   Returns the content pane, glass pane, layered pane, or root pane for this frame.
```
public void setContentPane(Container contenetPane)
```

```
public void setGlassPane(Component glassPane)
public void setLayeredPane(JLayeredPane layeredPane)
public void setRootPane(JRootPane rootPane)
```
Sets the content pane, glass pane, layered pane, or root pane for this frame.
```
public void remove(Component comp)
```
Removes the specified component from this frame.
```
public JMenuBar getJMenuBar()
public void setJMenuBar setJMenuBar(JMenuBar menuBar)
```
Gets or sets the menu bar for this frame.
```
public void setDefaultCloseOperation(int operation)
```
Sets the default operation when the user closes this frame.

JLabel (javax.swing)

A public class, derived from JComponent and implementing Accessible and SwingConstants, that represents a GUI display area for a string, an image, or both.

constructors

```
public JLabel()
public JLabel(String text)
public JLabel(Icon icon)
public JLabel(String text, int horizontalAlignment)
public JLabel(Icon icon, int horizontalAlignment)
public JLabel(String text, Icon icon, int horizontalAlignment)
```
Creates a label containing the specified icon and string, and using the specified horizontal alignment.

methods

```
public int getHorizontalAlignment()
public void setHorizontalAlignment(int alignment)
public int getVerticalAlignment()
public void setVerticalAlignment(int alignment)
```
Gets or sets the horizontal or vertical alignment of the icon and text.
```
public int getHorizontalTextPosition()
public void setHorizontalTextPosition(int position)
public int getVerticalTextPosition()
```

```
public void setVerticalTextPosition(int position)
```
Gets or sets the horizontal or vertical position of the text relative to the icon.
```
public Icon getIcon()
```
```
public void setIcon(Icon icon)
```
Gets or sets the default icon for this button.
```
public String getText()
```
```
public void setText(String text)
```
Gets or sets the text displayed on this button.
```
public Component getLabelFor()
```
```
public void setLabelFor(Component comp)
```
Gets or sets the component that this label describes.

JList (javax.swing)

A public class, derived from JComponent and implementing Accessible and Scrollable, that represents a GUI component that allows the user to select one or more objects from a list.

variables and constructs

```
public static final int HORIZONTAL_WRAP
```
Indicates that cells flow horizontally, then vertically.
```
public static final int VERTICAL
```
Indicates one column of cells (the default).
```
public static final int VERTICAL_WRAP
```
Indicates that cells flow vertically, then horizontally.

constructors

```
public JList()
```
```
public JList(Object[] items)
```
```
public JList(Vector items)
```
Creates a list that displays the specified items.

methods

```
public void addListSelectionListener(ListSelectionListener
listener)
```
Adds the specified listener to this list.
```
public void clearSelection()
```
Clears the selection (no items will be selected).

```
public void ensureIndexIsVisible(int index)
```
Scrolls the list to make the specified item visible.

```
public int getLastVisibleIndex()
```
Returns the index of the last visible cell.

```
public int getLayoutOrientation()
public void setLayoutOrientation(int orientation)
```
Gets or sets the layout orientation for this list.

```
public int getMaxSelectionIndex()
public int getMinSelectionIndex()
```
Returns the largest or smallest selected cell index.

```
public int getSelectedIndex()
public void setSelectedIndex(int index)
public int[] getSelectedIndices()
public void setSelectedIndex(int[] indices)
```
Gets or sets the selected index or indices.

```
public void setSelectionInterval(int from, int to)
```
Selects the specified index interval.

```
public Object getSelectedValue()
public Object[] getSelectedValues()
```
Returns the currently selected value or values.

```
public Color getSelectionBackground()
public void setSelectionBackground(Color color)
public Color getSelectionForeground()
public void setSelectionForeground(Color color)
```
Gets or sets the background or foreground color of the selection.

```
public boolean isSelectedIndex(int index)
```
Returns true if the specified index is selected.

```
public boolean isSelectionEmpty()
```
Returns true if no item is currently selected.

```
public void setDragEnabled(boolean flag)
```
Enables or disables the property allowing the user to select multiple items by dragging the mouse.

```
public void setListData(Object[] items)
public void setListData(Vector items)
```
Sets the contents of the list to the specified items.

```
public void setSelectionMode(int selectionMode)
```
Sets the selection mode for this list using ListSelectionModel constants.

JOptionPane (javax.swing)

A public class, derived from JComponent and implementing Accessible, that provides methods for creating standard dialog boxes.

variables and constructs

```
public static final int CANCEL_OPTION
public static final int OK_OPTION
public static final int YES_OPTION
```
    Return value if a specific button option is chosen.
```
public static final int CLOSED_OPTION
```
    Return value if the user closes the window without selecting anything.
```
public static final int DEFAULT_OPTION
public static final int YES_NO_OPTION
public static final int YES_NO_CANCEL_OPTION
public static final int OK_CANCEL_OPTION
```
    Specifies the types of buttons to use in the dialog.
```
public static final int ERROR_MESSAGE
public static final int INFORMATION_MESSAGE
public static final int WARNING_MESSAGE
public static final int QUESTION_MESSAGE
public static final int PLAIN_MESSAGE
```
    Specifies a message style.

methods

```
public static void showConfirmDialog(Component parent, Object
message)
public static void showConfirmDialog(Component parent, Object
message, String title, int buttonSet)
public static void showConfirmDialog(Component parent, Object
message, String title, int buttonSet, int messageStyle)
public static void showConfirmDialog(Component parent, Object
message, String title, int buttonSet, int messageStyle, Icon
icon)
```
    Displays a dialog box allowing the user to confirm an option. Uses the specified message, title, button set, message style, and icon.
```
public static void showInputDialog(Component parent, Object
message)
```

```
public static void showInputDialog(Component parent, Object
message, Object initialSelectionValue)
```
```
public static void showInputDialog(Component parent, Object
message, String title, int messageStyle)
```
```
public static void showInputDialog(Object message)
```
```
public static void showInputDialog(Object message, Object
initialSelectionValue)
```
```
public static void showInputDialog(Component parent, Object
message, String title, int messageStyle, Icon icon, Object[]
selectionValues, Object initialSelectionValue)
```
Displays a dialog box allowing the user to enter input. Uses the specified message, title, and message style. An initial selection and options can also be specified.

```
public static void showMessageDialog(Component parent, Object
message)
```
```
public static void showMessageDialog(Component parent, Object
message, String title, int messageStyle)
```
```
public static void showMessageDialog(Component parent, Object
message, String title, int buttonSet, int messageStyle, Icon
icon)
```
Displays a dialog box presenting a message. Uses the specified message, title, message style, and icon.

```
public static void showOptionDialog(Component parent, Object
message, String title, int buttonSet, int messageStyle, Icon
icon, Object[] options, Object initialValue)
```
Displays a dialog box allowing the user to make a general choice. Uses the specified message, title, button set, message style, and icon. An initial selection and options can also be specified.

JPanel (javax.swing)

A public class, derived from JComponent and implementing Accessible, that represents a lightweight GUI container used to organize other components.

constructors

```
public JPanel()
```
```
public JPanel(LayoutManager manager)
```
Creates a panel with the specified layout manager, which defaults to a flow layout.

JPasswordField (javax.swing)

A public class, derived from JTextField, that represents a GUI text field into which the user can type a password. The password itself is not displayed as it is typed, but a visual indication that characters are being typed is shown.

constructors

```
public JPasswordField()
public JPasswordField(int columns)
public JPasswordField(String text)
public JPasswordField(String text, int columns)
```
Creates a password field with the specified number of columns, initialized to the specified text.

methods

```
public char[] getPassword()
```
Returns the text contained in this password field.
```
public char getEchoChar()
public void setEchoChar(char ch)
```
Gets or sets the character that is displayed as the user types into this field.

JRadioButton (javax.swing)

A public class, derived from JToggleButton and implementing Accessible, that represents a radio button, used as part of a button group (ButtonGroup), to present a set of mutually exclusive options.

constructors

```
public JRadioButton()
public JRadioButton(String text)
public JRadioButton(Icon icon)
public JRadioButton(String text, boolean selected)
public JRadioButton(Icon icon, boolean selected)
public JRadioButton(String text, Icon icon)
public JRadioButton(String text, Icon icon, boolean selected)
```
Creates a radio button with the specified text, icon, and initial selection status (unselected by default).

JScrollPane (javax.swing)

A public class, derived from JComponent and implementing Accessible and ScrollPaneConstants, that represents a lightweight GUI container with a scrollable view.

constructors

public JScrollPane()

public JScrollPane(Component comp)

public JScrollPane(int verticalPolicy, int horizontalPolicy)

public JScrollPane(Component comp, int verticalPolicy, int horizontalPolicy)

  Creates a scroll pane displaying the specified component and using the specified horizontal and vertical scrollbar policies.

methods

public int getHorizontalScrollBarPolicy()

public void setHorizontalScrollBarPolicy(int policy)

public int getHorizontalScrollBarPolicy()

public void setHorizontalScrollBarPolicy(int policy)

  Gets or sets the horizontal or vertical scrollbar policy for this scroll pane.

JSlider (javax.swing)

A public class, derived from JComponent, that represents a GUI component that allows the user to select a numeric value by sliding a knob within a bounded interval.

constructors

public JSlider()

public JSlider(int orientation)

public JSlider(int min, int max)

public JSlider(int min, int max, int initialValue)

public JSlider(int orientation, int min, int max, int initialValue)

  Creates a new slider with the specified orientation, minimum value, maximum value, and initial value. The default orientation is horizontal, the default minimum value is 0, the default maximum value is 100, and the default initial value is the range midpoint.

methods

`public void addChangeListener(ChangeListener listener)`
Adds a `ChangeListener` to this slider.

`public int getExtent()`
Returns the range of values covered by the knob.

`public int getMajorTickSpacing()`

`public int getMinorTickSpacing()`
Returns the major or minor tick spacing of this slider.

`public int getMinimum()`

`public int getMaximum()`
Returns the minimum or maximum value of this slider.

`public int getOrientation()`
Returns this slider's orientation.

`public boolean getPaintLabels()`

`public boolean getPaintTicks()`

`public boolean getPaintTrack()`
Returns true if this slider's labels, tick marks, or track are to be painted.

`public boolean getSnapToTicks()`
Returns true if this slider's knob snaps to the closest tick mark when the user moves the knob.

`public int getValue()`
Returns this slider's values.

`public boolean getValueIsAdjusting()`
Returns true if the slider knob is being dragged.

`public void setExtent(int extent)`
Sets the size of the range covered by this slider's knob.

`public void setMajorTickSpacing(int value)`

`public void setMinorTickSpacing(int value)`
Sets the major or minor tick spacing for this slider.

`public void setMinimum(int minimumValue)`

`public void setMaximum(int maximumValue)`
Sets the minimum or maximum value for this slider.

`public void setOrientation(int orientation)`
Sets the orientation for this slider.

`public void setPaintLabels(boolean flag)`

`public void setPaintTicks(boolean flag)`

`public void setPaintTrack(boolean flag)`
Determines whether this slider's labels, tick marks, or track are to be painted.

`public void setSnapToTicks(boolean flag)`
  Determines whether the knob (and value) snaps to the closest tick mark when the user moves the knob.

`public void setValue(int value)`
  Sets this slider's current value.

JTabbedPane (javax.swing)

A public class, derived from `JComponent` and implementing `Accessible`, `Serializable`, and `SwingConstants`, that represents a GUI container that allows the user to switch between a group of components by clicking on a tab.

variables and constructs

`public static final int SCROLL_TAB_LAYOUT`
  Specifies a tab layout that provides a scrollable region of tabs when all tabs won't fit in a single run.

`public static final int WRAP_TAB_LAYOUT`
  Specifies a tab layout that wraps tabs in multiple rows when all tabs won't fit in a single run.

constructors

`public JTabbedPane()`

`public JTabbedPane(int tabPlacement)`

`public JTabbedPane(int tabPlacement, int tabLayoutPolicy)`
  Creates a tabbed pane with the specified tab placement and tab layout policy. The tab placement is specified using `SwingConstants`.

methods

`public Component add(String title, Component comp)`
  Adds the specified component to a tab with the specified title.

`public int getTabCount()`
  Returns the number of tabs in this tabbed pane.

`public Color getBackgroundAt(int index)`

`public void setBackgroundAt(int index, Color color)`

`public Color getForegroundAt(int index)`

`public void setForegroundAt(int index, Color color)`
  Gets or sets the background or foreground color of the tab at the specified index.

JTextArea (javax.swing)

A public class, derived from JTextComponent, that represents a multi-line area for displaying or editing text.

constructors

```
public JTextArea()
public JTextArea(int rows, int columns)
public JTextArea(String text)
public JTextArea(String text, int rows, int columns)
```
Creates a text area with the specified initial text and an initial size goverened by the specified number of rows and columns.

methods

```
public int getColumns()
public void setColumns(int columns)
public int getRows()
public void setRows(int rows)
```
Gets or sets the number of rows or columns for this text area.

```
public int getLineCount()
```
Returns the number of lines contained in this text area.

```
public boolean getLineWrap()
public void setLineWrap(boolean flag)
```
Gets or sets the property that determines if lines are wrapped in this text area.

```
public boolean getWrapStyleWord()
public void setWrapStyleWord(boolean flag)
```
Gets or sets the property that determines if lines are wrapped by words or characters (if they are wrapped at all).

```
public void append(String str)
```
Appends the specified string to the end of the document in this text area.

```
public void insert(String str, int position)
```
Inserts the specified string into this text area's document at the specified position.

```
public void setFont(Font font)
```
Sets the font for this text area.

JTextField (javax.swing)

A public class, derived from `JTextComponent` and implementing `SwingConstants`, that represents a single line area for displaying or editing text (often used as an input field).

constructors

```
public JTextField()
public JTextField(int columns)
public JTextField(String text)
public JTextField(String text, int columns)
```
Creates a text field with the specified initial text and an initial size governed by the specified number of columns.

methods

```
public void addActionListener(ActionListener listener)
```
Adds an action listener to this text field.
```
public int getColumns()
public void setColumns(int columns)
```
Gets or sets the number of columns for this text field.
```
public int getHorizontalAlignment()
public void setHorizontalAlignment(int alignment)
```
Gets or sets the horizontal alignment for this text field.
```
public void setFont(Font font)
```
Sets the font for this text field.

JToggleButton (javax.swing)

A public class, derived from `AbstractButton` and implementing `Accessible`, that represents a two-state button.

constructors

```
public JToggleButton()
public JToggleButton(String text)
public JToggleButton(String text, boolean selected)
public JToggleButton(Icon icon)
```

```
public JToggleButton(Icon icon, boolean selected)
public JToggleButton(String text, Icon icon)
public JToggleButton(String text, Icon icon, boolean selected)
```
Creates a toggle button with the specified string, icon, and selection state.

JToolTip (javax.swing)

A public class, derived from JComponent and implementing Accessible, that represents a text tip that is displayed when the mouse cursor rests momentarily over a GUI component.

constructors

```
public JToolTip()
```
Creates a tool tip.

methods

```
public JComponent getComponent()
public void setComponent(JComponent comp)
```
Gets or sets the component to which this tool tip applies.
```
public String getTipText()
public void setTipText(String text)
```
Gets or sets the text shown when this tool tip is displayed.

KeyAdapter (java.awt.event)

A public abstract class, derived from Object and implementing KeyListener, that permits derived classes to override the predefined no-op keyboard events.

constructors

```
public KeyAdapter()
```
Creates a new instance of a KeyAdapter.

methods

```
public void keyPressed(KeyEvent event)
public void keyReleased(KeyEvent event)
public void keyTyped(KeyEvent event)
```
Empty methods that should be overridden in order to implement event handling for keyboard events.

KeyEvent (java.awt.event)

A public class, derived from `InputEvent`, that represents an AWT keyboard event.

variables and constructs

```
public static final int VK_0
public static final int VK_1
public static final int VK_2
public static final int VK_3
public static final int VK_4
public static final int VK_5
public static final int VK_6
public static final int VK_7
public static final int VK_8
public static final int VK_9
```
   Constant values that represent the keyboard keys 0–9.

```
public static final int KEY_FIRST
public static final int KEY_LAST
```
   Constant values that represent the index of the first and last key event ids.

```
public static final int KEY_PRESSED
public static final int KEY_RELEASED
public static final int KEY_TYPED
```
   Constant values that represent the ids of a key being pressed, released, or typed.

```
public static final char CHAR_UNDEFINED
```
   A constant value that represents an event of a key press or release that does not correspond to a Unicode character.

```
public static final int VK_LEFT
public static final int VK_RIGHT
public static final int VK_UP
public static final int VK_DOWN
public static final int VK_HOME
public static final int VK_END
public static final int VK_PAGE_UP
public static final int VK_PAGE_DOWN
```
   Constant values that represent various keyboard directional keys.

```
public static final int VK_INSERT
```

```
public static final int VK_DELETE
```
Constant values that represent various keyboard editing control keys.
```
public static final int VK_NUMPAD0
public static final int VK_NUMPAD1
public static final int VK_NUMPAD2
public static final int VK_NUMPAD3
public static final int VK_NUMPAD4
public static final int VK_NUMPAD5
public static final int VK_NUMPAD6
public static final int VK_NUMPAD7
public static final int VK_NUMPAD8
public static final int VK_NUMPAD9
public static final int VK_ADD
public static final int VK_SUBTRACT
public static final int VK_MULTIPLY
public static final int VK_DIVIDE
public static final int VK_ENTER
public static final int VK_DECIMAL
```
Constant values that represent various keyboard number pad keys.
```
public static final int VK_PERIOD
public static final int VK_EQUALS
public static final int VK_OPEN_BRACKET
public static final int VK_CLOSE_BRACKET
public static final int VK_BACK_SLASH
public static final int VK_SLASH
public static final int VK_COMMA
public static final int VK_SEMICOLON
public static final int VK_SPACE
public static final int VK_BACK_SPACE
public static final int VK_QUOTE
public static final int VK_BACK_QUOTE
public static final int VK_TAB
public static final int VK_SLASH
```
Constant values that represent various keyboard character keys.
```
public static final int VK_PAUSE
public static final int VK_PRINTSCREEN
public static final int VK_SHIFT
```

```
public static final int VK_HELP
public static final int VK_CONTROL
public static final int VK_ALT
public static final int VK_ESCAPE
public static final int VK_META
public static final int VK_ACCEPT
public static final int VK_CANCEL
public static final int VK_CLEAR
public static final int VK_CONVERT
public static final int VK_NONCONVERT
public static final int VK_MODECHANGE
public static final int VK_SEPARATER
public static final int VK_KANA
public static final int VK_KANJI
public static final int VK_FINAL
```
Constant values that represent various keyboard command and control keys.
```
public static final int VK_UNDEFINED
```
A constant value for KEY_TYPED events for which there is no defined key value.
```
public static final int VK_F1
public static final int VK_F2
public static final int VK_F3
public static final int VK_F4
public static final int VK_F5
public static final int VK_F6
public static final int VK_F7
public static final int VK_F8
public static final int VK_F9
public static final int VK_F10
public static final int VK_F11
public static final int VK_F12
```
Constant values that represent the keyboard keys F1–F12.
```
public static final int VK_CAPS_LOCK
public static final int VK_NUM_LOCK
public static final int VK_SCROLL_LOCK
```
Constant values that represent various keyboard control keys.
```
public static final int VK_A
public static final int VK_B
```

```
public static final int VK_C
public static final int VK_D
public static final int VK_E
public static final int VK_F
public static final int VK_G
public static final int VK_H
public static final int VK_I
public static final int VK_J
public static final int VK_K
public static final int VK_L
public static final int VK_M
public static final int VK_N
public static final int VK_O
public static final int VK_P
public static final int VK_Q
public static final int VK_R
public static final int VK_S
public static final int VK_T
public static final int VK_U
public static final int VK_V
public static final int VK_W
public static final int VK_X
public static final int VK_Y
public static final int VK_Z
```
    Constant values that represent the keyboard keys A–Z.

constructors

```
public KeyEvent(Component src, int id, long when, int modifiers,
int keyCode)
public KeyEvent(Component src, int id, long when, int modifiers,
int keyCode, char keyChar)
```
    Creates a new instance of a KeyEvent from the specified source, having a specific type (id), time stamp, modifiers, key code, and/or key character.

methods

`public char getKeyChar()`

`public void setKeyChar(char character)`

Returns or sets the character associated with this `KeyEvent`. For events that have no corresponding character, a `CHAR_UNDEFINED` is returned.

`public int getKeyCode()`

`public void setKeyCode(int code)`

Returns or sets the code associated with this `KeyEvent`. For events that have no corresponding code, a `VK_UNDEFINED` is returned.

`public static String getKeyModifiersText(int mods)`

`public static String getKeyText(int keyCode)`

Returns a string representation of the `KeyEvent` modifiers key code (i.e., "Meta+Shift" or "F1").

`public boolean isActionKey()`

Returns a true value if this event is from an action key.

`public String paramString()`

Returns a string representation of the parameters of this event.

`public void setModifiers(int mods)`

Sets the key event modifiers for this event.

Locale (java.util)

A public class, derived from `Object` and implementing `Serializable` and `Cloneable`, that represents geographic-specific or political-specific information.

variables and constructs

`public static final Locale CANADA`

`public static final Locale CANADA_FRENCH`

`public static final Locale CHINA`

`public static final Locale FRANCE`

`public static final Locale GERMANY`

`public static final Locale ITALY`

`public static final Locale JAPAN`

`public static final Locale KOREA`

`public static final Locale PRC`

`public static final Locale TAIWAN`

`public static final Locale UK`

```
public static final Locale US
```
Constant values that represent locales based on countries.

```
public static final Locale CHINESE
public static final Locale ENGLISH
public static final Locale FRENCH
public static final Locale GERMAN
public static final Locale ITALIAN
public static final Locale JAPANESE
public static final Locale KOREAN
public static final Locale SIMPLIFIED_CHINESE
public static final Locale TRADITIONAL_CHINESE
```
Constant values that represent locales based on languages.

constructors

```
public Locale(String lang, String country)
public Locale(String lang, String country, String var)
```
Creates a new locale from the specified two-character ISO codes for a language and country. A computer and browser variant of a locale can also be included. These usually take the form of WIN for Windows or MAC for Macintosh.

methods

```
public Object clone()
```
Returns a copy of this locale.

```
public boolean equals(Object arg)
```
Returns a true value if this locale is equal to arg.

```
public String getCountry()
public String getLanguage()
public String getVariant()
```
Returns the character code for the name of this locale's country, language, or variant.

```
public static synchronized Locale getDefault()
public static synchronized void setDefault(Locale locale)
```
Returns or sets the default locale.

```
public final String getDisplayCountry()
public String getDisplayCountry(Locale displaylocale)
```
Returns the display version of the country name for this locale in either the specified or default locales.

```
public final String getDisplayLanguage()
```
```
public String getDisplayLanguage(Locale displaylocale)
```
Returns the display version of the language name for this locale in either the specified or default locales.

```
public final String getDisplayName()
```
```
public String getDisplayName(Locale displaylocale)
```
Returns the display version of the name for this locale in either the specified or default locales.

```
public final String getDisplayVariant()
```
```
public String getDisplayVariant(Locale displaylocale)
```
Returns the display version of the variant for this locale in either the specified or default locales.

```
public String getISO3Country() throws MissingResourceException
```
```
public String getISO3Language() throws MissingResourceException
```
Returns the three-character ISO abbreviation for the country or language for this locale.

```
hashCode()
```
Returns the hash code for this locale.

```
toString()
```
Returns a string representation of this locale.

Long (java.lang)

A public final class, derived from Number, that contains long integer math operations, constants, and methods to compute minimum and maximum numbers, and string manipulation routines related to the primitive long type.

variables and constructs

```
public final static long MAX_VALUE
```
```
public final static long MIN_VALUE
```
Constant values that contain the maximum possible value (9223372036854775807L) or minimum possible value (–9223372036854775808L) of a long in Java.

```
public final static Class TYPE
```
The Integer constant value of the integer type class.

constructors

```
public Long(long num)
public Long(String num) throws NumberFormatException
```
Creates an instance of the Long class from the parameter num.

methods

```
public byte byteValue()
public double doubleValue()
public float floatValue()
public int intValue()
public long longValue()
public short shortValue()
```
Returns the value of this Long as a Java primitive type.

```
public boolean equals(Object arg)
```
Returns the result of the equality comparison between this Long and the parameter arg.

```
public static Long getLong(String prop)
public static Long getLong(String prop, long num)
public static Long getLong(String prop, long num)
```
Returns a Long representation of the system property named in prop. If there is no property corresponding to prop, or the format of its value is incorrect, then the default num is returned.

```
public int hashCode()
```
Returns a hash code for this Long.

```
public static long parseLong(String str) throws
NumberFormatException
public static long parseLong(String str, int base) throws
NumberFormatException
```
Evaluates the string str and returns the long equivalent in radix base.

```
public static String toBinaryString(long num)
public static String toHexString(long num)
public static String toOctalString(long num)
```
Returns the string representation of parameter num in base 2 (binary), 8 (octal), or 16 (hexadecimal).

```
public String toString()
public static String toString(long num)
```

```
public static String toString(long num, int base)
```
Returns the string representation of this `long` or num in base 10 (decimal). The radix of the returned number can also be specified in `base`.

```
public static Long valueOf(String str) throws
NumberFormatException
```

```
public static Long valueOf(String str, int base) throws
NumberFormatException
```
Returns a `Long` initialized to the value of `str` in radix `base`.

Math (java.lang)

A public final class, derived from `Object`, that contains integer and floating point constants, and methods to perform various math operations, compute minimum and maximum numbers, and generate random numbers.

variables and constructs

```
public final static double E
```
```
public final static double PI
```
Constant values that contain the natural base of logarithms (2.7182818284590452354) and the ratio of the circumference of a circle to its diameter (3.14159265358979323846).

methods

```
public static double abs(double num)
```
```
public static float abs(float num)
```
```
public static int abs(int num)
```
```
public static long abs(long num)
```
Returns the absolute value of the specified parameter.

```
public static double acos(double num)
```
```
public static double asin(double num)
```
```
public static double atan(double num)
```
Returns the arc cosine, arc sine, or arc tangent of parameter num as a double.

```
public static double atan2(double x, double y)
```
Returns the component e of the polar coordinate {r, e} that corresponds to the cartesian coordinate <x, y>.

```
public static double ceil(double num)
```
Returns the smallest integer value that is not less than the argument num.

```
public static double cos(double angle)
```

```
public static double sin(double angle)
public static double tan(double angle)
```
Returns the cosine, sine, or tangent of parameter angle measured in radians.

```
public static double exp(double num)
```
Returns *e* to the num, where *e* is the base of natural logarithms.

```
public static double floor(double num)
```
Returns a double that is the largest integer value that is not greater than the parameter num.

```
public static double IEEEremainder(double arg1, double arg2)
```
Returns the mathematical remainder between arg1 and arg2 as defined by IEEE 754.

```
public static double log(double num) throws ArithmeticException
```
Returns the natural logarithm of parameter num.

```
public static double max(double num1, double num2)
public static float max(float num1, float num2)
public static int max(int num1, int num2)
public static long max(long num1, long num2)
```
Returns the larger of parameters num1 and num2.

```
public static double min(double num1, double num2)
public static float min(float num1, float num2)
public static int min(int num1, int num2)
public static long min(long num1, long num2)
```
Returns the minimum value of parameters num1 and num2.

```
public static double pow(double num1, double num2) throws
ArithmeticException
```
Returns the result of num1 to num2.

```
public static double random()
```
Returns a random number between 0.0 and 1.0.

```
public static double rint(double num)
```
Returns the closest integer to parameter num.

```
public static long round(double num)
public static int round(float num)
```
Returns the closest long or int to parameter num.

```
public static double sqrt(double num) throws ArithmeticException
```
Returns the square root of parameter num.

MessageFormat (java.text)

A public class, derived from `Format`, that is used to build formatted message strings.

constructors

`public MessageFormat(String str)`

Creates a new instance of a `MessageFormat` from the specified string pattern.

methods

`public void applyPattern(String str)`

`public String toPattern()`

Sets and returns the pattern for this `MessageFormat`.

`public Object clone()`

Returns a copy of this `MessageFormat`.

`public boolean equals(Object arg)`

Returns a true value if this `MessageFormat` is equal to arg.

`public final StringBuffer format(Object src, StringBuffer dest, FieldPosition ignore)`

`public final StringBuffer format(Object[] src, StringBuffer dest, FieldPosition ignore)`

Formats the specified source object with this `MessageFormat`, placing the result in dest. This method returns the value of the destination buffer.

`public static String format(String str, Object[] args)`

Formats the given string applying specified arguments. This method allows for message formatting with the creation of a `MessageFormat`.

`public Format[] getFormats()`

`public void setFormats(Format[] newFormats)`

Returns and sets the formats for this `MessageFormat`.

`public Locale getLocale()`

`public void setLocale(Locale locale)`

Returns and sets the locale for this `MessageFormat`.

`public int hashCode()`

Returns the hash code for this `MessageFormat`.

`public Object[] parse(String src) throws ParseException`

`public Object[] parse(String src, ParsePosition pos)`

Parses the string source (starting at position pos, or 0 by default), returning its objects.

```
public Object parseObject(String src, ParsePosition pos)
```
Parses the string source (starting at position pos, or 0 by default), returning one object.

```
public void setFormat(int var, Format fmt)
```
Sets an individual format at index var.

MouseAdapter (java.awt.event)

A public abstract class, derived from Object and implementing MouseListener, that permits derived classes to override the predefined no-op mouse events.

constructors

```
public MouseAdapter()
```
Creates a new instance of a MouseAdapter.

methods

```
public void mouseClicked(MouseEvent event)
public void mouseEntered(MouseEvent event)
public void mouseExited(MouseEvent event)
public void mousePressed(MouseEvent event)
public void mouseReleased(MouseEvent event)
```
Empty methods that should be overridden in order to implement event handling for mouse events.

MouseEvent (java.awt.event)

A public class, derived from InputEvent, that represents events triggered by the mouse.

variables and constructs

```
public static final int MOUSE_CLICKED
public static final int MOUSE_DRAGGED
public static final int MOUSE_ENTERED
public static final int MOUSE_EXITED
public static final int MOUSE_MOVED
public static final int MOUSE_PRESSED
```

```
public static final int MOUSE_RELEASED
```
Constant values that represent a variety of mouse events.

```
public static final int MOUSE_FIRST
```
```
public static final int MOUSE_LAST
```
Constant values that represent the index of the first and last mouse event ids.

constructors

```
public MouseEvent(Component src, int type, long timestamp, int
mods, int x, int y, int clickCount, boolean popupTrigger)
```
Creates a new instance of a `MouseEvent` from a given source, with a specified type, timestamp, keyboard modifiers, *x* and *y* locations, number of clicks, and a state value, if this event triggers a popup menu.

methods

```
public int getClickCount()
```
Returns the number of mouse clicks in this event.

```
public Point getPoint()
```
Returns the point location of this event, relative to the source component's space.

```
public int getX()
```
```
public int getY()
```
Returns the *x* or *y* location of this event, relative to the source component's space.

```
public boolean isPopupTrigger()
```
Returns a true value if this event is a trigger for popup menus.

```
public String paramString()
```
Returns a string representation of the parameters of this `MouseEvent`.

```
public synchronized void translatePoint(int xoffset, int
yoffset)
```
Offsets the *x* and *y* locations of this event by the specified amounts.

MouseMotionAdapter (java.awt.event)

A public abstract class, derived from `Object` and implementing `MouseMotionListener`, that permits a derived class to override the predefined no-op mouse motion events.

constructors

`public MouseMotionAdapter()`
Creates a new instance of a `MouseMotionAdapter`.

methods

`public void mouseDragged(MouseEvent event)`
`public void mouseMoved(MouseEvent event)`
Empty methods that should be overridden in order to implement event handling for mouse motion events.

Number (java.lang)

A public abstract class, derived from `Object` and implementing `Serializable`, that is the parent class to the wrapper classes `Byte`, `Double`, `Integer`, `Float`, `Long`, and `Short`.

constructors

`public Number()`
Creates a new instance of a `Number`.

methods

`public byte byteValue()`
`public abstract double doubleValue()`
`public abstract float floatValue()`
`public abstract int intValue()`
`public abstract long longValue()`
`public short shortValue()`
Returns the value of this `Number` as a Java primitive type.

NumberFormat (java.text)

A public abstract class, derived from `Format` and implementing `Cloneable`, that is used to convert number objects to locale-specific strings, and vice versa.

variables and constructs

```
public static final int FRACTION_FIELD
public static final int INTEGER_FIELD
```
Constant values that indicate field locations in a `NumberFormat`.

constructors

```
public NumberFormat()
```
Creates a new instance of a `NumberFormat`.

methods

```
public Object clone()
```
Returns a copy of this `NumberFormat`.

```
public boolean equals(Object arg)
```
Returns a true value if this `NumberFormat` is equal to `arg`.

```
public final String format(double num)
public final String format(long num)
```
Formats the specified Java primitive type according to this `NumberFormat`, returning a string.

```
public abstract StringBuffer format(double num, StringBuffer
dest,FieldPosition pos)
```
```
public abstract StringBuffer format(long num, StringBuffer dest,
FieldPosition pos)
```
```
public final StringBuffer format(Object num, StringBuffer dest,
FieldPosition pos)
```
Formats the specified Java primitive type (or object) starting at `pos`, according to this `NumberFormat`, placing the resulting string in the specified destination buffer. This method returns the value of the string buffer.

```
public static Locale[] getAvailableLocales()
```
Returns the available locales.

```
public static final NumberFormat getCurrencyInstance()
public static NumberFormat getCurrencyInstance(Locale locale)
```
Returns the `NumberFormat` for currency for the default or specified locale.

```
public static final NumberFormat getInstance()
public static NumberFormat getInstance(Locale locale)
```
Returns the default number format for the default or specified locale.

```
public int getMaximumFractionDigits()
```

```
public void setMaximumFractionDigits(int val)
```
Returns or sets the maximum number of fractional digits allowed in this `NumberFormat`.

```
public int getMaximumIntegerDigits()
```

```
public void setMaximumIntegerDigits(int val)
```
Returns or sets the maximum number of integer digits allowed in this `NumberFormat`.

```
public int getMinimumFractionDigits()
```

```
public void setMinimumFractionDigits(int val)
```
Returns or sets the minimum number of fractional digits allowed in this `NumberFormat`.

```
public int getMinimumIntegerDigits()
```

```
public void setMinimumIntegerDigits(int val)
```
Returns or sets the minimum number of integer digits allowed in this `NumberFormat`.

```
public static final NumberFormat getNumberInstance()
```

```
public static NumberFormat getNumberInstance(Locale locale)
```
Returns the `NumberFormat` for numbers for the default or specified locale.

```
public static final NumberFormat getPercentInstance()
```

```
public static NumberFormat getPercentInstance(Locale locale)
```
Returns the `NumberFormat` for percentages for the default or specified locale.

```
public int hashCode()
```
Returns the hash code for this `NumberFormat`.

```
public boolean isGroupingUsed()
```

```
public void setGroupingUsed(boolean toggle)
```
Returns or sets the toggle flag for the use of the grouping indicator by this `NumberFormat`.

```
public boolean isParseIntegerOnly()
```

```
public void setParseIntegerOnly(boolean toggle)
```
Returns or sets the toggle flag for the use of parsing numbers as integers only by this `NumberFormat`.

```
public Number parse(String str) throws ParseException
```
Parses the specified string as a number.

```
public abstract Number parse(String str, ParsePosition pos)
```

```
public final Object parseObject(String str, ParsePosition pos)
```
Parses the specified string as a long (if possible) or double, starting a position pos. Returns a number or an object.

Object (java.lang)

A public class that is the root of the hierarchy tree for all classes in Java.

constructors

`public Object()`

Creates a new instance of the object class.

methods

`protected Object clone() throws OutOfMemoryError, CloneNotSupportedException`

Returns an exact copy of the current object.

`public boolean equals(Object arg)`

Returns a true value if the current object is equal to `arg`.

`protected void finalize() throws Throwable`

The `finalize` method is called as the object is being destroyed.

`public final Class getClass()`

Returns the class of the current object.

`public int hashCode()`

Returns a hash code for the current object.

`public final void notify() throws IllegalMonitorStateException`

`public final void notifyAll() throws IllegalMonitorStateException`

Informs a paused thread that it may resume execution. `notifyAll` informs all paused threads.

`public String toString()`

Returns a string representation of the current object.

`public final void wait() throws IllegalMonitorStateException, InterruptedException`

`public final void wait(long msec) throws IllegalMonitorStateException, InterruptedException`

`public final void wait(long msec, int nsec) throws IllegalMonitorStateException, InterruptedException, IllegalArgumentException)`

Causes a thread to suspend execution for `msec` milliseconds and `nsec` nanoseconds. The `wait()` method (without parameters) causes a thread to suspend execution until further notice.

ParsePosition (java.text)

A public class, derived from Object, that is used to track the position of the index during parsing. This class is generally used by the Format class (and its subclasses).

constructors

```
public ParsePosition(int index)
```
   Creates a new instance of a ParsePosition from the specified index.

methods

```
public int getIndex()
public void setIndex(int num)
```
   Returns or sets the parse position.

Point (java.awt)

A public class, derived from Object and implementing Serializable, that defines and manipulates a location on a two-dimensional coordinate system.

variables and constructs

```
public int x
public int y
```
   The x and y locations of this point.

constructors

```
public Point()
public Point(Point pt)
public Point(int x, int y)
```
   Creates a new instance of a Point from the specified coordinates, the specified point, or using <0, 0> by default.

methods

```
public boolean equals(Object arg)
```
   Returns a true value if this point is identical to arg.
```
public Point getLocation()
public void move(int x, int y)
```

```
public void setLocation(Point pt)
public void setLocation(int x, int y)
```
Returns or relocates the position of this point.
```
public int hashCode()
```
Returns the hash code of this point.
```
public String toString()
```
Returns a string representation of this point.
```
public void translate(int xoffset, int yoffset)
```
Relocates this point to <x+xoffset, y+yoffset>.

Polygon (java.awt)

A public class, derived from Object and implementing Shape and Serializable, that maintains a list of points that define a polygon shape.

variables and constructs

```
protected Rectangle bounds
```
The bounds of this polygon.
```
public int npoints
```
The total number of points of this polygon.
```
public int xpoints[]
public int ypoints[]
```
The arrays of x and y locations for the points of this polygon.

constructors

```
public Polygon()
public Polygon(int[] x, int[] y, int np)
```
Creates a new instance of a polygon, initially defined by the arrays of x and y locations <x, y> and comprised of np points. The default constructor creates a new polygon that contains no points.

methods

```
public void addPoint(int newx, int newy)
```
Adds the point located at <newx, newy> to this polygon.
```
public boolean contains(int x, int y)
public boolean contains(Point pt)
```
Returns a true value if this polygon contains the specified point.

```
public Rectangle getBounds()
```
Returns the bonds of this polygon.
```
public void translate(int xoffset, int yoffset)
```
Relocates all of the x and y points of this polygon by xoffset and yoffset.

PrintStream (java.io)

A public class, derived from FilterOutputStream, that provides methods to print data types in a format other than byte-based.

constructors

```
public PrintStream(OutputStream out)
public PrintStream(OutputStream out, boolean autoflush)
```
Creates a new instance of a PrintStream on out. If the autoflush value is set to true, then the output buffer is flushed at every occurrence of a newline.

methods

```
public boolean checkError()
```
Flushes this print stream's buffer and returns a true value if an error occurred.
```
public void close()
```
Closes this print stream.
```
public void flush()
```
Flushes this print stream's buffer.
```
public void print(boolean b)
public void print(char c)
public void print(char[] s)
public void print(double d)
public void print(float f)
public void print(int i)
public void print(long l)
public void print(Object obj)
public void print(String s)
public void println()
public void println(boolean b)
public void println(char c)
public void println(char[] s)
public void println(double d)
```

```
public void println(float f)
public void println(int i)
public void println(long l)
public void println(Object obj)
public void println(String s)
```
Prints the specified Java primitive type, Object, or blank line to this print stream. When using a character, only the lower byte is printed.
```
public void write(int b)
public void write(byte[] b, int off, int len)
```
Writes a byte or len bytes from the array b, starting at index off to this print stream.

Random (java.util)

A public class, derived from Object and implementing Serializable, that produces sequences of pseudo-random numbers.

constructors

```
public Random()
public Random(long rnd)
```
Creates a new instance of a random class using the value of rnd as the random number seed. When the default constructor is used, the current time in milliseconds is the seed.

methods

```
protected int next(int b)
```
Returns the next random number (from the specified number of bits).
```
public void nextBytes(byte[] b)
```
Generates an array of random bytes as defined by b[ ].
```
public double nextDouble()
public float nextFloat()
```
Returns a random number between 0.0 and 1.0 in the specified primitive type.
```
public int nextInt()
public long nextLong()
```
Returns a random integer value from all possible int or long values (positive and negative).

```
public double nextGaussian()
```
Returns a Gaussian double random number with a mean value of 0.0 and a standard deviation of 1.0.

```
public void setSeed(long rnd)
```
Sets the seeds for this random number generator to `rnd`.

Rectangle (java.awt)

A public class, derived from `Object` and implementing `Shape` and `Serializable`, that represents a rectangular shape that is described by an `x` and `y` location, and a width and height.

variables and constructs

```
public int height
```
```
public int width
```
The `height` and `width` of this rectangle.

```
public int x
```
```
public int y
```
The `x` and `y` locations of the upper-left corner of this rectangle.

constructors

```
public Rectangle()
```
```
public Rectangle(Dimension dim)
```
```
public Rectangle(Point pt)
```
Creates a new instance of a `Rectangle` with an initial location of the corresponding values of `pt` or `dim`, with a height of 0 and width of 0. If neither `pt` nor `dim` are specified, then the initial location is <0, 0> and the height and width are set to 0.

```
public Rectangle(Rectangle rect)
```
```
public Rectangle(Point pt, Dimension dim)
```
Creates a new instance of a `Rectangle` with initial location and size values the same as corresponding values in `rect`, or with an initial location of the corresponding values of `pt`, and with a width and height corresponding to the values of `dim`.

```
public Rectangle(int width, int height)
```
```
public Rectangle(int x, int y, int width, int height)
```
Creates a new instance of a `Rectangle` with an initial location of <x, y> (or <0, 0> by default), and with a `height` and `width`.

methods

```
public void add(int x, int y)
```
```
public void add(Point point)
```
```
public void add(Rectangle rect)
```
Adds the specified point in space, defined by coordinates, a point, or the initial location of the specified Rectangle, to this Rectangle. This method may expand the Rectangle (if the point lies outside) or reduce the Rectangle (if the point lies inside).

```
public boolean contains(int x, int y)
```
```
public boolean contains(Point pt)
```
Returns a true value if this Rectangle contains the specified point.

```
public boolean equals(Object rect2)
```
Returns a true value if this Rectangle and the rectangle rect2 are identical.

```
public Rectangle getBounds()
```
Returns the bounds of this Rectangle.

```
public Point getLocation()
```
```
public Dimension getSize()
```
Returns the location or size of this Rectangle.

```
public void grow(int width, int height)
```
Increases this Rectangle by height and width pixels.

```
public int hashCode()
```
Returns the hash code for this Rectangle.

```
public Rectangle intersection(Rectangle rect2)
```
Returns the intersection of this Rectangle and the specified rectangle (rect2).

```
public boolean intersects(Rectangle rect2)
```
Returns a true value if this Rectangle intersects rect2.

```
public boolean isEmpty()
```
Returns a true value if this Rectangle is empty (height and width <= 0).

```
public void setBounds(int x, int y, int width, int height)
```
```
public void setBounds(Rectangle rect)
```
Resets the x and y locations, width and height of this rectangle to the respective values of rect or the specified values of x, y, width, and height.

```
public void setLocation(int x, int y)
```
```
public void setLocation(Point pt)
```
Resets the location of this Rectangle to the specified point.

```
public void setSize(Dimension dim)
```
```
public void setSize(int width, int height)
```
Resets the size to width and height, or the corresponding values of dim.

```
public String toString()
```
Returns a string representation of this Rectangle.

```
public void translate(int width, int height)
```
Adds the specified width and height to this Rectangle's width and height values.

```
public Rectangle union(Rectangle rect2)
```
Returns the union of this Rectangle and rect2.

Short (java.lang)

A public class, derived from Number, that contains integer math operations, constants, and methods to compute minimum and maximum numbers, and string manipulation routines related to the primitive short type.

variables and constructs

```
public final static short MAX_VALUE
```
```
public final static short MIN_VALUE
```
A constant value that contains the maximum possible value (32767) or minimum possible value (–32768) of an integer in Java.

```
public final static Class TYPE
```
The Short constant value of the short type class.

constructors

```
public Short(short num)
```
```
public Short(String num) throws NumberFormatException
```
Creates a new instance of a Short from the specified num.

methods

```
public byte byteValue()
```
```
public double doubleValue()
```
```
public float floatValue()
```
```
public int intValue()
```
```
public long longValue()
```
```
public short shortValue()
```
Returns the value of this Short as a Java primitive type.

```
public static Short decode(String str) throws
NumberFormatException
```
Returns the short representation of the coded argument (str). The argument can be coded in decimal, hexadecimal, or octal formats.

```
public boolean equals(Object arg)
```
Returns a true value if this Short is equal to the parameter arg.

```
public int hashCode()
```
Returns the hash code for this Short.

```
public static short parseShort(String str) throws
NumberFormatException
```

```
public static short parseShort(String str, int base) throws
NumberFormatException
```
Returns the string argument (str) as a short in base 10. The radix of the returned number can be specified in base.

```
public static String toString(short num)
```

```
public String toString()
```
Returns a string representation of this Short or num.

```
public static Short valueOf(String str) throws
NumberFormatException
```

```
public static Short valueOf(String str, int base) throws
NumberFormatException
```
Returns an instance of a new Short object initialized to the value specified in str. The radix of the returned number can be specified in base.

SimpleDateFormat (java.text)

A public class, derived from DateFormat, that allows for the parsing of dates to locale-based strings, and vice versa.

constructors

```
public SimpleDateFormat()
```

```
public SimpleDateFormat(String str)
```

```
public SimpleDateFormat(String str, Locale locale)
```
Creates a new instance of a SimpleDateFormat using the specified or default pattern and the specified or default locale.

```
public SimpleDateFormat(String str, DateFormatSymbols format)
```
Creates a new instance of a SimpleDateFormat using the specified pattern and format data.

methods

```
public void applyLocalizedPattern(String str)
```
```
public String toLocalizedPattern()
```
Sets or returns the locale-based string that describes this `SimpleDateFormat`.

```
public void applyPattern(String str)
```
```
public String toPattern()
```
Sets or returns the non-locale-based string that describes this `SimpleDateFormat`.

```
public Object clone()
```
Returns a copy of this `SimpleDateFormat`.

```
public boolean equals(Object arg)
```
Returns a true value if this `SimpleDateFormat` is equal to arg.

```
public StringBuffer format(Date date, StringBuffer dest,
FieldPosition pos)
```
Formats the specified string, starting at field pos, placing the result in the specified destination buffer. This method returns the value of the buffer.

```
public DateFormatSymbols getDateFormatSymbols()
```
```
public void setDateFormatSymbols(DateFormatSymbols symbols)
```
Returns or sets the date/time formatting symbols for this `SimpleDateFormat`.

```
public int hashCode()
```
Returns the hash code for this `SimpleDateFormat`.

```
public Date parse(String str, ParsePosition pos)
```
Parses the specified string, starting at position pos, and returns a `Date` object.

SimpleTimeZone (java.util)

A public class, derived from `TimeZone`, that represents a time zone in a Gregorian calendar.

constructors

```
public SimpleTimeZone(int offset, String id)
```

`public SimpleTimeZone(int offset, String id, int stMonth, int stNthDayWeekInMonth, int stDayOfWeek, int stTime, int endMonth, int endNthDayWeekInMonth, int endDayOfWeek, int endTime)`

Creates a new `SimpleTimeZone` from an offset from GMT and a time zone id. The id should be obtained from the `TimeZone.getAvailableIDs` method. You can also define the starting and ending times for daylight savings time. Each period has a starting and ending month (`stMonth`, `endMonth`), day of the week in a month (`stNthDayWeekInMonth`, `endNthDayWeekInMonth`), day of the week (`stDayOfWeek`, `endDayOfWeek`), and time (`stTime`, `endTime`).

methods

`public Object clone()`

Returns a copy of this `SimpleTimeZone`.

`public boolean equals(Object arg)`

Returns a true value if this `SimpleTimeZone` is equal to arg.

`public int getOffset(int era, int year, int month, int day, int dayOfWeek, int millisec)`

Returns the offset from the Greenwich Mean Time (GMT), taking into account daylight savings time.

`public int getRawOffset()`
`public void setRawOffset(int millisec)`

Returns or sets the offset from Greenwich Mean Time (GMT) for this `SimpleTimeZone`. These methods do not take daylight savings time into account.

`public synchronized int hashCode()`

Returns the hash code for this `SimpleTimeZone`.

`public boolean inDaylightTime(Date dt)`

Returns a true value if the specified date falls within daylight savings time.

`public void setEndRule(int month, int dyWkInMo, int dyWk, int tm)`
`public void setStartRule(int month, int dyWkInMo, int dyWk, int tm)`

Sets the starting and ending times for daylight savings time for this `SimpleTimeZone` to a specified month, day of a week in a month, day of a week, and time (in milliseconds).

`public void setStartYear(int year)`

Sets the daylight savings starting year for this `SimpleTimeZone`.

`public boolean useDaylightTime()`

Returns a true value if this `SimpleTimeZone` uses daylight savings time.

Stack (java.util)

A public class, derived from `Vector`, that represents a last-in-first-out stack.

constructors

`public Stack()`
   Creates a new instance of an empty stack.

methods

`public boolean empty()`
   Returns a true value if this stack contains no elements.

`public Object peek() throws EmptyStackException`
   Returns the item on the top of the stack, but does not remove it.

`public Object pop() throws EmptyStackException`

`public Object push(Object obj)`
   Returns and removes the item on the top of the stack (pop) or pushes a new item onto the stack (push).

`public int search(Object obj)`
   Returns the relative position of item `obj` from the top of the stack, or −1 if the item is not in this stack.

String (java.lang)

A public final class, derived from `Object` and implementing `Serializable`, that contains methods for creating and parsing strings. Because the contents of a string cannot be modified, many of the methods return a new string.

constructors

`public String()`

`public String(byte[] arg)`

`public String(byte[] arg, int index, int count)`

`public String(byte[] arg, String code) throws UnsupportedEncodingException`

```
public String(byte[] arg, int index, int count, String code)
throws UnsupportedEncodingException
```

Creates a new instance of the String class from the array arg. The parameter index indicates which element of arg is the first character of the resulting string, and the parameter count is the number of characters to add to the new string. The String() method creates a new string of no characters. The characters are converted using code encoding format.

```
public String(char[] chars)
```

```
public String(char[] chars, int index, int count) throws
StringIndexOutOfBoundsException
```

Creates an instance of the String class from the array chars. The parameter index indicates which element of chars is the first character of the resulting string, and the parameter count is the number of characters to add to the new string.

```
public String(String str)
```

```
public String(StringBuffer str)
```

Creates an instance of the String class from the parameter str.

methods

```
public char charAt(int idx) throws
StringIndexOutOfBoundsException
```

Returns the character at index idx in the current object. The first character of the source string is at index 0.

```
public int compareTo(String str)
```

Compares the current object to str. If both strings are equal, 0 (zero) is returned. If the current string is lexicographically less than the argument, an int less than zero is returned. If the current string is lexicographically greater than the argument, an int greater than zero is returned.

```
public String concat(String source)
```

Returns the product of the concatenation of argument source to the end of the current object.

```
public static String copyValueOf(char[] arg)
```

```
public static String copyValueOf(char[] arg, int index, int
count)
```

Returns a new String that contains the characters of arg, beginning at index index, and of length count.

```
public boolean endsWith(String suff)
```
Returns true if the current object ends with the specified suffix.
```
public boolean equals(Object arg)
```
```
public boolean equalsIgnoreCase(String arg)
```
Returns true if the current object is equal to arg. arg must not be null, and must be of exact length and content as the current object. equalsIgnoreCase disregards the case of the characters.
```
public byte[] getBytes()
```
```
public byte[] getBytes(String enc) throws
UnsupportedEncodingException
```
Returns the contents of the current object in an array of bytes decoded with enc. When a decoding format is not present, the platform default it used.
```
public void getChars(int start, int end, char[] dest, int
destStart)
```
Copies the contents of the current object starting at index start and ending at end into the character array dest starting at index destStart.
```
public int hashCode()
```
Returns the hash code of the current object.
```
public int indexOf(char c)
```
```
public int indexOf(char c, int index)
```
Returns the index of the first occurrence of the character c in the current object not less than index (default of 0). Returns a −1 if there is no such occurrence.
```
public int indexOf(String str)
```
```
public int indexOf(String str, int index)
```
Returns the index of the first occurrence of the string str in the current object not less than index (default of 0). Returns a −1 if there is no such occurrence.
```
public String intern()
```
Creates a new canonical string with identical content to this string.
```
public int lastIndexOf(char c)
```
```
public int lastIndexOf(char c, int index)
```
Returns the index of the last occurrence of the character c in the current object not less than index (default of 0). Returns a −1 if there is no such occurrence.
```
public int lastIndexOf(String str)
```
```
public int lastIndexOf(String str, int index)
```
Returns the index of the last occurrence of the string str in the current object not less than index (default of 0). Returns a −1 if there is no such occurrence.
```
public int length()
```
Returns the integer length of the current object.

```
public boolean regionMatches(boolean case, int cindex, String
str, int strindex, int size)
public boolean regionMatches(int cindex, String str, int
strindex, int size)
```

Returns a true result if the subregion of parameter str starting at index strindex and having length size, is identical to a substring of the current object starting at index cindex and having the same length. If case is true, then character case is ignored during the comparisons.

```
public String replace(char oldC, char newC)
```

Returns a new string with all occurrences of the oldC replaced with the newC.

```
public boolean startsWith(String str)
public boolean startsWith(String str, int index)
```

Returns a true if the current object starts with the string str at location index (default of 0).

```
public String substring(int startindex) throws
StringIndexOutOfBoundsException
public String substring(int startindex, int lastindex) throws
StringIndexOutOfBoundsException
```

Returns the substring of the current object starting with startindex and ending with lastindex-1 (or the last index of the string in the case of the first method).

```
public char[] toCharArray()
public String toString()
```

Returns the current object as an array of characters or a string. Is present due to the automatic use of the toString method in output routines.

```
public String toLowerCase()
public String toLowerCase(Locale loc)
```

Returns the current object with each character in lowercase, taking into account variations of the specified locale (loc).

```
public String toUpperCase()
public String toUpperCase(Locale loc)
```

Returns the current object with each character in uppercase, taking into account variations of the specified locale (loc).

```
public String trim()
```

Returns the current object with leading and trailing white space removed.

```
public static String valueOf(boolean arg)
public static String valueOf(char arg)
public static String valueOf(char[] arg)
public static String valueOf(char[] arg, int index, int size)
```

```
public static String valueOf(double arg)
public static String valueOf(float arg)
public static String valueOf(int arg)
public static String valueOf(long arg)
public static String valueOf(Object arg)
```
Returns a string representation of the parameter `arg`. A starting `index` and specified `size` are permitted.

StringBuffer (java.lang)

A public class, derived from `Object` and implementing `Serializable`, that contains methods for creating, parsing, and modifying string buffers. Unlike a `String`, the content and length of a `StringBuffer` can be changed dynamically.

constructors

```
public StringBuffer()
public StringBuffer(int size) throws NegativeArraySizeException
```
Creates an instance of the `StringBuffer` class that is empty but has an initial capacity of `size` characters (16 by default).
```
public StringBuffer(String arg)
```
Creates an instance of the `StringBuffer` class from the string `arg`.

methods

```
public StringBuffer append(boolean arg)
public StringBuffer append(char arg)
public StringBuffer append(char[] arg)
public StringBuffer append(char[] arg, int index, int size)
public StringBuffer append(double arg)
public StringBuffer append(float arg)
public StringBuffer append(int arg)
public StringBuffer append(long arg)
public StringBuffer append(Object arg)
public StringBuffer append(String arg)
```
Returns the current object with the `String` parameter `arg` appended to the end. A substring of a character array can be appended by specifying an `index` and `size`.

```
public int capacity()
```
Returns the capacity of this StringBuffer.

```
public char charAt(int idx) throws
StringIndexOutOfBoundsException
```
Returns the character at the specified index of this StringBuffer.

```
public void ensureCapacity(int min)
```
Sets the minimum capacity of this StringBuffer to be no less than min. The new capacity set by this method may actually be greater than min.

```
public void getChars(int start, int end, char[] dest, int
destindex) throws StringIndexOutOfBoundsException
```
Copies the characters at index start to end from this StringBuffer to dest, starting at index destindex.

```
public StringBuffer insert(int index, boolean arg) throws
StringIndexOutOfBoundsException
```
```
public StringBuffer insert(int index, char arg) throws
StringIndexOutOfBoundsException
```
```
public StringBuffer insert(int index, char[] arg) throws
StringIndexOutOfBoundsException
```
```
public StringBuffer insert(int index, double arg) throws
StringIndexOutOfBoundsException
```
```
public StringBuffer insert(int index, float arg) throws
StringIndexOutOfBoundsException
```
```
public StringBuffer insert(int index, int arg) throws
StringIndexOutOfBoundsException
```
```
public StringBuffer insert(int index, long arg) throws
StringIndexOutOfBoundsException
```
```
public StringBuffer insert(int index, Object arg) throws
StringIndexOutOfBoundsException
```
```
public StringBuffer insert(int index, String arg) throws
StringIndexOutOfBoundsException
```
Inserts the string representation of parameter arg into this StringBuffer at index index. Characters to the right of the specified index of this StringBuffer are shifted to the right.

```
public int length()
```
Returns the length of this StringBuffer.

```
public StringBuffer reverse()
```
Returns the value of this StringBuffer with the order of the characters reversed.

```
public void setCharAt(int idx, char c)
```
Sets the character at the specified index to c.

```
public void setLength(int size) throws
StringIndexOutOfBoundsException
```
Truncates this StringBuffer, if needed, to the new length of size.

```
public String toString()
```
Returns the String representation of this StringBuffer.

StringTokenizer (java.util)

A public class, derived from Object and implementing Enumeration, that manipulates string values into tokens separated by delimiter characters.

constructors

```
public StringTokenizer(String arg)
```

```
public StringTokenizer(String arg, String delims)
```

```
public StringTokenizer(String arg, String delims, boolean
tokens)
```
Creates a new instance of a StringTokenizer with the string initialized to arg, and utilizing the specified delimiters or the defaults (" \t\n\r": a space, tab, newline, and carriage return). If tokens is true, the delimiters are treated as words within the string and are subject to being returned as tokens.

methods

```
public int countTokens()
```
Returns the number of tokens present in this string tokenizer.

```
public boolean hasMoreElements()
```
```
public boolean hasMoreTokens()
```
Returns a true value if there are more tokens to be returned by this string tokenizer. hasMoreElements() is identical to hasMoreTokens() and is implemented to complete the implementation of the Enumerated interface.

```
public Object nextElement() throws NoSuchElementException
```
```
public String nextToken() throws NoSuchElementException
```
```
public String nextToken(String delims) throws
NoSuchElementException
```
Returns the next token in the string. nextElement() is identical to nextToken() and is implemented to complete the implementation of the Enumerated interface. New delimiters can be specified in the last method, and stay in effect until changed.

System (java.lang)

A public final class, derived from `Object`, that contains the standard input, output, and error streams, as well as various system related methods.

variables and constructs

`public static PrintStream err`

`public static InputStream in`

`public static PrintStream out`

Constant values that are the standard error output stream (stderr), standard input stream (stdin), and the standard output stream (stdout).

methods

`public static void arraycopy(Object source, int srcindex, Object dest, int destindex, int size) throws ArrayIndexOutOfBoundsException, ArrayStoreException`

Copies a subarray of `size` objects from source, starting at index `srcindex`, to dest starting at `destindex`.

`public static long currentTimeMillis()`

Returns the current system in milliseconds from midnight, January 1st, 1970 UTC.

`public static void exit(int num) throws SecurityException`

Exits the program with the status code of num.

`public static void gc()`

Executes the `gc` method of the `Runtime` class, which attempts to garbage collect any unused objects, freeing system memory.

`public static Properties getProperties() throws SecurityException`

`public static void setProperties(Properties newprops) throws SecurityException`

Returns or sets the current system properties.

`public static String getProperty(String name) throws SecurityException`

`public static String getProperty(String name, String default) throws SecurityException`

Returns the system property for name, or returns the value `default` as a default result if no such name exists.

`public static SecurityManager getSecurityManager()`

```
public static void setSecurityManager(SecurityManager mgr)
throws SecurityException
```
Returns or sets the security manager for the current application. If no security manager has been initialized, then a null value is returned by the `get` method.

```
public static int identityHashCode(Object arg)
```
Returns the hash code for the specified object. This will return the default hash code, in the event that the object's `hashCode` method has been overridden.

```
public static void load(String name) throws
UnsatisfiedLinkError, SecurityException
```
Loads name as a dynamic library.

```
public static void loadLibrary(String name) throws
UnsatisfiedLinkError, SecurityException
```
Loads name as a system library.

```
public static void runFinalization()
```
Requests that the Java Virtual Machine execute the finalize method on any outstanding objects.

```
public static void runFinalizersOnExit(boolean toggle)
```
Allows the execution of the finalizer methods for all objects, when `toggle` is true.

```
public static void setErr(PrintStream strm)
```
```
public static void setIn(InputStream strm)
```
```
public static void setOut(PrintStream strm)
```
Reassigns the error stream, input stream, or output stream to `strm`.

SystemColor (`java.awt`)

A public final class, derived from `Color` and implementing `Serializable`, that represents the current window system color for the current system. If the user changes the window system colors for this system and the window system can update the new color selection, these color values will change as well.

variables and constructs

```
public final static int ACTIVE_CAPTION
```
Constant index to the active caption color in the system color array.

```
public final static int ACTIVE_CAPTION_BORDER
```
```
public final static int ACTIVE_CAPTION_TEXT
```
Constant indices to the active caption border and text colors in the system color array.

```
public final static int CONTROL
```
Constant index to the control color in the system color array.

```
public final static int CONTROL_DK_SHADOW
```

```
public final static int CONTROL_SHADOW
```
Constant indices to the control shadow and control dark shadow colors in the system color array.

```
public final static int CONTROL_HIGHLIGHT
```

```
public final static int CONTROL_LT_HIGHLIGHT
```
Constant indices to the control highlight and light highlight colors in the system color array.

```
public final static int CONTROL_TEXT
```
Constant index to the control text color in the system color array.

```
public final static int DESKTOP
```
Constant index to the desktop color in the system color array.

```
public final static int INACTIVE_CAPTION
```
Constant index to the inactive caption color in the system color array.

```
public final static int INACTIVE_CAPTION_BORDER
```

```
public final static int INACTIVE_CAPTION_TEXT
```
Constant indices to the inactive caption border and text colors in the system color array.

```
public final static int INFO
```
Constant index to the information (help) text background color in the system color array.

```
public final static int INFO_TEXT
```

```
public final static int MENU_TEXT
```
Constant indices to the information (help) and menu text colors in the system color array.

```
public final static int NUM_COLORS
```
Constant value that holds the number of colors in the system color array.

```
public final static int SCROLLBAR
```
Constant index to the scrollbar background color in the system color array.

```
public final static int TEXT
```
Constant index to the background color of text components in the system color array.

```
public final static int TEXT_HIGHLIGHT
```

```
public final static int TEXT_HIGHLIGHT_TEXT
```
Constant indices to the background and text colors for highlighted text in the system color array.

```
public final static int TEXT_INACTIVE_TEXT
```
Constant index to the inactive text color in the system color array.
```
public final static int TEXT_TEXT
```
Constant index to the color of text components in the system color array.
```
public final static int WINDOW
```
Constant index to the background color of windows in the system color array.
```
public final static int WINDOW_BORDER
```
```
public final static int WINDOW_TEXT
```
Constant indices to the border and text colors of windows in the system color array.
```
public final static SystemColor activeCaption
```
The system's background color for window border captions.
```
public final static SystemColor activeCaptionBorder
```
```
public final static SystemColor activeCaptionText
```
The system's border and text colors for window border captions.
```
public final static SystemColor control
```
The system's color for window control objects.
```
public final static SystemColor controlDkShadow
```
```
public final static SystemColor controlShadow
```
The system's dark shadow and regular shadow colors for control objects.
```
public final static SystemColor controlHighlight
```
```
public final static SystemColor controlLtHighlight
```
The system's highlight and light highlight colors for control objects.
```
public final static SystemColor controlText
```
The system's text color for control objects.
```
public final static SystemColor desktop
```
The system's color of the desktop background.
```
public final static SystemColor inactiveCaption
```
The system's background color for inactive caption areas of window borders.
```
public final static SystemColor inactiveCaptionBorder
```
```
public final static SystemColor inactiveCaptionText
```
The system's border and text colors for inactive caption areas of window borders.
```
public final static SystemColor info
```
The system's background color for information (help) text.
```
public final static SystemColor infoText
```
The system's text color for information (help) text.

```
public final static SystemColor menu
```
The system's background color for menus.

```
public final static SystemColor menuText
```
The system's text color for menus.

```
public final static SystemColor scrollbar
```
The system's background color for scrollbars.

```
public final static SystemColor text
```
The system's color for text components.

```
public final static SystemColor textHighlight
```
The system's background color for highlighted text.

```
public final static SystemColor textHighlightText
public final static SystemColor textInactiveText
```
The system's text color for highlighted and inactive text.

```
public final static SystemColor textText
```
The system's text color for text components.

```
public final static SystemColor window
```
The system's background color for windows.

```
public final static SystemColor windowBorder
public final static SystemColor windowText
```
The system's border and text colors for windows.

methods

```
public int getRGB()
```
Returns the RGB values of this SystemColor's symbolic color.

```
public String toString()
```
Returns a string representation of this SystemColor's values.

Thread (java.lang)

A public class, derived from Object and implementing Runnable, that handles the implementation and management of Java execution threads.

variables and constructs

```
public final static int MAX_PRIORITY
public final static int MIN_PRIORITY
public final static int NORM_PRIORITY
```
Constant values that contain the maximum (10), minimum (1), and normal (6) priority values a thread can have.

constructors

`public Thread()`
Creates a new instance of a thread.

`public Thread(Runnable arg)`
Creates a new instance of a thread. `arg` specifies which object's run method is invoked to start the thread.

`public Thread(String str)`

`public Thread(Runnable arg, String str)`
Creates a new instance of a thread, named `str`. `arg` specifies which object's run method is invoked to start the thread.

`public Thread(ThreadGroup tgrp, String str) throws SecurityException`

`public Thread(ThreadGroup tgrp, Runnable arg) throws SecurityException`

`public Thread(ThreadGroup tgrp, Runnable arg, String str) throws SecurityException`
Creates a new instance of a thread, named `str` and belonging to thread group `tgrp`. The `arg` parameter specifies which object's run method is invoked to start the thread.

methods

`public static int activeCount()`
Returns the number of active threads in this thread's group.

`public void checkAccess() throws SecurityException`
Validates that the current executing thread has permission to modify this thread.

`public static Thread currentThread()`
Returns the currently executing thread.

`public void destroy()`
Destroys this thread.

`public static void dumpStack()`
Dumps a trace of the stack for the current thread.

`public static int enumerate(Thread[] dest)`
Copies each of the members of this thread's group into the thread array `dest`.

`public final String getName()`

`public final int getPriority()`

```
public final ThreadGroup getThreadGroup()
```
Returns the name, priority, or thread group of this thread.

```
public void interrupt()
```
Interrupts this thread's execution.

```
public static boolean interrupted()
```
Returns a true value if the current thread's execution has been interrupted.

```
public final boolean isAlive()
public boolean isInterrupted()
```
Returns a true value if this thread's execution is alive or has been interrupted.

```
public final boolean isDaemon()
```
Returns a true value if this thread is a daemon thread.

```
public final void join() throws InterruptedException
public final void join(long msec) throws InterruptedException
public final void join(long msec, int nsec) throws
InterruptedException
```
Waits up to msec milliseconds and nsec nanoseconds for this thread to die. The join() method waits forever for this thread to die.

```
public void run()
```
Method containing the main body of the executing thread code. Run methods can run concurrently with other thread run methods.

```
public final void setDaemon(boolean flag) throws
IllegalThreadStateException
```
Sets this thread as a daemon thread, if flag is true.

```
public final void setName(String str) throws SecurityException
public final void setPriority(int val) throws SecurityException
```
Sets the name of this thread to str or the priority to val.

```
public static void sleep(long msec) throws InterruptedException
public static void sleep(long msec, int nsec) throws
InterruptedException
```
Causes the current thread to sleep for msec milliseconds and nsec nanoseconds.

```
public void start() throws IllegalThreadStateException
```
Start this thread's execution, calling this thread's run method.

```
public String toString()
```
Returns a string representation of this thread.

```
public static void yield()
```
Causes the currently executing thread to pause in execution, allowing other threads to run.

Throwable (java.lang)

A public class, derived from Object and implementing Serializable, that is the superclass of all of the errors and exceptions thrown.

constructors

```
public Throwable()
public Throwable(String str)
```
Creates a new instance of a throwable object with the specified message (str) or none present.

methods

```
public Throwable fillInStackTrace()
```
Fills in the executable stack trace for this throwable object.

```
public String getLocalizedMessage()
```
Returns a locale-specific description of this object. Locale-specific messages should override this method; otherwise, the same message that the getMessage method produces will be returned.

```
public String getMessage()
```
Returns the detail message for this throwable.

```
public void printStackTrace()
public void printStackTrace(PrintStream stream)
public void printStackTrace(PrintWriter stream)
```
Prints the stack trace for this throwable to the standard error stream or to the specified stream.

```
public String toString()
```
Returns a string representation of this throwable object.

Timer (javax.swing)

A public class, derived from Object and implementing Serializable, that fires an action event after a specified delay. Often used to control animations.

constructors

```
public Timer(int delay, ActionListener listener)
```
Creates a timer that notifies the specified action listener every delay milliseconds.

methods

`public void addActionListener(ActionListener listener)`
   Adds the specified action listener to this timer.

`public int getDelay()`

`public void setDelay(int delay)`
   Gets or sets this timer's delay (in milliseconds).

`public void start()`

`public void stop()`
   Starts or stops this timer.

`public boolean isRunning()`
   Returns true if this timer is currently running.

TimeZone (java.util)

A public abstract class, derived from `Object` and implementing `Serializable` and `Cloneable`, that represents an amount of time offset from GMT that results in local time. Functionality is provided to allow for daylight savings time within a time zone.

methods

`clone()`
   Returns a copy of this `TimeZone`.

`public static synchronized String[] getAvailableIDs()`

`public static synchronized String[] getAvailableIDs(int offset)`
   Returns a list of all of the supported time zone ids, or only those for a specified time zone offset.

`public static synchronized TimeZone getDefault()`

`public static synchronized void setDefault(TimeZone tz)`
   Returns or sets the default time zone.

`public String getID()`
   Returns the id of this time zone.

`public abstract int getOffset(int era, int year, int month, int day, int dayOfWeek, int milliseconds)`
   Returns the offset from the Greenwich Mean Time (GMT), taking into account daylight savings time.

`public abstract int getRawOffset()`

```
public abstract void setRawOffset(int millisec)
```
Returns or sets the offset from Greenwich Mean Time (GMT) for this `SimpleTimeZone`. These methods do not take daylight savings time into account.

```
public static synchronized TimeZone getTimeZone(String id)
```
Returns the time zone corresponding to the specified id value.

```
public abstract boolean inDaylightTime(Date dt)
```
Returns a true result if the specified date falls within the daylight savings time for this `TimeZone`.

```
public void setID(String id)
```
Sets the id value of this `TimeZone`.

```
public abstract boolean useDaylightTime()
```
Returns a true value if this `TimeZone` uses daylight savings time.

URL (java.net)

A public final class, derived from `Object` and implementing `Serializable`, that represents a Web Uniform Resource Locator (URL).

constructors

```
public URL(String arg) throws MalformedURLException
```
```
public URL(URL url, String type) throws MalformedURLException
```
Creates a URL instance from a string argument, or by parsing a `type` (http, gopher, ftp) and the remaining base.

```
public URL(String proto, String source, int num, String doc)
throws MalformedURLException
```
```
public URL(String proto, String source, String doc) throws
MalformedURLException
```
Creates a URL instance using a defined protocol (`proto`), source system, destination port num, and document (`doc`).

methods

```
public boolean equals(Object obj)
```
Returns a true value if this URL is equal in all respects (protocol, source, port, and document) to `obj`.

```
public final Object getContent() throws IOException
```
Returns the retrieved contents as an `Object`.

```
public String getFile()
```

```
public String getRef()
```
Returns the name of the file (document) or its anchor this URL will attempt to retrieve.

```
public String getHost()
```

```
public int getPort()
```
Returns the name of the host (source) or the port this URL will attempt to connect to.

```
public String getProtocol()
```
Returns the protocol this URL will use in retrieving the data.

```
public int hashCode()
```
Returns the hash code for this URL.

```
public URLConnection openConnection() throws IOException
```

```
public final InputStream openStream() throws IOException
```
Returns a connection to this URL and returns the connection or a stream.

```
public boolean sameFile(URL arg)
```
Returns a true value if this URL retrieves the same file as the `arg` URL.

```
protected void set(String proto, String source, int num, String
doc, String anchor)
```
Sets the protocol (`proto`), source, port num, file (`doc`), and reference (`anchor`) for this URL.

```
public static void
setURLStreamHandlerFactory(URLStreamHandlerFactory fac) throws
Error
```
Sets the URL `StreamHandlerFactory` for this application to `fac`.

```
public String toExternalForm()
```

```
public String toString()
```
Returns a string representation of this URL.

Vector (java.util)

A public class, derived from `Object` and implementing `Serializable` and `Cloneable`, that manages an array of objects. Elements can be added or removed from this list and the size of the list can change dynamically.

variables and constructs

```
protected int capacityIncrement
```
The amount of element spaces to be added to the vector each time that an increase must occur. A `capacityIncrement` of 0 indicates that the list will double in size at every resizing.

```
protected int elementCount
protected Object elementData[]
```
The number of elements and the array containing the elements currently in this Vector.

constructors

```
public Vector()
public Vector(int size)
public Vector(int size, int incr)
```
Creates a new instance of a vector with an initial size of size (or using the default of 10). An initial capacityIncrement can also be specified.

methods

```
public final void addElement(Object arg)
public final void insertElementAt(Object arg, int index) throws
ArrayIndexOutOfBoundsException
```
Adds element arg to the end of this Vector or at a specific index. The capacity of the vector is adjusted if needed.

```
public final int capacity()
public final void ensureCapacity(int size)
```
Returns the current capacity of this Vector, or ensures that it can contain at least size elements.

```
public Object clone()
```
Returns the clone of this Vector.

```
public final boolean contains(Object arg)
```
Returns a true value if this Vector contains object arg.

```
public final void copyInto(Object[] dest)
```
Copies each of the elements of this Vector into the array dest.

```
public final Object elementAt(int index) throws
ArrayIndexOutOfBoundsException
```
Returns the element at location index from this Vector.

```
public final Enumeration elements()
```
Returns an Enumeration of the elements in this Vector.

```
public final Object firstElement() throws NoSuchElementException
public final Object lastElement() throws NoSuchElementException
```
Returns the first or last element in this Vector.

```
public final int indexOf(Object arg)
```

```
public final int indexOf(Object arg, int index)
```
Returns the index of the first occurrence of element arg, starting at index. A −1 value is returned if the element is not found.

```
public final boolean isEmpty()
```
Returns a true value if this Vector contains no elements.

```
public final int lastIndexOf(Object arg)
```

```
public final int lastIndexOf(Object arg, int index)
```
Returns the first index that object arg occurs at in this Vector, starting a backwards search at the specified index. If the object is not located, a −1 is returned.

```
public final void removeAllElements()
```

```
public final boolean removeElement(Object arg)
```

```
public final void removeElementAt(int index) throws
ArrayIndexOutOfBoundsException
```
Removes element arg and returns a true value. If the object requested is not located, a false value is returned. An element can also be removed at a specific index value, or all elements can be removed.

```
public final void setElementAt(Object arg, int index) throws
ArrayIndexOutOfBoundsException
```
Sets the element at the specified index equal to object arg.

```
public final void setSize(int size)
```
Sets the size of this Vector to size.

```
public final int size()
```
Returns the number of elements in this Vector.

```
public final String toString()
```
Returns a string representation of this Vector.

```
public final void trimToSize()
```
Reduces the size of this Vector to contain all of the elements present.

Void (java.lang)

An uninstantiable class that acts as a placeholder for the primitive void type in the Class object.

variables and constructs

```
public final static Class TYPE
```
The Void constant value of the void type class.

Window (java.awt)

A public class, derived from `Container`, that creates a graphical area that has no borders or menus and can be used to contain AWT components.

constructors

`public Window(Frame frm)`

Creates a new instance of a window that has a parent frame (`frm`). The window is initially not visible.

methods

`public void addNotify()`

Creates this window's peer.

`public synchronized void addWindowListener(WindowListener listener)`

`public synchronized void removeWindowListener(WindowListener listener)`

Removes or adds the specified window listener (`listener`) for this window.

`public void dispose()`

Removes this window and deletes any resources used by this window.

`public Component getFocusOwner()`

Returns the component from this active window that currently has the focus.

`public Locale getLocale()`

Returns the locale for this window.

`public Toolkit getToolkit()`

Returns the toolkit for this window.

`public final String getWarningString()`

Returns the warning string for this window.

`public boolean isShowing()`

Returns a true value if this window is currently visible on the screen.

`public void pack()`

Causes all of the components of this window to be laid out according to their preferred size.

`protected void processEvent(AWTEvent event)`

Processes the specified event for this window. If the event is a `WindowEvent`, then this method calls the process `WindowEvent` method of this window, otherwise it will call the parent class' `processEvent` method.

`protected void processWindowEvent(WindowEvent event)`

Handles any `WindowEvent` (event) generated on this window, and passes them to a registered listener for that event.

`public void show()`

Makes this window visible to the user and brings it to the front (on top of other windows).

`public void toBack()`

`void toFront()`

Sends this window to the back or front of other windows currently displayed on the screen.

WindowAdapter (java.awt.event)

A public abstract class, derived from `Object` and implementing `WindowListener`, that permits a derived class to override the predefined no-op AWT window events.

constructors

`public WindowAdapter()`

Creates a new instance of a `WindowAdapter`.

methods

`public void windowActivated(WindowEvent event)`

`public void windowClosed(WindowEvent event)`

`public void windowClosing(WindowEvent event)`

`public void windowDeactivated(WindowEvent event)`

`public void windowDeiconified(WindowEvent event)`

`public void windowIconified(WindowEvent event)`

`public void windowOpened(WindowEvent event)`

Empty methods that should be overridden in order to implement event handling for window events.

WindowEvent `(java.awt.event)`

A public class, derived from `ComponentEvent`, that describes a particular AWT window-based event.

variables and constructs

```
public static final int WINDOW_ACTIVATED
public static final int WINDOW_CLOSED
public static final int WINDOW_CLOSING
public static final int WINDOW_DEACTIVATED
public static final int WINDOW_DEICONIFIED
public static final int WINDOW_FIRST
public static final int WINDOW_ICONIFIED
public static final int WINDOW_LAST
public static final int WINDOW_OPENED
```
  Constant values that represent a variety of window event types.

constructors

```
public WindowEvent(Window src, int type)
```
  Creates a new instance of a `WindowEvent` from a specified source window and having a specific event type.

methods

```
public Window getWindow()
```
  Returns the source window that this event was triggered in.
```
public String paramString()
```
  Returns a string containing the parameters for this `WindowEvent`.